In the Shadow of Death

In the Shadow of Death

Restorative Justice and Death Row Families

Elizabeth Beck
Sarah Britto
Arlene Andrews

OXFORD
UNIVERSITY PRESS

OXFORD
UNIVERSITY PRESS

Oxford University Press, Inc., publishes works that further
Oxford University's objective of excellence
in research, scholarship, and education.

Oxford New York
Auckland   Cape Town   Dar es Salaam   Hong Kong   Karachi
Kuala Lumpur   Madrid   Melbourne   Mexico City   Nairobi
New Delhi   Shanghai   Taipei   Toronto

With offices in
Argentina   Austria   Brazil   Chile   Czech Republic   France   Greece
Guatemala   Hungary   Italy   Japan   Poland   Portugal   Singapore
South Korea   Switzerland   Thailand   Turkey   Ukraine   Vietnam

Published by Oxford University Press, Inc.
198 Madison Avenue, New York, New York 10016

www.oup.com

First issued as an Oxford University Press paperback, 2009

Oxford is a registered trademark of Oxford University Press

Library of Congress Cataloging-in-Publication Data
Beck, Elizabeth.
    In the shadow of death : restorative justice & death row families / Elizabeth Beck, Sarah Britto, and
Arlene Andrews.
       p. cm.
    ISBN 978-0-19-537569-5
1. Capital punishment—United States.
2. Death row inmates—United States—Family relationships.   3. Prisoners' families—United States.
4. Restorative justice—United States.   I. Britto, Sarah.   II. Andrews, Arlene Bowers.   III. Title.
    HV8699.U5B393 2007
    362.82'9—dc22   2006024007

9 8 7 6 5 4 3 2 1
Printed in the United States of America
on acid-free paper

*To offenders' family members
who suffer in silence*

Foreword

On a warm, humid Texas evening in October 1998, I stood by and watched as the state of Texas executed Jonathan Wayne Nobles. I was present mainly because, after corresponding with Jon for 11 years (along with a half dozen other inmates on death rows around the country), I was simply unprepared and unable to refuse the last request of a condemned man.

Jon was not one of the wrongfully convicted inmates that you've heard so much about in recent years. He was guilty as hell of a crime that he himself described as heinous and made no excuses for—the brutal, senseless killings of Kelley Farquhar and Mitzi Johnson-Nalley.

Standing on my left in the death chamber, holding my hand so tightly that I couldn't feel my fingertips for hours afterward, was Jon's aunt, Dona Hucka, the only blood relative who had ever come to visit him while he was in prison. His mother never made the trip. In fact she never even wrote, and Jon had only managed to locate her and say goodbye by phone the night before. Dona had driven all night from Oklahoma to be there.

A little over a year later I was back in Huntsville, outside the prison this time (thank God for small favors). The occasion was the execution of Larry Robison, and the hand that I held was that of Larry's mother, Lois, a retired third-grade schoolteacher.

Larry had begun behaving erratically and hearing voices when he was barely out of his teens. The doctors at the State Hospital for the Criminally Insane in Rusk, Texas, told Lois that though her son was indeed a paranoid schizophrenic, he was not a candidate for committal to any state-run mental health facility because he hadn't exhibited any violent behavior. A few years later Larry finally qualified. He killed his boyfriend and all four occupants of the house next door, including an 11-year-old boy. Another branch of the same Texas government cited "the rights of victims" when they found Larry competent to stand trial and sentenced him to death.

When it was all over Lois cried on my shoulder for a minute or two and then took a deep breath and wiped her face. Then she and her husband, Ken, almost immediately turned their attention to another prison facility on the other side of town where Lois's surviving son was serving a sentence for assault and robbery. From the beginning of his incarceration, Larry's younger brother, Steve, had endured verbal abuse from both inmates and corrections officers as the brother of a condemned child killer, and Lois feared that he would break under the pressure and "do something stupid" as she put it and endanger his chances at an upcoming parole hearing.

No one involved in the anti–death penalty movement in Tennessee will ever forget the family of Robert Glen Coe. Coe was handpicked by death penalty proponents in the government of Tennessee to be the first inmate executed by the state in over 40 years. There were other inmates who had been on death row longer, many of whom had long ago exhausted their legal options. But Coe's case was perfect from a public relations standpoint; he was white (defusing any charges of racial bias), he had confessed (making his case, at least in the eyes of the public, open and shut), and the crime he had been convicted of committing was sufficiently heinous—the kidnapping, rape, and murder of 8-year-old Cary Ann Medlin. In preparing for the execution the state had developed elaborate contingencies for the accommodation of witnesses. When the killing was over, members of the press and the Medlin family were ushered before the array of cameras and microphones that had been set up in the prison parking lot. Coe's brothers and sisters were offered no media access whatsoever and promptly escorted off prison property.

The victims' rights movement in this country is predicated on "humanizing" the stories of the family members of victims of violent crimes. They are dragged through the courts again and again, during every stage of a legal process that is necessarily exhaustive. When life and death are at stake, we the people owe it to ourselves to practice due diligence. The prosecutors will tell these folks who have already endured more than any human being should ever have to suffer that they honor the memory of their loved ones and that in the end they will receive closure.

I have encountered hundreds of victims' family members over my years of work against capital punishment. Most angrily denounced the activities of my fellow activists and myself from the other side of a police line, and I learned years ago that any attitude other than complete and total respect for their pain and their anger was counterproductive to the cause to which I've devoted most of my adult life. Sometimes they were on my side and for various reasons had chosen to deal with their grief by working to bring about an end to what they perceived as a cycle of violence that is pervasive in our society. Numerous support groups and membership organizations exist for murder victims' families today, whichever side of the street that they stand on.

But what about the Dona Huckas and the Robisons and the Coes? What about the hundreds of mothers, fathers, husbands, wives, brothers, sisters, sons, and daughters of Americans executed in this country every year? Most are innocent of any crime. All will carry the stigma of having been related to a "monster" with them for the rest of their lives. The guilt. The shame. They will bear all of this as well as the loss of their loved ones when the executioner pushes the button or pulls the trigger or flips the switch.

Is their anguish any less legitimate than that of the victims of the violent acts committed by the members of their families? Do we as a society even care?

In the following pages, the authors show us exactly why we should care about these families. They, too, have held hands and watched switches flip, but their work here moves beyond bearing witness. By letting the Dona Huckas, the Robisons, and the Coes of the world tell their own stories, they're creating space in our justice system for true reform and, in turn, true healing. We the people, they argue, bear responsibility not only for punishing criminals but also for repairing the lives of our fellow community members devastated by crime. Their vision of restorative justice brings everyone—victims or survivors and their families, offenders and their families, criminal justice professionals, and community stakeholders—to the table and out of the death chamber.

—Steve Earle
New York
April 2006

Acknowledgments

This book was a labor of love, which was made possible because of the support and generosity of so many people. Foremost we are indebted to all of the family members of offenders, who opened their homes, hearts, and wounds to us, and to the offenders, who were brave enough to talk with us. They shared their stories in the belief that it could make a difference for other families and society.

To the advocates who told us about their work with the family members of offenders and victims, we appreciate your time and all that you do to help others: Renny Cushing, Sandra Jones, Bruce and Julie Person, Bill Pelke, Susannah Sheffer, Peggy Sims, and Ed and Mary Ruth Weir. Dick Burr, Tammy Krause, Pamela Blume Leonard, and Howard Zehr have shown us that there is room for restorative justice in the traditional justice system, even in capital cases, and we are honored to share their work.

Numerous lawyers helped in the creation of this work by trusting us to talk with their clients, helping us make connections to offenders' family members, sharing their own stories with us, and reviewing vignettes and descriptions of particular cases for accuracy and for their inspirational work in the field. We owe special thanks to David Bruck and John Blume, who taught Arlene and countless others across the nation about family history and concerns in the legal and public arenas. We also particularly thank the dedicated individuals who comprised the former Georgia Multi-County Public Defenders' office, including the director Michael Mears (now the Public Defender Standards Council and the Georgia Capital Defender) and the Southern Center for Human Rights, including their former director Steven Bright. Other attorneys and defense team members who provided us support, insights, and stories along the way include Rachel Chmiel, Robert Lominack, Charlotta Norby, William Montross, Theresa Norris, Margaret O'Donnell, Mathew Rubenstein, Charlie, Sally, and most especially Timothy Floyd. We are also grateful to those who have mentored us in the mitigation process and showed us how to find the humanity in frailty, particularly Pamela Blume Leonard, Scharlotte Holdman, David Freedman, and Kathy Wayland.

Maura Roessner, editor extraordinaire, has gone above and beyond what anyone might have expected. Her wisdom and support have been invaluable and her belief in this project unwavering. We also appreciate the work of the copyeditors and production staff at Oxford University Press. We owe a very special thanks to Jason DeParle, David Freedman, Teresa Lyons, Charlotta Norby, Phillip Northman, Lauren Rich, and most especially Isabel Beck and Paul Eschholz, each of whom shared their expertise and time with us by reading and commenting on early drafts. Howard Zehr and Hugo Bedau contributed remarkable insights, and we are privileged by their participation. We are also thankful to Peter Lyons, colleague extraordinaire. Sandra Bloom, Jessie Harris-Bathrick, and Priti Shaw provided us with important insights into trauma.

The Georgia State University College of Health and Human Sciences–School of Social Work; Department of Criminal Justice, Central Washington University; University of South Carolina Institute for Families in Society; as well as individuals such as our great cheerleader William Le Matty provided financial support for our work. We are especially grateful for the assistance of numerous graduate and undergraduate students who helped with transcriptions of interviews, coding of data, footnotes, and often went above and beyond the call of duty so that we could meet deadlines. These students include Oluwakemi Adebayo, Blossom Birkebak, Nicholas Forge, Orianna Gatta, Shayla King, and Tammy Wilsker. We also received help from Kelly Abatis, Kelly Colbert, Janette Gagnon, Christine Gonzales, Kelly Hart, Kimberly Martin, Stacy Singer, and Charles Sterne. We are also grateful to Mary May Impastato and Krispen Harker. Friends who helped with the production include Cynthia East, Laura Switzer, and Mindy Wertheimer.

We are also indebted to a number of scholars who helped us personally or have paved the way through their research. They include Robert Bohm, John Braithwaite, Elizabeth Bruce, Ted Chiricos, Richard Dieter and the Death Penalty Information Center, Kenneth Doka, James Garbarino, Lorraine Gutierrez, Judith Herman, Denise Johnston, Rachel King, Michael Radelet, Cynthia Schultz, Dennis Sullivan, Larry Tifft, Mark Umbreit, Margaret Vandiver, Michael Vaughn, and Howard Zehr.

Other thanks go to Sherry Thacker for taking over Elizabeth's responsibilities at Congregation Bet Havarim when she was writing, to Sarah Brown, and to Atlanta Women Cycles and Jamie Higgins for starting it.

A special thanks to Steve Earle for the foreword to this book and for his undying advocacy for the rights of the oppressed, and to Pamela Blume Leonard for the afterword and for bringing the experience of offenders' families to us—without her there would be no book.

For everyone else who we have not listed, we appreciate your support and assistance with this project. Each of you helped to make this project better. We are solely responsible for any mistakes.

My life has been touched by the family members with whom I spoke and I will always carry a debt of gratitude to them. My debt to them is matched only by my debt to my own family. My mother, Isabel, has given me several lifetimes of support, as well as wisdom and the ability to work hard. My late father, Carl, gave me courage and the best parts of my soul. For my husband, Steve, this book is as much yours as mine; your calm, love, and constant belief in me make it so, and if that is not enough—I owe you for bringing rescue dog Francie to our home just when I wanted her least and needed her most. During my work on this book I thought about Ethan and how my parents gave me what I needed to do this and much more and how his amazing parents will do the same.

—Elizabeth

Writing this book highlighted the tapestry of human experiences, connections, and emotions that constitute family. My thanks to my family who is a constant source of love and support; my father, Paul, whose work ethic and academic example has always guided my work; my husband, Marwin, who makes me laugh and supplies me with everyday reminders that the world is a beautiful place; my siblings—friends I was fortunate enough to be born with, and my mother, Eva, who taught me the secret to life—forgiveness.

—Sarah

I learned about families who face death first from my husband, Stuart Andrews, who, soon after our marriage, took 2 weeks' leave from his regular job to tromp through cornfields and interview Klan members as he reconstructed a defendant's life history. Kathy Wayland and Scharlotte Holdman, mitigation specialists extraordinaire, have encouraged and taught me to explore deeply into the lives and social networks of people who face death.

—Arlene

Contents

Photos follow page 136

Note to Readers

This is not a typical book about the death penalty debate that focuses specifically on the pros and cons of capital punishment. Rather, our purpose is to highlight the experiences of capital offenders' family members. And while the many issues offenders' family members face will certainly add crucial elements to any debate about the death penalty, this is not the raison d'être of this book. Offenders' family members are important in their own right, and their stories and experiences provide insight into the complicated nature of the human condition. Though most readers will hopefully never have to experience the tragedy of either losing a loved one to murder or losing a loved one through capital punishment, many of us can relate as professionals working with or within the criminal justice or mental health system, parents, siblings, and community members to the many perspectives on guilt, vengeance, mercy, and forgiveness that are explored herein.

Throughout the book our exploration occurs within the constraint of the present criminal justice system—which, for better or worse, includes the death penalty. Our exploration is rooted in both the lived experiences of offenders' family members who were interviewed for this book and restorative justice theory, which views violent crime as an extreme violation of relationships and tries to find ways to hold offenders personally accountable while also addressing the needs of victims, offenders, and communities that arise from crime. The restorative justice-based policy suggestions examined throughout this book may lead to a reexamination of the utility of the death penalty for society, but even in the absence of a change in death penalty policy, numerous social issues related to the harms experienced by family members of offenders should not be ignored.

We hope that many different audiences will read and discuss this book, including

- Prosecutors and defense attorneys who frequently struggle with ways to honor the lives of victims throughout murder trials, do no further harm to victims, and address tremendous wrongs;

- Social workers, psychotherapists, and victim advocates who work with family members of both victims and offenders in their efforts to cope with murder and its aftermath;
- Criminal justice practitioners whose charge it is to represent the state in their interactions with the offender, victims' family members, and offenders' family members;
- Students of criminology, criminal justice, social work, sociology, psychology, and restorative justice who wish to begin to understand crime and punishment from a very personal perspective;
- Victims' family members who have suffered tremendously from the consequences of violent crime;
- Offenders' family members who are forced to deal with guilt, shame, anger, and love for their loved one as they face the isolating and at times debilitating process of their family members' trial and execution; and finally,
- Members of the general public who play critical roles in their communities where many social problems that lead to crime can be addressed.

Authors

Each of us came to writing this book after years of working with issues related to crime, social problems, and punishment. Two of the authors, Arlene Andrews and Elizabeth Beck, had professional experience working with family members of offenders on death penalty cases before the data collection for this book began. Elizabeth has worked as a consultant, mitigation specialist, and expert witness in developing offenders' psychosocial histories, which are used in the sentencing phase of death penalty trials. Most recently Elizabeth has worked with David Freedman to explore the impact of neighborhoods on offenders' development. Arlene has been an expert witness regarding the impact of child history on adult behavior in numerous death penalty trials in several states. In their work, Elizabeth and Arlene review records from schools, health care providers, child welfare agencies, juvenile and criminal justice systems, employers, military service, and other organizations involved in the defendant's life. They have interviewed numerous people who knew the defendant, including their primary caregivers, extended family, neighbors, teachers, social workers, foster parents, and a range of others familiar with the defendant.[1]

Sarah Britto has worked on several data collection projects, including the Capital Jurors Project in Florida that interviewed jury members in capital cases, and she has led research projects investigating the media's effect on fear of crime, punitive attitudes, civic engagement, and public policy. In reviewing the existing theory and research on restorative justice, she was inspired by the ethical grounding of this approach to justice and the promising results indicated in the literature.

Our work and research experience helped shape the data collection and theoretical orientation of this book. This work also guides our views regarding the social problem of violent crime, and although we try to guard against these particular subjectivities influencing our data collection efforts, these perceptions cannot help but shape the types of questions included in our interviews. These same experiences also aided us in gaining both access and acceptance among individuals that we interviewed.

Throughout our research, we offered every participant in our study the promise of confidentiality. Most individuals desired this discretion. Throughout the book when we refer to an individual by their first name only, we use a pseudonym. A few of the people that we interviewed wanted to have their real names published with their stories. For them we use both their first and last (real) names.

We interviewed 24 family members, and we held 2 focus groups with 12 individuals. We then interviewed 18 additional family members because they represented a specific experience, such as being children of the condemned, relatives of someone who was taken off death row, or family members who have become politically active. We also reviewed the social histories of 14 additional defendants whose legal team prepared mitigation evidence for sentencing in a death penalty trial.[2] Altogether, 55 families are represented, and their stories animate this book. We also talked with defense team members and leaders in restorative justice and the death penalty abolition movement. When conducting the interviews, we relied on the memories of the people that we talked with as well as their interpretation of events, and because both are fallible it is important to acknowledge this limitation. In cases involving longer narratives or specific legal information, we often verified the facts with a lawyer who was familiar with the case.

Two of the individual offenders found in the case studies are women, but because 97% of the individuals on death row and nearly all of the offenders throughout this book are male, we use that pronoun when we speak of offenders.[3] See appendix A for a detailed description of our research methodology.

Including Offenders' Families in Restorative Justice

Throughout the book we do not talk extensively about the death penalty debate or specific legal issues but focus on the offenders' family members and how they may fit into restorative justice practice. Before we begin this discussion, a brief review of several landmark Supreme Court cases that have shaped the current application of the death penalty cases is offered for the reader to understand the basic context of offenders' family members' lives. In the United States, the death penalty has been a part of our criminal justice system since its inception with the brief exception of the time period between the *Furman v. Georgia* Supreme Court decision and the *Gregg v. Georgia* decision.[4] In *Furman* the Supreme Court ruled that then-current death penalty law was unconstitutional because of the "arbitrary and capricious" nature of its application. Following *Furman*, 38 states and the federal government revised their death penalty statutes in an effort to ensure the fair application of the death penalty; specifically, trials were bifurcated to provide for a guilt phase where the guilt of a defendant is ruled on and then a separate sentencing stage where mitigating and aggravating circumstances can be presented to the court. *Gregg* provided a test of these new laws and effectively reestablished the death penalty in the United States in 1976. Numerous cases have since restricted the application of the death penalty, including no mandatory death penalty laws,[5] no death penalty in rape cases without an accompanying murder,[6] no death penalty for the mentally retarded,[7] and most recently no death penalty for individuals who committed the offense as a minor.[8] For readers who are interested, Appendix B provides an overview of the typical legal process in a death penalty case.

Though each of these cases represents legal precedents to most of us, to the offenders' family members the cases represent the life of their loved ones. Many social workers, counselors, and psychologists have long known that one of the first steps to healing, be it a societal ill or a personal nightmare, is storytelling. We listened to the stories of family members as they described life in the shadow of death and retell these stories. To contextualize their stories, we bring in research from social work, psychology, and criminal justice in the hope that examining how violent crime and capital punishment affect the lives of offenders' family members. We aim to provide insight into these and other social problems.

We place these stories in a discussion of healing the harm created by crime, and to do this we use the framework of restorative justice. Howard Zehr's seminal work on restorative justice theory, *Changing Lenses*, asked many readers to reexamine the notion of justice from the perspective of the "needs" of the involved parties.[9] Restorative justice posits that all individuals who are harmed by a crime have a right to voice their stories, receive help in meeting their needs resulting from the crime, and be included in the criminal justice process. Traditionally, restorative justice solutions attempt to meet the needs of victims, offenders, or community members, parties who are often called stakeholders, while still holding the offender accountable for the crime. From the reexamination of justice spurred by Zehr's book, hundreds of restorative justice programs have developed throughout the United States.

We believe it is time to again reexamine the issue of justice by including the perspectives of offenders' family members. Continuing in Zehr's tradition of building restorative justice theory, we ask readers to look through a different lens and examine the death penalty from the perspective of offenders' family members.

Structure of the Book

Restorative justice frames this 12-chapter book, divided into 3 parts. Part I introduces the reader to life in the shadow of death, restorative justice theory, and the family members of offenders in death penalty cases. We explore what these family members mean for social work, law, criminal justice, and sociology as well as for the larger philosophical study of a just society. In chapter 1 we discuss both the problems faced by offenders' families and why these issues are important to the understanding of justice in the United States. In chapter 2 we briefly trace the history of the restorative justice movement and discuss it in the context of death row families. Although it is obvious why victims' family members are central to a discussion of restorative justice, we make a case for including family members of capital offenders in restorative justice. Chapter 3 provides an in-depth portrayal of the multigenerational psychosocial histories of offenders' family members. We illustrate the deeply rooted pain haunting these families, which provides insight into them as individuals and into the homes that the capital offenders came from. Director of Investigation and Mitigation at the New York Capital Defender Office Russ Stetler has said that the answers to crime prevention are in these histories.

Part II captures stories, often in the family members' own words, and unearths the harms experienced by family members of capital offenders. Restorative justice theory posits that the first step to providing justice after a crime has been committed is to establish who has been harmed. These harms provide the groundwork to explore offenders' family members' needs. In chapter 4, we examine the various ways in which family members have been pronounced guilty and feel punished by society, the criminal justice system, and their communities. In chapter 5 we accompany a mother through the execution of her son and hear from other families whose lives have been destroyed by an execution. Chapter 6 recounts the voices of both minor and adult children and siblings of offenders. Some of the children were too young to understand the implications of their father's or brother's death sentence, whereas others stood by as he was executed. From grief to depression to post-traumatic stress disorder (PTSD), in chapter 7 we examine mental health issues and coping strategies as families struggle through the arrest, trial, sentencing, and execution of their loved one.

In part III we move beyond storytelling to examine the promise and problems of utilizing restorative justice solutions in capital cases. Chapter 8 explores how life changes when a death sentence is overturned through either commutation or exoneration. Family members talk about the impact of their loved one's commutation from death to life without parole. Readers will meet Joseph Amrine, an innocent man who spent 16 years on death row. Finally, in a unique case of restorative justice in action, convicted murderer William Neal Moore talks about the commutation of his death sentence and eventual parole that was made possible by the efforts of the victim's family members.

In chapter 9 we chronicle family members of victims and offenders who have organized at the local, state, and national levels. We also explore organizations that have provided support to death row families. Chapter 10 examines several ways restorative justice can touch capital cases, including defense-initiated victim outreach, a pioneering strategy that seeks to engage victims' family members and capital offenders in a restorative response to criminal proceedings. In chapter 11 we explore the role of the community in restorative justice and examine the ways institutions such as educational and mental health systems within the community have failed offenders and their families. We provide innovative models for addressing the harm associated with institutional failure and for bringing communities into the restorative process. In chapter 12 we look to the future and explore the many ways that restorative justice policy initiatives can help meet the needs of victim and offender families, offenders, and their communities.

We have also included two appendixes that elaborate on our research methodology and the basic operation of the criminal justice system in death penalty cases. Appendix A summarizes the interview, focus group, and case study methodology we used to gather and analyze information about capital offenders' families. Appendix B examines the process of a death penalty trial to provide a logical backdrop for the psychological journey these family members document for us.

Participants

Following is a synopsis of the 24 family members who participated in the general interview. Not included are family members who participated in the focus groups or were interviewed for a specific reason such as being a minor child of a death row inmate. Also not included are the 14 psychosocial histories that were used in the writing of this book.

Mothers

Barbara Longworth loves to laugh. Caucasian, in her mid-60s, she raised her children in a middle-class home. But since the death of her husband following her son's death sentence, her income level has dropped. Barbara worked for 25 years taking care of severely handicapped children in her home. Before her son was executed in 2005, Barbara never missed a visit to him in prison.

Betty never completed high school because she was forced to marry at age 14. She is Caucasian and in her mid-50s. Her husband beat her and her son horrifically; ultimately her son, Gale, killed his father. Gale is the "apple of her eye," and she visits him regularly in prison. Her son chose to forgo a jury trial and instead was tried before a judge who sentenced him to life without the possibility of parole.

Bridget, in her mid-50s, is an African American woman who lives in public housing and collects Social Security disability because of several physical and psychiatric disorders. She is very connected to her extended family and loves her son, Toby. She talks to him on the phone from death row as much as her money permits and saves her pennies to visit him.

Celia McWee is Latina and in her early 80s, though no one would believe her age if they saw her. She and her husband both worked professional jobs and raised three children. Her daughter died when she was in her 20s. Celia adored her son, Jerry, and has struggled emotionally since his execution in 2004.

Charlene is an African American woman living on Social Security disability. She presently takes care of her grandchildren. She visits her son, Travis, when her health allows. She has cancer and several other serious conditions and copes with life's hardships through her belief in Jesus Christ. She believes that the facts of her son's case will never be known because he agreed to a plea of life without the possibility of parole. For Charlene and her son, the possibility of the death penalty was so horrible that it left no other choice. She believes that her son may have played a minor role in the murder of which he is convicted.

Franny, who is Caucasian, was married at age 15 to escape the abject poverty of her family's home. Now in her mid-50s, she works at a convenience store and has recently remarried. She adores her son, Martin, and speaks to him regularly, but she seldom visits him in prison because she finds the visits incredibly stressful. Franny is very thankful that her son is not on death row, though he is serving a sentence of life without the possibility of parole.

Rose lives in an impoverished and isolated rural area and is a Caucasian woman in her 70s who did not graduate from high school. Though her husband was mentally ill, Rose had no idea what that meant and sought help for him from the snake handlers in their church. Rose loves her son, George, and visits him on death row when she can, but the prison is several hours away, and because of her age and income the trip can be very burdensome.

Georgia is a low-income African American woman who never finished high school and supplements her income by cleaning houses. She and her oldest daughter live together so that they can share the rent. Georgia is deeply religious and visits her son, Kenneth, on death row almost every week.

Jennifer, a middle-class Caucasian woman with a college degree is putting her daughter through college and regularly visits her son, Edward, in prison. She believes that he is innocent and that he did not get a fair trial because he chose to accept a plea bargain out of fear of a death sentence.

Marion, an economically struggling Caucasian woman who once lost her home, is in school trying to get her associate's degree in computers. She is in her 50s, and for many years she was married to an abusive man. Marion has spent a great deal of time in therapy getting over her past, which included abuse and incest. Marion loves her son, Mitchell, and visits him often on death row, though sometimes the visits can be tense because mother and son do not always agree and can be very critical of each other.

Mary is a small Caucasian woman in her 80s. She and her husband were in the middle class, and she was a stay-at-home mother while her husband was in the military. When her husband retired, he became a school administrator. She had one son who died in the Vietnam War and another who committed suicide. Her third son, William, is on death row, and she visits him every week that she can.

Pearl, an African American woman in her early 60s, is living on fixed income from her Social Security checks following a work-related injury. She had a daughter who was killed in a car accident in her late teens, and she is active in her church. She visits her son, Gilbert, who she loves, whenever she can get a ride to the prison since she cannot afford a car. Gilbert served close to 10 years on death row until he received a second trial, which led to a sentence of life without parole.

Sarah, a middle-aged, low-income African American woman, raised two children on a job that paid less than minimum wage. She is religious and active in her church. Her son Marcus's defense team speculates that she may have a substandard IQ. Sarah says she loves Marcus unconditionally but does not understand who he is after he became mentally ill. Lack of reliable transportation keeps Sarah from visiting her son on death row.

Vera, a Caucasian women in her mid-50s, is a public servant. She and her husband have a loving relationship, which they are now sharing with their granddaughter Kelly, the offender's daughter, who lives with them. Vera describes her family as a loving, touchy-feely one. She is very active in her granddaughter's after-school activities and is on the fundraising committee of the PTA.

Fathers

Karl is Caucasian and loves to cook for his three children, who he raised on his own as his wife died when his youngest was an infant. He once owned a small store and sold crafts that he made, but now he is in poor health, with emphysema and other lung-related illnesses. His family is extremely close, and one of his friends says that Karl would move in with his son, Nathaniel, if the prison would let him.

Matt is a college-educated, middle-class Caucasian man who raised three children. He is active with his grandchildren and was a leader in his church before his son's arrest. Matt and his son, Tony, were very close, and Matt and his wife visited their son regularly before his execution. His wife has not been the same since her son was killed, and he has sought counseling for his own depression.

Grandparent

Ivan, a middle-class artist, is also a survivor of a Nazi work camp who is in his 70s and in failing health. He helped raise his grandson, Timothy, the offender, because Timothy's mother had a debilitating illness. Ivan is very close to his grandson and is thrilled that he did not receive a death sentence. When Ivan's health permits, he visits Timothy regularly.

Siblings

Paul quit college when his brother was arrested. Now a store manager, he hopes to go back to school. He grew up in a working-class home and recently married. Because his brother, Jeremy, did not get the death penalty, Paul believes that justice has been served and understands that his brother will not get out of prison. The two seldom communicate.

Bonnie Coe grew up in severe poverty. Today she lives in subsidized housing and collects Social Security disability payments. She loved her brother, Robert, but seldom visited him in prison because she could not afford the trip. Today she is active in her church and very much misses Robert since his execution.

Mark is a middle-class African American man in his mid-40s. He grew up in a loving home with nine siblings. He and most of his brothers and sisters have gone to college. Mark did not visit his brother, David, often because David's severe mental illness often made him difficult to be around. Today Mark does public speaking on the death penalty and his brother.

Jan, married to a minister, is a middle-class African American woman in her 40s who is raising two boys. Like her husband, she graduated from college and works a professional job. She visited her brother, Adam, in prison when she could and misses him terribly since his execution. She believes that Adam's wisdom and dignity have given her the strength to withstand the pain of losing him.

Adult Children

Felicia Floyd is in her mid-30s, and she is married with two children. She is middle class with a master's degree and owns a small business. Before her father, Fred, was executed, she visited him regularly, but she maintained a level of distance from him to protect herself from the emotions associated with his impending execution, which occurred in 2001.

Cousin

Pat Seaborn, a retired Caucasian woman in her late 60s, has some college education, is middle class, and has been happily married for many years. She and her cousin, Ron, grew up in the same neighborhood, and she was terrified of her uncle, who used to beat Ron. Pat enjoyed her cousin's company and admired his intelligence. She was with him on the day of his execution.

Aunt

Patty is a very warm and spirited African American woman who likes to laugh. She owns a small home and is working class. She lives in a small town that she describes as very racist. After her sister died, she became the primary support person for her nephew, Luke, who she loved and has missed since his execution.

Part I

Shadow of Death

The effects of the death penalty on family members of capital offenders is a relatively new discussion in the literature and within the anti–death penalty community, which consists of lawyers who work on death penalty cases and those working to abolish the death penalty. It is particularly rare to see both restorative justice and capital punishment talked about together, yet we believe it is critical—to society, to the integrity of the justice system, and to the family members themselves—to explore the effects of a capital trial on family members and to bring these family members into a restorative justice process.

Because of the newness of applying restorative justice principles to death penalty cases, part I of this book provides background. The first chapter begins with an examination of what it means to live in the shadow of death because a loved one has been charged with a capital offense and explores why family members of capital offenders should matter to society. In this discussion it becomes clear that the death penalty is different for offenders' family members than any other form of punishment in the United States, and the punitive difference between life without parole and a death sentence is often borne by offenders' family members.

Restorative justice is most frequently used in nonviolent cases. In chapter 2 we provide an introductory rationale for its application to death penalty cases. We introduce the basic theoretical assumptions and stakeholders involved in typical restorative justice practice and argue that these assumptions can apply to murder cases and that the definition of stakeholder should be expanded to include offenders' family members. We explore restorative justice through real-life examples—stories of victims, offenders, and communities who come together to face the tragedy of murder and other serious crimes—and by examining key theoretical principles that explain why these processes may provide all involved with a sense of justice. Chapter 2 also highlights the research findings based on several restorative justice initiatives.

As individuals we have rich and multifaceted backgrounds that are based on our experiences, values, family, ethnicity, and a multitude of other factors. In chapter 3 we introduce many themes common in offenders' family members' backgrounds. Through short illustrations and longer vignettes, we tell about their childhoods, the turbulence of their experience with violence or mental illness, and their struggles with their loved one, the offender.

Our intention is that the first three chapters give readers an introduction to the experiences of offenders' family members and restorative justice. This introduction should help readers move forward in the book and critically examine their own ideas regarding restorative justice, its promises, pitfalls, and potential utility to help heal the wounds of violent crime.

1

Why Do Offenders' Families Matter?

The press called Martin's actions a "crime spree." Already convicted of armed robbery, Martin was facing the death penalty. In less than 2 weeks the jury would decide his fate, which his adoptive father, Phillip, felt powerless to influence. Phillip's faith in the criminal justice system had been shattered by the callousness of Martin's court-appointed attorney. Terrified that his son would be sentenced to die, Phillip did the only thing he felt he could do: in an act of faith and desperation, he asked God to take his life and spare his son's. In his garage with the car running, Phillip made the ultimate sacrifice to spare his son the ultimate punishment—he took his own life in a seemingly illogical effort to save his son. Unexpectedly his suicide turned out to be Martin's second chance at life. The jury, moved by Martin's loss, spared his life.

Learning that a loved one may have committed a horrible crime can rip a family apart. The death penalty is sanctioned in 32 states, the military, the federal criminal justice system of the United States, and nearly half of the countries around the world. In these places, while an offender's family reels from the impact of charges of a violent crime and as they begin to face their own feelings of anguish and powerlessness, family members must also confront the prospect of their loved one's death by execution.

When prosecutors decide to seek the death penalty in capital crimes, offenders' family members begin a new stage in their own lives, which they live in the shadow of death. This shadow covers all aspects of their lives and also influences how other people treat them. The knowledge that the state is seeking to execute their loved one and the reality of their impending loss changes family members' lives in numerous detrimental ways. Many suffer severe depression and trauma, face enormous financial challenges, and have difficulty participating in their own families and communities. Despite the fact that their lives are intertwined with the very public death penalty process and consequences, they are voiceless in the process. Perhaps the most insidious part of living in the shadow of death is the feeling that no matter what they do, few people care to see them, hear them, or extend compassion to them.

We do not want to minimize the anguish of crime victims or the horror of violence by drawing attention to offenders' family members; perhaps the worst experience a human being can imagine is the violent death of a child or the murder of a parent. Society aches for children who are lost to violence and grieves for sons and daughters who are robbed of their parents and hearts go out to their siblings and grandparents. We affirm that offenders should be held accountable and honor the rights of the victims to pursue justice, but our belief is that utilizing restorative justice to supplement the traditional justice system better meets these goals.

We maintain that crime victims' and offenders' family members, although deeply divided by violent crime, have similar experiences, including shared grief over the loss of the victim, isolation, trauma, depression, and frustration with the criminal justice system. Our work is driven by the belief that society's understanding of crime and punishment can be improved by exploring the effects of a capital charge on offenders' family members and that the pain of these relatives must be acknowledged and addressed to right larger societal wrongs.

The family members that we talked with represent individuals, long overlooked, who did not commit murder and yet are severely harmed by their interactions with the criminal justice system. In many ways the repercussions of the punishment of their loved one is internalized, and they, too, "feel punished by society." Family members' psychological and emotional responses to the crime and punishment often leave them depressed, and their feelings of fear, helplessness, and horror invoke trauma. One mother said, "There are no good days; there are days that are bearable and then the rest." Another mother described her life following her son's arrest and conviction as spent "pacing and crying, crying and pacing."

The media and the community can inflict further damage. The father of an accused inmate realized that "You [and your family] are viewed as guilty as soon as your son is arrested." A mother explained that when she left her house she felt scared because "You feel like someone is going to do something to you." This feeling of condemnation drives many families into isolation, and their isolation is reinforced at the trial, where the courtroom itself divides supporters of the offender and supporters of the victims.

Offenders' Families Matter

Readers may question why offenders' families matter and why they should be included in a discussion of justice and capital punishment. Indeed, there may be readers who believe that it is appropriate for the family members to feel condemned. Some might think that the offender's family is complicit in the crime because they raised a criminal, and others may lack sympathy for parents who raised children in abusive conditions. Some readers may support the notion of an eye for an eye, and given the suffering of the victim's family, they may see the offender's family members' pain as an appropriate extension.

Because murder and the death penalty bring up raw emotions, the perspectives of the offenders' family members are often overshadowed, and their pain has been lost in traditional discussions of capital punishment. Once a brother, sister, son, daughter, husband, wife, father, or mother commits a crime, the public regards him or her as a defendant, convicted felon, offender, or inmate.[1] To condemn his life, the prosecutor portrays his life as worthless. However, to family members he is still their child, father, brother, uncle, or nephew. They see him as a complex person who has done something terrible but is still human. Family members may be hurt by their loved one's actions, even enraged, but often their love is fundamentally unchanged.

Consider Sarah. Throughout her children's lives, this mother of three worked in the kitchen of her local nursing home. In 1998, her son Marcus killed the owner of the convenience store where she often bought a thing or two after work. When she fell short of money, the shopkeeper would front her what she needed; she considered him a friend. She mourned his loss and was devastated that it was her son who took his life. "He was my friend!" she incredulously repeated as she tried to grasp the magnitude of the situation. Still, she said of her son, "You don't stop loving him. You can't; that's not what a mother does." She blamed Marcus, and she blamed herself. She thought she had been a good mother because she loved him, cared for him, and met his basic needs, but when the crime occurred, none of that seemed real. Following Marcus's arrest, Sarah had to negotiate many feelings toward her son: concern, love, anger for his actions, confusion about mental illness, and her own feelings of torment on hearing his death sentence.

Offenders' families matter because, like Sarah, the loss of their loved one is personal. She was a hard worker, active in her community, and at the time of the interview she was raising her daughter's son as well. After the crime, her life began a downward spiral. She became depressed, was barely able to work, and lost the will to live. Perhaps most important, her depression took its toll on her grandson's life because she could no longer provide him with adequate care.

Family members matter because children are affected by the death penalty. We talked with several children of the condemned, some too young to comprehend why anyone would want to kill their "daddy" and others very aware of what a death sentence means. One adult child of an offender, whose father was arrested when she was a preteen, noted, "We live our lives under the black cloud of execution." Although research describing the negative effects of incarceration on children abounds, this is one of the first discussions of what it means to be a child of a parent on death row. Children of the condemned experience all the pain that a child of an incarcerated parent does, with another layer, unimaginable in its heaviness, heaped on their small shoulders.

Often family members are forced to simultaneously manage the effects of a death sentence and the parenting of other minor children. At best, the arrest keeps the parent distracted; at worst, the pain and anger that the family members experience influence the level of care they can give the children and changes the emotional context of the child's home life and development. Not only do these young siblings mourn the separation from their loved ones, but also they often feel the need to take care of and protect their mothers or fathers. The children often watch helplessly as all of their once-protective relationships begin to crumble.

Phillip, who took his life in his garage, was not the only family member who lost his desire to live. Nineteen-year-old Eliot was tried in a death penalty case in 1998. He and his younger brother, Brad, had always been very close. They supported each other through their father's abuse and tried to shield their mother from his violence. When Eliot received a death sentence, Brad, who was attending and doing well in college, was devastated. His mother, paralyzed by her own grief and confusion, was unable to support him. Brad attempted suicide. His mother saw Brad's suicide attempt as a wake-up call, but admitted that she remained too wrapped up in her own trauma to effectively reach out to him.

Not surprisingly, children in many families affected by a capital sentence are faring poorly. Some, like Brad, have harmed themselves or dropped out of school, and others become angry and destructive. Research suggests that because their parents are in prison, these children are at an elevated risk of entering the criminal justice system as offenders.[2]

Family members of capital offenders matter because the U.S. Constitution rests on principles of fairness and seeks to promote citizens' confidence in their government. Parents, siblings, cousins, and other relatives of capital offenders confront a strange dilemma as they address the moral development of their own children. They want their children to have respect for authority and the principles of justice, and yet their anger at the system often dominates their existence. They see the court system as stacked against them and view some policies and practices as gratuitous in their meanness. When the state tries to put their loved ones to death, the entire family system develops ambivalent or even hostile feelings toward their government and the justice system. When entire families lose faith in the criminal justice system, participatory democracy becomes increasingly difficult.

Family members matter because, when healthy, their contributions help sustain communities. A prime example is Barbara Longworth,[3] whose son Richard was recently executed for a capital crime. Since the time Richard was a child, Barbara has taken care of children with developmental and physical disabilities. Justin, one such child, has been with Barbara for 22 years, and though his speech is severely limited, he refers to Barbara as "Mom." She feeds him, bathes him, puts him to bed, and changes his diapers. She also comforts him when he is sad, and the two of them are often found sharing a laugh. Barbara's whole family views him as one of their own. The bond between Barbara and Justin is palpable, and the love must be making a difference because Justin's disabilities are so severe that he was not expected to live past puberty. Although Barbara was forced to give up another child due to the stress of Richard's incarceration, she continues to care for and love Justin as a son. Many other family members of offenders have faced similar challenges and choose to cut back on or withdraw from their community service work, either to focus on their loved one's case or because they were too depressed to participate.

Offenders' families represent a variety of backgrounds. Noted *New York Times* journalist Jason DeParle remembers visiting the parents of convicted murderer Robert Wayne Williams on the night he was executed. Williams was the first person executed in Louisiana following the reinstatement of the death penalty. DeParle's first and lingering thought was that the family was "so average." Robert's mother was in her 60s and was polite, kind, and horrified about what was happening to their son and the crime he had committed.[4] Not all offenders were raised in such average or loving homes. Many came from environments riddled with poverty and pain. Some were victims of horrifying child abuse, and others went to bed hungry for years. A number grew up in homes where the adults around them were unable to provide support and stability because they were dealing with their own demons: depression and other forms of mental illness, drugs and alcohol, and the aftermath of childhood or adult trauma. These families matter because they are members of our communities and in many cases their problems are symptoms of larger societal problems that have not yet been adequately addressed.

Most offenders who receive the death penalty come from oppressed and vulnerable populations that have a background of multigenerational poverty. Sarah, whose son Marcus killed the shopkeeper, worked several jobs at or below minimum wage so that she could provide food for her children. In cases like Sarah's, family members often weighed the consequences of not enough food or not enough supervision for their children, and food won. Sarah, like many other family members, never finished high school because she had to work to contribute to her parents' home. With little education, there were few options, and work was often exploitive. Sarah and other mothers like her were often unprepared and unable to put their energy into their child's emotional, cognitive, and spiritual development.

Several of the mothers we talked to left home and school when they began to menstruate because they feared that the rape they endured from their fathers, grandfathers, and brothers might result in a pregnancy. The consequences of murder compel us to ask how we as a society can intervene to break the cycle of violence. As their own stories reveal, executing a loved one does not break the cycle of violence but creates fresh wounds for these families, their communities, and future generations. By understanding families of capital offenders, communities gain greater insight into how to promote healthy, safe, and fulfilling environments. Restorative justice practice seeks just this kind of understanding by involving entire communities in responding to crime and preventing crime by addressing its root causes.

How Many Family Members Are There?

Since the first recorded execution in 1608,[5] 20,000–22,500 individuals have been executed under the legal authority of the American colonies or the United States.[6] Since the 1976 reintroduction of the death penalty in the United States, 1,042 inmates have been executed,[7] and currently, there are 3,370 individuals awaiting execution.[8] In the United States between 2004 and 2005, there were 123 individuals executed, and in 2004, another 125 individuals were sentenced to death.[9]

These are large numbers, but they do not represent all of the family members living in the shadow of death who feel as if they are also punished by the death penalty. Each person sentenced to death also brings an entire extended family to death row. For the purposes of this book, we have focused primarily on the immediate family of offenders, which includes fathers, mothers, husbands, wives, brothers, sisters, and children. We have also included aunts, uncles, grandparents, and cousins in special cases where these individuals raised the offender or were his primary support person. Although families offer varying degrees of support to offenders, each family carries the emotional, social, financial, and time burdens that come from having a violent offender as a relative. If we consider that most offenders conservatively have at least four family members in their lives—one parent, a sibling, a child, and a significant other—then currently in the United States 13,532 individuals are faced with the "invisible punishment" of being related to an individual on death row. If we look at actual executions in the United States since 1608, then over 90,000 immediate family members endured the punishment of watching their loved ones die at the hands of the state. Perhaps the most disturbing statistic is that since 1973 in the United States, 122 innocent people had served time on death row,[10] representing at least 476 family members.

Although the number of people sentenced to die is high, many more individuals with a capital charge get a sentence other than death because trials are avoided through the process of plea bargaining. Other defendants go to trial and receive life without parole or a lesser sentence, and a few individuals are found not guilty. But even in cases where the death penalty is not handed down, the families face, often for years as the case makes its way through the courts, the prospect of losing their loved one through execution.

All capital murder cases cast a long shadow of death over the offender's family. Close friends, church members, coworkers, neighbors, and community members also feel the effects of a capital charge, trial, and sentence. Finally, every capital case affects the quality of life in the community where the crime occurred and society at large. Focusing on the criminal trial and the execution can distract society from the root causes of crime and violence and foster fear and distrust. The emotional strain of calling on community members to serve on juries that ponder the worth of a person's life and the cost of processing a capital case through the criminal justice system drain a community's energy and may diminish its reserve of social capital and the potential for strong cohesion.

The Difference between Life in Prison and Death by Execution

Central to the awareness of the value of family members of offenders on death row is recognition of the many challenges these families face that are not adequately addressed by existing social services and the knowledge that these challenges are different from those faced by victims' family members and non–death row offenders' family members. By highlighting these differences we can begin to work on addressing specific issues related to having a loved one face capital punishment. Linda White has said, "There are more challenges with having a loved one on death row than being the mother of a murder victim." Linda's daughter, Cathy O'Daniel, was murdered in 1986, leaving behind a 5-year-old daughter.[11] Through her work with Murder Victims' Families for Reconciliation, an organization made up of family members of murder victims who oppose the death penalty, Linda has spent time with family members of capital offenders and has developed a great deal of firsthand knowledge about their experiences.

Linda explained that murder victims' families usually receive sympathy and compassion; they can talk about their loved one with pride; no one assumes that they are at least partially responsible for the death, and they usually are not forced to dwell on the parenting mistakes that they may have made. Moreover, they did not know in advance that someone wanted to kill their relative and that the state would not only sanction the death but also facilitate it. They do not have to worry about the psychological torture that they and their loved one face as they wait year in and year out for the execution to take place.

Family members whose loved ones receive a long prison sentence can usually accept and live with the court's decision. They grieve the loss of contact, they worry tremendously about the safety and well-being of their loved one in prison, and they are saddened by the missed opportunities. When the sentence is life without parole, family members are often devastated that the criminal justice system gives up on their loved one and immediately worry about who will visit him when they die. They may find little hope for redemption in the sentence, but eventually most families are able to cope. Some construct ways to foster relationships with their loved one in the very different environment of prison. Spared a death sentence, these families search for hope and healing in the prison visiting room. Life without parole frees families from the constant life-or-death struggle that demands all of their attention. As family members told us again and again, as long as there is life, there is hope.

In the chapters ahead we will explore, both theoretically and experientially, what a death sentence means for family members of the defendant. We hear relatives explain in detail the insidious and pervasive nature of a death sentence. One mother said, "You can't really grieve like you would [when there is death]. You grieve, but you grieve every day." Sadly, this mother knows the difference. Her 21-year-old daughter was killed in a traffic accident several years before her son's arrest for a capital crime. Reflecting on her children, she explained, "I got depressed when I lost my daughter, but I came out of it. I can't come out of this."

Summary

Fyodor Dostoyevsky once wrote, "The degree of civilization in a society can be judged by entering its prisons,"[12] and to this we would add "and by talking with the families of offenders sentenced to execution." Living with the knowledge that the state is trying to kill your loved one and that this action is supported by your community has devastating consequences. These consequences are compounded by the fact that society often turns its back on offenders' family members, shunning them from communal activities, shaming them into submission, and ignoring their stories of pain and suffering.

Existing in the shadow of death often brings emotional turmoil, thoughts of suicide, and numerous medical conditions related to living in a perpetual state of elevated anxiety. Available community resources are rarely appropriate because their workers have not been trained to handle the unique needs of this population, and traditional agencies do not offer outreach to connect with this population. Family members of offenders are therefore often left alone to deal with the execution and its associated financial strain, trauma, pain, and numerous family issues. Family members feel as if they cannot be seen or heard and are powerless to help their own relatives. This is why Phillip chose suicide and many other family members wrestle with similar choices.

Offenders' family members matter because their loss is personal and has devastating consequences for their entire family system. They matter because the siblings and children of offenders grow up with a shared sense of familial dread and in this context face increased risk for mental health problems and involvement in the criminal justice system. They matter because personal involvement with their loved one's capital case invariably results in the loss of confidence in the criminal justice system and the U.S. government, which is unhealthy for a democracy. They matter because some are active members of our communities who have contributions to make to society and find themselves unable to participate when bearing the burden of their loved one's execution.

Offenders' family members should also matter from a crime prevention perspective. The issues being faced by these families, such as poverty, racism, incest, domestic violence, drug and alcohol addiction, and mental illness, are often symptoms of larger social problems. These families may hold valuable information and insight into these issues. Society will never know—unless we listen and work with them to develop ways to address these issues.

Restorative justice solutions call for communities to develop mechanisms by which stakeholders can communicate. These conversations include discussions of the crime, the harm it produced, accountability and obligations, ways to meet the needs of everyone harmed by the crime, and ways to reduce the likelihood of future criminality. Offenders' family members should be included in these conversations—for their insight, because they have a family obligation to help, and because they, too, are wounded by the crime and capital punishment and their needs should no longer be ignored.

2

Understanding Restorative Justice

On April 19, 1995, Bud Welch's life changed forever. On that morning in Oklahoma City, Timothy McVeigh parked a truck loaded with a massive bomb in front of the Murrah Federal Building and killed 168 people, one of whom was Bud Welch's daughter Julie Marie.[1] Though Welch had opposed the death penalty his entire life, his first instinct was revenge. Bud revealed that "the pain I felt was unbearable. I was also filled with rage. I wanted Timothy McVeigh executed. I could have done it with my bare hands. I didn't even want a trial. I just wanted him fried."[2] Bud turned to drinking and smoking cigarettes to cope with his feelings. About 8 months later, he visited the bomb site; Bud describes how he "sat under the old elm tree where Julie used to park her car. I asked myself, 'Once they're tried and executed, what then? How's that going to help me? It isn't going to bring Julie back'—I finally realized that the death penalty was nothing more than revenge and hate. And revenge and hate are exactly why Julie and 167 others are dead."[3]

Three weeks after the bombing, Bud had seen an image of Bill McVeigh, Timothy's father, on television and immediately knew that one day he would have to reach out to this man. "I saw a deep pain in a father's eyes that most people could not have recognized. I could because I was living that pain. And I knew that some day I had to go tell that man that I truly cared about how he felt."[4] Three and a half years after the bombing, Bud met with Bill McVeigh and his daughter Jennifer. On September 5, 1998, at 10 in the morning, the two fathers spent some time in McVeigh's garden. They eventually made it inside to the kitchen table where Jennifer joined them.

> Earlier, when we'd been in the garden, Bill had asked me, "Bud, are you able to cry?" I'd told him, "I don't usually have a problem crying." His reply was, "I can't cry, even though I've got a lot to cry about." But now, sitting at the kitchen table looking at Tim's photo, a big tear rolled down his face. It was the love of a father for a son. . . . As I walked away from the house, I realized that until that moment I had walked alone, but now a tremendous weight had lifted from my shoulders. I had found someone who was a bigger victim of the Oklahoma bombing than I was, because

while I can speak in front of thousands of people and say wonderful things about Julie, if Bill McVeigh meets a stranger, he probably doesn't even say he had a son.[5]

Nothing will bring closure to Bud Welch, but for him reaching out to others and opposing violence and hate honors Julie's memory. By releasing his rage, he has made room for healing.[6] By recognizing the humanity in Bill McVeigh and his daughter Jennifer, he may also be helping them deal with their loss, but as Bud explains, "I wasn't doing it for Bill McVeigh, I was doing it for myself. It was a selfish thing on my part. But, as it turned out, it worked for all three of us [Bud, Bill, and Jennifer]."[7] Bud Welch has become an activist against the death penalty and a promoter of community involvement that is focused on healing and preventing violence.

Bud's efforts to stop the execution of Timothy McVeigh earned him scathing disapproval, but the fact that he didn't agree that an execution would provide justice for the victims' families shows that Bud may have understood something about the grieving process that the criminal justice system and many other victims did not. In a study reported by the Forgiveness Project, conducted 6 months after the bombing, 85% of victims' families and survivors wanted the death penalty for McVeigh. Six years later, things have changed dramatically. "The figure had dropped to nearly half, and now most of those who supported his execution have come to believe it was a mistake. In other words, they didn't feel any better after Tim McVeigh was taken from his cell and killed."[8] Yet capital punishment is often seen as the only fitting answer to such atrocities as the Oklahoma City bombing.

When an individual meets a violent death through crime, the entire community suffers. The victim's family members and friends lose not only their loved one and the future they planned to share but also a sense of security and trust in other people. Community members are shocked and disheartened when a murder occurs in their neighborhood, and they respond with sadness, fear, anger, and distrust. The criminal justice response focuses on arresting, convicting, and punishing the offender for his actions. During such tragedies, the losses suffered by the offender and his family members typically are overlooked. Restorative justice, by recognizing the connections and relationships (whether healthy, strained, or contemptuous) among offenders, victims, their family members, and the community seeks to address crime in a more holistic manner. It seeks to heal and strengthen communities by providing a restorative process for everyone affected by a serious crime.

Howard Zehr, a pioneer in restorative justice theory, practice, and scholarship, outlines the key principles of restorative justice: "1) crime is a violation of people and of interpersonal relationships; 2) violations create obligations; 3) the central obligation is to put right the wrongs."[9] Too often the criminal justice system loses sight of human nature, causing it to ignore many of the emotional consequences of the entire process. Even though the present criminal justice system leads to a verdict and a judgment that purports to right the scales of justice, the collateral damage can be staggering. The offender is often encouraged by his lawyers to deny or minimize responsibility. Though punished, the offender is rarely held personally accountable by publicly acknowledging his guilt, facing his victims, and offering an apology or the truth. In fact, the traditional justice system encourages many offenders to continue to deny responsibility, even in prison, and to blame others for their own actions. Restorative justice encourages offender accountability by stressing dialogue and truth-telling as central to putting things right and repairing personal relationships.[10]

Also in the traditional justice system, the victims' family members grieve for the loss of their loved ones and are often frustrated and harmed by their treatment throughout the criminal justice process. In death penalty cases, they suffer through years of appeals during which they constantly relive the morbid details of their loved one's death. Their counterparts, the offenders' family members, feel guilt, shame, embarrassment, and prolonged psychological torture of watching the state kill their loved one. Restorative justice aims to ease these harmful effects on the families of both victims and offenders. Before detailing the specifics of restorative justice, it is useful to first review the theoretical rationale behind the traditional system of justice that is currently in operation in the United States.

Retributive and Utilitarian Justice

Retributive justice and restorative justice are often seen as polar opposites. Retributive justice focuses on dispensing punishment equal to the harm of the original crime, whereas restorative justice seeks to promote the healing of all involved parties. Many scholars argue that restorative justice is antithetical to retributive justice and therefore there could be little possibility of solutions from each model coexisting.[11] Still others argue that the two systems are not mutually exclusive and that there may be room for punishment in restorative justice models and room for compassion and healing in retributive models.[12]

The philosophical rationale supporting capital punishment usually is based on two basic premises—retribution and deterrence. Superficially, retribution is simply revenge or repaying harm with an equal harm, but more nuanced interpretations of this concept also include punishment as a moral responsibility,[13] the therapeutic value of societal vengeance,[14] and the utility of such punishments for establishing the moral boundaries of a society.[15]

Retribution has roots in religious texts and in the moral philosophy of Kantianism (ethical formalism). Judaism, Christianity, and Islam include the principle of *lex talionis* or an "eye for an eye," a concept of punishment often described as "justifiable vengeance" that publicly demonstrates society's and the victim's right to revenge against an offender.[16] For many, vengeance serves an emotional need to see an offender suffer for the pain inflicted on one's friend or family members.[17] Whereas most modern societies have moved decidedly away from allowing victims to seek direct revenge, especially in cases of violent crime, the notion that this function can be institutionalized within the state still garners much support.

Still others have argued that retribution is useful to society because it provides an outlet for individuals' anger over the disruption to their community created by crime and disorder. A community that focuses its anger at a particular offender may also be drawn closer together because citizens generally agree that homicide is contrary to the community, and, despite any other differences community members may have, all can agree that individuals who commit murder deserve to be punished.

For Kant and philosophers of ethical formalism, the rationale behind the death penalty is not revenge but moral duty. Ethical formalism is based on the notion that all rational individuals are governed by moral principles, and a violation of these principles creates an obligation to reestablish a moral equilibrium. Noted criminologist Jeffrey Reiman explains rational individuals who commit murder cause their own death because they should be aware of the punishment. "He [the offender] authorizes his own execution thereby absolving his executioner of injustice."[18]

The utilitarian philosophical tradition, exemplified by scholars such as Mill, Bentham, and Hume, views punishment as a deterrent that seeks to change future behavior by influencing rational decision makers, who weigh the pain of punishment against the rewards of criminal behavior.[19] The example of an executed offender is intended to have a "general" deterrent effect on would-be offenders, who might refrain from criminal behavior to avoid execution. Rational individuals should choose not to murder or commit other crimes because they fear the death penalty.

Regardless of a philosophical position supporting capital punishment, both the severity and finality of its practice has resulted in limited use. One legal scholar argues that the death penalty should be reserved only for the "worst of the worst."[20] Whether this is currently the case in the United States is much debated. In fact, capital punishment has always generated extensive debate over issues such as morality, deterrence, cost-effectiveness, and racial or socioeconomic inequality.[21] Although the laws and procedures regulating its practice differ from state to state, most capital cases share some common elements, such as murder in the presence of aggravating circumstances, defendant access to state and federal appeals processes, and more media and public attention than similar non–death penalty cases.

Restorative Justice

Restorative justice evolved as a means to impose consequences on individual negative behavior while promoting positive alternatives that would prevent future criminality and help build stronger, more civil societies.

Although restorative justice is a developing theory about how to deal with crime at a societal level, it is also a social movement with roots in traditions and practices of several different cultures.[22] Therefore, no one restorative justice model encompasses all aspects of the movement. Rather, basic principles guide practices that can be adapted for particular communities and cultures.

Although the principles and ideals of restorative justice have long been present in the way indigenous people—such as the Maori of New Zealand, the Native American and the First Nations peoples of North America—do justice, restorative justice programming began in Canada in the 1970s as a response to two teen offenders who had vandalized several community members' properties. Working together, a probation officer, a coordinator of voluntary service workers, and a local judge developed the idea and process for offenders to meet the victims of their crimes. All parties thought this process would hold the offenders directly accountable for their behavior, give the victims the satisfaction of hearing an apology, and be less harmful to the offenders' future than juvenile detention.[23] Since this small beginning, the theory and practice of restorative justice have been reworked and tested many times.

Numerous restorative justice programs exist throughout the United States and the world, and there is no single formal process for accomplishing restorative justice or defined place and time when the process must occur. Rather, restorative justice is a philosophy that provides guidelines for creating processes and programs that fit the needs of particular communities and are flexible enough to meet the needs of diverse participants. The guidelines are that all restorative justice initiatives should provide the following: safe places for participants (stakeholders) to tell their stories; trained individuals to work with the stakeholders to establish the ways in which they were harmed and to explore their needs and obligations stemming from the crime; a focus on personal accountability where offenders are encouraged to take responsibility for their crimes, to understand the harm they caused their victims, their families, and their communities, and to develop ways to meet obligations that they incurred by committing a crime; and finally, for all stakeholders to work together to make sure that both needs and obligations are met.[24] In the majority of restorative justice programs throughout the world this process is accomplished through a meeting of the stakeholders, but it is not the only way to do restorative justice.

Theoretically, restorative justice starts with the recognition that crime disrupts social interactions among individuals and community members and causes harm. Criminal behavior is therefore seen as harming personal relationships between victims and offenders rather than solely violating the laws of the state. Even if the victim and offender did not know each other before the crime, the crime itself establishes a relationship immediately in need of repair. When crime is viewed as a violation of relationships rather than solely an offense against the state, it changes the focus from punishment to repair by taking care of the immediate needs of all the involved parties.[25]

Specifically, Zehr[26] defines restorative justice as involving all stakeholders in a process of exploring "harms, needs, and obligations" to try to repair relationships and "put things as right as possible."[27]

Restorative justice practitioners struggle with a common question: how can the needs of the victim and of the offender coexist? Restorative justice truly focuses on needs and obligations rather than mere retribution. The needs and obligations discovered in past research for both victims and offenders are shown in table 2.1.[28]

One of the guidelines for the practice of restorative justice is to provide an opportunity for various stakeholders to meet. For many victims, the feelings of loss, devastation, and rage that result from the violent murder of their loved one are directly connected to the offender and sometimes his family members. Consequently, there are times when victims' family members are compelled to meet with the offender or his family members. They desire a meeting because they need to have questions answered about the murder and the murderer's motives, to know about their loved one's final moments, to have the offender and his family understand who the victim was and how much the family grieves the loss of the victim, to hold the offender personally accountable and hear an apology, and in some instances, to offer compassion and forgiveness.

A dramatic example of the restorative justice process followed the assassination attempt on Pope John Paul II by Mehmet Ali Agca in 1981. Immediately after the shooting that placed him in intensive care, the pope forgave the shooter and asked others to "pray for my brother, whom I have sincerely forgiven."[29] His gesture provided a powerful message to Catholics and the larger world community about the importance of forgiveness and alternatives to revenge in response to violence. Two years later, during the Christmas season, Pope John Paul II visited Agca in prison and forgave him in person. The pope also reached out to Agca's family, meeting with both his

Table 2.1
Identified Needs and Obligations of Victims and Offenders

• VICTIMS	• OFFENDERS
—Safety and protection from the offender	—To be accountable for their actions
—Restoration of a psychological sense of safety	—To express remorse
—An opportunity to tell their story and be heard	—To tell their story and be heard
—Answers to questions about the crime	—To offer some kind of reparation of their actions
—Financial or symbolic reparation	—To explore the precursors to their criminal involvement
—Full accountability by the offender	—To address issues such as alcoholism, drug dependency, lack of job skills, mental health issues, etc.

brother and his mother. A larger message grew out of the pope and Agca's interactions—Christians and Muslims can solve differences through compassion and understanding rather than violence.

Although some victims or their family members want to forgive the offender, many do not. Victim autonomy is integral to restorative justice, and forgiveness is a choice for victims. Some victims have reported feeling harmed when their religious or other communities thrust forgiveness on them, suggesting that although victims should be encouraged to express their pain and their needs, they should never be coerced into participation, forgiveness, or even acceptance of an apology when they do not want to or in a way that does not feel appropriate to them.

Defining just who constitutes an offender's and victim's community and who is harmed by the crime has troubled many people working in the restorative justice field.[30] Few would disagree that at the least, the term *community* includes the family members of victims and offenders and their friends, faith community members, and neighbors. Studies of restorative justice programs have rarely explored and addressed the needs of community members. These needs include many of those already listed for both victims and offenders, as well as assistance in crime prevention so that events are not repeated, aid in combating the harmful effects of fear of crime, and opportunities to strengthen communities by building social capital and fostering efficacy for solving community problems.

The restorative justice approach acknowledges that involvement with the current criminal justice system often creates additional disorder in the lives of victims' and offenders' families and others and can increase crime by failing to address its roots.[31] Restorative justice seeks to engage all stakeholders in conflict resolution and build social capital that leads to crime prevention within families and communities.[32]

Because restorative justice focuses on individual and community needs, programs often grow out of grassroots initiatives and encompass a range of practices. Restorative justice may completely replace the traditional judicial procedure, allowing for a case to return to court if the process breaks down or the involved parties cannot reach an agreement, or it may be used to supplement the traditional justice system.[33]

This bottom-up development allows individual programs to meet the unique needs of their diverse communities. Most programs try to bring harmed parties together to address crime and its causes.[34] Bringing opposing parties together contrasts with a typical courtroom where symbolic and often literal lines are drawn between the involved parties. An offender sits with his defense team, opposite the prosecutor, both facing the judge. The aisle of the courtroom serves to divide victims' and offenders' family members and friends during the procedures. The rules of law as well as the formal roles of lawyers and victim advocates restrict the interaction among victim, the offender, and their respective families.[35] Nils Christie, a criminologist at the University of Oslo, argues that in our present criminal justice system the state has stolen the role of victim from the wronged party.[36] The theft denies the victim and related covictims (family members of the victim who are also harmed by the offense) the process of working through the harm. Telling one's story, expressing the pain caused by the crime, and having victimization validated often foster the healing process for crime victims.

An example of storytelling and its effects is found in the recent history of South Africa. On April 27, 1994, after years of resisting the Afrikaner nationalist government and its system of apartheid, enduring imprisonment, and having been branded a terrorist for his actions, Nelson Mandela became the first democratically elected president of South Africa.[37] As joyous as the occasion was for many South Africans and citizens of the world, Mandela faced what seemed an insurmountable task of confronting the violent injustices of the past while uniting a country to move forward. How could South Africa build a democratic society and at the same time deal with those who as government employees systematically oppressed, tortured, and murdered its black citizens? Some suggested a method similar to the Nuremberg Trials in Germany; others wanted blanket amnesty to be offered; still others wanted to ignore the past.[38] Out of this debate and ensuing compromise, the Truth and Reconciliation Commission (TRC) was created with the goal of laying the groundwork for South Africa using restorative justice principles to forge a new future by facing its violent past. The TRC, led by Archbishop Reverend Desmond Tutu of the Anglican Church, set out to hear the stories of victims' family members and seek truth from offenders. Those who came forward and admitted to their wrongdoings in a public forum (in a large public meeting hall, nationally televised) would be granted amnesty. By confronting the evil that transpired in South Africa, it was hoped that victims, offenders, and the country as a whole would come to know the truth of their histories and decide collectively to build a future where these atrocities would not happen again.

Tutu's description of the truth and reconciliation process in South Africa supports the idea of using restorative justice to build a new and different future: "Many who came to the commission attested afterward to the fact that they had found relief and experienced healing, just through the process of telling their story. The acceptance, the affirmation, the acknowledgement that they had indeed suffered was cathartic for them."[39] Other victims were not prepared for the process and were retraumatized when they relived their stories. Still others felt that some punishment should have accompanied the loss of their loved one's life. Over 20,000 victims told their stories, and 7,000 perpetrators confessed to crimes throughout the process, creating a national history of the violence used by both sides during the struggle against apartheid and for democracy. On accepting the report, Mandela stated:

> Dear fellow South Africans, accept this report as a way, an indispensable way to healing. Let the waters flow from Pretoria today as they flowed from the altar of Ezekiel's vision, to cleanse our land, its people, and to bring unity and reconciliation. We have looked the beast in the eye. We will have come

to terms with our horrendous past, and it will no longer keep us hostage. We will cast off its shackles, and, holding hands together, black and white will stride into the future, the glorious future God holds out before us—we who are the rainbow people of God—and looking at our past we will commit ourselves: "Never again! Nooit weer!"[40]

Even though the process was extremely controversial and was criticized by the African National Congress, many victims, and the National Party,[41] Mandela and others have argued that the proceedings showed South Africans and the world that the country wanted to create a united democratic government and move beyond the nightmare of apartheid. The use of restorative justice on such a large scale stimulated the movement worldwide and stretched its applications to involve extremely violent crimes.

The result of the growth of restorative justice has been the development of several popular models of programs that include family group counseling (FGC), victim-offender mediation (VOM), sentencing circles, and victim impact panels. Regardless of their particular form, parties to the crime verbally share their respective roles and thus reclaim ownership from the state. VOM models, used extensively in the United States and Europe, usually focus on the victim and offender, who are brought together to work out a reparations agreement whereby the offender meets the obligations created by the crime in an effort to repair the harm caused by the crime.[42] FGC, which began in New Zealand, includes family members of both victims and offenders and community stakeholders who confer "in deciding the resolution of a criminal or delinquent act."[43] All parties voice their opinions in a safe, facilitated setting. The process often begins with a discussion of the crime and its consequences, and then the group collectively develops a resolution that when successfully completed results in the acceptance of the offender back into the community. Sentencing circles are modeled after the practices of the First Nations people of Canada and are very similar to FGC, but the focus is wider: they include community members who are not connected to the crime, and they often bring together individuals harmed by similar crimes. Victim impact panels allow victims to tell their stories to groups of offenders and community members, often resulting in victim empowerment through storytelling and offenders learning about the consequences of their actions.[44]

In each of these models victims can express their pain and fear and the extent to which the criminal incident has impacted their lives. Offenders have the opportunity to explain and apologize for their actions and express sorrow and contrition. Throughout these encounters, the emphasis is on holding the offender accountable, reconciling affected parties, helping the victim and community regain a sense of control over their lives, and empowering communities to solve their own problems constructively.[45] In many cases a reparation agreement is made whereby the offender agrees to make amends. The reparation, especially in cases of violent crime, augments traditional punishment and is often symbolic, such as donating to a charity of the victim's choice, doing community service work to honor the victim's memory, or mailing a $1 check to the victim's family members on the anniversary of the victim's death. All parties are given the opportunity to ask questions and clarify specifics of the criminal event and the backgrounds of involved parties. Such encounters also give victims, offenders, and other stakeholders a chance to ask for or grant forgiveness if they feel it is appropriate.

Restorative Justice Research

In 1998, researchers Mark Umbreit, director of the Center for Justice and Peacemaking at the University of Minnesota School of Social Work, and his colleague Jean Greenwood reported that there were a growing number of more than 300 restorative justice programs operating in the United States. The majority of these programs focus on mediation between victims and offenders in property crime cases with juvenile offenders. As the number of programs increases, more researchers have attempted to evaluate them. Evaluations have generally included measures of victim and offender satisfaction, reasons for participation, perception of fairness among program participants, and the end result of the meetings for victims and offenders.[46] Additionally, some studies have attempted to compare the recidivism rates of juveniles participating in VOM programs with the rates of juveniles in traditional programs.[47] Umbreit and colleagues reported several key findings from over 100 studies of voluntary VOM programs,[48] including both victims and offenders report high levels of satisfaction with the process; the overwhelming majority of victims and offenders feel the process is fair for both sides; restitution or reparation was considered important by participants, but not as important as dialogue; offenders were more likely to follow through with reparations (of property, monetary, or symbolic) than offenders in other programs; and finally, recidivism rates were generally lower than in comparable groups receiving traditional criminal justice punishments.

Although restorative justice is the focus of much current research and correctional policymaking, few of these programs focus on violent crime. Many researchers, politicians, and representatives of restorative justice programs argue that its utility is limited to property crimes and less serious violent crimes.[49] Violent offenders, particularly those committing homicide, are often considered beyond the reach of the healing process involved in restorative justice. Recently such notions have been challenged by several diverse groups throughout the world,[50] and many programs have developed out of responding to victims' requests to meet with their perpetrators, even in cases involving capital crimes.[51] For example, the TRC in South Africa demonstrated the value of applying restorative justice to violent crimes, even offenses that were heinous in nature, for victims, communities, and offenders.[52] Although we do not argue that amnesty should be granted to violent offenders who confess, we believe that important lessons can be learned from South Africa. The few studies conducted in the United States concerning extreme violence and restorative justice have very promising results for victims and offenders,[53] and these studies point to the possibility of restorative justice and retributive justice solutions being used in combination.

An example of a restorative justice program that is coupled with retributive justice is found in Mark Umbreit's exploration of the Victim-Offender Reconciliation Program (VORP) in mediating encounters between offenders and victims in five case studies involving extremely violent crimes.[54] A professional mediator performed an extensive needs assessment and had private meetings with both offenders and victims before the encounter. Offenders and victims had various reactions, but none of the participants regretted participating in the process. Some of the positive outcomes mentioned by respondents included the opportunity to apologize and forgive, a lessening of the intensity of anger felt as a result of the crime, a movement toward healing and peace, and a sense of involvement among community members.

Caren Flaten, a youth counselor in Anchorage Alaska, studied seven juvenile cases using VOM in crimes that included murder, attempted murder, and burglary.[55] Like Umbreit's study, all participants went through extensive preparation before the mediation sessions, including journaling and meeting with the facilitator to process the feelings and questions they had for each other before the meeting. Again, both victims and offenders reported high levels of satisfaction with the mediation, mentioning such specific benefits as aid in the rehabilitation process, a chance to tell one's story and express emotions, a chance to have questions about the crime answered, the personalization of the victim and offender, opportunities for apology and forgiveness, fear and anger reduction, and healing. All of the participants agreed that mediation was appropriate for serious crimes. A study of 22 violent offenders involved in a VOM project in Canada found similar results.[56] Both victims and offenders expressed a high level of satisfaction with the encounter, and many victims left feeling they had more control over their lives.

Practitioners and theorists alike stress the importance of all parties preparing for restorative justice meetings because without preparation victims run the risk of being revictimized by the meeting. Often individual needs must be addressed before a beneficial meeting can occur. Before a meeting, victims, offenders, and community members should clarify what they need to say to the other parties and the questions they would like to ask. They may even want to role-play these questions with a trained facilitator to get comfortable with the emotions brought up by discussing the crime. Properly trained facilitators are critical to this process.

Is Restorative Justice Compatible with the Death Penalty?

Capital cases create special challenges for proponents of restorative justice. The death penalty, with its goals of retribution and deterrence, seems antithetical to such restorative justice goals as taking individual accountability, creating dialogue, repairing harm, and fostering healing for all involved parties. Proponents of the death penalty often argue that cases involving extreme violence, including murder, are beyond the scope of restorative justice. In capital cases, the victim is dead, so there is no relationship to be repaired, and the harm to the victims' family members is too extreme not to punish through traditional methods. For these cases, many may ask: What purpose is served by restorative justice?

Even among death penalty abolitionists, the use of restorative justice in capital cases presents problems. In response to a study by Umbreit and Vos that described the benefits of using "victim offender mediation/dialogue sessions" with offenders on death row in Texas, death penalty scholars Radelet and Borg argued that "such programs have no place on death row. If the state is truly interested in promoting restorative justice between killers and the families of their victims—as we think it should be—the first step it needs to take is to abolish the death penalty and stop promoting the false belief that capital punishment is an effective way to foster the healing of families of homicide victims." They argue that the very premise of restorative justice is to restore individuals: victims, offenders, and community members. Execution disrupts this difficult process in many ways and "creates an entirely new group of profoundly injured people: the offender's family."[57]

Despite the incongruity between the application of the death penalty and the goals of restorative justice, there still remain the needs of other individuals involved in the crime and the criminal justice process that results in an execution. Although Radelet and Borg correctly assess the situation that restorative justice can never function completely and properly in a system where offenders are executed, Umbreit and Vos describe a program that deals directly with the needs of victims and offenders in their current situations, which includes a capital sentence and execution. The issue largely becomes one of timing: do we wait to abolish the death penalty before using restorative justice to attempt to address the needs of victims' and offenders' families, or do we begin to work with them in the shadow of the death penalty?

Another concern among some death penalty abolitionists is that restorative justice work, although important, will deflect attention from the movement to abolish the death penalty, thereby impeding the effort to end capital punishment. To this we suggest that it is also possible that restorative justice work will bring to light complex issues that will be critical to the debate over the death penalty. The current irony of the capital punishment debate is that the individuals arguably most impacted by the death penalty—the offenders' family members—are absent from the debate.

It is our belief that there are openings in the death penalty process where restorative justice would be helpful to all involved parties and that create new concepts of what is possible when confronting murder. The restorative justice model deserves to be considered in the death penalty debate.

Currently little research exists examining the programs in many states that attempt to incorporate restorative justice into work with victims and offenders in death penalty cases, but initial studies show promise. Using in-depth case study analysis, Umbreit and Vos assessed the use of restorative justice in capital cases.[58] The authors studied the experiences of five individuals (three relatives of the murder victim [covictims] and two offenders) who participated in VOM. Both offenders and victims' family members met extensively with a professional mediator before the encounters took place, and everyone reported satisfaction with the process. The experience served to humanize both offenders and victims' family members and gave both sides a chance to tell their stories and offer accompanying apology or forgiveness if desired. Finally, the encounter was described as healing by all who were involved.

Although the process was ultimately healing, it was not easy. In meeting each other, they faced their worst fears and talked their way through it together. Not all victims' family members granted forgiveness, and most did not leave entirely unburdened, but each left in a better place than where he or she started. As one victim participant noted after the execution, "[J]ust because [the offender] is gone, doesn't mean that the hatred and that anger and rage is going to be gone, it has to be displaced, and this program helps you take it from this place to this place and get rid of it."[59] Another victim in this study explained, "It's very easy in a crime as horrible as that one to not really be able to place blame anywhere . . . and so for me it was important to establish some level or some balance of accountability among everyone, and not no one and nothing."[60] These participants stress the importance of accountability and having the offender admit his wrongdoing so that all parties could begin coping with the crime.

In the most extensive study to date, Umbreit and colleagues analyzed case studies and interviews with 79 offenders and victims in programs in Texas and Ohio.[61] All of the participants were victims, their family members, or offenders in serious cases of violent crime, including homicide. In three of the cases the offender was on death row. Participants reported high satisfaction levels with the dialogue, and 80% of the participants felt the "program had a profound effect on their lives. Victims, family members, and offenders alike reported feeling more at peace and better able to cope with their lives."[62] These results indicate that even in cases where retributive justice—punishment in the form of incarceration or a death sentence—is used by the state, restorative justice offers something for victims, their family members, and the offenders that is missing in other systems. Three recent studies by the authors of this book also suggest that models of restorative justice should begin to include offenders' family members.[63]

Summary

Crime creates multiple and serious harms, and instead of feeling supported by the criminal justice system, individuals, including victims, often feel aggrieved and frustrated. Recognizing that harms victims, offenders, their loved ones, and communities experience are wounds which are often aggravated in the present system, theorists and practitioners looked for other ways to address crime. They developed restorative justice, a needs-based approach to addressing crime. Restorative justice recognizes that the relationship between the victim and offender is damaged by crime and tries to involve both parties in communication to seek ways to repair harm, meet obligations, and reduce recidivism.

The two most important components of restorative justice programs are voluntary participation and extensive pre-encounter preparation. In cases of property crime, the goal is for offenders and victims to negotiate a reparation agreement, and in violent cases the focus is on the dialogue itself and the healing power it might offer. Often the victim and victims' family members want information that only the offender could supply: they want to know all the details, the motives, the what-ifs, and they want to tell offenders how the crime has changed their lives. Similarly, some offenders desire a chance to take personal responsibility for their actions and apologize to those they have hurt. Forgiveness, although not a required outcome, is offered spontaneously by some victims and appears to help both victims and offenders in their healing processes. For all involved parties, the process is extremely painful, but the studies cited in this chapter suggest that the outcomes justify the process.

The death penalty creates challenges for proponents of restorative justice. The traditional justice system's rationale for the death penalty— retribution and deterrence—is not based on repairing relationships and does not match with such restorative justice processes as personal accountability and dialogue between involved parties. An offender given a death sentence is often portrayed as someone beyond redemption and as a monster not worthy of human life, whereas restorative justice recognizes that he should be held accountable for his actions and be required to meet obligations. Restorative justice can also create concerns for opponents of the death penalty, some of whom have noted that in addition to process issues (including the fact that the victim may be deceased), restorative justice programs take attention away from the inhumanity of the death penalty and the abolition movement.

However, the significance of the Umbreit and Vos study should not be ignored.[64] The authors found that of the five individuals who participated in VOM, all described healing effects. Given the preliminary success of restorative justice studies, we believe it is important to explore additional applications of restorative justice in response to violent crime, particularly to offenders' family members, an often-overlooked group profoundly impacted by the crime. Examples like Bud Welch and Bill McVeigh,

Pope John Paul II and Mehmut Ali Agca, and the TRC in South Africa all offer the promise of justice that is more inclusive than a typical criminal justice sentence. In these very important cases, justice meant addressing the harm caused by crime through dialogue and building better communities to prevent future crime and promote social justice. We believe there is similar potential for restorative justice to address the needs of offenders' families in other serious cases.

Throughout the book we use exploratory empirical data to assess the needs of offenders' family members and explore different ways that restorative justice is already being used and might be expanded in capital cases, and we place specific focus on offenders' family members. We hope that these ideas combined with the extensive work by other scholars and professionals will help better address the specific needs of victims, offenders, and community members.

3

Meet the Families

Several days after her fourteenth birthday and not long after her first menstrual period, Lesa was married to a man who smelled and was dirty. Her mother not only had signed for Lesa's marriage but also had arranged it. Lesa speculates it was because of the influence of her grandmother: "Grandmother's view was that all women were bad. They were nothing more than whore hoppers. I think my mother got scared, and married me off right after my first period so that nothing could go wrong."

Lesa recognizes that her mother didn't have an easy life. She suffered from severe depression and horrible headaches, which Lesa believes were caused by spurs in her sinus cavity and a deviated septum that was never treated. Her mother also never received hormones after a hysterectomy. Her mother felt neglected and strained by her time alone because her husband, Lesa's father, was always working extra hours, or stretching the grocery budget by hunting or fishing. Lesa doesn't believe that her mother was cruel, even though she could be verbally abusive; she just had, as Lesa said, "a number of issues which made life very difficult for her and those around her."

In contrast, Lesa had a special bond with her father and often waited for him to come home from work because he always had some sort of trinket for her in his lunch box. When Lesa's mother started to make plans for her to marry Bob, Lesa was horrified. She tried to avoid the marriage by threatening to tell her father how she really felt about Bob, but her mother slapped her hard across the face and said, "If you mention this to your Daddy in any fashion except that you want this to happen, I will divorce your Daddy." Not wanting to hurt her father, Lesa stayed quiet and married Bob in what she described as a "rinky dink church down the street."

Although Lesa's family was poor, they were nowhere near as poor as the family that she married into. Her husband brought Lesa home to a small, roach-infested trailer, which had neither air conditioning nor a washer and dryer. For the first two nights of their marriage Lesa avoided sex. The idea scared her, and when she saw her husband's penis she grew terrified: "I was a child thinking how could it possibly fit? I had tried to use a tampon and that would not fit." On the third day, Bob lost all patience and raped his wife multiple times. Lesa recalls, "I was bleeding, and everything in me felt like it was torn up. When I went to the bathroom, I would cry because of the pain." Throughout their marriage, Bob never stopped raping Lesa and beating her as well. Lesa explained that if the dinner, or his clothes, or anything else he demanded was not just so, then he would beat her. She tried to create a pleasing household for Bob, but they simply had no money. Bob spent his earnings on poker machines, and Lisa's grocery allowance was limited to $20 a week from her mother.

About a year after their marriage, Lesa gave birth to Bobby. Every time Bob tried to raise a hand to Bobby, Lesa would throw herself between her son and husband. The brutality of the beatings escalated. One time, Lesa recalled, her husband choked her until she passed out, while her son attempted to protect her by beating his father with a plastic bat. Lesa left her husband seven times, but each time she was forced to return because either Bob would find Bobby and steal him from her or she would have no other place to go.

Lesa's mother died 7 years after the marriage, in 1984, and Lesa never asked her mother why she pushed her into marrying such a brute. When Lesa returned from the funeral, she had changed. That night she served her husband his dinner as usual. He was unhappy with the mashed potatoes and knocked the table over. This time, Lesa did something she had never done before: she spoke back to him. After receiving a hideous beating, Lesa got a knife and left for the eighth time. Then, while Lesa filed for divorce on the grounds of cruelty, Bob received supervised custody. Shortly after the divorce was finalized, Bob kidnapped Bobby and took him out of the state. It took Lesa three agonizing weeks to find her son and get him back.

On her own and without a penny, Lesa was terrified by life and desperate. However, not long after her divorce she met and married Greer, an older man who was kind to her and Bobby. After their wedding, Greer changed, and although he did not hit her, he became verbally abusive to Bobby. Bobby was torn between his father, who had brutalized his mother, and his stepfather, who was mean to him. Much to Lesa's chagrin, Bobby began to spend days with his father and eventually moved in with him. Bob continued to beat Bobby, and eventually the violence escalated between them to the point where Bobby "snapped"—he picked up a gun and killed his father and his father's girlfriend.

Today Bobby is on death row. If he had been several months younger when he committed murder, his sentence would have been commuted to life without parole, but Bobby killed his father after he turned 18, and he was not affected by the 2005 Supreme Court ruling that ended executions for juveniles. Lesa visits her son every week, and mother and son are very devoted to each other; today Lesa is very clear when she says, "I won't make it if they kill my child."

Lesa, like many mothers found in this book, loved her son and wanted what was best for him, but she lived her life against a backdrop of abuse, chaos, and pain. Not all of Lesa's choices were wise, but she did the best she could. She believes that she is the other victim of the murder, yet she does not absolve herself for her role in her son's mistakes as she knows that his deadly violence was a response to his own victimization and her inability to change things.

Referring to family members of capital offenders, especially parents, as the "other victims" can be considered contradictory to recognizing the role that the offender's home life played in the development of his criminal behavior. However, as we saw with Lesa, the parents themselves are often victims of grim social histories and intergenerational abuse. We explore the family members' histories in this chapter because it provides context for their stories and grounds for bringing them into a restorative justice process.

We begin the discussion with a brief review of the published research on capital defendants' families. Data from the psychosocial histories of 14 offenders and selected interviews of other offenders' family members are used to introduce the following four family themes:[1]

- *Excessive violence and neglect with ineffective protection.* These are families who were ravaged by abuse and neglect and did not receive support from battered women's programs or Child Protective Services.
- *Lack of education and support about mental health issues, including substance abuse.* A number of family members saw troubling behaviors from the offender, including talking to himself, but the family members were unsure about what they were seeing or where they might go for help. In some cases, when they did seek assistance, the help was inadequate.[2]
- *Unprepared caregivers and family disarray.* A number of parents said that they were raising their sons while they were raising themselves. These individuals got married devastatingly early, some as young as 14. They were unprepared to be parents, and the behaviors that occurred within the household, such as abuse and drug use created disarray.
- *Institutional barriers to equality.* Many family members were dealing with the lasting effects of racism, classism, and segregation.

These patterns do not represent an exhaustive list of the types of family issues experienced in the homes in which capital offenders were raised and do not represent every family system we found. They do, however, shape the themes that occurred over and over among the families we interviewed. After our exploration of the themes, we turn to what theory tells us about the effects of family issues on individual development.

Themes in Past Research on Capital Defendants' Family Histories

When capital defendants' lives are examined, a number of risk and resilience factors emerge. Social scientists have long studied precursors in the personal and family histories of people who commit murder,[3] and some of these studies look particularly at people sentenced to die. In a comprehensive critique of published studies about factors in the lives of death row inmates, forensic psychologists Mark Cunningham and Mark Vigen found the population to be overwhelmingly male and disproportionately African American.[4] Intelligence levels were low to average, and educational attainment was low (half did not finish high school), which is comparable to individuals found in the general prison population. One difference, however, is that among the death row inmates with low intelligence, their levels were likely to be very low. Death row inmates had far higher rates of psychiatric disorders and neuropathological conditions than the general population and somewhat higher rates than the general prison population. The researchers found high rates of substance abuse and intoxication by death row inmates at times proximal to the capital crime.

Cunningham and Vigen also learned that within the inmates' family histories, paternal abandonment, foster care and institutionalization, abuse and neglect, and parental substance abuse were common. Social work researcher Dorothy Van Soest reported similar psychosocial histories. Van Soest and her colleagues examined the histories of 37 men executed in Texas in 1 year and found that compared to rates in the general prison population, the men were more likely to have been physically, sexually, or emotionally abused; neglected; raised in poverty; exposed to family alcohol or drug abuse; and diagnosed with posttraumatic stress disorder, mental retardation, or school behavior problems.[5]

Providing specificity to Cunningham and Vigen's and Van Soest's works, Harvard Public Health researchers David Freedman and David Hemenway examined the psychosocial histories of 16 men on death row and found that all of them experienced some type of family violence.[6] In 14 cases, they found multigenerational family histories of physical abuse. In three cases the defendant was beaten to the point of losing conscious; three defendants were victims of incest, and four experienced sexualized physical abuse. Fifteen of the defendants witnessed intimate partner or other family violence in their own homes. In 14 of the cases the men grew up in homes where family members were polysubstance abusers. Each of the conditions found in the Freedman and Hemenway study can itself be a significant obstacle to healthy development; taken together, they are alarming.

Few studies compare the backgrounds of defendants convicted of murder who are sentenced to die with those who are given other sentences. In one, researchers Schaefer and Hennessy examined national data files about executed capital offenders and compared descriptors in their life histories with those found in a New York study of homicide offenders in the general population.[7] Though the samples were not directly comparable, the findings suggest that executed offenders may be more likely to have neuropathy, psychiatric illness, substance abuse, and child abuse histories than other violent offenders.

Themes in Family Background

Our research supports these findings, and tables 3.1 and 3.2 explore the factors found in the sample of 14 offenders' case histories.[8]

Table 3.1 provides a list of 21 factors present in the childhood histories of the 14 capital defendants. The list includes all of the factors reviewed in the published research, such as violence and drug use, as well as other factors not previously named, such as religious abuse and exposure to health risks.

In table 3.2, the offenders are given pseudonyms, and the factors that affected their development are indicated. By way of a quick review, table 3.2 shows that all of the defendants came from homes in which drug or alcohol abuse occurred, and 13 were victims of physical or sexual abuse. Depression or mental illness affected 13 defendants or their family members. Ten grew up in poverty. Seven experienced religious extremism. Most of the offenders experienced more than half of the factors. The table also shows the factors present in the lives of each of the individual offenders. For example, the table shows that Jamal grew up in an environment were he experienced all of the factors but sexual abuse.

Violence and Neglect

It is no surprise that many capital offenders come from homes filled with abuse and neglect. The maltreatment and interpersonal violence in these households was often very severe, involving guns, knives, or boiling water. One father in our study set his son's pants on fire while the boy was wearing them. Common practices in two of the interviewed families included leaving children outside, sometimes for days, following a beating, and in several cases drunken fathers shot at the children's feet as a way of reminding them who was in charge of the household. What follows are stories of abuse—experienced by three mothers, Theresa, Betty, and Lynn—and its multigenerational effect on their families.

On hearing these stories, it can be hard not to wonder why the mothers stayed with their tyrannical and violent husbands. A defense lawyer that we spoke with gave us Theresa's answer.[9] Her rationale was surprising. This lawyer said that Corbin, the offender, and his siblings had all described the beatings, sexual abuse, and bullets that marked their home life with their father. Sometimes the children stayed outside in the woods near the home to escape their father, and other times he sent them there. Everyone in Corbin's family knew that Theresa felt trapped and yet was unable to leave. Perhaps, they speculated, she was afraid.

However, Theresa finally admitted that she had what might be considered a good reason for not leaving—she did it to protect the children. She explained that she had been married before she met Corbin's father, and that her first husband beat her when he was drunk. The first time she required hospitalization, she filed for divorce on the grounds of cruelty, but her husband, who was politically connected in their small town, received sole custody of her

Table 3.1
Selected Factors Present in the Childhood Histories of 14 Capital Defendants

Trauma and Violence
>Childhood severe physical abuse
>Exposure to severe or chronic domestic violence
>Exposure to murder, attempted murder, or threats to murder
>Exposure to suicide, attempted suicide, or threats to suicide
>Exposure to school and community violence
>Exposure to war and/or displacement related to war
>Combat trauma

Sexual Abuse and Exploitation
>Childhood sexual abuse
>Childhood exposure to pornography
>Sexual assault after childhood
>Participation in pornography or sex industry (by force or voluntary)

Psychological Abuse and Terrorism
>Degradation and humiliation by caregivers
>Intimidation and threats of harm
>Caregiver's abuse of pets and property
>Forced isolation
>Corrupting, causing children to engage in immoral or illegal acts
>Dominance by caregiver, disallowing development toward age-appropriate autonomy
>Unpredictable caregiving (fluctuations of indulgence and harshness)

Abandonment, Shunning, Isolation, or Rejection
>Abandonment by father
>Abandonment by mother
>Abandonment by other primary caregiver
>Avoidance by peers and others due to stigma associated with real or perceived characteristics of the defendant or defendant's family
>Rejection by certain family members or peers; scapegoating
>Social isolation due to restrictions of living environment, shyness, or emotional withdrawal
>Shunning by others related to poor dental health, hygiene, or other similar factors

Mobility and Unstable Relations
>Frequent residential relocation and school and caregiver changes
>Homelessness
>Changing household composition, people come and go
>Household chaos, i.e., absence or insufficient order in the home (e.g., no organized meal times, no regular place to sleep, inadequate housekeeping)

Unreliable Caregivers
>Attachments that are few in number, weak, and frequently changing
>Insecure attachment bonds; anxiety about who cares; yearning
>Psychologically unavailable or detached caregivers (e.g., physically present but emotionally distant due to depression, substance abuse, self-absorption, apathy, dislike of child)
>Absence of or insufficient unconditional love

Table 3.1 (*continued*)

Parental Inadequacies

Father and/or mother absence for reasons of abandonment, incarceration, illness, work (e.g., military, seasonal work, work-related travel)

Parental criminality, addiction, mental illness, physical illness, disability

Parental ignorance regarding healthy child-rearing practices

Role reversal, i.e., child assumes responsibility for parent

Perpetual unresolved hostility between parents

Inadequate Social Supports

Unavailable or unskilled social network members in times of need

Unavailable or conflicted peer relations

No one to reliably provide comfort through healthy touch, listening, affirming, giving tangible assistance, advice, companionship

Social isolation, loneliness

Norms of extreme self-sufficiency

Loss and Unresolved Grief

Death of caregivers: normative (e.g., death of older grandparent); premature and unexpected (e.g., early disease); traumatic (e.g., by murder or accident)

Death of friends and loved ones

Loss of caregivers and loved ones due to divorce, incarceration, or departure

Severe disappointment (e.g., failure in sports or use of talent, loss of hope/dreams)

Inadequate support for mourning and grief subsequent to loss

Poverty and Deprivation

In utero and early infancy deprivation of physical and/or emotional nurture

Childhood neglect

Material deprivation (inadequate housing, food, clothing, medical care, transportation)

Psychosocial and physical health correlates of poverty

Family economic insecurity due to chronic unemployment or underemployment, gambling, excessive debt

Lack of supervision and positive discipline

Lack of private space or personal possessions

Religious Abuse

Sexual or physical abuse by intensely religious parent or minister

Cult or separatist group participation by parents, caregivers, or self

Barriers to spiritual development

Alcohol or Drug Abuse

Parental alcoholism or other forms of alcohol abuse

Fetal alcohol effects and syndrome

Parental use of illicit drugs

Parental abuse of medications or other chemicals

Parental abuse of "medications" to alter child's mood or behavior

Table 3.1 (*continued*)

Head Injuries, Learning Disabilities, or Mental Retardation
Diagnosed, misdiagnosed, or undiagnosed atypical learning abilities
Problems in intellectual functioning
School behavior problems
History of head injury

Mental Illness or Emotional Disturbance
Diagnosed, misdiagnosed, or undiagnosed mental disorders
Dysfunctional stress adaptations
Ineffective or harmful mental health treatment

Chronic Physical Illness, Injuries, or Disabilities
Physical conditions (e.g., neurological, endocrine, others) that affect behavior
Cognitive, speech, or language impairments
Residence with someone who has prolonged illness or disability

Exposure to Health Risks
Exposure to neurotoxins such as lead-based paint or contaminated water
Residence near biological and chemical hazards
Exposure to preventable diseases (e.g., those caused by vermin, lack
   of immunization, poor hygiene, unsafe sexual practices)
Injuries or death of loved ones due to risk-taking behavior such as gun play,
   speed driving, daring acts

Gangs
Participation in gangs or ad hoc groups that commit illegal activities

Exposure to Crime
Commission of detected or undetected crimes by parents or caregivers
Early delinquent acts
Incarceration, including solitary confinement

Out-of-Home Placement
Foster care
Residential treatment facility
Juvenile detention or institution for juvenile offenders

Institutional Abuse and System Failure by the State
Inadequate educational support
Inadequate support from child welfare system
Inadequate support from juvenile justice system
Inadequate support from mental health care system
Inadequate support from criminal justice system
Inadequate support from disabilities, special needs, and health care system

Discrimination or Oppression
Discrimination by race, ethnicity, or national origin
Discrimination by gender and gender roles
Discrimination by gender identity or sexual orientation
Real or perceived domination by another person or group

Table 3.2
Selected Factors Present in the Childhood Histories of the 14 Capital Defendants or at Least One Close Family Member

	Offender													
	Alfred	Arnold	Darius	Donnie	Garth	Graham	Jamal	Jonathan	Gale	Martha	David	Tommy	Yvette	Willie
Victim	Own child	Unknown women	Male store clerk	Employer	Female neighbor	Female neighbor	Father	Male store clerk	Father, step-mother	Husband, father	Grand-mother	Mom's drug supplier	Own children	Police officer
Factor														
Alcohol or other drugs	X	X	X	X	X	X	X	X	X	X	X	X	Early	X
Poverty	X	X			X	X	X		X	X	X	X		X
Domestic violence	X	X			X	X	X		X	X		X	X	
Mental illness	X		X	X		X	X			X		X		
Depression	X	X	X		X	X	X	X	X				X	X
Learning disability/ mental retardation		X		X		X	X				X			
Religious extremism					X		X	X	X	X			X	X

(continued)

35

Table 3.2 (continued)

	Offender													
	Alfred	Arnold	Darius	Donnie	Garth	Graham	Jamal	Jonathan	Gale	Martha	David	Tommy	Yvette	Willie
Physical abuse	X	X		X	X	X	X	X	X	X	X	X		X
Sexual abuse	X	X			X					X	X		X	X
Mother	Absent	Corrupt*	Absent, raised by grandparents	Weak, died	Weak, caring	Weak, caring	Corrupt	Weak, caring	Corrupt	Weak	Absent, raised by grandparents	Corrupt	Weak, caring	Absent
Father	Brutal	Corrupt	Unknown	Caring	Brutal	Brutal	Brutal	Brutal	Brutal	Brutal, corrupt	Unknown	Unavailable	Corrupt	Weak
Parent marital	Divorced	Divorced	Never married	Married	Divorced	Separated	Divorced	Married	Divorced	Divorced	Never married	Divorced	Divorced	Divorced
Parent style	Chaos	Chaos	Nurturing grandparents	Caring	Rigid	Neglect	Chaos	Rigid	Chaos	Rigid	Rigid	Chaos	Rigid	Rigid

*"Corrupt" signifies the parent had a corrupting influence on the child, e.g., gave the child alcohol or drugs, taught the child to steal or commit other crimes.

toddler son. With no custody restrictions, he moved himself and their son to another state. Theresa has not seen her child since then. She does not know whether he is alive and if his father ever beat him like he beat her. When her second husband began beating their children, she continued to stay with him; she was terrified that if she left that he might receive custody of the children, and she would be more powerless than ever to protect them.

Another mother, Betty, tried to leave her husband, Angus, whose brutality broke her and her children's bones and spirits and often left them unconscious. During a particularly savage attack on the children, Betty ran to her neighbor's house for help. Her neighbor placed her in his truck and headed to the house for the children. When Angus saw them approaching, he grabbed his gun and shot and killed the neighbor. Shockingly, Angus served only a couple of years in prison for the crime. After the children were grown, Angus decided that he no longer wanted to be married to Betty, so they divorced. Angus married a string of women, including one who had a romantic attachment to his son, Gale. When Angus fathered another child, the first that was not Betty's, Gale became enraged that his father might inflict more harm on a child. The two argued, and Gale shot and killed Angus and his wife.

A third mother, Lynn, did manage to leave an abusive relationship, but she could not protect her son. Lynn married young in life to escape the sexual abuse in her family of origin, and when her marriage did not work, she took her young son and left her husband. Divorced and with a child, she met another man, Dean, who she married, and together they also had a son, Alfred. Dean was an alcoholic who had a head injury that left him prone to irritability and violent outbursts. He beat Lynn badly. After 2 years, she took her kids, including Alfred, and moved out of his house and back to her mother's home.

On leaving Dean, Lynn worked as a waitress and tried to make ends meet. When Dean came and forcibly took Alfred, she was terrified at the thought of fighting to get him back. Her only comfort was that she believed that Dean was living with his mother, who had always been good to Alfred, so she trusted he would be well cared for there.

Alfred actually lived alone with his father, where he was sexually abused and beaten, including a time when his father broke Alfred's leg. Several times Child Protective Services intervened, placing Alfred with his paternal grandmother, but she eventually returned him to Dean each time, believing that "a boy should be with his daddy." Even when he lived with Dean, Alfred saw his grandparents often and developed relationships with his cousins, aunts, and uncles. Although his grandmother and extended family cared deeply for Alfred, it never occurred to him to tell anyone that there were problems when his father drank.

Dean kept steady jobs, presented himself to his mother as managing well, and drank mostly on weekends. He had a steady stream of live-in girlfriends and short-term wives. Alfred was expected to call each of these women "Mama," and he developed a fondness for most of them, but each inevitably left because of his father's drunkenness and brutality.

Multiple changing and conflicted relationships, inadequate protection, and ambivalent caregiving created a ripe environment for Alfred to develop serious emotional problems. As Alfred matured, his marriage and a steady job seemed to indicate that he was getting his life on track. Unfortunately, with the financial stress of being a new father, Alfred started taking methamphetamine to enhance his job performance, an idea he picked up from his supervisor and senior employees in the company. On a Saturday afternoon when Alfred was withdrawing from the drugs, he napped on the couch while his young son slept in the next room. The boy awoke and started to cry. Alfred first tried to comfort him, and when the child did not stop crying, Alfred went into a violent rage, shaking his son and eventually throwing him, causing a fatal head injury. These family histories clearly illustrate the intergenerational effects of violence.

Unprepared Caregivers and Family Disarray

During our interviews, a number of the mothers said that they still were growing up themselves when they had their first child. Lesa and Betty were each married when they were 14; two others were married at 15, and three at 16. The children born to such homes often experienced unprepared caregivers and chaos. This was certainly the case for Arnold and his mother, Carol.

When Carol was growing up, her mother worked two shifts to support her children and a violent, alcoholic husband who was in and out of the home. For Carol's mother, divorce was difficult because her religion prohibited it, so she did not take action until her husband finally started living with another woman in a different state. Carol left the chaos of her mom's house when she was only 16 and married Joey, who was 18. She was drinking at least a six-pack a day by the time Arnold was born, the fourth of seven children. Neighbors describe their home as a place of chaos where both parents often were drunk, hosted neighborhood pot parties, and fought brutally. The children were hit, but more often they were just ignored. Joey managed to keep a minimum wage job, and Carol managed to keep appearances together enough so that when Child Protective Services periodically checked in after reports of abuse and neglect, they were unable to find evidence of misconduct, and a finding of abuse was never filed. Arnold's school identified him as in need of special education, and Carol did go to meetings at the school when they asked her to come because she wanted to be a good mother.

Despite Carol's intentions, Arnold's primary caregiver was an older brother, who taught him to steal. By age 12 Arnold was drinking and sniffing glue regularly. About that time Carol, at her sister's urging, joined a church, got sober, and left her husband. Carol was determined to guide her children in the right direction, but they had never learned to respect her.

After he turned 14, Arnold never went a day without some sort of drug, except when he was incarcerated and had access to drugs only sporadically.

He spent most of the time from age 16 to 21 behind bars. Even though his family life was chaotic, when he was released, he always migrated home, a home where crisis and confusion were tolerated. While serving a sentence for auto theft, Arnold escaped; while on the run, he raped and killed two women in two different states. During his trial, neuropsychological assessments revealed organic brain damage and clear signs of fetal alcohol effects that had never been diagnosed.

Crushed by her feelings of guilt associated with her inadequate parenting starting in utero, Carol began developing serious stress-related health problems. Arnold calls her almost daily from prison, and they pray together over the phone. She visits every few months because she lives 300 miles away. She and her children are intimidated by the legal system. They were confused about the people who came to their house to talk with them, often not knowing who was from the prosecution and who was with the defense. His brothers have been in trouble with the law, and the idea of testifying in court about their home life and asking for mercy for their brother made them anxious. The family accepts Arnold's guilt, though they never could have imagined that he would commit such crimes.

Raising children is hard work, and it is frightening to think that those responsibilities fall to young teenagers without a support system and a great deal of unresolved trauma and pain. Today mothers like Carol are living with the nightmare and guilt of their own mistakes. Yet the mistakes that they made were not malicious; rather, they were an effort to cope with the pain and fear found in their families of origin.

Psychiatric and Neurological Disorders

Psychiatric and neurological disorders affect the family lives of offenders in serious ways. In most cases family members knew prior to the capital crime and subsequent trial that their loved one had severe problems, and they had worked hard to ensure treatment. Often they would spend their own money to augment care or fight for his institutionalization when his behavior showed signs of violence; when they could not get help, they tried to keep him under their watchful eyes. In several cases, the offender lived with family members who understood the disorder and its severity. Other family members, however, did not understand what was happening to their loved one. Even with little comprehension of what mental illness was, they were all too aware that his bizarre behavior was a problem, but they were helpless in how to address it.

Jamal's parents' views of his mental illness were clouded by their religious perspective. Raised in a strict fundamentalist church, his parents were forced to marry following an unplanned pregnancy when Jamal's mother was only 17 and his father 18. The couple fought violently from the beginning; by the time Jamal was 10, his parents had left the church and divorced. His father had developed serious alcohol dependency, and his mother, believing that a woman should have a man to take care of her, ended up in revolving relationships. Jamal lived alternately with his mother and father.

When Jamal began to show signs of psychotic delusions, his parents' religious beliefs told them he was possessed by demons and that he needed to be cleansed by God. They sent him to live with his grandparents, who belonged to an independent church. The church was apocalyptic, advocating membership by invitation to a select few and separatism from most of the world. His grandparents believed Jamal was evil. His school recognized him as emotionally disordered, but because he was a quiet child who caused no problems, his problems were never accurately diagnosed. By the time he was a young adult, Jamal frequently conversed with various spirits who lived inside him.

Jamal's father thought his son was odd but blamed it on his ex-wife's side of the family. Jamal's mother saw his "demons" as a message from above. In this context, it is not surprising that his schizophrenia went undiagnosed until he followed the spirit who told him to kill his father and he faced a capital trial.

After his arrest, Jamal's mother even said that if he was put to death, it would bring him closer to God. She assisted the defense team, but she was prepared for any outcome, suggesting that the state could do what it wanted, but the real outcome was up to God. Though the defense team prepared for a capital trial, the prosecutor accepted a guilty plea, and Jamal received a life sentence.

In many cases, the psychological issues of offenders and their family members are not as apparent as they are in Jamal's. There are situations in which everyone knows that something horrible had happened in the offender's past, but they had no idea that the trauma could cause a serious psychiatric illness. This was the case for Darius. Although born to a crack-addicted mother, Darius was surrounded by caring family members and friends from the time he was a small child. He was sent from Washington, D.C., to North Carolina to live with his mother's grandparents—his great-grandparents—when he was just a few months old. The adjustment was hard—he cried constantly and banged his head, but his great-grandparents took good care of him and raised him in a caring community and church.

By the time Darius was a teenager, his great-grandparents were becoming frail with age; he did well so long as they gave him structure, but like others born to crack-addicted mothers, he had problems with self-regulation. During his teenage years Darius stayed with his grandparents and several aunts and uncles in rotation so that no one seemed to be particularly in charge, though his uncle went regularly to meetings with teachers. Darius maintained average grades and graduated from high school with plans to go to the local community college. Then, one night when he was 18, he and his buddies got drunk and decided to race their car with another on a country road. The car Darius was in skidded and slammed into a tree, and his three best friends were killed instantly. He saw the top of his lifelong friend's head sheared off. Darius, a passenger in the rear seat, walked away with hardly a bruise, but the posttraumatic stress from this event destroyed his life and sense of self.

Darius felt guilty and responsible for his friends' deaths, and from that time on, he was lost. He never really worked; he simply drifted, and he began using drugs and alcohol. Every year on the anniversary of the accident and his friends' deaths he drank himself into oblivion. It never occurred to anyone in his family that he had a mental disorder induced by the accident. His family knew he was depressed, but they did not know the implications of such a prolonged depression. They sought help for him from the local mental health center, but his condition was misdiagnosed: he clearly had posttraumatic stress disorder, but they treated him only as a resistant substance abuser.

Following the accident that killed his friends, Darius felt he had no one he could go to for emotional or social support. He did not want to hurt or upset his elderly great-grandparents, who were his primary caregivers. Before his capital crime, Darius's aunts and uncles thought he was okay, but they were horrified to learn that he was one of three men who killed a liquor store operator. The assault occurred when Darius had been on a 5-day binge of drinking and smoking pot. He and his other friends went to the liquor store to rob the owner. One of the defendants pulled the gun and shot the owner when he threatened to shoot them.

Darius's great-grandparents died soon after his arrest. One aunt visits him regularly and feels guilty and lost about how to help him. The entire family feels shame and confusion. It seemed to them that Darius walked away from the car accident unscathed, yet they had no idea how much harm had actually occurred.

Many parents are lost when they try to manage a child's emerging problems associated with psychiatric or neurological conditions. Parents' inability to address these problems are exacerbated when there are problems and failures in the mental health system.

Institutional Barriers to Equality

Sarah, who we met in chapter 1 (her son killed a local shopkeeper), provides a strong example of institutional barriers to equality as her and her son's lives were shaped by segregation and labor practices that ensured their poverty. Sarah lived "across the tracks" in her small town of 20,000 people. The railroad tracks divided the town: on one side were the town center and the middle-class and wealthier homes; on the other was Sarah's enclave, mostly made up of low-income African Americans.[10] The city had no public transportation, and the only vehicle Sarah had was an unreliable old car, which meant that her children were unable to access any jobs or other opportunities in the city center, several miles from their home. The only amenities within walking distance were several churches and a convenience store attached to a gas station.

Without a high school education, Sarah worked at a menial job. In the late 1990s her company was sold, and the new owner reduced her wages significantly to just below minimum wage. This wage reduction was possible because Sarah lived in a right-to-work state, a strategy designed to keep unions out of areas by indicating that workers are employed "at the will" of the employer. Consequently a worker could be fired for any reason other than those protected by federal law, so voicing a concern about wage reduction was out of the question to Sarah, who believed that she had no other options. Without job protection or pay for absences, Sarah was afraid to take a day off work and accompany Marcus to a mental health appointment. One appointment Sarah scheduled after Marcus started displaying disturbing behavior, including carrying on lengthy and vociferous conversations with himself. Marcus went to the mental health center at the designated time, but left before he saw the doctor. It is difficult to say what might have happened had he seen a doctor, but we do know that Marcus shot and killed a man just weeks after failing to get help at the mental health center. He was later diagnosed as schizophrenic.

Not all capital offenders come from families with extreme abuse and the type of challenges that Lesa experienced. Like Sarah, there were a number who had to deal with the persistent stresses, strains, and corrosive effects of poverty and racism. Graham's mother, Tina, cobbled together a living for herself and her family in their rural South Carolina community. Tina maintained a tiny wooden sharecropper's house in a tobacco field, where she raised Graham and his two siblings as a single parent. Picking crops was one of the few jobs available for African Americans in the early 1960s, and when Tina was pregnant with Graham she was in the fields while planes flew overhead, dropping chemicals on the produce. Graham was undoubtedly exposed to toxins in utero.

As the son of a sharecropper, Graham spent his childhood in strict segregation and finished only a few years of school. More than once, white boys drove down the dirt road to his house and yelled, "Dance, nigger, dance!" while they fired bullets at his feet. By his teens, Graham had developed severe mental health problems, including persistent psychotic delusions, which may have been prompted by his exposure to toxins. Before he was 20, he spent time in prison for theft.

On his release, as he was walking to his mother's house, he stopped at the home of an elderly white woman who was the grandmother of one of the boys who used to call out racial slurs and shoot at him. He robbed her and shoved her hard enough to cause her death. Though the racist attacks of his youth did not directly lead to the crime, the entire context of Graham's life was marked by poverty and racism and the toxic environment they created. Graham needed support to stay in school, and he needed treatment for his psychotic delusions. Instead his severe poverty ensured that he received neither.

Again and again, family members express shame about what it was like to be among the poorest in their communities. Roy's foster parents were told that Roy's family had to burn tires in the fireplace to stay warm. Garth moved to California to escape his poor roots, only to be labeled a hillbilly. The families describe feelings of marginalization and exclusion, a sense of separation from the mainstream of their communities, which in turn affected their ability and inclination to reach out for help when problems arose.

In today's society, many families can meet their food, shelter, and transportation needs, but they cannot afford health care. The implications of this are profound. When a family notices odd behavior in a loved one, it is difficult to engage a therapist, and psychiatric hospital stays are aborted when Medicaid runs out. Moreover, there are times when it is impossible to pay for the antipsychotic drugs that can make the difference between a productive or destructive life for so many people with mental illness. Poverty alone does not cause someone to commit capital murder, but it is often enmeshed with other issues, such as mental health disorders and violence. Poverty compounds problems to further limit access to care and support.

Family Effects on Individual Development

Individuals are affected by their families; Lesa blames herself for not leaving her husband, and Carol knows that her problems with drugs and alcohol affected her son's development. Some individuals leave very harmful families relatively intact, while other individuals leave hurting and, like sticks of dynamite, self-destruct or hurt others. To provide a context for understanding the home lives of offenders and their family members, we review the literature that explores the ways in which families impact the development of their members.

Families are elaborately complex, interdependent social systems that tend to be influenced by the social norms of their immediate culture and the larger society around them.[11] One of the most important functions of a family is providing a place where an individual learns to love and be loved through his or her attached relationships. Primary attachments are unique relationships that children form with those persons they regard as their sources of security and survival.[12] Young children adore their primary attachments and do whatever they can to be near them. Likewise, attached caregivers are passionate about their children in a mutual bond. When attachment does not occur because an adult attachment figure is not available or unable to provide such care, the child is likely to have problems in social relationships throughout their lives.

Through attached relationships, people develop their capacity for empathy—the root of social responsibility, conscience, and positive moral behavior.[13] Another cornerstone in early development is the growth of self-regulation in behavior,[14] a capacity acquired through nurturing and social learning. Children deprived of attached relationships are at risk of not developing empathy, behavioral regulation, and social responsibility.

Critical to a family's interaction is its ability to communicate. In healthy families, members know how to share joy, sorrow, affection, anger, and a host of other feelings. These families solve problems by collaboratively identifying the problems, exploring alternative solutions, sharing decisions about what to do, evaluating the effect of decisions, and trying again if necessary. They negotiate, compromise, reciprocate, and manage conflict; as a result, they adapt to adversity in constructive ways.

In contrast, some families may have a variety of dysfunctional communication patterns. For example, children who engage in crime tend to come from homes with high turmoil, inconsistent consequences for behavior, or excessive coercion by parents.[15] These children learn to coerce others to get their way, the parents respond with increasing coercion, and the cycle escalates as the child becomes more resistant. The stress mounts. Without help from outside resources, the family is at risk for serious problems.

For healthy development, families must seek to provide children with a stable environment because children are at risk of problematic developmental outcomes if they experience instability. Instability can include environmental instability (e.g., frequent residential moves or changing household members, changing child care or schools), lack of clear structure (e.g., irregular daily routines or inconsistency in parental expectations), and unpredictability of events (e.g., parental temper outbursts or unexplained parental absences).[16]

To survive, families must gather resources to meet physical needs, such as food, shelter, clothing, hygiene, health care, and transportation. Even against a backdrop of scarcity, healthy families distribute these resources among their members with emotional support and a sense of belonging. They take particular care of vulnerable family members.

Families who have been historically denied adequate resources or have become marginalized fare less well. They suffer the burden of disparities. Many feel politically impotent, economically oppressed, and psychologically helpless in community arenas outside the comforting circle of their own family and friends. They struggle with unemployment or poor job conditions, racial and ethnic discrimination, inferior schools, deprivations of child and elder care, and insufficient physical and mental health care. Children deprived of basic nutrition or health care, regardless of the reasons for it, are at risk of suffering poor development.[17] One of the most robust predictors of crime and delinquency is a background of persistent poverty in childhood, particularly in the early years.[18] This in no way implies that poor families cannot be healthy or raise outstanding children, but that poverty brings a unique set of obstacles to families.

Families must adapt to life changes that are expected, such as a young adult child leaving home, a job change, or death of an elderly parent. They must also adapt to unexpected changes, such as when a storm damages the house or a family member is robbed. If the stressors include a serious threat to life or involve a major loss, they are considered catastrophic or traumatic.

Some families are stunning in their ability to overcome adversity. Froma Walsh, one of the country's leading scholars on families, emphasizes that a family's fundamental beliefs about itself guide the ways its members interact with one another and the outside world.[19] She identifies several core beliefs that characterize families that manage to be resilient in the face of difficulty. These include *trust*—faith in the dependability of and loyalty to one another; *coherence*—the belief that life has meaning and is manageable despite continual shifts; *respect* for individual differences and autonomy; a sense of *shared history and identity*; *positive outlook*—commitment to persevere and hope for the future; *acceptance* of things that cannot be changed; and belief in *transcendence*, a greater whole beyond oneself, and *spirituality* that is dynamic and provides support. When families lack these attributes, problems can become crises and crises can become devastating.

Resilient individuals are able to confront life's challenges and emerge stronger than they were before the crisis. They are neither merely survivors nor rugged individuals oblivious to the pain. Rather, they have absorbed the challenges in ways that they learn from and use their lessons to handle future problems. Resilience helps explain why some children survive childhood abuse without mental illness or a propensity for abusive behavior and are able to rise above their origins in poverty.[20]

In contrast, vulnerable individuals succumb in various ways to the forces of acute or chronic stress; their responses are maladaptive. They may develop physical illnesses, particularly heart disease and immune system deficiencies, or even a range of mental illnesses, including those specifically linked to stress, like posttraumatic stress disorder or mood disorders, such as depression or anxiety. In extreme cases, their minds seek to block the perceptions that induce stress, and they dissociate or develop other psychotic or perceptual distortions. Grasping for relief from the stress, they may externalize their distress and develop oppositional patterns of behavior, such as using physical force or engaging in manipulative or subversive activities that are illegal.

Resilience seems to evolve from both biological and social sources. The individual capacity to manage physical stress is regulated by biochemical functions that genetically vary among individuals and are apparent soon after birth. In addition, the individual can acquire certain conditions that inhibit the biological capacity for stress management, as in the case of certain head injuries, brain tumors, constant exposure to highly demanding stressors, alteration from the use of chemicals or medications, or development of some physical diseases that compromise the endocrine system.

Families play a major role in buffering stress and fostering resilience among their members. By providing affection, discipline, stable resources, and respectful communication, they can promote a child's empathetic and prosocial development. Unfortunately, many defendants have families that have faced multiple chronic problems that interfere with their capacity to provide consistent and healthy child developmental support.[21] Additionally, the lives of capital offenders are often unique in that few had access to supports that would have buffered the effects of their families. Protective factors include such benefits as a consistent adult who cares (like a teacher or minister), an above-average IQ, or access to programs aimed for children at risk. These factors tend to be woefully absent in the lives of offenders; this is due in part to the fact that barriers to equality or the chaos at home provide little opportunity for these factors to be present.

Summary

All of the offenders' family members in this book have faced extreme difficulties in their lives, even before their loved one committed a capital crime. Too often, these families did not have the knowledge or resources to cope with these difficulties. Four common themes that manifested themselves in the personal stories of offenders' family members were violence and neglect, teenage pregnancies for mothers who were unprepared for parenthood, psychiatric and neurological disorders, and institutional barriers to equality, including poverty, racism, and gender discrimination. All of these problems affected parents' ability to get the resources that their children desperately needed. Many of these problems were intergenerational and therefore represented family norms and diminished the ability of any one family member to intervene and break the cycle.

Many offenders grew up in a subculture marked by endemic violence and deprivation, and their parents knew that these were dangerous conditions for children's development. Parents did not see any other options for a better life, however, and they often coped by downplaying problems when they occurred. Additionally, even though a healthy attached relationship is critical to human development, many offenders' family members had no idea how to provide this—often because they did not have any sort of model from their own family and were too busy working, defending themselves or their children from brutality, or lost in their own hallucinations or addictions to form the necessary connections. Many lacked the communication skills to support their children's ability to manage conflict and learn negotiation. As a result, self-regulation was not supported in their children's development; under a confluence of circumstances, their children committed murder.

Offenders' families replay their life decisions over and over: "What if I had brought him to live with me?" "What if I had followed through with filing charges so that his father would be prosecuted for domestic violence?" "What if I had found a good psychiatrist for him?" They cannot go back, but their experiences can shed light on how communities, social service agencies, and schools can support children, adolescents, young adults, and families as they cope with life challenges. Their experiences also provide a warning for what happens when pain and harm are not addressed. These families needed help from outside sources with issues like mental illness, domestic violence, religious abuse, learning disabilities, and substance abuse as well as the basics of providing their children with adequate shelter, nutrition, and a stable environment long before the capital crime occurred.

For some of these family members, talking about their pain and articulating the numerous difficulties they have lived through is the first step toward breaking the cycle and reaching out to others for help. Unfortunately, there are currently few resources that provide family members with a safe place to talk about their issues and address their needs. A restorative justice process is needed whereby family members can freely express their guilt, shame, secrets, and pain associated with their own lives as well as their loved one's case without fear of censure. Family members have obligations to put their homes in order and seek assistance with the many issues that plague their households, including substance abuse, mental health issues, and violence. By doing so they will be making amends to their own communities, but it is unreasonable to expect that they will be able to meet these obligations without help, especially while they are simultaneously trying to manage the threat of their loved one's execution.

Although being a parent should get easier as children grow older, for these families—most of whom had painful lives before the crime—life became exponentially harder. Part II of this book explores the numerous harms incurred by family members as they interacted with the criminal justice system in capital cases.

Part II
Storytelling

A critical component of restorative justice is storytelling. To understand crime, its causes, and its consequences, it is necessary to allow those who have been affected—stakeholders—to speak in their own words. Part II explores offenders' family members' lives following the crime through their own voices and perspectives. We asked family members to tell us about the consequences of crime and how they are coping with having a loved one charged with a capital crime, their experiences with the criminal justice system, changes within their family and community dynamics, and their feelings toward the victim and his or her family members. They responded to our questions with candor, eloquence, raw emotion, and information that we never could have imagined. Their stories were not easy to tell, and they were often difficult to listen to, because they provide a very personal perspective about murder and the death penalty that contradicts many popular notions. By listening to their voices, we can begin to understand the harms experienced by family members in the context of death penalty trials, and this understanding is critical to bringing these family members into a restorative justice process.

Therapists and restorative justice theorists and practitioners know that telling one's personal story is one of the cornerstones of healing. Through storytelling, harms can be articulated, and the process of connecting harm and damage with specific needs and ways to address these needs can begin. Because of the significance of storytelling, it is not surprising that although our interviews were not meant to be therapeutic, many of the family members expressed gratitude for the opportunity to tell their stories and to have someone listen. For a number of the family members, the interview process was the first time they told their story to a person who did not have an agenda other than to hear and understand them. Moreover, storytelling can promote action, and family members felt validated by our belief that their words are important.

In chapters 4 through 7, we take the interviewees' descriptions of their experiences and offer interpretations through the lens of our own professional training in social work, criminal justice, and psychology.

We seek to shed light on this overlooked segment of the population, as well as identify the numerous ways they are harmed to better understand how a restorative justice process may be beneficial for them. Their stories speak to the death penalty and its effects and consequences, and their words offer new insight into the nature of crime and punishment.

4

Death Penalty Trials

At age 25, and after a great deal of hard work, Paul appeared to have gotten his life on track. He had grown up in a difficult home environment, which he summarized as "Mom was absent, and Dad was having problems." Paul's father was authoritarian, demanding, and at times abusive. Money was tight since Paul's father was an itinerant preacher whose earning capacity was limited by a degenerative health condition, and Paul's mother worked hard at a job that barely paid a minimum wage. As the oldest son, Paul had the responsibility of taking care of the household and his sister and two brothers. Paul described his days as being a mother and father to his siblings and his evenings as a scrutinized son, for when his father came home, he would expect a report. If things did not go well during the day, then Paul's father would generally beat the kids, with his fury largely directed toward Paul's younger brother Jeremy.

In high school, Paul realized that the only hope for a better life was to take action. He asked the Christiansons, a family from his church, if he could move in with them, and they agreed. Then Paul started going to the local mental health clinic and using therapy to come to terms with the issues in his past and "to let go of some of the baggage that I had been carrying around." After high school, Paul started college and worked at a fast food restaurant, a job he enjoyed. He had a healthy network of friends, was active in his church, and was starting to heal the wounds of his childhood.

All of Paul's progress suddenly halted when Jeremy was arrested. When Paul came home that day, he had a feeling that something was wrong. He recalls, "The phone rang, and it was my aunt. I could tell immediately by the sound of her voice that things were bad. She told me, 'we don't know if we can find your brother, and we think he is dead.' She said, 'I think your parents are at the police station.'" Paul immediately went to the station and learned that Jeremy was okay but had been arrested for killing Mr. Miller, an elderly and prominent member of the community, during an attempted robbery. The details of the crime were particularly heinous; Jeremy not only shot Mr. Miller in his own home but also boastfully compared his actions to those of a violent character in a movie that was popular at the time. Paul was stunned. He had been worried about Jeremy, who he saw as unruly and running with a fast crowd, but never as a murderer.

In an instant, Paul's world changed. His family was facing a crisis and had to confront the reality that they were in a heated public situation. The murder of Mr. Miller had gained national attention, and Paul stated, "It would be commonplace to have NBC, CBS, ABC, or FOX calling." Media correspondents would come to their house or Paul's place of work, hoping to catch a glimpse of the family. Things became so intrusive that Paul's coworkers would create decoys so that he could leave work in privacy.

His public life was difficult, but Paul's home life was torturous. His family members were all "emotional wrecks. I mean just bawling. You walk through the house and you start crying, and you don't even know why." For Paul, the thought of his younger brother being executed was as painful as his grief for the Miller family.

The public scrutiny and private stress affected Paul's ability to function. At the time of the murder he was in college and working. After the crime, he explained, "I had to quit school because I was failing everything. I went from A's to F's overnight." Paul's social networks unraveled; friends started disappearing, and Paul was surprised by how many of them were from his Christian circles, including the pastor. Paul confided that his life began to feel surreal: "Suddenly your world is turned upside down. Your friends are your enemies, and your enemies are your friends. Like there is a prominent person in town who was bitter rivals with Mr. Miller. He came to our defense at several different times. That is almost like a sickening feeling."

Paul's relationship with his community changed so profoundly that venturing outside of his home became a burden. "Oh it's terrible. You feel ashamed, embarrassed, intimidated, scared." He added that to this day, leaving the house can still evoke these emotions.

Painfully, he admitted, "For years and even now, I would get strangers walking up to me saying, 'You're Jeremy's brother, aren't you?' Then they'd ask something stupid, like, 'Did he really shoot him while he was eating his breakfast?' And you end up feeling like you are Snow White in the forest scene where she is running, and everything is after her."

Paul's other two siblings were in ninth and tenth grades at the time of Jeremy's arrest. In school they were harassed and threatened; classmates called them names, defaced their lockers, and made death threats. Eventually, things got so bad that the principal suggested that it was in the children's best interest to leave the school. Paul recalls, "There was no other school for them to go to. The principal suggested home schooling for both of them, but there was too much stress at home for that."

Against this backdrop Paul and his family prepared for Jeremy's trial. They agreed that Jeremy needed to be severely punished for what he had done, even if it meant spending the rest of his life in prison. Though most members of his family favored the death penalty at that time, none wanted to see Jeremy die. They all knew another side of Jeremy and understood the hardships he endured growing up.

A death penalty trial changed the life of every family member with whom we spoke. The disruption experienced by these family members was immense, even in families where the offender had behavioral problems and had been in trouble with the law in the past. Though the first reaction to the crime is invariably shock and profound sorrow for the victim and the victim's family members, this grief is quickly overshadowed by the threat of losing their loved one. This threat is traumatic, and the pain can be debilitating. Moreover, family members rarely have the financial or emotional resources to manage all of the changes occurring in their lives.

Having a loved one face the death penalty results in family members being singled out in the media and in their own communities. It is ironic that as more attention is focused on them, these families become increasingly isolated, and few community resources exist that target their needs. Rarely are offenders' family members given assistance in navigating the process involved in a death penalty trial, and the confusion often elevates their already high stress levels. After a death sentence is pronounced, they are left alone to live in the shadow of death, facing such issues as shame, fear, depression, trauma, suicide, stress-related health problems, and the constant threat that the state will soon execute someone they love.

Jeremy was fortunate to be assigned a legal team that was among the most competent in the country, but even with the best of lawyers, a death penalty trial takes its toll on all those involved. During the trial, the crime, including very specific and gruesome details, are relived in public, and the media scrutiny is intense. Under these conditions family members must assist the legal team and prepare for mitigation in the sentencing phase.[1] Mitigation often involves telling painful family secrets, and Paul assumed most of that burden in his family though it meant conflict with his father. The two never agreed on the nature of their home environment. On one hand, Paul wanted the jury to understand that he and his siblings grew up in an abusive environment, and that abuse contributed to Jeremy's violence. On the other hand, Paul loved his father and worried that by telling Jeremy's story he would jeopardize his relationship with his father. The decision to testify was not difficult for Paul to make, but it was very painful to implement.

Paul's testimony and support of Jeremy's legal team played a critical role in Jeremy's defense. Paul was always nervous before meeting with the lawyers because he believed that Jeremy's life depended on what he said to them. Paul revealed, "I would be anxious all day waiting for [the meeting] to happen. . . . [T]hen after it was done, I would just start crying. Not because they were hard on me. It was just that I would have to rethink all that stuff."

Paul developed trusting relationships with members of the legal team with whom he "bared his soul." Because of the length of the trial process, when two members resigned from the team for other jobs, Paul felt abandoned and feared that they left because they had lost faith in the case. Unfortunately, no one anticipated his concern and thought to tell him that this was an inaccurate assumption. In addition, changes in the legal team also meant that Paul had to dredge up and relive the same difficult stories for each new member of the team. The whole process "was a sickening emotional roller coaster."

For Paul and his father, reliving their past in front of lawyers was hard enough, but processing their long-suppressed emotions was excruciating. The family, forced to confront issues without sufficient time or support to deal with their feelings, had no way to integrate the freshly opened wounds into their lives. Paul observed, "Family members are changing, and a great deal of pain is getting stirred up" during the legal process: "Dad's blaming himself, and Mom is blaming herself, and neither of them is saying it, but they were on the inside, and it is destroying them. Mom thinks they were too hard as parents, and Dad thinks they were too soft. From all of this, Dad was suicidal, and Mom was really suicidal. I was fearful. I was calling my mom and dad every day. I really did not think my dad would make it. I really thought he would have taken his own life."

The lowest point for Paul's father, when he came closest to harming himself, was a result of a miscommunication with the legal team. On that particular day, Paul's father believed that he was going to court for the first day of Jeremy's trial, but it actually turned out to be a hearing to examine legal questions surrounding electrocution, a very disturbing possibility. Paul's father explained that on that day he felt so low that he almost wished the police officer had ended Jeremy's life at the time of the arrest. He confessed, "I see how this is stretching out, hurting us all. I am ashamed of that, but when you listen to them [the lawyers] describe to you point-by-point, blow-by-blow how the electric chair is going to take your son, you think things like that." Paul's father was plagued by the gruesome details that he heard that day and by his thought that things might be better if Jeremy had died.

Following the trial, which took several years, Paul and his family experienced another devastating miscommunication. They had been told that they would receive a contact visit with Jeremy, and everyone was thrilled and anticipating the moment that they could touch him again. However, the prison's concept of a contact visit and the family's vision could not have been more different. On their arrival, the family was shocked to find Jeremy chained, shackled, and halfway across a room on the other side of a barrier. Because there was no glass partition, it was considered a contact visit by this prison's administration—and that was the closest Jeremy's family had come to him in the years since his imprisonment.

Jeremy and his family were more fortunate than most of the families described in this book. His expert legal team avoided the death penalty. Despite this positive outcome, the family still carries scars from the trial and the possible execution of Jeremy. To this day Paul cannot walk into a courtroom without having a debilitating physical response. He clearly suffers from symptoms consistent with posttraumatic stress disorder (PTSD). Although Paul has a steady job and he and his father have reconciled, he regrets that he still has not returned to college. Paul's sister has received her GED, but his other brother, forced to drop out of school in the tenth grade, has become an alcoholic and has drifted in and out of jail.

Like Jeremy's family, family members of offenders who must go through a death penalty trial with their loved one often find their own lives being placed under a microscope by the media and members of their community and suffer immensely from guilt by association. Additionally, these family members are profoundly affected by their interaction with the criminal justice system and wrestle with seemingly unfair processes and arbitrary procedures. These experiences are intensified for individuals who perceive racism, classism, or ignorance of mental health issues among members of the court.

Guilt by Association

Family members of capital offenders say they are treated as if they themselves committed a horrible crime. Each family member we interviewed felt as if they were being punished along with their loved one, and these punishments included intense negative media coverage, being ostracized in their churches and communities, verbal threats, and disrespectful treatment by members of the criminal justice system.

Media Scrutiny

One of the many ways that a free media serves society is to provide information about crimes, arrests, and court proceedings.[2] When presented accurately, such information contributes to the general public's ability to make informed decisions about their personal safety and broaden their views regarding such matters as crime prevention strategies, criminal justice policies, and punishment. Conversely, when a crime story is sensationalized, it is likely to generate a public response based on fear.[3] Sometimes the media simply give a mixed message; they refer to the person as "the defendant" before a trial even begins and convey a sense of guilt with headlines such as "Murderer Caught" and "Crime Solved." Because crime has built-in drama, crime stories—especially brutal ones—get extensive coverage. This coverage often pits "evil" offenders against "good" victims.[4] As a result, the community context as well as the social and psychological factors that led up to a crime are often omitted.

Most family members recognized that the media have a legitimate and important role to play, but they also had strong negative feelings about the media. To triangulate and verify their experiences with the media, we reviewed available newspaper coverage involving the cases of the loved ones whose family members we interviewed. We found substantial variation in the tone of the actual news accounts about the crimes and trials.[5] Some reports described the facts in a straightforward way. This was seen in the newspaper account of Jeremy's arrest, despite his incendiary remarks when he likened himself to a notorious fictional killer. Other cases with far less material were sensational, presenting only limited perspectives of both offenders' and victims' family members.

Most of the family members described media coverage as "horrible." The nature of the coverage, the amount of coverage, and occasionally even harassment by members of the media were disturbing. Family members largely agreed that the most devastating part of media coverage was story content that made their loved one look like a "monster," "villain," or "dirt," while providing an incomplete picture of their loved one. Family members wanted their loved one's story told in context and hoped for a complete and accurate portrayal. Family members wanted newspaper readers to know that in addition to committing a horrible crime, their relative also was a highly decorated war veteran or a loving father.

Consider the example of William, a Vietnam veteran, who killed a police officer when he was stopped for a traffic violation and experienced a post-traumatic flashback. As the police officer approached him on a country road, William's mind flashed to Vietnam, and at that moment he was no longer in his community but in Vietnam, where he had to protect himself. He grabbed a hunting rifle from his car and killed the approaching armed stranger. William's mother, Mary, now in her 80s, explained that William suffered from PTSD and that he was receiving treatment at the Veterans Administration hospital. However, as Mary learned, PTSD is not easily treated, and some people are never symptom free despite efforts by the medical community and the patient's own desire to heal.[6]

William did want to heal. In addition to seeking treatment, he opted to live in an isolated area in the country as a way of reducing stimuli and stress to quell his PTSD symptoms. Prior to serving in Vietnam, William graduated from college with dual degrees. As a youth, he helped elderly neighbors mow their lawns and do other chores. His father was a school principal and his mother an active community volunteer. The media, however, ignored these aspects of William's life and misconstrued his isolationism, describing him as a militia survivalist. Stories also "had him eating out of garbage cans," a sensational claim that both William and his mother dispute. Most important, the media made no attempt to educate the public about PTSD, including the limitations of treatment and the fact that it should be considered a public health concern.

The media's inaccurate depiction of William had a demoralizing effect on Mary and her community. Embarrassed by the media portrayal, Mary, who had previously been a community activist—chairing the local hospital's fundraising committee—felt forced to relinquish her public position after the murder and arrest. Even though she had initiated a fundraising dinner and built it into a money-making gala, she believed that people would find her unworthy of retaining this position. Her fear was that others would associate her with the crime and also might believe that she let her son go hungry. She explained that she would not let anyone, particularly a child of hers, go hungry. She saw the image of her son eating out of a garbage can as an attack on both of them, and her feelings of shame caused her to withdraw from her community. As a result of the crime's public nature, Mary and other family members faced both the perception that they were being looked at differently and the reality of community members changing their behavior toward them. Their lives became shrouded in shame.

In another example, Mark, a public servant and a brother of a death row inmate, also viewed the publicity as hurtful. "It made me feel anxious," he confided. "It made me feel self-conscious knowing that the family and David [the offender] were getting that kind of publicity. Some of it was one-sided. I guess it [the publicity] made me feel angry and depressed. Things were twisted [in] the ways he was portrayed—like he was a monster."

In David's case, the media did have material to create a monster—David murdered two people outside of a shopping center and minutes later entered a police station saying that he wanted the death penalty for what he had done. During his trial, David testified that he committed the crime because he was depressed and wanted the state to kill him, becoming what is known in the criminal justice system as a "volunteer," a defendant who wants the death penalty. He explained that he was too much of a coward to kill himself and wanted the state to do it for him.[7] Several newspapers cited quotes from a letter in which David said that he might kill again and that he must die. David claimed that he had no remorse and that he committed murder to get what he wanted—the death sentence.

The newspaper stories accurately stated that David was depressed and a paranoid schizophrenic, but they missed a number of critical details necessary to understand him and his motives. First, the papers did not report David's statement that he was "God's personal psychiatrist," a comment that sheds light on his mental health and the validity of his other statements. Additionally, the papers neither ran stories to explain mental illness and schizophrenia nor did they report that David sought help for his mental illness and was released from a psychiatric hospital shortly before the crime. They also didn't mention that David was a local sports hero who was in college on a sports scholarship when he experienced his first schizophrenic break from reality.[8] They neglected to report that at age 20 David started talking about religion in ways that could be considered odd and one day walked away from a game, saying that God disapproved of sports. They did not write that David was lost in a world of hallucinations when he committed murder. They also failed to say that his family desperately worked to secure adequate mental health care, experienced the health system as inadequate, and were frustrated when the hospital continually discharged David before they believed he was ready. Never was it mentioned, as in other documented cases, that David was often discharged on the first day that his care was not covered by health insurance.[9] Although his family knew that he needed care for his schizophrenia and did what they could to support him, they did not have the resources to treat his illness and protect David and his victims.

Except for the few family members who totally blocked the media out of their lives, most had examples of times when they were devastated by seeing printed accounts of the crime and trial. One mother said that when she read the paper it was "terrible. I would read and cry, just hurting. I can't explain when I read the paper what it did to me, and sometimes the newspaper would put a little more in it than what actually happened."

Sometimes the family members saw the media coverage as downright macabre. One accompanying story about an execution included a picture of the hearse leaving the correctional institution with the driver and his passenger laughing. Another time a statement in the editorial portion of the local paper about another condemned killer declared, "Stick a needle in Spivey's arm and put him to sleep permanently."[10] Such statements were particularly hurtful, as family members knew that a neighbor had written them.

Family members grew to fear the media and were disturbed by unpredictable intrusions. Marion, an offender's mother, remembered, "What gets you is, you are driving down the road and all of a sudden you hear it on the radio, and you don't know it is going to be on the radio. It's like a knife being stuck in your chest and turned." One younger sibling described the terror of being home with a babysitter because her parents were at her brother's trial, when a message panned across the bottom of the television screen announcing that her brother had received a death sentence and would be executed.

The families also feared the power that the media have to sway the opinions of their consumers. Several worried that unflattering and incomplete media coverage would influence a trial's outcome because the media provided the community with information that may subsequently be used by jurors in a court of law to pass judgment on their loved ones. These family members did not believe that the jury selection process would remove individuals who had been biased by the media, and in cases where a change of venue had been denied, that fear was particularly potent.

Community Hostility

Community responses to the crimes often had numerous negative effects on family members. Perhaps the most harm occurred when Paul and Jeremy's younger brother and sister had to drop out of school with no other options for an education. Other family members also reported problems within children's schools. Mark indicated that his nephew's elementary school teacher suddenly changed her attitude toward the young student—previously encouraging and kind, she became cold and critical following news reports about his uncle. Karl's son was in high school at the time Karl committed murder, and his son's girlfriend, who was in the ninth grade, had to change schools after being tormented by such name-calling as "killer's girlfriend." A sister reported that a cousin of hers walked into her history class only to find her relative's picture on the board because his impending execution was part of the day's current events lesson.

Sometimes the community's hostility occurred much closer to home. It was not uncommon for one offender's mother to find human feces on her doorstep or to receive death threats following newspaper articles about the crime, trial, or the aftermath. For this family, the newspaper accounts continued throughout the 19 years between arrest and execution. Each year on the anniversary of the murder, the paper ran a picture of the victim's family visiting her gravesite.

For most family members, the attacks were verbal. A sister of an offender likened the attacks to "being in the big ocean and being drowned by everyone around. It was like they were pushing us under . . . every time we come up they [the media and community] would push our heads back under." On rare occasions, family members were physically attacked. Bonnie Coe, whose brother, Robert, was convicted of murdering a child, recalled her parents' truck being shot at. Bonnie further indicated that she lost her job because of the publicity and community response. The administration at her place of employment "didn't come out and say that they fired me because I was his sister. I know that is what it was because I did a good job. I worked overtime; I worked the hours that they asked me to; and then it came out in the paper. People were whispering and talking, and they called me in the office and told me that they did not need me anymore."

Although most family members never experienced any overt violence, many lived in fear of it. Sarah, an African American mother, said that she felt comfortable in her own African American neighborhood, but when she would cross the tracks to the white side of town to do her errands, she felt fearful. She reported, "I was scared, too, about being his mother. Like doomed. You feel like someone is going to do something to you."

Another defendant's family with young children in the home received threatening phone calls regularly. Georgia, a single, low-income mother who worked several jobs, used to spend her nights awake in a chair in her living room. She explained, "I sat up because I was afraid to go to sleep, and I was watching over my family. I brought the kids into the living room—two were on the sofa and one was on the floor—and I would sit in the chair all night long." Eventually the African American religious leaders in her community took a public stance in support of the family and asked the city to provide additional patrols to the neighborhood.

The religious community, however, is not always so supportive. "The church can make a big difference, [but] they turned their back on him," explained one of the mothers interviewed. Similarly, Paul said that the minister of his church stopped him on the street recently to ask how Jeremy was doing. Paul replied, "I appreciate your concern for Jeremy, but you did nothing when we needed you, so we really don't need to be talking to you about it now." Other family members responded with anger to their religious leader when he or she promised to pray for them but ignored their loved one awaiting execution. Celia McWee observed, "It's not me that needs the prayers; it is my son, but they don't mention him." Bonnie stated that she and her family wanted to start attending church again as a way of gaining emotional support and a spiritual connection following the arrest. However, as she looked around for a spiritual community to join, she said that they "kind of shunned us when they found out we were his family." Mark said that his sisters had been pillars of the church, giving time and money, and yet "in their moment of pain, they did not feel like the church reached out to them and comforted them." Another participant left his church because of its pro–death penalty stand.

Each of the family members in this study suffered from guilt by association. Media portrayals, members of their communities, churches, and educational system all reinforced their own guilty feeling associated with the murder. Some family members faced threats of violence, loss of employment, loss of friends, and ostracism in their community, whereas other family members only perceived negative hostility toward them. Whether the negative attention was real or perceived, these family members frequently suffered alone as they internalized feelings of shame. Even though the hardship caused by the community and its institutions, including churches and the media, was difficult, it paled in comparison to the pain caused by the criminal justice system. Not only did their loved one's fate lie within that system, but also disillusionment cut deeper as it affected family members own views about their country.

A Broken System

Like many individuals living in the United States, the offenders' families generally viewed the criminal justice system positively before the arrest. Those of color and those living in small towns with a history of corruption were the most skeptical, but most of the family members that we talked with believed at the time of the arrest that justice would be served. Those who believed that their loved one was guilty accepted that he would be punished, although they prayed for a sentence less than death. Some even helped police capture their loved one, believing their cooperation would help solve a horrible crime, prevent other crimes, and help their loved one avoid the death penalty. Family members were often frustrated and angered by the actions of their loved one's lawyers, the way the police and prosecution handled evidence, judges' behavior, or the ways that race influenced the criminal justice process. They experienced a profound feeling of disorientation from the entire criminal justice proceedings. Unfortunately, almost everyone interviewed for this book, whether or not their family member was guilty, lost faith in the American criminal justice system after becoming intimately involved in its processes. Matt, a father and successful businessman, summed it up: "When you are brought up with a certain ideal and way of thinking about this country and then you find out that everything you have been taught is not true, that is when you get agitated and upset like I do. In this country you are guilty if you are arrested: period. And your family is, too . . . you have to prove your-self [as a family member] innocent, and the press will not help you." Another father explained, "If every parent in this country knew how easy it was for a district attorney and judge to convict their child, the death penalty would not last 15 minutes."

James Liebman and his colleagues Jeffery Fagan and Valerie West echoed these sentiments when, after the chair of the U.S. Senate Committee on the Judiciary asked them to statistically analyze error rates in 4,578 capital cases adjudicated from 1973 to 1995, they declared that, "The capital system is broken."[11] They found that errors were made in 68% of all cases, and that the errors were so serious that sentences were reversed for 82% of those inmates, often after they'd spent years on death row.[12] In many cases, once the evidence was presented properly in a new trial or hearing, a different, less severe sentence was handed down. Lawyer incompetence was the largest cause of error, followed by suppression of evidence. Although the Liebman et al. study did not specifically examine race, other studies have found race to be a significant factor in determining who gets the death penalty and support the conclusion that the administration of the death penalty is unfair.[13] Family members' concerns with the criminal justice system mirror those of the research.

The Defense Team and Lawyers

In a death penalty case there are usually two attorneys, the lead attorney and the second chair, and their skill levels range from excellent to appallingly incompetent. Examples of death penalty attorneys' abysmal behavior abound. Lawyers have been heard calling a client a racial epithet, observed sleeping during the trial, and even seen at the trial inebriated.[14] Lawyer incompetence *can* result in an overturned sentence on appeal, but there is no guarantee of this, and the years spent on death row while the appeals process goes forward place enormous stress on defendants and their family members. Not knowing if their loved one will ever get off death row makes the years fraught with anxiety and feelings of powerlessness. Family members see that mistakes are being made, but they are uninformed about standards for legal practice, and they have nowhere to turn. When they raise questions with their loved one's attorney, they are often rebuffed.

Although the inclusion of mitigating and aggravating evidence is what makes the death penalty constitutional, in many cases ineffectual defense teams barely present mitigating evidence.[15] One psychotic defendant, who lives with constant hallucinations and companion "genies," was sentenced to die after his defense attorneys presented only one mitigation witness. The hallucinations and genies were never mentioned, and the essence of the mitigation, less than two trial transcript pages, argued that the defendant "came from a broken home." On appeal, skilled attorneys presented the case and introduced evidence that on many occasions the stepfather cruelly beat the defendant, stripping him naked and tying him across the passageway of the front porch and beating him with a mule whip while his mother screamed, "You're going to kill him!" The genies started to visit after such beatings, when the 10-year-old boy would hide—naked and bleeding—in the woods beyond his house. Such dissociation is a known posttraumatic reaction,[16] and this defendant lived in a state of permanent dissociation. In appeal, the defendant was found to be so mentally ill that he could not comprehend life or death and thus could not be executed.

Sometimes, as in the above example, the new evidence is heard, but this is not always the way it goes. Richard Longworth never received a second hearing on his claims of ineffective counsel, which included the fact that evidence related to his family background and his own mental state and drug use at the time of crime was never raised by his attorney. In addition, his attorney placed himself squarely in the center of a conflict of interest. Richard's mother, Barbara, describes her son's attorney as a "buffoon" and said that he did absolutely nothing to help Richard. Part of the reason that the attorney never raised the mitigation evidence is because he was also representing Richard's family. At some point during the case, Richard's attorney convinced Barbara and her husband that they, too, needed representation. Fearing the unknown, the family retained their son's lawyer. The attorney took the position that it would be better for them if mitigating evidence were never raised. Barbara blames herself for her son's poor representation and explained that "you feel stupid, you blame yourself. I feel like my whole family was raped by the system. And we were, and we were left feeling so stupid." For years appellate attorneys sought to undo the damage with a new hearing for Richard. Failing to get his case heard again, Richard was executed in 2005.

Our research revealed additional examples of attorney incompetence, including lawyers who did not follow leads suggested by family members, attorneys who were not even sure of their client's name, and others who acted like there was nothing to be done because guilt was clearly established. Family members knew that they were part of an adversarial system. They expected the prosecutor to work zealously to convict their loved one. What devastated members was the inadequacies of their family member's advocate.

Evidence

Family members raised numerous concerns about the handling of evidence in their loved one's judicial proceeding. Particularly troubling were questions about the admissibility and suppression of evidence, the handling of new evidence, coerced confessions, codefendants who received reduced sentences for information related to the crime, and plea bargains. In the case of Robert Coe, suppression and admissibility were key concerns. In 2000, Robert was executed *without* physical evidence linking him to the crime. His attorney argued that Robert was executed while holding a valid legal claim that likely would have exonerated him if a jury had heard it. In 1979, Robert, who was mentally ill, was arrested for child molestation and murder. Given his history of exposing himself, he seemed a likely suspect. Robert had been diagnosed with schizophrenia and had spent years in a psychiatric hospital. He grew up in a home where he was battered, beaten with a leather strap, and left outside for days. Robert never fully escaped his childhood trauma, harboring an intense fear of authority. While he was in police custody and without an attorney present, Robert did what many people with mental illness are known to do—he became passive and agreed with his aggressor (in this case, the police) to end the aggression.[17] With a signed confession, Robert was convicted of the crime in 1981 and sentenced to death. His trial attorney fought to show that Robert was incompetent to stand trial due to insanity but spent very little time and effort investigating whether Robert had actually committed the crime.

By the time appellate attorney Paul Bottei was assigned to the case in 1995, the point at which new evidence could be admitted had passed. There was, however, important new evidence to be heard. Witnesses had identified Craig (a pseudonym), a man with a history of making inappropriate sexual advances to young children, as the person who abducted the victim. Shortly after the child's abduction, Craig was seen with fresh bloody scratches on his neck, and he had no alibi for the time when the murder occurred. Moreover, tire tracks at the crime scene were identified as being consistent with Craig's car tires, not with Robert's car. Evidence left on the victim's body did not match any of the samples obtained from Robert. The police also took bloody clothing and bedding from Craig's home for testing, and no one informed the defense of the presence of this evidence. Bottei and his legal team, years after Robert had been convicted, discovered the existence of the bloody clothing and bedding. It is not known whether the bloody evidence was lost or deliberately suppressed by the state. What is known is that the state suppressed their existence. The state never revealed the fact that the evidence had even been collected, something that they are legally required to do.

In his motion requesting a stay of execution to the Tennessee Supreme Court, Bottei asserted, "The state of Tennessee convicted Robert Coe of murder and got the jury to sentence him to death by losing or destroying critical evidence, which would have exonerated him." Bottei further argued, "Robert Coe's claim of constitutional error has been given short shrift by the lower courts, with the trial court erroneously claiming that it had given Robert Coe an 'evidentiary hearing' on the matter when he has never had this case heard on the merits by any court in the State."[18]

The Tennessee Supreme Court overruled the claim, stating that its job was to look at constitutional violations and not evidence. Robert's sister reflected, "Every day I think about Robert's execution, and I know that if the evidence had been brought up things would have been different. It's a horrible feeling." For Bottei, it was incredibly frustrating to have compelling evidence that Robert had not committed this horrible offense and not have anyone listen. Bottei believes that the court system contains multiple layers that can each be affected by human error, and once an error occurs, the system does not always allow the opportunity for it to be corrected. It is unthinkable to Bottei and Robert's sisters that Robert lost his life because evidence was suppressed or lost through human error. Robert's sister Bonnie said that there is "nothing like knowing that your brother was put to death like a dog for something he did not do."

Martina Correia is terrified that the same things may happen to her brother, Troy Davis. Martina is a wiry African American woman who is proud of her military service. Her boundless energy has been somewhat hampered by her struggle with cancer. Every day Martina works and prays for justice for her brother. She believes justice for him would begin with a hearing on new evidence. Troy was arrested in 1989 for killing police officer Mark Allen MacPhail. This shooting took place in a Burger King parking lot when MacPhail came to the aid of a homeless man who was being harassed. Following the testimony of nine witnesses for the prosecution, Troy was convicted of the murder and sentenced to death.

Since the trial, six witnesses have recanted their testimony, including those who provided the most damaging testimony against Troy. In addition, other witnesses who do not point to Troy as the assailant have come forward. Troy and his family are deeply concerned that the new evidence will never be heard in a court of law, and their concern has been exacerbated by the 1996 enactment of the federal Antiterrorism and Effective Death Penalty Act.[19] The act seeks to streamline the appeals process for death row inmates in part by limiting the time frame in which a defendant can present new evidence as well as significantly raising the bar for the presentation of new evidence.[20]

Another hurdle that Troy needs to overcome is that courts tend to view recantations with skepticism because people come forward—as a witness for either the defense or prosecution—for a variety of reasons, ranging from the notion that speaking up is a moral obligation to a response to pressure from the police or community or simply fear. Therefore, in exploring the efficacy and validity of a recantation, it is important to place it in context. If the court allowed a new hearing on the evidence, then information regarding the recantations and other evidence would be raised suggesting that Troy did not commit the crime. Following is a description of some of the inconsistencies associated with the investigation of the murder that could be raised at trial.

If a hearing were to be held, it would be argued that 16 witnesses were at or around the Burger King during the shooting. All agree that one of the individuals was hassling a homeless man named Larry Young, but stories have changed as to what happened next and whether Young's aggressor was the one who shot MacPhail. Some witnesses state that two men approached the altercation. Troy and his lawyers assert that there was another man nicknamed "Trace" (a pseudonym) who they have identified as both harassing Young and committing the murder.

The defense believes that Trace pulled the gun. Afraid that he might get caught, Trace went to the police to pin the shooting on Troy.[21] Troy and his lawyers believe that the police viewed this information as reliable and as a result proceeded to influence witnesses so that their accounts mirrored the information that Trace provided. Troy's attorneys assert that from the moment that Trace walked into the police station—despite the inconsistencies in his story—the investigation worked to find evidence that supported his rendition of the murder. Specifically the defense believes that it is able to show that witnesses' statements on the evening of the shooting changed to support Trace's story following his visit to the precinct.

For example, on the night of the shooting, all the witnesses claimed that they did not see what had happened. The witnesses said that things happened quickly, and when they looked up, there was bedlam. Later, however, Mr. Williams, one of the witnesses, changed his testimony dramatically. At the crime scene, Williams said he had a hard time seeing what was going on because of the tint on his car windows. When the police asked him to identify the shooter, he said he could not. During the trial, Williams identified Troy as having committed the murder. Following the trial he stated in a sworn affidavit, "I have no idea what the person who shot the officer looks like." He added that he did not want to testify at the trial, but the authorities told him that he must.

Williams was not the only witness told that he must change his testimony. The defense team asserts that other witnesses were "threatened in order to secure their cooperation and to adopt the investigator's rendition of the facts."[22] Witness Dorothy Ferrell was on parole when someone from the district attorney's office came to see her. She was told that the DA's office would help her if she would assist them in the case. Ferrell stated that she was afraid that if she did not do what the police wanted, she would be sent back to jail. After the trial, Ferrell said that she had not told the truth.

Martina knows that it will be very difficult to get a hearing on the evidence, yet she still devotes a great deal of time and energy to making this happen. She has become a one-woman public relations firm; she sends faxes, e-mails, and packages about Troy and his case to churches, local and national abolition groups, and civil rights leaders and organizations. She has overseen the development of the Web site www.troyanthonydavis.org. She has called and written television news shows and radio stations. She has sought attention from individuals ranging from Oprah Winfrey to the mayor of her city. She networks at local and national conferences, churches, community meetings, and civic centers. She is constantly on her cell phone, and, at times, she has had to pay dearly when she exceeded her monthly minutes. She has changed the way she lives her life to fight for her brother. Martina loved every aspect of her life in the military: the uniform, the work, the regimentation. After Troy's sentence, however, she resigned, believing that the need to devote herself to her brother's case and abolition activities would interfere with military regulations.[23]

At the time of this writing, Davis's appeals for a new hearing were before the judges of the Eleventh Circuit Court of Appeals. According to Troy's Web site, a ruling is expected at any time. The site also notes that if his appeal is denied, the case will go to the U.S. Supreme Court, and if denied there, an execution date will be set so that "Troy Davis could have less than a year left."[24]

Another evidence issue that troubles families is flawed or false confessions. Governor George Ryan of Illinois echoed these concerns in January 2003 when he commuted the death sentences for all individuals in Illinois. Following 13 exonerations in the state of Illinois and a review of all cases, Ryan declared the capital system broken. He cited a review of 10 years of cases in a single Illinois county that showed 247 instances in which the self-incriminating evidence by the defendant was shown to have been either thrown out of court or held insufficient content to convince a jury of conviction.[25] False confessions are often related to external factors that occur during the interrogation and include duress, coercion, intoxication, fear of violence, and threat of extreme punishment. Moreover, false confessions are more likely to occur in cases where individuals have low IQs, mental illnesses, and other mental impairments.[26] Though the actual frequency of false confessions is currently debated by researchers, it is accepted that false confessions do occur.

In several of our cases, defendants signed confessions prior to representation, and in each case, family members had questions about the ethics or validity of the confession. For example, Robert Coe's family believes that his mental health was so fragile and the effects of his family trauma so pronounced that he signed a confession out of intense fear of the police. Paul Bottei, Robert's appellate attorney, explained that transcripts from the confession are full of the classic signs of a false confession. Such signs include leading questions, monosyllabic responses from Robert, and the fact that the police had a great deal of information about the actual murder from the medical examiner. In another case, Jan, a sister of a defendant, said that the statement her brother made in his confession was strange and sounded nothing like him. When the case was heard on appeal under the guidance of a competent attorney, a handwriting expert testified that the accused did not write the statement. Despite this evidence, the sentence was upheld.

Pitting codefendants against each other to obtain state's evidence is common practice in the criminal justice system, but it was also cited by Ryan as one of the reasons he commuted the death sentences of all death row inmates in Illinois.[27] Ryan explained that after reviewing cases he found that "co-defendants who are equally or even more culpable get sentenced to a term of years, while another less culpable defendant ends up on death row."[28] There were several cases in our study population where this occurred, leaving the defendant's family members dismayed and incredulous.

On July 6, 1991, Jerry McWee and codefendant George Scott entered a convenience store to rob it. Jerry had been a police officer and emergency medical technician, but his life had taken a downward turn when he left his wife for another woman and lost his job due to a back injury. Jerry shot the convenience store clerk, and Scott shot a second man soon after. On his arrest, Scott cooperated with the authorities and testified against Jerry, who was sentenced to death and executed in 2003. Scott originally denied that he received any sort of deal from the prosecution, a denial he later recanted when he admitted that he did testify as part of a plea bargain in exchange for a life sentence. The difference in sentences is particularly striking because Jerry expressed an enormous amount of remorse for his actions and had no criminal history, whereas Scott expressed no remorse and has been described "as a career criminal with a lengthy criminal history."[29] For the sake of getting a capital conviction, prosecutors often overlook the human beings involved in the crime and difference in their characters. In many cases, repeat offenders who know how to work the system and "turn state's evidence" by telling their version of the crime to the prosecutor first receive reduced sentences, while more naive codefendants get more severe punishments.

The final issue surrounding evidence that distressed the families involved plea bargains. When capital offenders strike plea bargains, they trade the possibility of presenting evidence that may exonerate them for the assurance that they will not be executed. Family members described the decision for their loved one to take a plea as a Faustian bargain, that is, one that requires giving up one's soul. They must choose to gamble with their loved one's life and try to get a fair trial or agree to a plea bargain to avoid the possibility of death. Charlene, whose son pleaded guilty, explained the motivation of this bargain, "If it had not been a death penalty case, it would have been completely different. He would have gone to trial and had the opportunity to defend himself. Because it was a death case, we had no choice but to take the plea because the thoughts of losing him were so drastic."

Charlene went on to say that many things that happened the night of the murder never came out in court because the threat of death made it impossible to risk a jury trial. This mother agrees that her son must pay a price for what happened that night, yet he should not pay the punishment for all who were involved. She believes that the murder was gang related, and because it was pinned on a single shooter, her son, the dangerous activities of gangs continue without rebuke. Charlene constantly second-guesses herself about encouraging her son to take a plea bargain and will always wonder if she is the reason he will live out his life in prison and that the gang continues to create problems in her community.

A very different kind of plea bargain occurred in Shareef Cousin's case. At age 16 Shareef was charged with capital murder and several unrelated carjackings. His mother begged and borrowed for money to pay a private lawyer, who suggested that he plead guilty to the carjacking and in exchange the capital murder charge would be dropped and Shareef could go to a boot camp where he could get a GED, be out in a few years, and resume a normal life. Shareef's mother advised him to plead guilty even though he denied the charges. To his mother, it was not an issue of guilt or innocence; it was an issue of her son's life or death. Indeed, the lawyer had a point when he argued that Shareef would be safer in boot camp than he would be in his gang- and drug-infested neighborhood. Shareef and his mother were devastated, however, when his lawyer's prediction did not come true. Shareef received 20 years for the carjacking and still faced a capital trial. Ironically, the capital case against Shareef was eventually dismissed because a videotape showed Shareef at a neighborhood basketball court during the murder and carjacking. Even though the evidence produced showed that he was not guilty, he still had to serve 10 years of a 20-year sentence for the carjacking to which he pleaded guilty. Although plea bargains may be an expedient way to move cases through the criminal justice process, these cases illustrate that they can sacrifice defendants' due process rights. When lawyers fail to present exculpatory or mitigating evidence, it not only hurts their client but also devastates defendants' family members and leads them to the conclusion that the current criminal justice system does not produce justice.

Judges

Family members often watch trials vigilantly and observe everything, from technical legal maneuvers to the nuanced facial expressions of the judge and jurors. They know that one of the most important elements of a fair and respected justice system is the judiciary. The judge presides over the courtroom and is supposed to apply the law impartially. Experience has caused many defendants and family members to come to believe that impartiality is not always achieved. In fact, research about the justice system supports their claims that judges are not always impartial. Specifically, studies have shown that some judges have personal biases and have articulated racial, ethnic, or gender bias.[30] Earlier in this chapter, we introduced David, a paranoid schizophrenic who committed two murders to receive the death penalty. Although it is impossible to know whether the judge in this case was biased, David's lawyer and family believe that this judge overstepped his boundaries. Mark, David's brother, explains, "The judge helped David get the death penalty at every turn," and David's lawyer agreed. In fact, the judge handed him his death sentence during the hearing to decide if David was mentally competent to stand trial. In the state where the crime occurred, mental competency is determined in a hearing by a jury. As the hearing wrapped up and the jury deliberated, David's attorney had no choice but to leave the courtroom because he had been subpoenaed to appear in another part of the state. Thereafter the jury returned to say that David had been found competent to stand trial. Incredibly, the judge invited David, without the presence of his lawyer, to plead guilty and receive the death penalty. Mark was enraged by the judge's behavior as he watched David sign his life away. Although at that time David was asking for the death penalty, his brother knew that if he was properly medicated he wouldn't have done so.

Families were often concerned about the evidence that a judge would or would not allow into the courtroom. One mother explained that her son's ex-wife, a witness for the prosecution, testified that he had beaten her during their marriage. The defendant denied the accusation and asked that police records be pulled to verify her story. When records were not found, the defense asked that the testimony be stricken from the record. The attorney and family were shocked when the judge denied the objection and allowed unsubstantiated claims into the record, which might have influenced the jury. Family members are acutely aware of the power that judges have and in many ways see them as the symbol of the criminal justice system. When family members question a judge's decision, it taints their view of the entire system.

Race and the Criminal Justice System

Both the United States and its criminal justice system have a long, well-documented history of racial discrimination. Numerous studies describe unequal treatment of minorities and whites in the criminal justice system. These studies contain information on racial profiling, police brutality, police apathy toward minority communities, prosecutors and judges valuing white victims and defendants more than their minority counterparts, unequal sentencing practices, and discriminatory treatment in jails and prisons.[31] Most African Americans are well aware of the facts and know, for example, that more whites than African Americans use crack in the United States but proportionately more African Americans are arrested.[32]

The clearest discussion of race and the death penalty is found in the empirical research of law researcher David Baldus and his colleague Charles Pulaski. In the 1980s, Baldus and a team of scholars statistically analyzed all of the death-eligible cases in several places, including Philadelphia County, Pennsylvania, and in the state of Georgia, for numerous variables, including procedural facts and characteristics of the murder. They found that one-third of African Americans on death row in Philadelphia County would have received life sentences in other counties, and that when all else was equal, a death sentence was 4.3 times more likely to be given when the victim had been white.[33]

Little has changed since the 1980 study. A 1990 analysis of 28 studies by the U.S. General Accounting Office found a "remarkably consistent" pattern of racial disparity.[34] Additional studies showing racial bias were conducted in Indiana, Maryland, New Jersey, North Carolina, Virginia, and Pennsylvania as well as within the federal system.[35] Finally, vile anecdotal stories such as that of Ray Anthony Peek, whom the judge called a "nigger" from the bench, highlight the racism confronting African American defendants.[36]

One needs only to look to the U.S. Supreme Court to put such findings in context. In 1987 in *McCleskey v. Kemp* (1987), the Supreme Court reviewed and accepted the accuracy of Baldus's findings in Georgia, thereby affirming that race affected sentencing. However, the Court saw systemic racial bias as inevitable and ruled that racial bias against a specific defendant must be present to influence the outcome of a case. Because the Supreme Court suggested that endemic institutional racial discrimination does not matter in a death penalty case, it is hardly surprising that the African American family members we talked with believed that race played a significant role in their loved one's arrest, charge, and prosecution.

Pearl explained that when a neighbor called her to say that her son had been arrested for murder, "I asked who the [victim] was, and she told me a white lady, and that is when the death penalty hit my mind. I have not been right since." Pearl's feelings are backed up by evidence. The General Accounting Office found that in 82% of the studies on capital murder, the race of the victim influenced the decision to seek death. Since 1976 nearly 1,200 people have been on death row for killing a white person and just over 200 for the murder of an African American.[37]

When African American family members were asked about the role of race in their loved one's case, each of them looked at the interviewer askance; for them, the case was *about* race. One mother said that she has watched the paper carefully since her son's arrest and has noticed that when a murder occurs, if the accused is African American, then the death penalty is often sought, but it is sought less often if the accused is white. Georgia, another mother, indicated that it is difficult to look around the visiting room and to see so many black families. She states that "when you see that, you can't help but believe that something is not right in the system."

In four of the cases we examined, an African American defendant was sentenced before an all-white jury. In at least one of the cases, the prosecutor supported his case by building on race-based fears. The young man had been apprehended while wearing a T-shirt featuring a rap star. The prosecutor held up the shirt and likened the defendant's actions to the actions of a notorious rapper. Family members found this aspect of the trial racially provocative. They were also horrified to hear the prosecutor in his closing arguments describe African Americans' entrance into the United States as part of the immigrant experience.

Race plays out in other ways in capital cases. Patty explained that her nephew's "inexperienced first lawyer found that he had come to a small Southern prejudiced town, and there was a black boy who raped, kidnapped, and murdered a white girl. So naturally he [the out of town lawyer] was not going to get any support." She added that a black juror did not want to give a sentence of death, but eventually the juror succumbed, stating that she could not take the pressure and racial epithets from the other jurors.

African American family members struggle with having the children in their lives respect authority while their lives have been clouded by the biased application of laws affecting their loved one's case. A sister stated, "It is so sad when you tell a child that the color of his skin may affect the way some people respond to you, and then you point to my brother for verification." Throughout the history of the United States, the justice system has been mired with examples of racial discrimination. This is especially evident with capital punishment, where the wounds to the African American community caused by the appalling history of lynching and institutional racism are not allowed to heal.

Untouchable

Unlike the victims' family members, offenders' family members can visit their loved ones. Some victims' family members would give anything just to lay eyes on their loved one again. Offenders' family members are able to do this, but their visits are not without difficulty. They often spoke of the distance, humiliation, and even physical pain associated with their prison visits. Franny's son is in the general prison population because he was spared death, but she does not visit frequently because of the ordeal of the visit. The night before the 7-hour car ride to the prison she cannot sleep because she is so anxious about how she will find her son. Prison procedures ensure a new obstacle almost every time. She does not know if the prison personnel will hassle her, or if she will actually be able to see her son. Twice she has gone for her visitation and been denied the opportunity to visit due to bureaucracy within the prison.

Several cruel developments cast especially dark shadows on Franny's visits. Two weeks before the trial, she had to tell her son that his father had committed suicide. She felt powerless. She was unable to hold him, touch him, or even give him a sweater to ward off the cold. She then elaborated that as if her visit was not bad enough, in the most intimate of moments of shared sorrow, the guards abruptly cut it short. She said, "When he needed to cry just at the most crucial time for us, they made us separate. It breaks everything— the bond and everything. You're not in a setting to give or receive comfort." Years later, her other son was killed during a work-related accident. This time, the prison chaplain broke the news to her imprisoned son, but she again found herself trying to console him through a glass partition.

The glass partition, a shatterproof symbol of separation, caused physical as well as emotional pain for some of the family members we talked to. Two elderly family members indicated that they have a difficult time hearing their loved one across the partition, and to compensate they had to crouch down to the small, waist-high opening, a position that strained their already fragile backs. Another younger family member has problems with a disc in her back, and the crouching left her in severe pain for days following a visit.

Visitation is viewed by the prison system as a privilege, and like most privileges, this one can be taken away. Lesa, whose story began chapter 3, explained that while her son was in jail awaiting his trial, he asked her to bring him a pair of high-top tennis shoes as he was having trouble with his ankles and thought that the support offered by the high-tops might help. She signed in and walked through the guard area into the visitation room with the new shoes visibly displayed. Her son tried on the shoes and asked that she take his jail-issued shoes home as he did not think the authorities would allow him to keep two pairs of shoes. As she was leaving the jail, and in a moment of confusion, fear, and poor judgment, she placed the shoes under her sweater and discarded them on prison property after she left the building. By the time she turned the key over in her car, she was surrounded by corrections officials. She was told that she had taken government property and that her visits would be revoked indefinitely. After she called for many months and wrote weekly, the administrator of the jail told her if she stopped contacting him, she would be able to visit her son 1 year after the incident. She felt like she had no choice other than to agree, even though this meant that she and her son were unable to visit during his trial and for several months following his death sentence. Not being able to communicate with him face to face following his death sentence was excruciating for Lesa, who could only imagine how her son was taking the news at that time. For Lesa, the glass partition would have been a welcome trade-off for seeing her son.

Summary

The lives of offender's family members often change abruptly when their loved one is charged with a capital crime and faces the death penalty. Family members find their roles shifting from friend, neighbor, congregant, and community leader to outcast or criminal by association; sometimes this even occurs in cases where their loved one is later found not guilty. The social and communal fabric of their lives unravel as they perceive that they are being punished along with their loved one.

Offenders' family members face intense media scrutiny as the story of the offender and their family is simplified and sensationalized. Rather than including complex social issues that may have led to the crime, most media coverage of capital offenders paints them in simple terms, such as monster, villain, or deranged hermit. Too often, issues such as mental illness and addiction are demonized rather than explained. The truth is painful enough, but when it is distorted and sensationalized, family members suffer additional trauma, and their standing in the community is further diminished.

Family members of offenders perceive hostility from their communities. For many these perceptions are based on strange looks, finger pointing, conversations that stop when they walk by, children being asked to leave the public school, ostracism from church groups, and, in extreme cases, threats of violence or actual attacks. Others do not experience overt hostility but still imagine the way that community members must feel about them. Whether imagined or faced directly, the consequence of community hostility is isolation. Without community connections, offenders' family members' chances of reaching out to get help with legal issues, trauma, or depression are restricted.

Family members also face problems within the criminal justice system and are continuously amazed at how complicated and arbitrary the process is.

They expressed concern with the handling of evidence and plea bargaining, prosecutors who were more interested in convictions than justice, judges who were biased, defense attorneys who were incompetent or did not have enough time to devote to the case, and the way that poverty and racism seemed to shape the outcome of cases. Clearly, to these families, the criminal justice system is not living up to the goals of fairness and punishment only for the guilty.

Our narratives illustrate what many other researchers have concluded: the system is broken. The legal system is confusing, and offenders' family members are provided with few resources to help navigate it. Overwhelmingly, offenders who are poor, uneducated, minorities, or mentally ill are more likely to end up on death row than their counterparts. These biases contribute to offenders' family members feeling disenfranchised by both the criminal justice system specifically and the United States generally. Finally, not only is punishment meted out to offenders, but also family members bear the punishment. Some have even suggested that their punishment is more intense than the offenders'—they have to live with not only the impending execution but also its aftermath.

The harms incurred by offenders' family members should be central to restorative justice programs aimed at capital cases. A restorative justice framework could provide support to offenders' family members who need someone to listen and help them process their experience so they do not feel isolated. Offenders' family members need changes in the criminal justice system that address issues of due process, unfairness, and racial discrimination. They also have obligations to fulfill related to the crime, but their potential to provide needed answers to victims' family members, inform community members of the conditions that lead to crime and make suggestions on ways crime could be prevented, and help the offender be held personally accountable by facing up to the wrongdoing is ignored. Offenders' family members need to be heard in their communities and in the debate over the death penalty. They are profoundly affected by crime and death penalty trials, yet their voices are silenced because too often they are judged guilty by association.

5

"You Didn't Punish Him, You Punished Me"

In March 2004, Celia McWee received a phone call from her son, Jerry, who was on death row because in 1991 he and his codefendant George Scott robbed a convenience store and killed the clerk. The call was the most difficult one Jerry had ever made because he had to tell his mother that he had been served, indicating a warrant stating that he would be executed in less than 1 month. Upon Jerry's call Celia was confused, asking, "Served what? What have you been served?" She told us:

> I had no idea what he was talking about even though we often talked
> about who got served. I knew what served meant, but he still had to
> explain it. He said "a warrant—I got served a warrant." I remember that
> I was sitting there holding my grandchild on my lap when Jerry called.
> I remember calling my grandson's mother and telling her that she needed
> to come and pick up the baby. I don't remember much until she got here,
> and then I just broke down. I stayed like that all day.

At some point Celia collected her emotions long enough to call Jerry's four children to tell them that the family would have a contact visit the next weekend, the first one in over a decade. Celia did not mention the warrant because Jerry wanted to tell his children himself, but the children knew; Jerry's 26-year-old daughter, Misty, realized: "There was only one reason for us to have a contact visit. I knew that. I didn't say anything, but when I hung up the phone, I started to scream."

Celia also knew what happened to an inmate immediately after they have been served. She played and replayed the details in her mind. She imagined Jerry leaving the warden's office, where he was given his death warrant, and she imagined his escort to a lockdown cell where he would live out the last few weeks of his life as policy dictated, under suicide watch. Because of the suicide watch there would be light on constantly, and the guard would walk in often to make sure Jerry did not harm himself. She knew that Jerry would pass the cell that had been home for 13 years. He would not be able to say goodbye to friends or have the comfort of his few possessions—a rosary, a radio, and a family scrapbook. On the last evening of his life he would be transferred 100 miles away to the death house in Columbia, South Carolina. Throughout this time Jerry would be given a spiritual advisor who would visit regularly, perform the last rites of his Roman Catholic faith, and witness the execution. But Celia did not know what would happen next or the visitation policy for an inmate under warrant. She called the warden and learned that she could visit daily, and at some point after the execution Jerry's belongings would be released. She could call the prison a week or two following the execution to find out when she could pick them up. Prison regulations would not allow Jerry to pass on his few belongings, like his television set, to other inmates who could use them, a detail that saddened him and his mother.

Living several hours from the prison and having a car with over 200,000 miles on it, Celia began staying with a friend who lived near the prison in Moncks Corner. For 3 weeks, she would drive to the prison and stay in Moncks Corner for 4 or 5 days and then return home for a day or two to check on her house and take care of funeral arrangements.

Some of Celia's visits with Jerry were lighthearted and others very serious. She and Jerry disagreed about his final moments, and this created an undercurrent of tension. Celia wanted to be in the execution chamber, but Jerry wanted to spare her the pain of watching him die. She felt strongly about being there because she was still haunted by the horrible moment she found out about her daughter Joyce's death. On December 31, 1979, Joyce was brought to the hospital emergency room and pronounced dead on arrival, but the family in the waiting area did not know her status. Eventually a doctor informed them that she was gone. Celia felt as if she was robbed the opportunity to say goodbye to her child and could not go through that again. For Celia, being in the execution chamber with Jerry was essential to her self-preservation. She explained, "I don't think I could cope with it, for someone to tell me he's gone. For them to come up there to outside the prison to make the announcement—I have gone through it with my daughter, and I can't—I don't think I can do it a second time to hear someone say that he is gone." Jerry finally agreed to allow his mother to witness his execution.

After visits with Jerry, nights in Moncks Corner were long. Here Celia would drop the facade of strength that she maintained for Jerry's sake. She would stare at the TV for hours, never sure what she was watching. She barely ate, and when she was able to sleep, it was fitful.

On April 15, Jerry's family met with him for their final visit. Jerry told everyone that he loved them and instructed his only son to look after his three sisters. His last hug was to his mother, and his two oldest daughters agreed that seeing their grandmother turn her back and walk away was excruciating. Jerry's oldest daughter, Wendy, noted that while she and the rest of her family had each other, her heart truly broke for her father, who had no one and had to take the steps away from his family on his own. Red-eyed and sick with grief, the family members could not believe that these were the final "I love you's."

Not long after the family left, Jerry was transferred to the death house, and on the way out he offered the warden a heartfelt word of thanks. In Columbia, Jerry's family, friends, supporters, and lawyers gathered for a prayer service.

At the service, Jerry's lawyers spoke about their client's remorse, as well as his kind and selfless demeanor. They also discussed the unique legal issues associated with his case. Specifically, during the trial, the jury had asked the judge to clarify what would happen if Jerry were not given the death sentence, and the judge did not answer. Because the Supreme Court subsequently ruled that juries have the right to know the options, there was hope that the Supreme Court would overturn Jerry's sentence or rule that a new trial be conducted.[1] The prayer service was followed by a candlelight vigil outside the governor's home. The next day, April 16, was eerie—a long, surreal day.

From the death house Jerry was allowed to make phone calls. His final goodbye came at 5:30 P.M., when one of the children's cell phones rang. As her siblings talked to their father, Misty nervously awaited her turn. As her time concluded, she had a sick feeling as she relinquished the phone to the next person. After they hung up, the children joined the anti–death penalty activists and friends as they picketed and held vigil outside the prison.

At the death house, Celia stood in the observation room, weeping. Eventually the curtain opened, and she saw a freshly shaven Jerry strapped to a gurney with intravenous tubes stretching to a nearby wall. He looked at his mother just long enough to blow her two kisses, and she returned one of them. She listened intently, with a mother's sorrow, as Jerry read his final statement, in which he expressed remorse for his family and the victim's and stated, "I only wish things could have been different. I would give anything if only that had been the case."[2]

Outside the prison, at 6 P.M., Misty could no longer withstand the pain, and her knees buckled beneath her as she desperately sobbed. At 6:18 P.M. on April 16, 2004, Jerry was pronounced dead and became the 908th person executed in the United States and the 30th person in South Carolina since 1976. At 6:30 P.M. a prison official came outside to announce that the State of South Carolina had carried out its mandate. Soon after that, Celia, Jerry's spiritual advisor, and his lawyers exited the building. The next day's newspaper report about the execution included a statement from the victim's family that said April 16 was not a time to rejoice, and they asked people to please pray for the soul of Jerry McWee.[3] A few days later during the funeral service for Jerry his spiritual advisor said that Jerry went peacefully.

Conversant in death penalty and execution, Celia remains haunted by Jerry's last moments. She has not found comfort in Jerry's spiritual advisor's proclamation that he went peacefully. She asks herself over and over "how does he know" that, and indeed she might know more than him. Celia had reason to wonder. Although the seemingly peaceful technique of lethal injection has replaced vivid electrocution in every state but Nevada, it is not necessarily a painless event, but looks that way because of a paralyzing agent. Nine states, including Georgia and South Carolina, have adopted a protocol based on three injections. The first injection is Pentothal, an ultra short-acting barbiturate. The second is a paralyzing drug that stops breathing, and the third stops the heart. Some doctors speculate, and research confirms, that an individual may feel tremendous pain during lethal injection but be unable to express it because of the paralyzing agent.[4] For this reason, a proto- col that includes a paralyzing agent is not permitted in pet euthanasia. At present California does not use a paralyzing agent, and an anesthesiologist ensures that the inmate is sufficiently sedated. However, executions sched- uled for the early part of 2006 were put on hold because the state had not been able to secure the services of an anesthesiologist. Doctors are refusing to participate in executions because it violates their medical ethics.

As one would expect, the first few months following Jerry's execution were difficult for Celia, but as time went by, her life has become excruciating. Initially she responded as many do to a loved one's death. Sleepless, she felt hollow and lonely. She tried to maintain her daily habit of getting up and reading the newspaper. She knew that it was important for her to leave her home, so every few days she would force herself to go somewhere even if only to the dollar movies. Several times a week she turned on the computer to see what was going on in the death penalty community or stay in touch with her online friends. But unlike the typical grieving process, Celia's pain has grown steadily worse.

Almost a year later, there are days when she does not pick up the newspaper from her front yard and weeks when she does not leave the house. Everything around her feels empty. She tried to visit another inmate on death row so that she could see her friends and support someone who had no family, and yet, "No matter how many people were in the room, it was so empty without Jerry." She hates to let the inmate down, but she cannot bring herself to go back.

State executions like Jerry's are bizarrely unlike any other death in that they are precisely calculated: the state scripts and announces the time and method of death, and the executioners choreograph and practice the final hours and moments leading up to it. Many people remember where they were when President John F. Kennedy or John Lennon were shot, though few indi- viduals have ever looked at their watches and said, "In exactly 5 minutes from now, someone I love will stop breathing." The certain knowledge of the time and method of an inmate's death puts unique strains on his loved ones.

Many families feel like the state is punishing them for their loved one's crime when an execution is carried out. Offenders' family members must for- ever live with the knowledge that someone intentionally killed their relative. They must also live with the fact that the death was planned for years, sanc- tioned by the government, and often supported by community members. These feelings compound their grief and isolation because few people can relate to these experiences, and perhaps even more devastating, few caregivers are trained to deal with the psychological trauma that family members fre- quently face after an execution.

To better understand execution and its effects on the families of the condemned, we consider three aspects: (1) the ritual and history of execution;

(2) the effects of an impending execution on individuals and familial relationships; and (3) the aftermath of execution. From our analysis, it is clear that families are severely damaged by executions and do not have adequate resources available to help them cope. Restorative justice is offered as a starting place for helping families with trauma, depression, and more practical needs (like transportation).

Ritual

In recent years the word *ritual* has acquired positive connotations suggesting healing, spirituality, or celebration, but the term is also associated with violence and terror, as in the phrases "ritual abuse" and "ritualistic torture." No matter what one's opinion is about state-sanctioned execution, undeniably it is a process associated with routine and ritual, and it is one that has taken many public and private forms in the United States and abroad.[5]

As recently as the twentieth century, drawn to the spectacle and community activity, audiences flocked to public executions, which were often staged in public arenas and town squares. They came with the illusion that they were experiencing the theater of justice. In reality, they were witnessing the power of the state over the individual.[6] Before the death penalty was abolished in European countries, public officials intended for the executions to impart a moral, deterrent effect, but records show the crowds often missed the point and responded with compassion or admiration for the person who would soon be put to death.[7] The condemned became a character in a larger-than-life drama, and his last words took on particular significance on the public stage. Crowds waited to hear what the condemned would say when he or she had an audience and nothing to lose. Would he curse or repent?[8]

In early U.S. history, the state intended public hangings to be serious, somber events and opportunities for the community to express its condemnation and hear moralistic sermons. By the beginning of the nineteenth century, however, executions had become festivals with drunken, irreverent crowds and illegal activity such as gambling at the hanging site. Even more troubling for public officials was the change in the attitude of the crowd as they too began to show support for the condemned.[9]

The last state-sanctioned public execution in the United States occurred in Owensboro, Kentucky, in 1936, where 20,000 people gathered to watch Rainey Bethea hang. The day was a macabre festival, with hot dogs and drinks for sale, people camping, and the crowd jeering and cheering as Bethea spoke his final prayer.[10] The press captured the unruly atmosphere, and the resulting sense of public shame helped move executions from public to private spaces.[11]

As executions became private, concern also arose about the methods of execution to the point that governments sought what psychiatrist Robert Lifton and journalist Gregg Mitchell have called "the ultimate oxymoron—the humane killing."[12] In the 1800s, stoning, burning, and beheading were largely replaced by hangings and firing squads. With advances in technology in the early twentieth century, it was thought that electrocution would be more in keeping with modernity and compassion because it was quicker and less prone to error, an assumption upheld by the Supreme Court when it ruled that electricity could produce instantaneous and painless death. The gas chamber was the first method to mimic sleep, but its use was never widespread.[13] Today, despite medical evidence to the contrary, lethal injection appears to be sterile and peaceful, and thus consistent with the concept of execution as a concealed, somber, and private event. The great irony in "humane killing" is that although retribution and revenge is touted as one of the primary reasons for execution, there has been an attempt to minimize and mask the human suffering of the condemned.

Notification

From an administrative standpoint, Jerry McWee's execution went smoothly. The run up to it, however, was atypical because unlike Jerry, most inmates and their lawyers know when a death warrant is on the horizon. Depending on where a case is in the legal process and past actions of the court, the legal team can approximate when a warrant will be served. However, the legal issues associated with Jerry's case made it difficult to predict an impending warrant, so he and his family were caught completely off guard. In the beginning of 2004 it seemed to the McWee family and the defense team that nothing would happen with the case until at least the following fall. They were all shocked when a death warrant was issued in the spring. The family had no time to prepare themselves for their impending loss. Although the McWee family may have wanted more time to prepare, other family members perceive the foreknowledge of an execution warrant as equally difficult.

The belief that a warrant would be forthcoming was very hard for Adam's sister Jan. She recounted what it was like for her and her family when Adam's appeals came to a close, signaling that a warrant would soon follow: "He had written me that March and told me he wouldn't live to see his next birthday and asked me if I would tell the rest of the family. It was kind of like your most dreaded fear becoming a reality because you spend all those years thinking and praying that it won't come to this. It was Easter, and you think, 'Okay, that is not a good time to tell Mom that her son is going to be executed.' . . . And then of course there is Mother's Day. You can't tell her before Mother's Day."

Eventually Jan and her brother made an arrangement. They picked a time and date for Jan to go to their mother's house and wait for Adam's call. That way Adam could tell his mother and know that she would not be alone. Although their mother had time to digest the information prior to the issuing of a death warrant, she did not sleep well for several months following that call as she begin what is called the deathwatch.

Final Days and Deathwatch

Margaret Vandiver, a researcher who has expertise in the area of capital punishment, writes that the suffering of families of the condemned spans a number of years. This pain is ratcheted up to crisis level when a death warrant is issued and reaches an apex in the final few days before execution.[14] Vandiver's research is consistent with our own, and the five family stories that follow illustrate the long-term crisis experienced by families during and after a deathwatch and execution.

On April 26, 2001, Ron Spivey was placed under death warrant in the state of Georgia, where policy sets the execution date 10 days after the warrant has been served. Ron's sole family support was his cousin, Pat Seaborn, with whom he grew up. Pat always had a soft spot for Ron because she had been horrified by his abusive father. Though she lived in another state when Ron was arrested, she eventually returned home to Georgia. Over the years, she faithfully visited Ron on death row, and their relationship grew much closer.

When Ron was under warrant leading to his March 16 execution, Pat spent the 10 days visiting him and working with his lawyers to get a stay of execution. They were 10 grueling, exhausting days of frantic legal work divided by sleepless nights. On the day of the execution she recalled her arrival at the prison: "There was an officer at the gate, who asked what my business was here today. I said my name, and I just dissolved. His eyes filled with tears. When I had to go through that gate and tell the prison officials that I was there for my cousin's death, I fell apart. I just lost it."

Pat remembered: "We had started to say our goodbyes, and the lawyer came in and said 'we got a stay.' I was like 'we got to stay where?' She said 'no, a stay of execution.' We could not believe it. The warden extended our visit because we were all so happy; even he was happy, as this would have been his first execution. You go through the euphoria for about 6 weeks, and then it's awful."

Pat explained what it was like for the reality to hit—the realization that the euphoria was doomed: "You say good-bye, you walk out of the room, and you think you will never see him again, and then you know tomorrow you get a stay, and you have to go back and say goodbye again. To say it one time is all you can do. Nobody can understand what it is like to do that."

Ron was served his final death warrant 10 months later. "I was just as wrecked as the first time," Pat recalled, stunned that she was in the middle of a deathwatch again. "No one should have to go through a deathwatch twice." Reflecting on the final moments, she recalled: "I still see the shift change during deathwatch. I still see the employees leaving with tears in their eyes saying goodbye to Ron. I still see the corrections officer saying to me 'I have been here 9 years, and that man is my friend, and I am going to miss him.' I asked someone on the death team if they would be going with Ron all the way to the execution chamber, and he said to me, 'if I had to go there, I would have to quit.'"

The final hours of the deathwatch were incredibly difficult for Pat. Her heartache caused her to feel physically ill. The warden suggested that perhaps she leave the prison. Anger shot through her anguish, and she retorted, "I don't care how bad I feel, I am staying here until the end because this is the last time I will see my family member because you are going to kill him." After the execution she explained unapologetically "So I was awful. But I had to be mad to go through it a second time."

Felicia Floyd and Pat happen to be friends and neighbors, and Felicia also had to say goodbye to her father twice after a stay was granted. She recalled the process of doing this as "hideous and unthinkable." On the final day of her father's life, Felicia unexpectedly did not have the support of her family for her last visit and goodbye to her father. This happened because the execution was abruptly moved from 7 P.M. to 4 P.M. Her husband and children had planned on coming to the prison in the late afternoon, but because Felicia and her father were not notified of the time change until well into the day, they were unable to get word to her family in enough time for them to make it to the prison. Frustrated and alone, Felicia added fury to the long list of emotions that ravaged her that day.

Sadly for families, such last-minute schedule changes are not uncommon and are just one of the many ways that the system demonstrates that it is oblivious to the torment of offenders' family members. Tony's family expected a contact visit at 3 P.M. on the day before his execution. When the family called the prison to confirm the visit, they were told the visit would be at 2 P.M. and shorter than previously scheduled. As Tony's father, Matt, tried to sort things out over the phone, he heard the prison guards laughing in the background. "This may have been a joke to them," he recalled, "but not to me." When the family entered the visitation room, Tony was behind glass. It took a call to the warden to get the contact visit, and the time that was lost due to the negotiation was never recovered.

Things deteriorated the next morning when the family came for their final visit, scheduled from 7 A.M. to 9 A.M. Although they arrived promptly, they were not escorted into the visitation room until well past 7. At 8:15, the prison officials informed them that the visit was over. Caught up in protesting their abbreviated time, the family lost the moment to truly say goodbye. Matt described this double loss, saying, "I didn't realize what happened at the time, but my wife informed me that she never got to say goodbye. They just took him out and left us standing there. We don't have a marker on the grave yet. She just can't put a marker there. But I think if we had closure" [his voice trails off and the thought that it might be easier for his wife if she had been able to say goodbye is not spoken]. He added simply, "She lives with this thing every day."

When Luke's mother died during his time on death row, his Aunt Patty became his primary support. Patty and her other sister, Lucy, are spirited women who love to laugh and recount the fun times they shared with Luke. While he was under a death warrant, the aunts had their first contact visit with Luke in 18 years. During these visits, they "could hug and kiss him and have a wonderful time." However, what joy they could extract from these moments was shattered during one of the visits when Luke told them that the nurse had come to see him to evaluate his veins for the lethal injection.

The execution day came more quickly than anyone thought it could. Though Luke assured his aunts that he was tired and ready to die, he still maintained a will to live. He explained that although he could not stand another day on death row, he would happily choose to live the rest of his life in prison. Patty shared their final moment together with us:

> We saw him after he had eaten his last meal, and they had him in a holding cell. When you go down to the holding cell, you feel so empty. There is no hope. We sat on the bench and talked to him. We talked through a little hole, and he was all shackled. That was really hard. As he was leaving, I told him "don't look back, just follow the light and keep going." The final thing he said was, "Don't you all worry about me. I'm ready to die. The life I'm living is not life. They're ready to kill me, and I'm ready to go. Now I don't want any of you to leave here crying." Oh, I held my tears until I got around the corner, and then I nearly passed out. Then we stayed on the bench until they announced that he had died.

Despite the insensitive bureaucracy that often governs these rituals, a single kind gesture can mean the world for a grieving family member. All of Jan's and her family's visits with her brother occurred through glass, even during the deathwatch. On Jan's last visit before Adam's execution, she was able to touch his hand. She describes this touch as an act of mercy from a prison guard. As the visit drew to a close, the guard kindly turned his back, and she and her brother were able to use that moment of privacy to reach through the opening in the glass and touch each other's hands. Their mother, who had not been able to touch her son for years, was never given such an opportunity.

Executions tend to occur in waves, with several taking place in a short period. They are scheduled without regard for sacred seasons, which compounds the crisis of a deathwatch and the pain that comes with anniversaries. At one point in South Carolina, six offenders were executed between December 4 and January 22, and several of the family members we interviewed lost their loved one during this block of time. In the previous year, another inmate whose family's story is in this book was also executed in early December. In 2001, five inmates were part of an execution schedule that occurred during the holiday season from October 25 until January 24, 2002, in the state of Georgia. Although Jerry's execution took place in the spring, he was under warrant during lent and Easter, and the parallel between the religious practice of lent—penance, prayers, and sacrifice preparing for the anniversary of Christ's death on Good Friday and their own preparation for Jerry's death was disturbing to his Catholic family.

Clemency

Following a warrant it is not uncommon for lawyers and family members to launch campaigns for clemency appeals, a process that is the inmate's last chance for life. Local and national anti–death penalty organizations distribute information about the condemned and ask individuals to support clemency efforts through letter-writing campaigns, faxes, and protests directed to the governor or the Board of Pardons and Paroles or in federal cases to the president. Most of the time, the probability that clemency will be granted is scant; the efforts are symbolic rather than practical. Family members, however, keep their hopes alive, and in some cases, the chance of a good outcome at a clemency hearing seems better than at others. Because the policy of the Georgia Board of Pardons and Paroles is to take the desires of the victims into consideration, Fred Gilreath's family, including his daughter Felicia Floyd, had high hopes that his clemency hearing might result in a change of sentence.

Fred had been on death row for 21 years. He has two grown children, Felicia and Chris, who each have children of their own. Felicia and Chris know what it means to be crime victims. Fred, a violent husband and father, shot and killed his wife (their mother) and father-in-law in 1979, when Felicia and Chris were children. Family members raised them separately, and Chris wanted his father dead. When Felicia was a teenager she visited and forgave her father, and they enjoyed a newfound relationship for the last 15 or so years of his imprisonment. Felicia cautiously introduced her children to her father but never fully explained to them who he was. About a year before Fred's execution, with his wife's encouragement, Chris went to see his father for the first time. His father asked for forgiveness, and although Chris struggled with it, he chose to forgive him. The two began to develop a relationship, and soon Chris, his wife, and their son were visiting on a bimonthly basis. Chris's son grew to love his grandfather and looked forward to the time that they spent together.

Once Fred's death warrant was issued, Felicia and Chris teamed up with his lawyers and devoted themselves to trying to save his life. They began by holding a press conference in which they explained that they were already crime victims and they did not want the state of Georgia to make them orphans. By going public, they hoped to build momentum for their cause and win influence with the Board of Pardons and Paroles. Renny Cushing, then director of Murder Victims' Families for Reconciliation, an organization made up of individuals who have lost loved ones to crime and do not support the death penalty, came to Georgia to offer help. Their clemency appeal was well organized and garnered a great deal of support.

Nine days of organizing work culminated in an emotional meeting with the board. Fred's lawyer advised the children that they plea for their father's life, suggesting that they talk about their relationship with their father and the reconciliation they had found. Felicia did so but later regretted her decision, wishing that instead she had gone in as her mother's daughter.

She said: "I wanted to say if there is a victim it is me. My mother missed my graduation from high school and from my master's program; she missed the birth of my children, my marriage. I wanted to go in as my mother's daughter. I wanted to be portrayed as a family member asking for mercy. What I wanted to get across was that I was a victim, and I found that forgiveness had healed me, and that any further violence would add to this terrible legacy. It would not bring me peace but destroy the healing that I found through the years." Felicia believes that her approach would not have made a difference in the outcome, but she wishes that the members of the board and observers in the courtroom had heard this part of her story.

Imploring the board Christopher said, "If my mother could talk now, she would say she did not want him to die, we have lost enough. . . . We don't want to lose anymore."[15] Two of Fred's aunts also joined in their pleas, and his attorney reminded the board that the victims' relatives "do not want this to happen."[16] Even with this organized support, there were major problems with the clemency hearing. First, one of the board members was out of town and chose to make his decision based on the file; he did not even listen to a recording of the proceedings and sent his vote by fax. Second, and perhaps more unsettling, was the fact that two of the board members appeared to have a conflict of interest. They were under investigation by the state's attorney general's office, as it had been alleged that they improperly accepted money from a state vendor. Because the attorney general's office is responsible for defending any challenges to a death sentence, it was easy to see why Fred's family members and lawyers would question whether these members of the board could examine the issues in an impartial and unbiased manner. The family was not surprised, but still heartbroken and outraged when the death sentence was not commuted to life without the possibility of parole. However, they were astonished and angry when the board returned a statement chastising them for pleading for Fred's life.

Felicia and Chris tried to show that they loved, honored, and deeply missed their mother while working to heal and develop a forgiving relationship with their father. The board rejected their pleas, leaving them devastated about the decision and questioning whose interest the board was trying to protect.

Execution

The execution itself is the culmination of the criminal justice ritual. Executions are usually the end of a long series of legal appeals designed to ensure due process in the courts. When the legal process is exhausted, the correctional system's execution team practices and rehearses the death procedure. Despite the strong focus placed on this moment, the actual execution can go awry, as it did in the case of Ron Spivey and others.

It is incomprehensible that Ron would have killed a police officer for $20 during a poolroom brawl, yet a number of things about Ron's life were beyond comprehension, including that his father locked him in cupboards, beat him, and threatened his life as a child.[17] Ron was first hospitalized for psychiatric disorders at age 15 and was released after several weeks without having received any treatment, even though according to his cousin, Pat, the admitting doctor recommended a 2-year commitment and shock therapy. Ron's life was forever marked by his father's abuse, his own mental illness and its inadequate treatment, his alcoholism, and contradictions. Ron was kind when he was on his medicine, but paranoid and aggressive when off. The prison system tends to be particularly hard on inmates who kill police officers; nonetheless the prison guards and administration liked Ron.

In March 2001, Ron was scheduled to die by electrocution, but in winter 2000, for crimes committed after May 1, 2000, the Georgia General Assembly had abolished the use of the electric chair.[18] Prompted by the state's move to lethal injection, Ron and his defense team won a stay of execution for the Georgia Supreme Court to determine the constitutionality of the electric chair. Justice Leah J. Sears writing for the majority stated, "Electrocution offends the evolving standards of decency that characterize a mature, civilized society."[19] Ten months later, when Georgia had made the changes necessary to implement lethal injection, Ron received a second death warrant, and the *Augusta Chronicle* ran an editorial titled "Stick It to Him."[20]

On January 24, 2002, Ron was executed, but his final minutes became the subject of heated controversy. It quickly became apparent that the amount of drugs injected in his veins was inadequate to kill the 6-foot-6-inch man; for 7 minutes, he remained lucid, awaiting death while a larger dose of drugs was prescribed and eventually administered.[21] His need for a physician to administer additional drugs reignited the debate over the role of medical personnel in executions. The American Medical Association's position is that "as members of a profession dedicated to preserving a life when there is hope in doing so a [physician] should not be a participant in an execution."[22] Therefore, for the most part, physicians and their governing bodies limit their execution activities to declaring the time of death. The doctor's duties, however, go beyond that scope when an execution is flawed, including doctors being called in to the execution chamber to insert an intravenous needle when a vein cannot be found.[23] Pat, Ron's cousin and the closest person to him, indicated that she thought Ron, an ardent opponent to the death penalty, would have been pleased that his death raised questions about the morality of execution and the humanity of lethal injection, yet to this day she continues to be horrified by the way Ron spent his last 7 minutes.

Neither Pat nor Felicia witnessed the executions of their loved ones, but they did what most family members in Georgia do: they waited across the street at a truck stop for the lawyers who witnessed the execution to call them and say it was over. Felicia was particularly anxious because she knew that the execution of Jose High, which occurred days before her father's, had been botched.

She was sick with worry, hoping and praying that her father's execution would be smooth.[24] Even though there were no such problems with Fred's execution, she still remembers the tremendous stress it brought her.

The family members' pain grows as the date approaches. Unfortunately, because of the trauma associated with executions, for many the heightened pain does not lessen with time, and in some cases the pain is more pronounced years after the execution.

Postexecution

Execution and Personal Items

For family members, the pain does not end when the last drop of lethal fluid has done its job. Macabre events continue to punctuate the grieving process, eviscerating any momentary sense of peace the family may have found. Such a moment occurred when Patty, Luke's aunt, received her nephew's belongings in the mail. "I began to unpack the box, and there was his wet towel and washcloth that he used right before he was executed. I screamed." For Patty, the wet towel was too vivid a reminder of his last few hours; she could visualize him in the shower with restraints under the watch of an armed guard.

Jan saw it as surreal that she was planning her brother's funeral while he was still alive. Although people often have input in their final arrangements, no one but family members of condemned people write advance obituaries and funeral programs with the date of death. Like Celia, Jan shuffled between visits to her brother and making funeral arrangements; sometimes the two activities merged, as when she explained, "I sent him copies of the obituary, and at one point during a visit, we started talking about the funeral service and the obituary, and that was one of the weirdest things. It was so hard."

Like Patty, Jan was unexpectedly confronted with the reality of her brother's belongings. The box that was sent from the prison included his sneakers, socks, a stocking cap that he wore for warmth, and a signed copy of the execution warrant. Jan recalled looking at the warrant and thinking: "You think someone really had to do this. They had to sit down and put in black in white and with their signature that somebody was to be killed. It is like no chances, no more anything; just kill this person. The piece of paper said the date and time for when the execution was ordered; it's barbaric." The warrant made it profoundly clear that the state had deliberately set in motion the mechanism that resulted in her brother's death.

For Celia, the most grotesque reminder of the execution was a package she received from the funeral home. Inside was Jerry's prison jumpsuit, which had been cut off of his body after he was put to death. Celia is not sure what to do with such an object of abject contempt, yet it is the last thing that Jerry wore and one of the few physical links to him.

Receiving personal items after a loved one's death is usually a difficult event. This is especially the case for families whose loved ones met with a violent death. For families of murder victims, their personal effects may include bloody clothes, whereas offenders' family members are likely to receive a death warrant indicating homicide as the cause of death and the clothes their loved one wore during the execution. Restorative justice's goal to minimize trauma and help families by providing them with information would support giving a warning to families as to what they might expect with their loved one's effects. Although the experience still will be painful, they can prepare for it and if desired have someone help them through the process.

Living with an Execution

The tragedy of an execution, as with any death, does not end with the funeral. The execution continues to stress the family members whose lives are already steeped in pain. In fact, in three of the families, the primary support person for the executed man could not go through with an interview. Jan explained that her brother and her mother were always very close. While her brother had been alive, her mother talked with him on the phone, visited regularly, and talked about him often. Three years after his execution, she still cannot mention his name.

Matt laments that 2 years after his son's execution his wife is still devastated and not the person that she was while her son was alive. She forgets things and is often so distracted that she is unable to follow a conversation. She has gained a dangerous amount of weight, and the medicine that she takes for depression has not lifted her spirits. She was 57 when the execution occurred, and her "whole personality has changed," so much so that her daughter recalled that when her brother was executed, "I lost my mother as well." For Matt, it is also difficult; he lost his son, his wife has withdrawn, and his daughter is still mourning. He worries about the changes in his daughter, who has become quiet and has lost some of her spirit, though she keeps going for the sake of her children. To deal with his own issues related to his son's execution, Matt takes medication for depression and has received a great deal of pastoral counseling, saying that he is "grateful to the Lord" for putting the pieces back together.

The fact that the execution occurred during the first week in December indefinitely changed the entire holiday season for this family. Thanksgiving now marks the deathwatch and Christmas the execution. For others to celebrate these holidays as happy occasions further isolates this family from the pulse of their community and undermines any possibility of holiday celebration. Matt worries about his children, who have the dual role of creating meaningful holidays for their own children while mourning the death of their brother.

One year after Jerry's death, Celia's life is very different. Specialists in family caregiving recognize that in many situations family members are forced to devote a good portion of their day-to-day lives nurturing a loved one who is impaired or close to death. When death does occur, sometimes it is followed by a sense of relief that the suffering has ended, but it also leaves a large void. Death has brought not only the loss of the individual but also a loss of routine and purpose.

At the moment Celia feels as if her life lacks meaning. She is a widow, mother, grandmother, and great-grandmother. Her children and grandchildren all live within an hour's drive and prior to Jerry's execution she was a babysitter, cook, and doting MeMaw (the name the grand- and great-grandchildren call her). After she retired, time was measured by her Saturday visits to Jerry. On Fridays, she would prepare for the visit by tanking up her car with gas and collecting $10 in quarters for the vending machines. She would also go to the beauty shop to get her hair done, wanting to look her best as a way of reassuring Jerry that she really was doing well.

Now her children and grandchildren call and ask her to their homes for dinner, but going anywhere is laborious and being around people gives her a hollow feeling. A trip to a restaurant reminds her of the things that Jerry will never again enjoy. Her nerves are frayed and her spirits dampened. Celia has a good day if she gets out of the house. Because being around people is difficult, her refuge is the 99-cent movie theater. She does not like to cry around people, but at home she cries often, and because she worries that her sorrow will depress others, she has isolated herself even more. She has lost weight, her face has become pale and drawn, and she looks like she has aged 10 years in just 1 year.

Celia used to take great pleasure from her grandchildren; now they exacerbate her difficulties. When they come to visit, she is hypervigilant about their safety. She always provided a careful watch over the children, but now she is obsessed with their well-being. Celia no longer wants the kids to go outside because a car might hit them. She knows that the children are cautious and well behaved, the street is quiet and buffered by a large front and back yard, but that makes no difference. She feels that she is unable to protect them in the safety of her own home, just as she was unable to protect her adult son. Because keeping them safe from unforeseen circumstances is a heavy burden, her time with the grandchildren has become a constant source of worry. As a result, she has chosen to see very little of them.

As an anti–death penalty activist, Celia used to provide support to family members and even organized a conference for them. She supported family members during trials and had an e-mail list that kept people throughout the state posted about trials, clemency hearings, and executions. She held vigil at the governor's home or outside the prison during an execution and negotiated with the prison warden for the delivery of Christmas presents and visits with the family members. Although Celia adamantly believes in the cause, she has lost her sense of efficacy. After being unable to save her own son, her work feels like a futile effort.

Celia knows that she cannot go on this way and has sought mental health care. Unable to figure out the system, she called a friend who helped her make an appointment at the community-based mental health clinic in her area. She did not mind waiting 2 weeks for an appointment or that the intake process took 5 hours. At the clinic she told everyone that she did not want them to try to talk her out of the guilt the way her friends and family do. Celia does not want to hear that she was a good mother, or that she has no reason to feel guilty; rather, she wants the fact that she holds feelings of guilt validated.

Although it has been difficult, Celia is appreciative of the therapy. In therapy, she realized that she had misjudged many of her relationships with her grandchildren; she had been critical of the grandchildren because she did not think they visited Jerry enough. She was resentful that Jerry's children appeared to be moving forward with their lives. She now knows that they hurt as much as she did. "How could they have not? They loved Jerry, and he was their father," she explained. Celia also knows that she should have paid more attention to their needs and behaviors. Her granddaughter Misty has been in life-altering pain, yet Celia was not there to support her.

Celia lost her ability to provide direct care to her great-grandchildren and the people who had once depended on her. One of her greatest regrets was her inability to care for her dog, a family pet that had been with her for years. He mostly lived outside, and as Celia said, "He wanted nothing more than to be loved." Overwhelmed by his presence and unable to give him anything, Celia sent him to the animal shelter. She does not know what happened for sure, but she is pretty convinced that the dog met the same fate as Jerry. She lost her drive to support others and, in some ways, views herself as an executioner.

Shared Punishment

In many cases in this book, after receiving a death sentence, the inmates were ready to die. They told family members that they were tired or that life on death row was no sort of life at all. For others, self-preservation kicked in, and still others wanted to spare their families the agony of an execution. In contrast, none of the family members ever felt ready to say goodbye. They saw the execution and the ritual surrounding it as monstrous and pointless, an endeavor that punished the wrong people.

Ron knew that his cousin, Pat, was angry, so in their final moments together, while he had an intravenous port in his hand, he said to her, "Okay, kid, I don't want you to be mad. I don't want you to be bitter. I don't want you to be sad, because I'm okay." According to Pat, the greatest irony is that the wrong person is hurt during an execution. "You must be punished when you take a life, but by executing him, you didn't punish him, you punished me," she confided. "Ron said he was so tired of this place [prison] and that execution would set him free. I am punished. His daughter is punished. The people that loved him are punished. But not him. Each time a warrant comes down, we relive the whole thing. Every one of those memories just came tumbling back. You know that someone else is suffering just like you suffered." Felicia remembers having similar feelings during her father's last days. "He was ready to go," she recalls. "The only thing that made him question going was the relationship that he had with my brother after all of these years. He had gotten close to his grandchildren, and I think that he felt that my brother still needed him."

Punishment does not stop with the execution of the inmate. Many family members feel as if the state missed the mark and are instead punishing them. Robert Coe's sisters talked about the reverberations of his death sentence and execution on family members, agreeing that not only they were hurt, but also their children were. They felt torn about the toll that their support of Robert and his claims of innocence had on their families. The sisters find few things worse than imagining his last hours. His final moments were dignified, but he was scared and frustrated that the evidence that would have likely exonerated him was never allowed to surface.

The pain of execution reverberates throughout the family. The children of Robert's sisters, who were at times neglected because of their mothers' preoccupation with Robert, may still feel effects. Pat feels the pain anew each time an execution occurs; Felicia worries about her bother; and the list goes on and on. Yet all of the family members who experienced an execution said in one way or anther that their peace was in knowing that their loved one, the offender, is now spared the pain associated with the death penalty. As Pat says, an execution is a missed mark.

Summary

The rituals of execution are full of contradictions and irony. The execution process requires a recognition of humanity in the offender that the media and the criminal justice system have spent years trying to deny. A "humane killing" requires that the offender understand what an execution means, recognize the difference between right and wrong, and specifically comprehend why they are being executed. Prior to execution an inmate lives in a sub-human world—he is a number who is fed through a slot in his cell door, who a jury and judge have determined does not deserve to live. Then, when the deathwatch begins, people affiliated with the state begin to acknowledge his humanity. He receives visits and is given a spiritual advisor who has a great deal of access to him and with whom he can spend considerable time. He is given a meal of his choice, sometimes one that would have been too expensive for his budget prior to incarceration. In exchange for this treatment, the state trusts he will go to his death in a cooperative manner and appear as if he has merely fallen asleep. To family members, these contradictions smack of hypocrisy.

The inmates associated with our study did comply with the state's wishes, but their families have had difficulty coping with the execution. They remember that the defendant was a human being worthy of love. For their loved one's sake they have adhered to the requirements and vagaries of the state's control, visiting when allowed, helping calm the condemned, dealing with the body when the state's job was done, and trying to carry on with their lives in the aftermath of the execution.

But they are haunted by the peculiarities associated with the execution, including that on their last visit their loved one looked healthy and his body never showed that he was hours from death. They find it unsettling that they planned his funeral service while he was still alive. They hate having to make a decision about whether to witness the execution, and the conversation and negotiation with the offender over this decision are extremely difficult. Whether or not they choose to witness, they forever have a mental image of someone who earns his salary from their taxes killing their loved one.

They mourn the death of their loved ones without the support of their community. Their grief is not publicly acknowledged. Although close friends and family may come to a funeral service, their neighbors generally do not bring casseroles and offer condolences. They suffer alone and are full of shame. Not only have they lost their loved ones, but also many feel like they have lost their sense of purpose. Prior to the execution a number of family members enjoyed regular visits with their loved one, and much of their energy was focused on their incarcerated relative. Once the execution has been completed, they lack the peace that they believe their family member has found in death. They feel as though they, not their loved one, have been punished.

Their enduring pain calls out for the healing effects of being brought into the restorative justice process, but even here they are in a no man's land. Are they family members of the offender, or has the cycle of violence repeated itself and made them family members of a victim of violence? Following an execution, offenders' family members desperately need help to process their grief as well as the rage and anger they feel toward the system. Restorative justice solutions seek to intercede in the cycle of violence by preventing future violence.

6

Children of the Condemned

Andre was good at everything he did. He was bright and talented at football and basketball. He grew up in public housing with his six siblings and a single mother in a violent, drug-infested neighborhood. By age 13, he had tried both crack and intravenous drugs, which made him happy. Using drugs made him feel like "somebody." After becoming addicted, Andre's life teetered between his desire for drugs and his attempts to quit. When he was clean, he turned to religion. For a while he was attending church regularly, trying to stay off drugs and live his life by the teachings of Jesus Christ. In church he met and fell in love with the woman who would give birth to his first son, Jeffery. Despite his intentions of being a good father, the intensity of his addiction won out. Andre left the church, his wife, and his infant son and once again began using and selling drugs.

By the early 1990s, when Andre was arrested on a federal charge that included gang activity, drug dealing, and murder, he had fathered five children by three women. He did not know his oldest son Jeffery well since the boy's mother shielded her son from his father's activities. Still, Jeffery maintained a relationship with his paternal grandmother, so he had at least some connection to his father. Andre was much closer to his two youngest children, and he had a particularly close relationship with his youngest son, Dray, who lived with him for a number of years.

Today Jeffery is 18 years old and Dray is 15. The boys do not know each other very well, but the similarities between them are unmistakable—each looks very much like his father. They are extraordinarily polite, so that when the interviewer called to make arrangements to meet them, each of the boys addressed her as "ma'am," thanked her for her interest, rearranged their schedules to meet with her, and provided detailed instructions to their homes. When complimented on their good manners, the two boys independently credited their mothers and their father. Stark differences, however, exist. Jeffery is quiet, has been raised in the church, and takes matters such as his virginity very seriously. His clothes are fashionable, but conservative—baggy jean shorts and a buttoned-up shirt. In contrast, Dray is gregarious, athletic, and popular with the girls; wears very baggy clothes and several chains; and has pierced ears.

Also, the ways the boys deal with their father's death sentence are quite opposite. Dray tries to deal with things very directly, whereas Jeffery is more cautious, sidestepping any discussion of painful issues. Dray worships his father and is outspoken in his feelings for him. Jeffery, on the other hand, is profoundly curious about his father but more reserved.

Jeffery met his father when he was five or six and his father was in prison. The visits were important to their relationship, not so much because of the time they spent together—it was difficult to connect through the glass—but because Jeffery saw in his father "a picture of himself when he grew up." They shared the same features, the same walk, and several other mannerisms, and Jeffery felt instantly connected to this stranger, a larger version of himself.

Their developing relationship was seriously altered when Andre was transferred out of state 8 years ago. Since that time the contact between the two has been limited to bimonthly phone calls. Jeffery is always happy to hear his father's voice. But because Andre is using a phone card with limited time, the calls are short and largely unsatisfying. Typical calls last between 3 and 10 minutes, and the phone time is shared between Jeffery and his mother. Andre does not say goodbye before he tells Jeffery that he is proud of him, warns him not to make the mistakes that he has, and encourages him to take care of his mother. Often Jeffery will pass the phone to his mother, and sometimes his parents talk about him. The feeling of joint parenting is "really good" to Jeffery. He explains that when they are on the phone, it is a moment when he feels like he is in a "normal household—a household with two parents, like everyone else has."

Jeffery has taken Andre's advice and stayed out of trouble. He knows his father made "bad choices," and he knows how easy it would be for him to slip up as well. He hears his father's voice in the back of his mind, making the consequences of bad behavior all too clear. Moreover, his father's pride in him feels good, even over the phone, and Jeffery will not risk disappointing him. As Jeffery explains, "[I] work hard to not end up like him. It is motivating, and it feels good to tell my Dad how I am doing." Now a senior in high school, Jeffery is currently weighing the options between college and military service.

While Jeffery realizes that he is very much like his father and wants to do well by him, he finds Andre to be somewhat of a mystery. Their short phone calls hardly help cultivate a father-son bond. Jeffery would like to tell him about girls and things like that, but there is never enough time. He does not even really know what kind of crime his father committed. He often asks about the crime, and Andre always said that he would tell him when he was old enough to understand. Jeffery's mother believes that Andre is afraid to tell Jeffery the truth, both because he is ashamed of his crime and because he does not want to risk his relationship with his son. Jeffery finds it strange to know that he has so much in common with his father without really knowing him.

Dray recently moved, and the boys now go to the same school, where they are enjoying getting to know each other. For Dray, this recent change of school and neighborhood is a step up. His new home is in a less violent area, and kids do not carry guns at his new school. In some ways, Dray's progress toward adulthood has been more precarious than Jeffery's because he had the added risk of living in a violent neighborhood. Jeffery's friends are largely involved in the church, but Dray's best friend is in juvenile detention with several felony charges. In addition, this friend's older brother was shot, and Dray's uncle, a surrogate father and firefighter, was murdered. Both Jeffery and Dray have strong mothers and share the love of their paternal grandmother, who will not put up with adolescent shenanigans.

They both credit their father with keeping them out of trouble. Dray calls his father "Diddy," and says that "Diddy is helping me to do a 360 from where Diddy was. Diddy says 'you see the wrong way, look at me. I am going to show you the right way.' " Dray's relationship with his father is deep. To Dray, Diddy is his coach. Dray believes, "My dad is coaching me how to rise. My family, his family, we're a team." He proudly continues, "Diddy helps me with all my problems whether it be a girl, school, or a sports problem. I might be at home dwelling on something, and Diddy will call and he'll help me. He always tells me 'education is first.' He put that in me. No coach ever did that." Serious about his education, Dray knows that a football scholarship is within reach but that he must maintain his grades and test scores to receive one.

Although Andre's advice was always important to Dray, sometimes it was difficult to implement. When Dray was 9 years old, he and his mother went to counseling for his "anger problem." Dray says that the counselor gave him the language to understand how he was feeling. In support, his father helped him see the implications of his problem while giving him the motivation to address it. Today Dray has learned to better control his temper and calls himself a "chill dude," and because Andre counseled him to stay active, he has thrown himself into sports.

Despite the intensity of his feeling toward his dad, Dray is profoundly aware of his father's physical absence and pending fate. Dray says that it is especially hard to be on the field or court and see the other mothers and fathers in the stands. It is also hard to go to the banquets, where he often receives awards such as most valuable player, with just his mother. He has developed a game time ritual where he looks at the stands, keys in on an empty seat, taps his chest twice with his fist, and flips his wrist and points his index finger to an empty seat. That way he evokes the spirit of Diddy. After the game, he knows that he will talk with his father about the plays and rehash the highs and lows. Although Dray perceives his father as his coach, he has never had the opportunity to interact with him on the field or court. Dray says that he would be happy to put all of his "talent in a bottle and give it away" if he could play one game of basketball with his father.

At 15, Dray's life is shadowed by his father's impending execution. He fears the day but feels confident that he will be able to continue without his dad. He has grown up a lot in the years his father has sat on death row, and reflecting on his young life, he explains: "I might be wild. If [they had killed my father earlier] I would not have any of those trophies up, but certificates saying

I graduated from juvenile detention center. But Diddy kept my head on straight. He said, 'don't go down that road—that is not the right road.' If I knew he was already gone, I would be like 'whatever, don't tell me anything because I lost my father at an early age.' Now I am older and wiser, but I have to be a man when he goes. I got nieces to look after, and I can do something with my football."

Jeffery does not deal with the reality of his father's pending execution as directly as his brother does. His mother told him about his father's death sentence several years ago, and he has since spent a great deal of time in tears. The tears eventually dried into denial. Now when asked about his father's sentence, Jeffery says it is "life in prison." When asked what he thinks will happen to his father, he says that "he will spend the rest of his life in prison."

Both of the boys are well aware that their father needs to be punished for what he has done, and both accept the fact that Andre will spend the rest of his life in prison. For Dray, that means he will always be there; he will be his coach for the times that he needs him most. Life in prison would give Jeffery time to get to know this person with whom he has so much in common. That, however, is unlikely—Andre's appeals are running out.

The Administration on Children, Youth, and Families of the U.S. Department of Health and Human Services has targeted children of inmates for special services, such as relationship-building skills, support groups, and therapy for the children. They also recommend parenting classes for inmates.[1] But these programs often overlook children whose parents face a death sentence. Dray and Jeffery's case clearly shows that children of the condemned may have a greater need for support than children of incarcerated parents, as they not only have to deal with the all the stressors that children of other incarcerated parents face but also they must contend with the threat of their father's death by execution.

This chapter is based on interviews with eight children of the condemned, four of whom were minors at the time of the interview, and two siblings who were minors when their brothers were sent to death row. Table 6.1 indicates the children, their age at the time of interview, and the type of relationship that they had with their loved one. We begin the chapter with a review of the research on children of incarcerated parents and then turn to interviews with the children. We end with Robert Meeropol's story of how he used his parent's execution to shape his contribution to society.

Research on Children of Incarcerated Parents

In 1999, the Bureau of Justice Statistics estimated that one in every 50 children in the United States had a parent in state or federal prison.[2] The effects of the parent's incarceration are profound for children and society. Children of incarcerated parents are five times more likely to go to prison than those without

Table 6.1
Children and the Relationship with Death Row Parent

Name	Age at Interview	Relationship	Parent's Status
Dray	16	Father, custodial parent before arrest. Highly engaged post-arrest.	Death sentence
Jeffery	18	Father, love, but limited engagement pre- and post-arrest.	Death sentence
Kofie	16	Father, love, but limited engagement pre- and post-arrest.	Death sentence
Teria	8	Father, love; treasures visits with her father and his letters but does not understand where her father is.	Awaiting death penalty trial
Misty	Over 21	Father, custodial parent before arrest; love, but she found it difficult to adjust to parenting behind bars.	Executed
Wendy	Over 21	Father, custodial parent before divorce; love, but she found it difficult to adjust to parenting behind bars.	Executed
Felisha	Over 21	Father, custodial parent before arrest; love, but she maintained an emotional distance for protection.	Executed
Robert	Over 21	Mother and father, does not really remember his parents, though he does remember prison visits. Believes that he was born into a happy loving home.	Executed
Michelle	Over 21	Brother, lived with her older brother who she adored until his arrest when she was a preteen.	Executed
Betsy	Over 21	Brother, lived with her older brother who was her protectorate until his arrest when she was a young adult.	Death sentence

The relationship is based on our subjective determination from the transcripts and interviews.

a parent in jail.[3] The intergenerational effect of incarceration is such that newspapers occasionally run stories of children who have met their fathers for the first time when they ended up in the same prison system.[4] Criminal behavior in children often follows a number of warning signs, which include aggressive, hostile, or antisocial behavior; use of drugs and alcohol; running away; and school truancy. A number of studies show that many children respond to their parent's incarceration by engaging in these same activities.

Additional studies find that boys of incarcerated parents are over-represented among youth who receive mental health treatment. A study of adolescents receiving mental health care finds that 43% of youth in treatment had a parent who was incarcerated. Moreover, these adolescents had higher rates of conduct disorder then children in the general population (a disorder often associated with criminal behavior that includes difficulty following rules and aggressive behaviors), attention deficit disorder, and problems with role performance. It is not surprising that these youths also have higher rates of school suspension and expulsion as well as arrest.[5]

In 1992, psychiatrist Stewart Gable reviewed the literature on children of incarcerated parents and found five major themes.[6] (1) Parent-child separation is likely to cause trauma for the child, and this trauma comes from two sources: the severing of the relationship and loss of income. (2) Following parental incarceration, nonspecific behavioral problems emerge, and the manifestations and symptoms of these behaviors are specific to the child's developmental phase. (3) Some children will feel stigmatized, which can be harmful to their development, and African American children may feel as if the high incarceration rates of African Americans result from a race-based stigma and prejudice. (4) Deceiving children about their parent's incarnation is widely practiced, even though the literature indicates that it is harmful to a child's development. (5) Most children do not show severe antisocial behavior at the time of their parent's arrest. Boys near puberty at the time of parental incarceration, however, are at greater risk for engagement in antisocial behavior. This risk tends to occur in the presence of other risk factors, such as parental substance abuse and mental illness, as well as poverty, child abuse and neglect, and transient living situations. Statistically, the risks for parental incarceration and engagement in antisocial behavior often coincide.[7]

Denise Johnston, co-cofounder of the Center for Children of Incarcerated Parents, built on Gable's work to explore the effects of incarceration on children from a developmental perspective (see Table 6.2). She observed profound effects at each stage. During infancy (ages 0–2), when children should be developing attachment and trust, separation from the parent can induce impaired parent-child bonding. In early childhood (ages 2–6), as children's cognition advances and they can imagine things and they move toward greater autonomy and initiative, separation from their parent can induce separation anxiety and related developmental regression. If the parent becomes incarcerated while the child is in middle childhood (ages 7–10), when a child is developing industry and productivity, the traumatic stress reactions can induce developmental regression and poor self-concept, leading to long-term emotional and behavioral problems. Early adolescents (ages 11–14) who lose a parent to incarceration may have difficulty acquiring the emotional and behavioral regulation that is expected at that age.[8]

Sometimes the effects can be mediated by protective factors—characteristics of the child and his or her environment that promote healthy development and mitigate risk factors. Protective factors include having the presence of a loving adult and being a child with intelligence and a happy disposition, which makes other people want to be around them.

Table 6.2
Possible Developmental Effects of Parental Crime, Arrest, and Incarceration in Children

Developmental Stage	Developmental Characteristics	Developmental Tasks	Influencing Factors	Effects
Infancy (0–2 years)	Limited perception, mobility, and experience. Total dependency.	Development of attachment and trust.	Parent-child separation.	Impaired parent-to-child bonding.
Early childhood (2–6 years)	Increased perception and mobility. Improved memory. Greater exposure to environment. Ability to imagine. Incomplete individuation from parent at younger ages.	Sense of autonomy and independence. Sense of initiative.	Parent-child separation. Trauma.	Inappropriate separation anxiety; other developmental regression. Impaired development of initiative.* Acute traumatic stress reactions; survivor guilt.
Middle childhood (7–10 years)	Increased independence from caregivers. Increased ability to reason. Peers become important.	Sense of industry. Ability to work productively.	Parent-child separation. Enduring trauma.	Developmental regressions. Poor self-concept. Acute traumatic stress reactions. Trauma-reactive behaviors. Impaired ability to overcome future trauma.
Early adolescence (11–14 years)	Organization of behavior in pursuit of distant goals. Increased aggression. Puberty. Increasing abstract thinking.	Ability to work productively with others. Control of expression of emotions.	Parent-child separation. Enduring trauma.	Rejection of limits on behavior. Patterning of trauma-reactive behaviors.

Late adolescence (15–18 years)	Emotional crisis and confusion. Adult sexual development and sexuality. Formal abstract thinking. Increased independence.	Achievement of cohesive identity.** Resolution of conflicts with family and society. Ability to engage in adult work and relationships.	Parent-child separation. Enduring trauma.	Premature termination of the dependency relationship between parent and child. Characteristic legal socialization. Intergenerational crime and incarceration.***

* *Developmental regression:* sequence of developmental reactions to stress/trauma at all ages. A documented deterioration in any aspect of development or reported loss of skills, however transient.

** *Achievement of cohesive identity:* adolescence developing the related ability to successfully engage in adulthood. This includes formal and abstract thinking, achieving some form of independence and self-sufficiency; acquiring work skills, and functioning in sexual relationships.

*** *ICD-10 (International Classification of Diseases, 10th revision) and DSM-IV (Diagnostic and Statistical Manual of Mental Disorders, 4th edition) legal socialization:* legal socialization is the process through which adolescents acquire attitudes and beliefs about the law. It is critical in shaping adolescents' perceptions of the law, rules, and agreements among members of society, as well as the legitimacy of authority to deal fairly with citizens who violate society's rules based on previous types of interactions with the law, *MacArthur Foundation Research Network on Adolescent Development and Juvenile Justice; http://members.cox.net/lmcoon/salarycap.htm#24*

Source: Denise Johnston, "Effects of Parental Incarceration," in *Children of Incarcerated Parents*, ed. Katherine Gable and Denise Johnston. New York: Lexington Books, 1995.

Incarcerated fathers like Andre seek to be a part of their children's lives. This interaction, if managed properly, can serve as a protective factor and minimize the child's chance of following in their footsteps. In a study of incarcerated men, social work researcher Creasy Hairston found that 80% of incarcerated fathers wanted to strengthen and improve their parenting skills. These fathers indicated that they wanted to be better parents to their children than their parents were to them, and they wanted a better life for their children than their own.[9]

Parenting from Prison

Personal interactions from prison can take the form of letters, phone calls, and visits. Calls are limited because of the prohibitory high cost of using prison phones, and visits are often difficult because of the long distances many families have to travel to the prison, the emotional drain associated with a prison visit, and the lack of physical contact. All of the children desired more from their parent(s) than the visitation situation would permit. Yet no matter how limiting the barriers, the interactions are priceless to the children and often essential to their development into adulthood. The story of Jerry McWee's children, Misty and Wendy, exemplifies the importance and numerous challenges of maintaining a relationship with a father on death row.

Prior to 1988, Jerry had what Wendy called "the ideal family." He worked as an emergency medical technician, and his wife was a stay-at-home mom. Wendy and Misty were born in 1974 and 1976 and have two younger siblings, Heather and Jerry Jr., with whom we did not speak. According to the sisters, they often did things as a family, and the children in the neighborhood enjoyed spending time at their home. In the late 1980s, however, Jerry had an affair with a younger woman and soon divorced his wife. The family was devastated. Not long after the divorce, Jerry suffered a debilitating back injury that forced him to quit his job and go on disability.

The children's lives changed dramatically with the divorce. Their mother, previously a stay-at-home mom, took several jobs to support the family, and Wendy and Misty took over the household responsibilities of child care, meals, and cleaning. The pressure was too much for Misty, whose unresolved anger at her parents led her to begin cutting herself with razors. She moved in with her father, at the age of fourteen, because she was looking for more structure than she had with her mother. Misty recalled that "my father was great. He got up every morning and fixed me breakfast, took me to school every day, was there for me when I got home, and helped me with my homework." While living with her father Misty stopped cutting herself and worked hard to restrain her bad temper. Wendy continued to live with her mother. Although she never stopped "loving her father to death," she was angry with him for leaving and breaking up their family. Life was not easy for Wendy, who was now a senior in high school. Without Misty's help, Wendy became what she called "the second parent" to her younger siblings. "I signed all report cards, their papers, and their excused absences. Mom was working two jobs. I was cooking and cleaning, and it was such a big role for me to do."

When Jerry was arrested for murder, Misty moved back in with her mother and was furious at her father for "doing what he did and leaving her." Not long after Misty's return, Wendy quit high school, married, and moved out of her mother's home. Misty now found herself in charge even though she desperately needed her own authority figure. As she explained, "There was no one to make us go to school, so we didn't." By the time Misty was in tenth grade, she dropped out of school. Jerry Jr. also dropped out when he reached the tenth grade, and Heather only made it to the ninth grade.

The years following Jerry's arrest and sentence were very hard on his children, especially Misty. Though Misty refrained from cutting herself, she began to lose control of her temper. Rather than unleashing her fury on other people, she diverted it and began punching things until her hands would ache. She was not actively suicidal, but she never stopped wishing the Earth would "swallow her whole." Misty resented the fact that she could not lean on her imprisoned father as she sorted through her own behavior and "demons." Misty explained, "If you needed your father to talk to, you could never call him up and say 'hey I had a bad day, and I need a hug' or 'this boyfriend of mine did something, and I need you to have a talk with him' or 'I feel so angry that I can't stand it.'"

Prior to his arrest, talking with him had helped make things better, but now she was on her own. As Wendy explained: "You don't want to air out your problems. You did not want him to think that it was so bad for us. You had to try to keep everything on a positive beat. . . . He'd say 'I want to know everything,' but I mean why do you want us to sit here and tell you all of this bad stuff that's happening when you know you cannot do anything? Then you feel like you are punishing him, so you don't mention it. But there are lots of things that you wish you could have talked with him about." Misty added, "What can he do anyway? If you do tell him it's not like he can put his arms around you and make it better or give you comfort. He can't do that from behind the glass."

Wendy believes that from prison it was next to impossible for Jerry to maintain his parental authority. She said, "I don't think he wanted to voice his opinion too much, risking that we may not come back and see him. I think it was just too hard." When disagreements occurred, the children felt terribly guilty. After one disappointing visit with her father, Misty told us sarcastically, "Gee, like I just made his day!" Even though Misty and Wendy's interactions with their father had constraints, the love, care, and support that he showed them provided a great deal of stability for the girls, particularly Misty, who has struggled with grief, anger, and depression since Jerry's execution.

Misty and Wendy were not the only children struggling to have a meaningful relationship with a father in prison. Kofie, the 16-year-old son of a man on death row, feels the absence of stability and a male role model in his life. He and his father, Eric, who were never close prior to the arrest, are struggling to develop their relationship now. Eric was arrested when Kofie was very young, so Kofie has no memories of living with his dad. When asked what he knows about his father, Kofie answers, "Not a whole lot, but I know I love him, and he loves me." Kofie visits his father about every 2 weeks. He wakes up at 5 A.M. on visiting days, which gives him time to iron his clothes meticulously, a visiting day ritual; then he usually goes to the prison with his grandmother, and the three of them visit for about an hour.

Each visit is an earnest attempt to solidify their relationship. His father is always happy to see him and tells him that he loves him, and Kofie loves sharing his accomplishments but is honest about his problems as well. In fact, the two often discuss things like Kofie's "anger problem." Kofie also knows that it is better to get things out in the open because his grandmother will tell his father how he is *really* doing. Still, he recognizes that most visits do not include intimate conversation about feelings and support. What he likes the best is being told that his father is proud of him. At the same time, he also believes that his father's assessment may be a bit superficial because "he does not really know me." Just the feeling that both his mother and father care about him is important and makes him feel like other children who have two parents, even though neither is able to devote the time to him that he needs.

Each visit is no easier or less awkward than the last one. Kofie says, "I feel like I miss him. He is in handcuffs and that makes me angry to see them. I try to control the anger. The glass makes me angry, too. It would be different without the glass. I could hug him, talk to him, and we could really talk."

Kofie does need to talk. His life is full of confusion and fear. He does not really have a stable home environment and is constantly bounced between his mother, his aunt, and his grandmother. He likes being with his aunt best, but she has responsibilities that make it difficult for her to care for him full time. When he is with his mother, she tends to ignore him. He is terrified of the possibility that his father will be executed. He naively believes that if his father were not in prison that the two of them would live together, and he would have a home and a safe place to share his feelings. "If Dad was here, we could talk. We could spend time together. We would be going to the mall, hanging out—doing things that boys do." Kofie's anger management counselor has told him that he needs a male mentor to do some of the things that a father might, but he has been unable to find one. At the time of our interview, Kofie thought his girlfriend might be pregnant, and he was happy about the possibility of being a father at age 16. Several months following the interview, we received word that Kofie's girlfriend was not pregnant, and that Kofie is presently serving time in juvenile detention. Like Misty, and to a lesser extent Wendy, it is clear that Kofie needed more guidance from his father than his father was able to provide, and it is also clear that his father needed support to learn how to play a more active role in his son's life.

Not all children are able to visit their incarcerated parent, and in these cases the relationship becomes more difficult to sustain. Parents on death row often try to compensate for their absences with letters and phone calls— communication the children treasure. When the interviewer asked 9-year-old Trina if she received letters from her father, Trina ran out of the room and came back smiling and holding the letters close to her chest. Although she has no memory of touching her father, the love found in these letters shows him as deeply engaged in her life.

Robert Meeropol's memory of his parents is reinforced by the letters he received as a very young boy. He and his brother, Michael, are the sons of Ethel and Julius Rosenberg and are the only children in the United States who have lost both parents to execution. The high-profile nature of the Rosenbergs' arrests, trials, and executions created more powerful feelings among a wider group of people than most other cases. The public debate regarding the Rosenbergs has made the relationship between them and their parents very public—including the publishing of 100 prison letters between the boys and their parents. The letters are found in *We Are Your Sons: The Legacy of Ethel and Julius Rosenberg*.[10]

The Rosenbergs' letters to their children are much like letters that were shown to us by the children interviewed in our study—all tended to contain a discussion of developments related to appeals, encouragement, and an outpouring of love. For example, in a letter dated July 11, 1952, Julius Rosenberg writes, "I want you to know I am interested in learning about the day camp, the swimming and activities that you and Robbie will be indulging in. . . . So let's hear good reports of your progress. As for me I keep reading, and writing, and working on our case."[11] In a letter to "Sweetest Children" dated September 25, 1952, Ethel shares a personal moment: "When Daddy was in to see me on Wednesday, we babbled like a couple of kids ourselves, marveling first over one of you and then over the other, we dearly wish for you to know how proud we are of the fine job both of you are doing, . . . developing into healthy, happy people. All my love— Mommy."[12]

The Rosenbergs' book of letters also included the parents' final letter, addressed to "Dearest Sweethearts, my most precious children," and concluded, "We wish we might have had the tremendous joy and gratification of living our lives out with you. . . . We press you close and kiss you with all of our strength."[13]

The Rosenbergs influenced their children's individual values and their opportunities, and Ethel and Julius's last letter to the boys provides a prescient belief that this would occur. In this letter the parents also wrote, "Your lives must teach you, too, that good cannot really flourish in the midst of evil." Robert Meeropol, a committed social activist, lawyer, and author, lives by those words—he has spent most of his life working to ensure the human rights of all. The parents wrote that they had solace in their knowledge that the boys would be surrounded by a community. Although Robert recognizes that aspects of his childhood were traumatic and painful, he believes that he gained as much as he lost. He attributes this to his genetic disposition toward optimism and "the nurturing of so many good and caring people." This nurturing included committed social activists who rallied behind Robert and Michael as a way of showing support for their parents, their enrollment in progressive schools and summer camps, and their interactions with their adoptive parents, Anna and Abel Meeropol.

In 1954 the Meeropols were awarded custody of Robert and Michael. They were social activists and supporters of the Rosenbergs who, Robert speculates, gave up their membership in the Communist Party so that the courts would look more favorably at their petition to adopt the boys. The imprint of the Meeropols' social activism endures, and many remember Abel's contribution—the penning of "Strange Fruit," the antilynching song, made famous by jazz vocalist Billie Holliday. The Meeropols provided love and support and engaged Robert's passion for progressive politics.[14] Their home was full of cultural and intellectual stimulation, warmth and security, and social activism. They were part of what Robert calls a community of supporters, who cared for him and his brother as well as provided financial contributions for college and summer camp. "After my parents were killed, my brother and I became to some degree children of the movement that fought to save them."

All of the children we interviewed said that their father's arrest robbed them of their childhood. Wendy and then Misty had to share the role of parent in the McWee household. Kofie moves from home to home. Robert and his brother spent time in an orphanage. At age 16, Dray worries about providing for his family. But perhaps none of the children took on more responsibility than Carley. At age 19, she no longer receives guidance and support from her father; rather she is his only caretaker.

Carley was 15 at the time of her father's arrest and has always believed that he is innocent and never received a fair trial. She finished high school and credits her large support system—her mother, who divorced her father prior to his arrest, and her four grandparents—with helping her through her depression following the crime. By all ostensible measures, Carley is happy and productive, yet she is very clear that her father's arrest took away her childhood. For the first year following his arrest, Carley guarded herself at school, always waiting for disparaging remarks about him from other students. She was anxiety ridden, suffering with the irrational belief that she might have prevented the whole thing. She had to force herself to focus on getting through each day. "I cried all the time," she remembers. "I couldn't go to bed. I wasn't sleeping. I wasn't eating. I didn't care about anything. I went to school, but I didn't care. It was hard, but for the most part I put on a happy face around people—I really did! I made myself go to school as it did no good to sit home and dwell on it."

From age 15 to 18 Carley was unable to have regular visits with her dad because she lacked transportation, which made her difficult teenage years worse. As soon as she turned 18, however, she began to visit him regularly. Since then she has become very active in his court case. She spends up to 20 hours per week researching information on the Internet regarding his case and similar cases. She also spends time talking to his trial attorney, his appellate attorney, and even the prosecutor. Carley has asked the appellate attorney if she could read a transcript of the trial, and he has told her she is welcome to come to his office any time. Apprehensive about confronting the details of the murder, she has not made the time to do so. But she knows that she needs to read it because it is critical to understanding how best to help her father. Carley is aware that her and her father's roles have switched: she no longer seeks support from him; instead she is father's primary support and legal advocate. She feels the weight of the responsibility and freely acknowledges that she has taken on this role herself. She desperately wants justice to be served and her father to survive, even if the best she can do is a sentence of life without the possibility of parole. Like other children she lives her life under what Felicia Floyd called the "black cloud of execution."

Execution: A Child's View

Children deal with the threat of execution in several ways. When interviewing them, we learned that some tried to ignore or deny it altogether; others saw it is as a distinct possibility and sought to address it pragmatically. Most handled it similarly to their adult family members, focusing on their relationship with their fathers and only occasionally allowing the threat of execution to emerge. Those who have lived through an execution still struggle to cope with the loss. Jeffery and Kofie both categorically deny the possibility of execution. When asked about what sentence his father received, Jeffery did not mention death. When his mother mentioned the pending execution, he broke down. The guardian who introduced us to Kofie said that without question Kofie has a clear understanding of where his father is and that several family members have talked with him about the death sentence and what it meant. Yet when asked, "What does death row mean?" Kofie simply said that his father "should not be there." When asked what happens there, he snapped, "I don't know nothing about death row!" He even denied knowing where his father was. During the course of an hour-long interview, Kofie talked about his relationship with his father and the death of his grandfather with elegance and detail, but when the interview turned to his father's execution, he became defiant, and his body language changed to express discomfort and anger.

Other children actively prepare for their fathers' executions. Dray explained, "I treasure my dad because I don't know when that day might come when they will off him. I try to keep myself together because I want to be prepared for it if it does occur." Dray believes that if Andre were to be executed, he would then be the head of his extended family, which includes his grandmother and two nieces. This belief further motivates him to excel in sports and in school.

Felicia Floyd, who we met in the previous chapter regarding when her father, Fred, was executed for murdering her mother, prepared for his execution by maintaining an emotional distance from him. Although she brought her children to the prison to meet him, she wanted to protect them from feeling like they were losing family and never explained to them that he was their grandfather.

Felicia, however, worries about her brother Chris, who did not exercise her level of restraint. Chris, who we did not interview but who appears in Rachel King's book *Capital Consequences*, had been estranged from his father for most of his life because his father was an alcoholic, abusive, and had killed his mother. For most of his life Chris was furious and expressed no desire to see his father. In 1996, Chris met Beth, and they fell in love, married, and had children. With the birth of their first son, Beth became increasingly concerned about Chris's repressed anger. Believing that he needed to see his father to deal with and release his anger, she suggested that Chris visit Fred. She did not think that reconciliation was necessary, but that some kind of interaction was.[15]

After the visit, Beth said that Chris "seemed different to me."[16] Chris had been struck by the changes in his father, who was no longer scary but instead was a rather devout and humble old man who wanted to reach out to his son. Chris not only grew to love his father and to fight for his clemency but also began to rely on him. He and Beth and their son, Christian, visited Fred often, and Christian, in particular, grew to love his "pappy." Beth called Fred an inspiration, summarizing the new relationship in the following way: "He gave Chris a lot in the way of memories. He talked to Chris about his mother. Fred also told us [stories] about his childhood. It helped Chris understand why Fred was the way he was. Fred had a really horrible upbringing. It put Fred in a different light and made Chris think that maybe he would have been capable of the same thing. Everything about our time together was healing."[17]

When Fred was executed, Chris and his family were devastated; they have taken the execution very personally, and their quality of life has suffered. Felicia believes that his pain was a result of Chris letting himself get so deeply attached. Felicia has rebounded much better, although her life was still hurt by the loss of her father through execution and her self-imposed distancing from him.

Robert Meeropol remembers the feelings associated with his parents' arrest and eventual execution as a "vague and generalized anxiety." He explains that "to a 3- or 4-year-old, it is a vague mystery. You can't really figure out what it is, but you know it is real bad and threatening. You can't put your finger on it, but it was powerful and pervasive. Something was hovering in the background at all times. I knew this had something to do with my family, and that things could get worse."

During the 4 years before the Meeropols were awarded custody of Robert and his brother, things did get worse. The boys were shuttled from relative to relative, including time with their Grandmother Tessie, whom Robert described as "sour and nasty," and they spent several months in a children's shelter. Robert tried to be normal, but bottled up his feelings. He did not want to call attention to himself and hoped to escape notice. Robert did not have the option of telling anyone that he was the son of Ethel and Julius Rosenberg because their names evoked strong reactions from everyone, reactions that were hardly comforting.

Jerry's execution was torturous for Misty. Prior to her parents' divorce, Misty was a shy and well-behaved child, but after the divorce and her father's arrest and execution, her personality has changed. Since the execution, she no longer has the same capacity for restraint. She has gotten into street fights, struck her mother, and resumed cutting herself. She is plagued by nightmares, which sometimes wake her. She often tries to ward off sleep because the anticipation of her dreams scares her. She explains that she is depressed and has lost the fight to get herself together, confessing, "I don't care. I feel like the most important thing in my life was taken away from me. I don't care what happens to me—I really don't." Nearing the first anniversary of Jerry's execution, Misty once again took out a sharp object and cut herself. The wound was so bad that she required hospitalization. She no longer sought mere release—this was a suicide attempt. Things have not improved since her release from the hospital. In fact, her life continues to spiral downward; she has served time in jail, and her family is concerned about her new friends and boyfriend.

Children facing their father's execution respond in several ways, including withdrawal, denial, anger, involvement in criminal activity, and even in a limited number of cases by transforming their pain, confusion, and anger into positive action. These children all need help communicating with their incarcerated fathers, understanding his crime and society's reaction to it, and coping with the loss that comes with execution. Society should recognize the risks that executing fathers and mothers poses to the lives of their children, and when a decision is made for an execution to take place, society should own the responsibility of providing resources for these children so that they can cope with the execution.

Siblings with a Brother on Death Row

Michelle describes her childhood as idyllic; she was a daddy's girl, though both parents adored her. Her two older sisters were already out of the house for most of her childhood, and she idolized her older brother, with whom she played everything from Superman to baseball. He helped her set up her

Barbie Playhouse at Christmas and encouraged her violin lessons. Several months after her 11th birthday, Michelle's older sister picked her up from school and told her that her brother had been arrested for murder; he and a codefendant robbed a store and killed the owner.

Michelle had been introduced to the death penalty before her brother's crime when she was home watching a movie on TV about an accused individual and his family. She remembers comparing herself to "those poor people" thinking, "God, we're so lucky that nothing bad has happened to us. We're so lucky that our life has been good." Not long after seeing the movie, however, her brother was arrested, and she became one of those poor people.

Days after the arrest, Michelle's parents sent her to Florida to live with relatives, who tried very hard to keep her distracted and happy. Despite being taken on outings to the beach and to amusement parks, Michelle hated being isolated from her immediate family. She recalled, "I would cry at night because I wanted to be with my family; I wanted to go home."

Several months later, Michelle returned home. Her father picked her up at the airport with flowers, but her home had changed. "It was never quite the same. It was like there was a piece missing, and there was just kind of a sadness that was over everybody. Mom was in her own little world. She was just sad—all the time. She was quiet. She didn't laugh as much as she used to. She'd get in her good moods, and then she'd get in a funk. When she was in a funk, she was sad all the time. She would sleep all the time. She would cry by herself. She would get mad at small things. And I know dad was always different."

After Michelle's brother went to death row, life got even more difficult at home, and her parents became more distracted. Her mother's energy and spirit disappeared; she just went through the motions of living. Her father became so withdrawn that attempts to interact with him felt strained. "They still took care of me the way they should have. But it was different. I hate saying this, but I remember just doing my own thing. They wanted to take care of me and make sure that I did the right thing, but I didn't really depend on them. I couldn't they weren't really there, and I did not want to burden them."

Michelle also felt as though she had become a caretaker because she spent a great deal of her time worrying about her mother, who she would attempt to console by telling her that everything would be okay. She thought her father would be fine because he always seemed strong, but 8 years after his son's arrest he died from a heart attack. Michelle became extremely depressed; she dropped out of college and came home to be with her mother. In reality, she needed her mother's company as much as her mother needed her.

Worrying about one's parents was something that Michelle would not wish on anyone: "It is stressful and sad." Her way of coping with this situation was to shut down. "I learned to close myself off and not talk about the problems I was having," she confesses, "so that I wouldn't lay any more burdens on them." Being closed down made it difficult for her to have any normal relationships because she did not want to share her feelings or show vulnerability. Knowing that her coping strategy was "not normal," Michelle sought therapy. Even though it seemed to be working, she quit after she broke down crying in one of her sessions. She reflected, "I don't know if I was embarrassed or if I just didn't want to cry. I don't like to cry. And so I didn't go back. I probably should have gone back, but I just can't bring myself to."

One of the other coping mechanisms that Michelle used was always to appear quiet and collected. She always wanted to look "normal," so she never left the house without focusing on her physical appearance, and it was her hope that if she always wore nice clothes and looked like she fit in, no one would focus on her feelings. Michelle explains that her preoccupation was "very shallow," but keeping a normal appearance "was important as it was kind of a protective shell."

Betsy's home life, like Michelle's, provided her with love and support, but unlike Michelle, Betsy grew up in a neighborhood filled with crime, drugs, and gangs. Her brother Jim was her protector, and he used to ride his bike up to her school to escort her home and keep her safe from the older kids who used to harass and beat up on the younger ones. Betsy and Jim would return from school to a "house full of love." Her single mother put food on the table and love and laughter in Betsy's life, in spite of the fact that she had to go to work at 5 A.M. and often did not return until 6 P.M.

In the early 1990s, the household stability started to erode when Betsy's mother broke her back and went on disability, and doctors prescribed morphine for pain. Not long after her mother's accident, the police showed up at Betsy's door with questions about Jim. Later he was apprehended, tried, and convicted of first-degree murder and sentenced to death. From the moment of his arrest, Betsy had no one left to protect her. Her mother was barely able to take care of herself. She became hooked on antidepressants and morphine for her back. "Following the death sentence," Betsy explained, "my mother reached for the pills. She could barely walk, and she could barely talk. Her words were slurred, and she lost her memory." Eventually the combination proved lethal. In 2004, when Betsy was 22 years old, she found her mother dead on the living room couch. The official cause of death was an "adverse reaction to drugs."

Today Betsy is a mother to her own infant daughter, and she takes care of her three brothers, including Jim, who is on death row. She talks to lawyers and plans to use money from her mother's life insurance to hire a lawyer to defend Jim. Twenty thousand dollars, however, buys little in terms of a death penalty appeal. "I would give my life so that my brother could see the light of day again." She told us, "I would give anything to keep him alive. Just so I could see him behind glass, I don't care. I would give anything to keep him alive."

When asked if she thought about what will happen when her brother is executed, Betsy responded, "I don't know what will happen to me. I have lost my world. I have lost my mother. I would have lost my brother, and I would just have a portion of it [her world]—my daughter."

Too many siblings of offenders on death row lose their childhood because of a death sentence. Their parents are overwhelmed with the legal case, and they are often left to take care of the household while trying to manage their own trauma and depression. These siblings must cope with their parents' grief and related health concerns, which, as the stories of Michelle and Betsy illustrate, means that while their brother is on death row they may lose a parent to a stress-related illness. While all of the stories express pain and sorrow and a number of the family members are debilitated by their losses, one man, Robert Meeropol, found a way to use his voice and to turn the pain felt by children whose family members are executed into action.

Finding a Voice

It has taken Robert nearly 40 years to figure out how to be the son of the Rosenbergs as well as the Meeropols and to overcome "my fear, harness my anger, and transform the destruction that was visited on my family."[18] Up until 1974, Robert Meeropol remained private about his heritage, with only his immediate family knowing that he was the son of Ethel and Julius Rosenberg. That changed, however, when his brother, Michael, called late one evening to explain that a new book had been released. Not only had the author printed Rosenberg family letters without Robert and Michael's permission, but also he had edited the letters so that references to the children were removed, making it look like "our parents loved communism more then they loved their children."[19] Moreover, the author implied that Michael and Robert had "rejected their parents' values."[20] Despite the fact the Rosenbergs went to their deaths steadfast in declaring their innocence and that Robert and Michael believed them, the book took the position that the Rosenbergs were guilty.[21] Now that Robert's and Michael's personal property was being used to hurt their family, they chose to go public—not only to protect their property but also to clear their parents' name. They determined that the only way to clear their names was by championing a campaign to pressure the government to reopen the Rosenberg file and to release all sealed documents, documents that the sons—along with others—believed would exonerate the Rosenbergs.

The decision to go public was not easy. Robert was concerned for his family because he did not know whether his public stance would endanger his children and subject them to harassment. He also worried about the quality of his own life, believing that from the moment he went public he would go through life with a neon "Rosenberg" sign above his head. Despite their reservations, Michael and Robert chose to meet with an attorney to get assistance with their copyright claim and with their Freedom of Information Act suit against the government agencies that were keeping sealed documents containing information about their parents. This effort evolved into a national campaign to reopen the documents. To help finance this campaign, Michael and Robert made numerous public appearances throughout the country.

To take a public stance after living in private for so long was monumental. As Robert explained, "For as long as I could remember we'd suffer what was said about our parents in silence. We never had the opportunity or emotional freedom to give voice to our opinions about our parents' trial and execution."[22] By the end of the campaign to reopen the case, over 100,000 pages of documents were still classified. Although many of the released documents spoke to inappropriate and even illegal acts on the part of the judiciary, Robert and Michael were no closer to publicly establishing their parents' innocence. Today, Robert still feels good about the effort, confiding that "publicly acknowledging my heritage, confronting my fears and making this effort was personally powerful for me."

Robert's public stance was life-changing. During the course of his work, he met individuals who had been harmed or imprisoned because of their progressive political activities, and he learned that many of these individuals had children. Robert determined that he wanted to devote his life to helping children like himself, "children in this country who were suffering because of the targeting of their progressive activist parents."[23] He launched the Rosenberg Fund for Children (RFC) in 1989 to meet their needs. The RFC makes grants to children for school tuition, college, and summer camp; therapy; and music, photography, and riding lessons as well as many other enrichment activities. Grants are also available for travel to see an imprisoned parent. The RFC sponsors weekend retreats for the children to meet each other, share stories, and help them cope with trauma. Like restorative justice programs, the RFC has taken a needs-based approach to helping children who are targeted because of their parent's politics. The children determine what they would like and then request help from the RFC to obtain it. It is hoped that their involvement might break down some of the children's isolation, and the long-term affects of the trauma and depression they may experience.

Today Robert marvels "at how lucky I was to have found my life's calling." He reflects that his "parents' resistance inspired a movement. That inspiration has survived their execution." Both Robert and Michael were nurtured and cared for by an entire community as they lived through their parents' executions. Robert hopes the RFC will become that nurturing community for other children. According to Robert, the RFC works to provide concrete benefits to "children and families while being firmly grounded in activism. By connecting the children to a support network, we could facilitate the development of a progressive community."[24] To him the RFC is the vehicle to defeat "the destructive social forces that killed my parents."

Robert believes that given the context of his life, he had three choices: accepting defeat, striking back, or following the road he took. He used his anger to develop something positive, a process that he calls "constructive revenge." Robert's concept involves stopping those institutions that take away human rights as defined by the United Nations Human Rights Convention. Article III of the convention states that "everyone has the right to life, liberty and security of person."[25] This article centers his work for the abolition of the death penalty. He knows that his story is unique, but he also believes that all children of the condemned have moral authority because to them the death penalty is personal—the life of their loved one is being threatened; therefore, they hold the power to make change, and their voices should be heard.

Summary

Children of an incarcerated parent face increased risk for dropping out of school, drug use, depression, and their own involvement in the criminal justice system. These risks are compounded for children whose parent, brother, or sister is on death row because they must deal with the additional stressors of an impending execution and because they are often left out of programs designed to help children of incarcerated parents in the general prison population.

These children are the death penalty's dirty little secret. The death penalty is designed to punish offenders who commit heinous crimes, but the reality is that much of the burden of this punishment is shouldered by the offender's children or siblings and the actual execution may increase the likelihood of negative outcomes in their lives. By ignoring these children's needs, society sends them the message that they are not worthy of support because they are the children of the worst criminals. Society makes it clear to them that the pain they are caused as a result of the death penalty does not matter. The children of capital offenders are hidden victims and in many cases are primed to live out the self-fulfilling prophecy of society's belief about their families.

This book illustrates numerous cases of adults struggling to manage to live in the wake of a family member's death sentence; to expect that children would react any differently is misleading. Solutions using restorative justice principles would focus on providing family members, parents and children, a safe place to talk where they can develop strategies to work together to manage the numerous challenges they regularly face. Children desperately need help navigating the numerous ups and downs of maintaining and developing their relationships with their father or brother on death row. A trained professional could assist these families with educational materials on parenting and the death penalty, information and referrals concerning treatment for depression and trauma, and facilitation of communication between all family members.

A counselor or a support group could help family members and their loved ones on death row learn to communicate in a meaningful way within the confines of prison visitation, letters, and restrictive phone calls. Much more should also be done to help these children cope with the isolation, anger, fear, sorrow, and confusion associated with their loved one's crime and impending execution.

The RFC provides a constructive example of a way to begin addressing the needs of the children of the condemned. Though not officially a restorative justice program, the RFC honors the needs-based philosophy of restorative justice. The children of the condemned need assistance with trauma, education, and enrichment activities, and they need an opportunity to meet each other and bond. Some of the children that we interviewed want to be able to constructively confront the forces that killed or seek to kill their parents. Robert Meeropol believes that children of extraordinary circumstances have moral authority. In one way or another, all of the people with whom we spoke chose to talk to us because they hoped that the sharing of their stories would support the abolition of the death penalty, educate the general public about the devastating consequences of the death penalty on offenders' family members, as well as provide information and support to other family members so that they would not feel alone. The children's stories indicate that the death penalty produces numerous long-term negative consequences on their lives and that these consequences may outweigh any of the negligible benefits of execution.

Children especially need help understanding and adapting to the death by execution of their father or brother. The intense anger they feel over their loss may manifest itself in behavior that is harmful to others or self-destructive or with a great deal of hard work it can be transformed into something that is healing. Without community support and programs like RFC to assist them with processing their pain, society runs the risk of continuing a destructive cycle and losing these children's potential to be fully contributing members of society.

7

Psychological Distress

Sarah's nightmare began several months before her birthday. Her son Marcus—in his early 20s, unemployed, and living with her—began acting increasingly strange. He had always been somewhat withdrawn and exhibited odd behaviors in school, and then Sarah observed that he was having audible conversations with himself, complete with elaborate gestures. When she saw him arguing with himself, she knew it was time for help. Uneducated about mental health symptoms and treatment, she took her son to the local emergency room and waited with him until he saw the doctor.

Marcus left the emergency room with a referral to a mental health clinic, where Sarah dropped him off for his appointment. She had wanted to come in with him because she was concerned that he would not follow through, but she had to be at her job. When Sarah's children were small, she had begun working in the kitchen of a local nursing home, where she earned as much as $6.25 an hour. At about the same time that Marcus began exhibiting bizarre behavior, another company bought the nursing home and slashed her wages. She could not afford time off. But her instinct was correct. When Marcus entered the clinic, he sat in the waiting area without giving anyone a copy of his referral. No one questioned him, and eventually he became frustrated and left.

When Sarah asked Marcus about his appointment at the clinic, he became angry with her, insisting that he was not crazy. When Sarah told him that he needed help, the enraged Marcus left for his father's house in a neighboring state. He returned to Sarah when his father also pressured him to get help. Sarah told him he could stay only if he sought treatment. Not long after, Marcus then left the house, robbed a local store, and shot and killed the shopkeeper.

Although identified immediately, Marcus was not apprehended right away, and Sarah was terrified that the police would find him dead or that he would be killed when they tried to apprehend him. Worse still, the prosecutor had already announced that she would seek the death penalty. For Sarah, Marcus's life was already over—and effectively, so was hers.

On the day of the murder, Sarah lost much more than a son, as the impact of the crime invaded her own sense of being at every level. During Marcus's time in jail pretrial, trial, sentencing, and years on death row, her birthdays came, and went and she had no idea that they had occurred. She worked during the day; at night she sat in the back of her house with the curtains closed. Often she only slept when a friend or family member would spend the night. Her blood pressure was out of control for the first time in her life, and she could not focus on any aspect of her life. She had lost all meaning. Friends and family were concerned that she would kill herself. Sarah turned to scripture and prayer. Although her faith kept her from suicide, it did not give her the wherewithal to put her life back together.

Though she was suffering intensely, Sarah was not the only family member in pain. She said that her nephew, who had been very close to Marcus, had not been the same since the murder; he had withdrawn from everyone and everything. Family relations had fragmented as well. The family used to get together and celebrate holidays, but not any more. Sarah said, "It is just too hard. It is too hard to remember that someone is missing."

Through her pain, Sarah grieved for the shopkeeper. Before his murder she had frequented his store, and she always looked forward to seeing the kind man she called her friend. On several occasions when she ran short of money he would loan it to her. She felt horrible for his family, and until the trial, she empathized deeply with his wife. When Sarah was on the witness stand pleading for Marcus's life, she looked to the victim's family members and thought she saw the shopkeeper's wife laughing. From that moment Sarah stopped caring about the other woman. She remained very sad about her friend, the kindly shopkeeper, and for the rest of his family, but she could no longer muster sympathy for the victim's wife.

The trial period was grueling. Sarah did not sleep for a number of days before she testified—she knew that what she said would help determine if her son lived or died. Members of the defense team recalled her testimony as powerful in its poignancy. She was dignified on the stand and as she walked out of the courtroom. But with the courtroom door safely closed behind her, she let out a wail—a sound primal in its pain. At times she still feels that wail inside of her, and she confides that she is often so sad she feels like her heart is going to explode.

Since Marcus was sentenced to death, things have gotten much worse. She started drinking and said "I could feel myself dying and see myself killing myself. I would not go out of the house. I knew that I would die alone in that room [her bedroom]." During the interview, she said that things had improved somewhat but was quick to point out, "I cry and pray, pray and cry, and sometimes I pace." But she was no longer drinking herself to death.

Two years after her son's sentencing, Sarah's life was bleak; she literally had not been able to open the heavy curtains in her house since the murder. Once social and active in her church, she now largely divided her time between work and her bedroom. She felt afraid to go outside of her neighborhood; she could tolerate the pointing and whispering, but she expressed anxiety that someone might harm her. More difficult perhaps than the fear was the guilt that still plagued her: "At first I thought I did a good job" as a parent. She worked double shifts around holidays to buy the children presents; she raised them in the church; she loved them. All that means little, for "now I feel a lot of the time that it was my fault what happened."

She has taken down all of the pictures of Marcus. About once a month she pulls them out of the storage box under her bed and slowly looks through them. This ritual seems to undermine any progress she may be making. "When I look at the pictures, it is a setback; it will take 4 or 5 days until I am okay. . . . It is hard—I really can't explain, but everything is hard. I get set back." As she describes her life, it becomes clear that for Sarah a good day is a hard one, and a bad day is unbearable.

She has not been able to see Marcus in 18 months because her car will not make the 2-hour trip to the prison, and friends' cars seem to be equally unreliable. Her phone calls with her son are maddening: "It is like talking to someone else, a stranger. He talks real low and mumbles something, and I ask him what he says, and he says nothing. It is not him that is in his body." Sarah lost her son not only to prison but also to mental illness. The only way she gets through is by "reading scripture because it keeps your mind positive."She warns: "If you let your mind go negative, you will go crazy and it may kill you."

Almost a year after this interview, a member of Marcus's defense team received a call from Sarah's sister, who said that several nights earlier Sarah had a dream that God's hand beckoned her toward Him. When she told her sister about the dream, Sarah said she did not follow the hand because she was afraid, but if that hand ever came back she would follow it. Life had simply become too painful. Several nights later Sarah died in her sleep, and though the official cause of death would never be identified as a broken heart, that is what her family believes caused her death.

Against the backdrop of Sarah's story, it is important to consider how a death sentence affects family members' mental health. Like Sarah, most of the family members who experienced acute psychological distress also had symptoms of depression and trauma. They told of lives marked by deep grief and families imploded by a lack of coping mechanisms.

The family members' experience with their pain is told in this chapter, and to understand the psychological processes associated with the intensity of their sorrow, we explore published research related to the family members of capital offenders' experience with grief and theories related to grief and bereavement. Specifically we look to two explanations of loss—nonfinite loss and disenfranchised grief—to explain the profound nature of the hurt. Next we look at depression and trauma symptoms among the people that we interviewed as many of the family members experienced these difficult psychological states.

Broken Hearts: What Grief Research Tells Us

John Smykla, a political scientist who has studied criminal justice issues, including the death penalty, for close to 30 years, argues that all people involved in the circle of capital punishment, including offender's family members, are victims. Smykla interviewed 40 family members of death row inmates representing 8 cases, and he found that the family members in his sample experienced prolonged suffering and distorted grief reactions. Smykla found similar grief symptoms in family members who had a relative on death row for as little as 6 months and as long as 6 years, indicating that the reaction was distorted.[1]

A typical grief reaction, such as one that follows a death due to natural causes, occurs shortly after the loss and usually fades with time and adaptation to the fact that a loved one is gone but life continues.[2] *Distorted grief* is a term used to describe pain that is so consuming that it changes the personality and life of the bereaved. In the *American Journal of Psychiatry,* Eric Linemann reported six ways distorted grief reactions manifest in individuals and become detrimental to one's social and economic well-being. These include acquisition of medical illness, alterations in social relationships, disruptions in social interactions, depression, conduct that is without emotional expression, and overactivity without a sense of loss—that is, keeping busy (with sometimes risky behaviors) to avoid a sense of loss.[3] Reasons for the distorted grief found in the Smykla study can be understood by looking at the experience of nonfinite loss and disenfranchised grief among death row families.

Nonfinite Loss and Disenfranchised Grief

Katherine Norgard is a psychologist and adoptive mother of a man who was on death row, and she knows firsthand that the pain accompanying a capital charge does not lessen with time. She likens her feelings of grief to prolonged suffering, but calls it chronic sorrow.[4] Because of the prolonged nature of a death sentence, and in contrast to a death by natural causes, Norgard and other family members do not move through the stages of grief that ultimately lead to healing.[5]

When Norgard talks about chronic sorrow she is describing *nonfinite loss,*[6] a term coined by Elizabeth Bruce and Cynthia Shultz, researchers who work in the area of grief, loss, and adaptation to explain the prolonged suffering in which an individual is lost between two world. The first world is the pain that is known, and the second is what happens when an inevitable dreaded future event occurs to make the ache even more intense.[7]

Nonfinite loss has three aspects. First, the loss is continuous and often follows a major event. For the family of capital offenders, the loss usually begins with the crime and arrest. In some cases the family members in our study began their loss with the onset of their loved one's mental illness or alcohol and drug addiction, and a capital crime was the culmination of this process. The continuous nature of the loss is reinforced by the years of appeals and reminders such as another execution within the state, which drives home the nearly inevitable ending to their own family member's life. In the cases we reviewed, the average length of time between arrest and execution was 12 years. To family members who may struggle, as Sarah did, just to get through each day, those years are an eternity. Celia McWee, whose daughter died tragically and whose son was executed, said, "There is no comparison. When Joyce died, we thought that was the worst thing imaginable, but this is much worse. All of those years of waiting for the phone to ring and to hear it's time." Since the execution, she added, it has "only gotten worse." Clearly the years of nonfinite loss have heightened the difficulty of handling the death.

The second part of nonfinite loss is when developmental expectations are not met. For example, many parents raising a child with physical disabilities grieve anew each time their child "should" be achieving a milestone that his or her disability prohibits—learning to ride a bike, going on a first date, graduating from college. Similarly, parents of capital offenders grieve each time their loved one misses a social milestone. Most family members mourn the fact that their loved one will never marry, have children, or often even finish high school. Barbara has a son on death row, and she stopped going to high school graduations, weddings, and other family celebrations. When her son's best friend graduated from college, she could not face the ceremony even though the families had been extremely close ever since the boys were young. Not only would the ceremony remind her that her son would never graduate, but also it was heartbreaking to be around individuals with whom she and her family shared a history. "It's just too hard," she sighed. "It makes me think about the time that we had together as families and the way my son played with their children. Now their son has a life, a future, and mine has a death sentence. I cannot look at [my friend's] children and not feel like a hole has swallowed me up."

The third part of nonfinite loss is the loss of one's own hopes and ideals. Those who experience nonfinite loss question who they could/should/might have been if a particular experience had not occurred. For example, a mother who has lost her son through execution or a death sentence might also experience a sense of loss of her own role, hopes, and ideals as a mother. In this regard, one mother called her online support community the "if only's,"[8] explaining that all family members with a loved one in prison live their lives repeating "if only." If only he were not in prison, I might have seen him graduate, or if only he had listened to me about his friends, I might have been a grandmother. Additionally, several family members said that they lost their belief in God when this occurred.

For family members of capital offenders, the nonfinite nature of their experiences is compounded by the nature of the death. Researcher Margaret Vandiver argues that family members of capital offenders experience "chronic dread," a term that she uses to describe the anticipatory grief associated with execution, aggravated by the perception that people in respected positions want to violently kill a loved one.[9]

Vandiver's emphasis on the type of death associated with execution speaks to the work of Kenneth Doka on grief and bereavement. Doka, who has written over a dozen books on grief, defined the phrase *disenfranchised grief*, which occurs when a loss cannot be openly acknowledged, publicly mourned, or socially supported.[10] Doka and others have found that when disenfranchised grief occurs, the emotions of the bereaved are intensified so that the person often experiences high levels of distress and disorganization, as well as prolonged grieving, and healing becomes more difficult. The overwhelming majority of family members in our study who had been through an execution experienced disenfranchised grief. They were unable to share their grief with others, and rather than feeling supported by their community in their time of loss and need they felt isolated, angry, and ashamed.

Psychologist Bronna Romanoff and her colleagues found that grief is most effectively addressed with the help of community support and when the relationship between the dead and the mourners is acknowledged by others in the community.[11] The public sanction of execution denies social support to the mourners of the deceased, which in turn disenfranchises their grief. Any remaining community support for family members of executed offenders occurs within their private circles at best. From a public perspective, the offender is often portrayed as such a monster that few could imagine the existence of mourners. Even if the community acknowledges mourners, some people discount or ridicule their feelings. This was poignantly illustrated in 2005, when Barbara and her two daughters held vigil outside the death house with family, supporters, and anti–death penalty activists waiting to hear about their relative's final moments. On the other side of the lawn, a crowd gathered, seemingly supporters of the death penalty; the group cheered at 6 P.M., the appointed hour of the execution, and jeered at the hearse as it drove the body from the prison grounds.

This example speaks to the adversarial nature of capital cases and shows how it further complicates the process of grief for offenders' family members. In the courtroom and media, stories about victims tend to emphasize only the good and stories of defendants only the bad. The entire matter is cast as good versus evil without regard for the complexity of human life. The offender's family members try to refute the charge that he is the worst of the worst by embellishing their loved one's good qualities. Eventually, the offender's struggle for justice and fight for his life overwhelm his family, and the person on death row often becomes the center of the family. The fact that he is now a target for death necessitates that the family work to save him, almost placing him in the position of a martyr. Moreover, the all-consuming focus on saving the offender's life often exacerbates the distorted or disenfranchised grief reaction. Because the offender has in some cases taken on the role of center of the family, the family members no longer pursue other interests or relationships that could buffer the effects of their loss.

Depression and Trauma

Because nonfinite loss and disenfranchised grief predominate in the lives of death row families, depression and trauma symptoms are common and can be debilitating and dangerous. Given that Smykla described symptoms of depression and trauma in his study, we decided to test the validity of his findings by screening the 24 family members involved in our general interview for these symptoms.[12] Not surprisingly, most had experienced at one time or another, after the arrest, a prolonged fragile state of mental health. One mother has been living in misery since her son's arrest 9 years earlier. For a number of years she was so unhappy that she wanted nothing more than to end her own suffering, and she contemplated suicide. Yet she could not imagine bequeathing to her 11-year-old daughter the agony of losing her brother and her mother, and she knew that if she ever did anything to herself that her daughter would have to perish with her. In retrospect, she realized that it was "crazy" and unthinkable to harbor such thoughts and never came close to acting on her urges, but the fantasy brought relief. She explained, "That is how you think. This makes you so crazy that that is how you think—anything for relief, anything to make it go away." Today she is proud of her youngest and thrilled for the life that she is developing, but the thoughts of ending both of their lives remains vivid in her memory.

Depression

Depressive disorder, as described by the *Diagnostic and Statistical Manual* (4th ed., revised) (*DSM-IV-TR*), is characterized by the following: a 2-week period of depressed mood or loss of interest in pleasure; significant weight gain or weight loss (more or less than 5% of body weight within a month); significant changes in appetite, insomnia, psychomotor agitation, or retardation, that are significantly noticeable by others nearly each day; feelings of worthlessness or excessive guilt; diminished capacity to concentrate or indecisiveness; and recurrent thoughts of death. Major depressive disorder or clinical depression may be acute and marked by a single event, or it can be recurrent, or chronic, in which case the symptoms may be persistent. Clinical depression is distinct because it is persistent and often marked by morbid preoccupation and even psychotic symptoms.[13]

Dysthymia, often referred to as "double depression" when diagnosed concurrently with a major depressive episode, involves prolonged but slightly milder experiences of depressed mood for significant portions of the day and for up to 2 years. It may include symptoms of poor appetite, insomnia, low energy, low self-esteem, feelings of hopelessness, and difficulty concentrating. The concept of dysthymia may be a meaningful way of psychologically understanding the ongoing nature of loss experienced by family members of capital offenders. Depression and dysthymia are significant illnesses that deeply diminish the quality of life for the sufferer and also affect those who love him or her as they become less emotionally available and can be difficult to be around.[14]

To assess depression in family members, we asked 24 family members who participated in the general interview if they ever received a diagnosis of depression since their family member's crime. Those participants who had never been diagnosed as depressed were asked to respond to questions in the Beck Depression Inventory, an instrument that assesses depression.[15] We did not administer the inventory to participants who had actually been diagnosed with depression because we thought that the questions might be emotionally straining while providing minimal additional data.

In the general population, depression affects 1 in 8 women (12%) and 1 in 16 men (6%).[16] We found significantly higher rates in our group, which are detailed in table 7.1.

Following their loved one's arrest and death sentence, 15 (63%) of the 24 individuals in our original study were categorized as depressed Each of the 15 diagnosed participants reported that his or her symptoms lasted at least 1 year, with the average being about 5 years, indicative of high rates of dysthymia. Ten of 24 (42%) indicated that they were presently depressed and did not anticipate it lifting in the near future.

Out of the 24 family members, 7 identified themselves as completely debilitated by depression; 3 had lost their job, and 1 of those 3 has also lost her home. Marion explained that after her son's death sentence she was unable to work, open her mail, or pay her bills: "I lost everything. . . . I became a burden on my family." Three of the parents interviewed had each experienced the death of a child prior to their son's arrest, and all three said that the loss associated with the arrest was much more difficult: "I got depressed when I lost my daughter, but I came out of it."[17] Other family members described their feelings in the following way: "There have been no good days since his arrest. There are days you can bear. There are days when you have hope, and then there are the rest of the days." Their grief often had physical manifestations. One mother confided, "The pain inside was so deep that I could not even breathe," and another said that she felt "filled up all of the time" and that this feeling was physically painful.

We then looked more closely at the duration of the depressive symptoms. Six of the 15 individuals had been depressed following the notification of their loved one's arrest and remained so for several years but were not symptomatic at the time of the interview. Three of these family members talked about the lifting of their depression and offered explanations for its passing. Matt lived through his son's execution and recovered through pastoral counseling. Patty became the primary support to her nephew Luke, who was executed after his mother had died. As Luke's aunt, she was deeply saddened and depressed following his death; however, she recovered with the support of friends and family. Marion, whose son is still on death row, has recovered from her depression after seeking medical and psychological treatment. Today, she has thrown herself into death penalty abolition work.

The remaining three who had recovered from depression had loved ones who received sentences of life or life without parole. These family members explained that the sentence was difficult and that they were deeply saddened to have a loved one incarcerated forever, but once the death penalty was

Table 7.1
Participants and Psychological Distress

Name	Primary Support to Defendant X=Yes	Sentence	Symptoms Consistent with Trauma >1 year X=Yes	Depression >1 year X=Yes	Symptomatic at Time of Interview X=Yes	Belief that Primary Support Person had Psychological Distress X=Yes
Barbara	X	Executed	X	X	X	NA
Betty	X	LWOP	X	X	X	NA
Bernard	X	Life+years				NA
Bonnie	X	Executed	X	X	X	NA
Bridget	X	Death	X	X	X	NA
Celia	X	Executed	X	X	X	NA
Charlene	X	Life+years	X	X		NA
Felicia	X	Executed				NA
Franny	X	LWOP	X	X		NA
Rose	X	Death	X	X	X	NA
Georgia	X	Death	X	X	X	NA
Jennifer	X	Life+years				NA
Joseph	X	Resentenced from death to LWOP	X	X		NA

Joyce		Executed				X
Pat	X	Executed				NA
Marion	X	Death				NA
Mark		Death				X
Mary	X	Death	X	X		NA
Matt		Executed	X	X	X	X
Patty		Executed				X
Paul	X	LWOP	X	X		NA
Pearl	X	Death	X	X	X	NA
Sarah	X	Death	X	X	X	NA
Vera	X	Death				NA

LWOP = Life without parole.

avoided they were eventually able to move on. One mother whose son received a sentence of life without parole remained depressed at the time of the interview, which took place 10 months after her son's trial.

Of the 15 diagnosed with depression, 4 family members recognized that they were depressed but did not seek help. Their reasons for not seeking treatment varied. One was opposed to mental health care, whereas a few believed that medicine or counseling would not make a difference. Still another said they had no place to turn or that they could not afford treatment. The others with depression had talked to a health care professional about their symptoms. Of these, several sought help from their local community mental health center. Although Celia McWee and Paul were happy with the care they got, Pearl, who received both medicine and counseling, was not. Pearl credits the medicine with allowing her to work but says the counseling "made things worse." Rather than receiving individual attention, she was placed in general group therapy. She felt totally alone and isolated because others in the group were worried about such problems as spousal fidelity. In contrast to the life-or-death trauma that she was experiencing, these problems paled. Not only was she unable to relate to the other members of her group, but also they and the group leader were totally unprepared for the magnitude of her problem.

Pearl was one of five interviewees who were taking medicine at the time of the interview. She continued to exhibit symptoms of severe distress, but indicated that the medicine was helping. Similarly, Betty, a mother, explained that without the medicine she could not brush her hair, get dressed, or leave her house. Even though the medicine helped her function at a basic level, it did not alleviate her chronic sadness. Betty's medicine has made life bearable, but its lack of effect for her and so many others suggests that something else is going on, which the data led us to believe is trauma.

Trauma

It is not uncommon for individuals who have been diagnosed with depression and other psychological states to fail to respond to treatment because they have been misdiagnosed, and in fact trauma can be masked in more traditional diagnoses, such as depression, or it can be commingled with other illnesses.[18] The treatment dictated by the misdiagnosis seldom addresses the symptoms of trauma. While the depression or the other psychological states may subside through drugs or therapy, the trauma remains unresolved. Though drugs such as selective serotonin reuptake inhibitors (e.g., Prozac), have had good results for depression, drugs used to treat trauma have not had the same success until very recently.[19]

Judith Herman, a professor of clinical psychiatry at Harvard University and an international expert on trauma, describes trauma as "an affliction of powerlessness. At the moment of trauma, the victim is rendered helpless by overwhelming force."[20] As a result, traumatic events leave people without a sense of control, connection, and meaning and can have a profound impact on their lives. According to Herman, the impact occurs as traumatic events "overwhelm human adaptation to life."[21] Based on the event (i.e., rape and other violence, murder and other tragic and unexpected loss, or participation in war), individual differences surrounding the person (support system, genetic makeup, and willingness to seek support), and a host of other factors, the effects of a traumatic event range from fairly benign for some individuals to debilitating for others.[22]

When trauma occurs, the basic assumptions held by all individuals tend to shatter, including the beliefs that one is basically a good person, that some level of fairness exists in the world, and that a certain degree of safety can be counted on. When these assumptions are questioned, individuals begin to experience an existential crisis, in which one's place in the world and of one's own efficacy begins to seem lost. To work one's way out of an existential crisis, meaning needs to be made from the situation, and this process is facilitated by meaningful human interaction.[23] Symptoms such as distress may linger beyond the traumatic event, causing stress, pain, and disorder.

Presently, the only discussion of trauma, in the clinical handbook for all mental health disorders, the *DSM-IV-TR*, is for posttraumatic stress disorder (PTSD), and the symptoms of it can be in some cases life threatening and often are quite debilitating.[24] However, most offenders' family members do not fit the clinical assessment of PTSD because it requires what are considered gateway criteria, including (1) that "a person experienced, witnessed, or was confronted with an event or events that involved actual or threatened death or serious injury or a threat to the physical integrity of self or others"; and (2) that the person's "response involved intense fear, helplessness, or horror" (feelings that are common to the family members that we interviewed).[25]

Although meeting the criteria for number 2 is straightforward, the criteria for number 1 is a bit more difficult because accepted examples found in the psychiatric literature include rape, war, and witnessing or experiencing a loved one's violent death. Although family members of the condemned believe that they are witnessing a prolonged violent death of a loved one, their experience can be discounted by society given the acceptance of execution and the belief that lethal injection lacks violence. However, when Celia witnessed Jerry's execution, there was no doubt in her mind that what she was seeing was cold, calculated homicide. Similarly, Nashville singer/songwriter and Grammy Award winner Steve Earle witnessed the lethal injection of a man who befriended him from death row, and Earle describes it the following way: "At very best, it's terrifying. It's torture. It was for me. I don't think I'll ever recover from it. I have absolute waking nightmares about it."[26]

The combination of family members' fear, powerlessness, and horror provide a potent recipe for trauma and suggest that PTSD might occur. Consider that all of the family members said that they experienced intense fears, which emanated from execution and its threat, the criminal justice system, and their own communities. Family members felt both helpless and powerless; they could not assist defense attorneys, they could not do anything about judges who did not follow procedures, and they did not have the resources to hire high-profile lawyers who might give their loved ones a chance in the legal system.

Family members admit to feelings of fear and powerlessness, but their feelings of horror were most profound. Virtually all of them described the events as a nightmare and an experience they would "not wish on their worst enemy." The horror also came from sources other than the impending loss of life; a number of family members were incredulous that people existed who actually wanted to kill their loved ones. Franny explained, "I would look around the courtroom and think, 'You want to kill my child. This is my child.' It's just so awful. It is so awful that you cannot describe it."

Given the presence of fear, helplessness, and horror, we decided to determine if symptoms of PTSD were found in the 24 general interviews with family members in our study. In order to do this we did a post hoc analysis where we analyzed the interview transcripts to find evidence of specific thoughts, feelings, or behaviors associated with this disorder. We used *DSM-IV-TR* criterion for PTSD, and the Davidson Trauma Scale, a commonly used diagnostic tool to look for the presence of PTSD in our sample.[27] The *DSM-IV-TR* defines the symptoms of PTSD as (1) intrusive emotions and memories, responses after a triggering event, and nightmares; (2) avoidance of stimuli or psychic numbing that involves feelings of detachment and staying away from relationships, and stimuli associated with the event; and (3) hyperarousal that involves an exaggerated startle reaction, explosive outbursts, extreme vigilance, irritability, panic symptoms, and poor sleep.[28] For a clinical diagnosis, the symptoms must last at least 3 months.[29] We ensured that our matching of text and symptoms was reliable by using two independent reviewers, who placed the same quotes in the same categories over 90% of the time.

The details of the family members' experiences with intrusion, avoidance, and hyperarousal are noted in table 7.2 and very briefly described here. Nine family members experienced intrusiveness; for Matt and Paul, the intrusions involved panic attacks following benign encounters with the criminal justice system. Five family members experienced avoidance and numbness, one of whom lost her ability to cry, even following the death of her favorite sister. Five family members had increased arousal, with most of them experiencing explosive outbursts and trouble sleeping. Each of the 16 family members experienced at least one of these states and did so for a period of greater than 3 months.

While intrusive symptoms, avoidance, and hypervigilance are used to diagnose PTSD, there are other feelings and behaviors—such as irrational guilt, social isolation, substance abuse, and cognitive changes such as shattered assumptions about the world (e.g., from secure to unsafe)—that also mark the disorder. In addition, many health issues are related to trauma, depression, and stress.[30] In table 7.3, we examine some of those issues and see that all of the

Table 7.2
Prevalence of PTSD Symptoms Found among 16 Family Members

Symptom	Number of Participants Chronically Affected	Examples Found in the Literature	Participant's Experiences
Intrusiveness	9	Recurring thoughts that do not go away	Two participants said that they spent hours walking and pacing and reading scripture to make the thoughts go away.
		Response to stimuli	Two participants had panic attacks with traffic violations or a summons for jury duty.
		Inability to focus	One mother said she would be in the car and not sure where she was going or what she was doing.
		Nightmares	Three participants went through significant periods where they sought to avoid sleep because of nightmares.
Avoidance of stimuli, and numbness	5	Avoidance of places associated with event	Two family members drove out of their way to avoid the crime scene or place where their loved one was arrested.
		Diminished interest in activities	Two family members no longer had an interest in going to church or participating in community activities. One indicated that she lost interest in sex.
		Feeling detached or numb	One mother said that she lost the ability to cry, and the extent of this recently surprised her when she did not cry following the death of her favorite sister.
Increased arousal and hypervigilance	5	Explosive outbursts	One mother said, "I am very mad now; it is like my whole personality has altered."
		Panic attacks	Five participants experienced such attacks.
		Trouble sleeping	Five had trouble sleeping.
		Hypervigilance	Celia could not babysit for her grandchildren for over a year as she had an irrational fear that something might happen to them.

Table 7.3
Manifestations of Cognitive and Emotional Symptoms Related to PTSD Found among a Subset of Family Members

Symptoms	Number of Participants Effected	Examples Found in the Literature	Participant's Experience
Cognitive changes	All	Shattering of basic assumptions	All lost at least one of the following: safety, fairness, and/or the belief that he/she was a good mother/person.
		Guilt	All but one family member felt an enormous amount of guilt.
Social isolation	14	No longer interacting with friends	Very few family members maintained friendships that they held prior to the events.
		Ending participation in community endeavors	Several family members quit their church or community activities because they saw themselves as unwelcome or unworthy.
		Removing oneself from their families	Franny was one of several mothers who withdrew from family members, and she did not interact with her daughter or grandchildren for 3 years. A focus group participant had not celebrated a holiday since his son's arrest.
Serious alcohol or drug use	2		Only two family members said that they abused alcohol following their loved one's arrest. None reported drug use.
Physical illnesses	10	Inability to control conditions	Five participants lost their ability to control diabetes or high blood pressure.
		Worsening of conditions	In three cases, either emphysema worsened or cancer spread.
		Stress-induced conditions	Two participants had heart attacks.
		Death	Four participants discussed a stress-related death (usually from cancer or heart attack, always of the offender's mother or father) that the participant attributed to the events.

families experienced a shattering of basic assumptions; 14 family members isolated themselves socially; 10 experienced a decline in their physical health; and 2 developed serious drug or alcohol problems.

Recently, researchers have begun to differentiate between PTSD and complex PTSD. John Briere, the director of the Psychological Trauma Program at the University of Southern California Medical Center, and Joseph Spinazzola, an expert in the field of trauma and the director of the Trauma Center at the highly respected Justice Resources Institute, describe complex PTSD as a cluster of psychological symptoms that occur as result of multiple, extended, highly invasive or highly shameful events. Complex PTSD includes experiencing altered self-capacities, signaled by overwhelming emotions that cannot be controlled and the loss of an ability to interact interpersonally. Those who suffer from complex PTSD exhibit cognitive and mood disturbances—negative self-perceptions, self-hatred, low self-esteem, feelings of helplessness and aggression, emotional outbursts, and lack of emotional regulation. Overdeveloped avoidance responses, similar to PTSD but more pronounced, might range from substance abuse to complete dissociation. Somatoform distress can arise when intense psychological distress manifests itself physically and cannot be traced to any medical or physical condition (stomach pains, gastrointestinal complaints, fatigue, etc.). Last, traditional PTSD symptoms may also occur.[31]

Complex PTSD may be a more useful description than traditional PTSD because it often involves a highly shameful event that may undermine family members' ability to talk openly and gain resolution. This parallels the secrecy that often surrounds issues of family violence or incest. When secrecy or isolation is coupled with the ongoing and overwhelming sense of powerlessness that is inherent in the experience of death row, the result is often trauma symptoms, which diminish the person's quality of life.

The feelings of shame and isolation are so strong for family members that some are judged by their communities and others experience guilt. For many, these feelings are intertwined and become overwhelming. Psychiatrist James Gilligan explains this dangerous combination: "To be overwhelmed by shame and humiliation is to experience the destruction of self-esteem; and without a certain minimal amount of self-esteem, the self collapses and the soul dies."[32]

All but one interviewed family member described intense guilt. Marion, the one who did not experience guilt, explained that she made a lot of mistakes as a young mother and that many of these mistakes were the consequences of the inadequate parenting she had received as well her experience of childhood abuse and incest. She has spent numerous years in therapy working on her issues and coming to these insights. She concludes that she did the best that she could under the circumstances and that she could not blame herself for her inadequacies because she came about them honestly. She always had only the best of intentions as a mother.

Celia and Marion are friends, and Celia is jealous of Marion's lack of guilt. Celia even feels guilty for giving birth to Jerry. Paul blames himself for his brother's crime. "I felt like it was my fault that it happened, and I had that on me for a long time, and I couldn't shake it. I actually thought it was my fault. So much grief for what [my brother] had done. I mean we all felt like we had the gun in our hands that day. It was ridiculous because we did not, but it felt that way. Our blood killed their blood. It just really tore us up. I particularly felt very guilty because I wasn't more active in trying to get help [for him before the crime]. . . . We felt bad about, you know, like a double depression and double grief—that something terrible had happened to people in the community."

Coping

Of the 24 general interviews only 9 family members did not experience depression or trauma symptoms. We examined their interview transcripts to determine strategies, character traits, or other protective factors possessed by these family members. As indicated on table 7.1 Bernard, a grandfather, and Jennifer, a mother, faced the prospect of their loved ones' death penalty trial; however, in each case the trial and death sentence were avoided as a result of a plea bargain. In two cases the individual we interviewed was not the primary support to the defendant and therefore may not have been as emotionally impacted. In two cases, we found that the primary support person to the offender was not part of the nuclear family of the interviewee and thus may have shared less of an emotional attachment and history or may have found comfort in their own immediate family. Pat Seaborn was Ron Spivey's cousin, and Patty was Luke's aunt, so that even though they loved their relatives, they did not have the same bond as if they had raised him or lived with him.

Two others who were the primary support person to the offender did not experience trauma or depression and had strong support systems at home. Vera has forced herself to stay optimistic and strong as she is raising her son's preteen daughter. She gets a sense of meaning and joy from her granddaughter and loves having her, but she fights her feelings of sadness and anxiety because she views depression as a luxury she cannot afford because it will further damage her grandchild. Finally, Felicia Floyd made a conscious decision to distance herself from her father to avoid any psychological distress associated with his execution. Although she was profoundly sad following the execution, she never experienced debilitating psychological distress.

Two others, Matt and Marion, have since worked through their emotions. Each had been severely depressed, and each had positive results from a combination of medication and counseling. Marion also credits her improved mental health to the sense of purpose that she got from doing abolition work.

To address their psychological distress, all family members said they prayed, but their sense of its efficacy varied. Some said they prayed because it was all they could do. Barbara Longworth, known for a clever sense of humor that is part of her coping strategy, joked that she is still waiting for God to hear her. Barbara and her son were close to Jerry McWee, and shortly before his scheduled execution, she told Jerry to please give God a message for her: "Tell him to start listening! I'm talking, but he's not hearing." She then corrected herself, and in a more somber tone, added, "Well, really none of us have heard anything." Other family members said that they would be lost without prayer, and all but one of the family members who clung to the power of prayer were also among the 15 of the 24 general interviewees who exhibited depression and trauma symptoms. The father who sought pastoral counseling, however, credits it and his belief in God with getting him beyond his severe depression and anxiety, which had previously interfered with his work. He also does not believe that traditional therapy would have been meaningful because "when something this bad happens, you have to believe in God." He explained that the only hope for finding meaning in something this senseless and tragic is to seek God's will. He believes that his son is with God, and that thought provides him comfort.

Strained and Shattered Family Systems

Several patterns emerge when a family is dealing with a capital trial. As we saw, the defendant's family members tend to feel distorted grief, which, when coupled with the trauma associated with a capital charge, often created chaos within the family unit. Family members reported denial, avoidance, blame, splintering among members, and in some cases the breakdown of an entire family system. Few families seem to weather the turmoil together and act collectively to meet the needs of each other and the offender.

In some families, the primary pattern is denial. Family members deny that the family has ever had any problems, and they deny that their loved one committed a crime even in the face of overwhelming evidence. Other family members place full responsibility on a codefendant or stand by an alternative explanation. Because it was difficult to get family members to talk about their roles in splintering relationships, our data for this section are primarily based on interviews with defense team members and with individuals who were expert witnesses in these cases. When possible, we followed up on these stories by reviewing court documents.

Mike's family is an extreme example of denial.[33] One of his attorneys explained that in 1992, Mike, who had a history of pedophilia, was arrested for the murder of a young child. Mike confessed and has never denied his guilt. Not long after his arrest, his attorney hired an experienced social worker whose job it was to create a psychosocial history of Mike's life. The social worker discovered that he grew up in a family riddled with problems that began in utero. He was conceived when his mother was in a full body cast and on a morphine drip for a broken back resulting from a car accident. Her husband had drilled a hole in the cast so that he could have intercourse with her.

Five months into her pregnancy, after daily doses of morphine and regular consumption of alcohol, Mike's mother learned that she was pregnant. She wanted an abortion, but her husband forbade it. The social worker was non-judgmental toward the family and suggested over and over that they did the best that they could against a difficult backdrop of poverty, disability, chronic pain, addiction, and abuse.

The family would hear none of it. They insisted that Mike's childhood was normal, and he was not guilty. Despite Mike's early and consistent confession and reams of documents evidencing the issues in his home, his parents shut out the truth. In fact, they called the district attorney and offered to testify that the defense team made up evidence regarding the family's dysfunction. They also claimed that Mike was always a normal child, despite the fact that his childhood behavior was so bizarre that a number of school officials and neighbors testified about his instability.

Mike's parents now visit him in prison regularly. In a structured environment where he is removed from any stimuli that could trigger his pedophilia, Mike functions better than outside, and thus these visits reinforce his parents' view that he is sane and that he received good parenting. While his parents remained unified, their denial was troubling for his siblings, who testified about their difficult home life even though they feared that their parents would never forgive them.

For family members trying to balance the agony of their past with maintaining family relationships, avoidance of difficult issues is one of the primary strategies. A capital trial, however, can threaten to permanently disrupt that balance. A defense lawyer told us about Andrea, who was able to escape from her family's destructive patterns when she moved away and established a successful career in law enforcement. Following her brother's arrest, she was asked by his defense team to help them develop the family's psychosocial history. She reluctantly agreed and spent hours talking about their childhood, recalling neglect, rape, and a host of terrifying abuses. She had explicitly told the defense team that they had one session to ask all of their questions because she believed that she would pay too high a cost to her own well-being to have to relive her memories a second time. Moreover, she feared that if she spent too much time recalling the past it would jeopardize her relationship with her parents, and she might be unable to control the anger and feelings brought out by the questions. In fact, it is common for survivors of childhood abuse to protect their parents in the hope that they can finally forge a normal relationship.

Other family members assign blame. They feel miserable and look for ways to blame others for their misery—the prosecutor, the judge, the media, and the defense attorneys. Sometimes they blame other family members. An expert witness told us about a woman who faults her parents for her brother's crime. Following his arrest, she lashed out at her parents and presently is not speaking with them. Her father did have a large role to play in her brother turning to criminal actions, as he was a violent alcoholic with other mental health disorders. Since his son's arrest, he has sought mental health treatment for his problems and has become a constructive member of society. He desperately wants to make amends, but his daughter refuses to interact with him.

Intrafamilial murder, such as patricide, can truly destroy a family because some family members see themselves as victims while others take the side of the offender. Gale grew up in an extremely violent home. His younger sister was largely spared because their parents were divorced during most of her childhood. When Gale killed his father and accidentally his father's new wife in a shoot-out, his sister grieved for her father and aligned herself with the murdered wife's family. When Gale's sister sat with the victim's side of the family in the courtroom, her biological mother was hurt and angry. Gale's sister and mother have tried to avoid each other, but their paths have crossed and the ensuing confrontations are ugly.

Many family members fear their relationships will disintegrate if they discuss their past with each other. Sadly, these fears are very real as several families who spoke openly experienced a breakdown in their family relations. For other families, finally talking about their issues brought them closer. As discussed in the beginning of chapter 4, Paul talked about his decision to testify about his father's abuse in an attempt to save his brother Jeremy's life. Paul knew that by testifying he might irreparably damage his relationship with his father, but he preferred that to not taking an active role in the defense. Mitigation experts (members of the defense team whose job it is to collect and analyze mitigation evidence) have said that it is not uncommon for one family member—usually a sibling but sometimes another relative— to take on the responsibility of disclosing family secrets. Most people would find it difficult to risk losing a relationship with a family member to try to save another's life. Yet in the aftermath of Paul's decision to testify for Jeremy, he and his father have a healthier relationship than ever before and have agreed to disagree about some of the family dynamics. Sometimes disclosure of a secret is followed by a collective sigh of relief—relief that this person spoke and therefore no one else in the family had to do so and relief that the information was finally out in the open.

Some families cling together, rallying around their accused member. They diligently search for good lawyers, monitor the justice process, visit the defendant, and stand by as needed. They spend their savings and refinance their homes to offset the expenses. They cry, reminisce, and reflect on a hundred "if-only-we-had-done-this-or-that" speculations. Distant family members may come back into the fold, facing the shame but uniting to defend their family's solidarity. They say things like, "I don't agree with what he did, but he's family. I'm gonna be there for him" or "We love him unconditionally." A brother said that he and his family held monthly meetings in which they would talk about their family member's case and strategize about family and community involvement. They assigned roles and coordinated a grassroots defense; for example, one person was designated the spokesperson with the media, another the liaison to the defense team. Their coordinated effort united them as never before.

In addition to shaping family interactions, capital punishment can have an intergenerational effect because trauma can be transmitted from one generation to the next. As psychiatrist and trauma expert Sandra Bloom notes: "Our lives are reenactments not only of our own buried traumatic experiences, but also [those] contained in our family history."[34] Not surprisingly, research conducted on family members of Holocaust survivors shows that children who grow up knowing of their parents' trauma often internalize this trauma.[35] Some feel the trauma as if it were affecting them—that is, they are in the camp with their parents—and others feel only the effects of their parents' diminished capacity, pain, and bereavement. The literature supports that these children often have a difficult time forming intimate relationships because they have not fully differentiated their own experiences from their parents' pain. Although capital punishment is not truly comparable to the Holocaust, parents of capital offenders are often awash with feelings of pain and bereavement for an extended period of time, and some of them are raising young children against this backdrop. While mothers and fathers feel like they are in prison with their sons, the children around them may feel the same.

Charlene is very worried about her grandson, who lives with her; since his uncle's arrest, he has become withdrawn. She is sure that some of it is because he misses his uncle, but she also is concerned that her grandson is paying a price because she is less available to him given the strain that her son's sentence has placed on her and her preoccupation with capital punishment. Though she tried to cover her feelings by filling the house with gospel music, her grandson intuitively knows that she is not herself and is unable to give him everything he needs to thrive.

Summary

Life in the shadow of death places unique strains on offenders' family members that often result in extreme psychological distress for individuals and their family system. At best, the unique strains carried by these family members are managed through a combination of staying active, talking with other relatives, and connecting with available mental health and spiritual resources. At worst—which, sadly, we saw more of in our interviews—these strains are not managed and result in depression, trauma, and associated health problems, which in the most severe cases ended in death caused by stress-related illnesses or suicide.

The grief experienced by offenders' family members as a result of a death sentence and eventual execution of their loved one is not processed the same way as typical grief. Offenders' family members experience nonfinite loss and disenfranchised grief—leaving them in a perpetual state of anger, sadness, remorse, and inability to move forward toward healing. Their loss is experienced over a period of several years, and for some families decades, with the constant knowledge that the worst is yet to come. Once the execution is carried out, they still cannot mourn in a normal way because friends and neighbors do not recognize their loss. The anger from the fact that the state killed their healthy relative, coupled with the fact that few people understand what they are going through and empathize with their experiences, furthers their sense of isolation. We met family members who could not recover from the experience even many years after an execution.

The majority of individuals in our study were currently experiencing or had experienced since the death sentence symptoms consistent with clinical depression. A large percentage were also suffering from symptoms consistent with PTSD and complex PTSD. Many did not seek medical or psychiatric help because they were afraid or because they did not know that resources existed to help them. When they did seek help, it was often only the depression that was diagnosed; rarely was trauma recognized and treated.

As the many stories in this book have illustrated, offenders often come from families that are dealing with intergenerational issues, such as addiction, incest, and physical abuse. Even without these issues, most families are unprepared for the stress a capital charge and an execution place on their family systems. While trying to cope with the stress of a capital charge and the individual psychological distress, these families must also decide whether to share their family's dirty laundry by participating with the mitigation team. Although sharing this information is often critical to mounting a case for a sentence less than death, for many families revealing these family secrets is traumatizing. These family members bare their souls and are then left to put the pieces of their traumatic history back together under the shameful glares of their neighbors and without any professional help.

Howard Zehr is clear in his work that trauma, crime, and restorative justice are interrelated. During a traumatic crisis, individuals feel as if they have lost all identity, meaning, and relationships.[36] In assessing the harms of crime, it is critical to include the trauma experienced by both victims and offenders as a result of the crime and criminal justice system. It is clear that interacting with the capital system produces devastating consequences for offenders' family members. Society must take responsibility for the consequences the system inflicts on all families and provide support. Future chapters explain how restorative justice can be used to help meet the needs of all parties involved in violent crime and to make sure the criminal justice system meets the obligations it creates by imposing the death penalty and severely harming offenders' family members.

Bud Welch, President of the Board of Murder Victim Families for Human Rights, with daughter Julie Welch, victim of the 1995 bombing of the Alfred P. Murrah building in Oklahoma City.

Bill Babbitt, Founding Board member of Murder Victim Families for Human Rights and brother of Manuel Babbitt, executed May 4, 1999.

Defense-Initiated Victim Outreach Founders (l–r): Richard Burr, Howard Zehr, and Tammy Krause. Courtesy of Craig Spaulding.

Robert Meeropol, son of Ethel and Julius Rosenberg (executed June 19, 1953).

Reverend William Neil Moore, former death row inmate.

Richard Longworth, executed April 15, 2005 at age 36, with mother Barbara Longworth.

Kathi Crosby and Barbara Longworth at anti-death penalty vigil.

Jerry McWee, executed April 16, 2004 at age 51.

Vigil for Jerry McWee.

Martina Correia, sister of Troy Anthony Davis, awaiting ruling from the Eleventh Circuit Court of Appeals on innocence claim.

Pat Seaborn, cousin of Ron Spivey, executed January 24, 2002 at age 62, with Emmy Award-winning actor and Ron Spivey supporter Ed Asner.

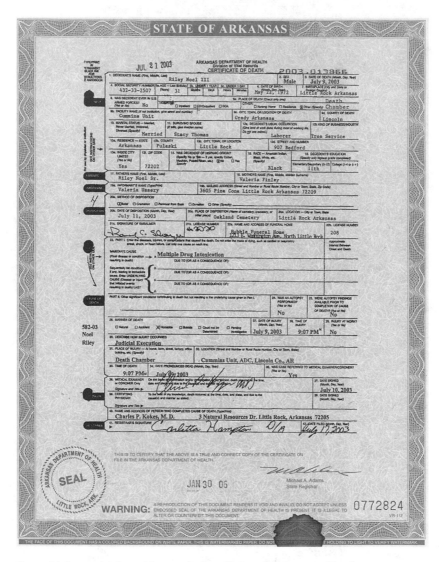

State of Arkansas death certificate indicating "homicide" as cause of death.

Part III
Restorative Justice

The stories of offenders' family members' experiences with the death penalty process explored in part II clearly establish that offenders' family members suffer enormous consequences as a result of inadequate social support systems, their loved ones' crimes, and the community and criminal justice system's responses to the crime. In the spirit of restorative justice, part III tries to move forward by recognizing these harms and establishing specific needs of offenders' family members, exploring the obligations of all individuals involved in the process, and searching for restorative justice solutions that connect needs with obligations. We also attempt to reflect on the concerns and needs of victims' family members, the offender, the general public, and the criminal justice system. Given the serious nature of capital crimes, restorative justice programs and initiatives in this area are not intended to replace the operation of the traditional criminal justice system but to augment its practices.

Applying restorative justice to capital crimes is relatively new territory, currently being navigated by theorists and practitioners like Howard Zehr, Mark Umbreit, Tammy Krause, and others. Our efforts in part III rely not only on interviews with offenders' family members but also on the research and practice of pioneers in this area—offenders, victims, lawyers, mitigation specialists—and other concerned individuals to explore several different ways to include restorative justice principles in capital cases.

We specifically explore how (1) social systems have failed offenders and their family members prior to the crime and ways that these systems can be changed or repaired, (2) family members' needs are met when the death penalty is averted, (3) family members attempt to make amends on their own, and (4) family members can participate in formal restorative justice programs. Because restorative justice practice is relatively new in the area of serious felony crimes and because we are introducing a brand new set of actors to the process (family members of offenders), we view part III as a starting point for the exploration of specific initiatives for restorative justice in serious crime as well as a repository of ideas for others working in the field to draw from when developing practice and policy in the future.

8

Life Is Different

Life is different for William Neal Moore. Not too many years ago, Moore, a convicted murderer, sat praying in the deathwatch cell in state prison in Jackson, Georgia. Seven hours before his scheduled execution he was granted an emergency stay. Moore is still praying, but now his surroundings have changed, and he is no longer waiting for the state to kill him; today he is a minister to a congregation in Rome, Georgia. In a truly unique and remarkable circumstance, Moore, with the help of the victim's family, his family and friends, and community members, convinced the Georgia State Board of Pardons and Paroles to commute his death sentence to life in prison. Several years later he was released on parole, and he has dedicated his life to helping others.

"Death is different," a phrase used by the U.S. Supreme Court to describe the death penalty, captures its irreversible finality. This irreversibility makes capital punishment fundamentally different from any other legal alternative. This chapter focuses on how family members of the convicted perceive alternative sentences to the death penalty, including life without parole. From a restorative justice perspective, it is important to establish whether the death penalty does more harm to involved parties than its alternatives, and we try to address that question by exploring the lives of offenders and their family members who faced a death sentence but whose verdict was overturned or changed. Our exploration is based on a rephrasing of death is different; in the upcoming pages we ask "Is life different?"

Moore's story shows that life is different in two compelling ways. First, one can see the power of redemption in the relationship between victim and offender. Second, Moore's narrative gives us some insight into how life is different for victims' family members who apply restorative justice principles in their own healing journeys.

From Death to Life in the Legal System

There are several ways in which a death sentence can be overturned; the two most common are commutation and reversal. Commutations, a change to a lesser sentence, are administrative decisions that most often come from the state's Board of Pardons and Paroles after a death warrant has been signed. The Board of Pardons and Paroles is an advisory board to the governor on death penalty commutations, but in many states the governor is legally bound to follow their recommendations. The most notable commutation in recent years was Governor Ryan's sentence conversion of all 167 of Illinois's death row inmates, which he made, not because of the merits of any individual case but, because he believed that the criminal justice system in Illinois was flawed, and therefore the risk of executing an innocent person was great.[1] Ryan's commutations saved the lives of five innocent individuals who were subsequently shown to be not guilty and freed from death row.[2]

Other commutations occur as a result of the U.S. Supreme Court interpretations of the constitution. For example, the Supreme Court determined that the execution of members of a specific population—such as minors in *Roper v. Simmons* (2005), and people with mental retardation in *Atkins v. Virginia* (2002)—is no longer constitutional,[3] so all of the individuals on death row who were under age 18 at the time of the crime or found to be mentally retarded have been taken off of it.

Unlike such cases of sweeping sentence changes, most commutations are given to individuals and are generally decided on the specific legal issues of the case or the offender's personal story. These commutations can be granted for legal and humanitarian reasons. Once a death warrant is signed, it is not uncommon for family members and legal teams to organize and ask supporters to send letters, e-mails, and faxes to the executive branch and the pardon and parole board. Sometimes family members will have the opportunity to meet with the review body. This was the case for Felicia Floyd and her brother, who hoped for a humanitarian commutation when they asked the Georgia Board of Pardons and Paroles not to orphan them by executing their father. Some commutations result in exoneration or release with time served, but in most cases the sentence is changed to life without parole.

In contrast to a commutation, a reversal of sentence tends to result from the appeals process or the postconviction process. Specifically, the offender alleges that he was not given a fair trial for such reasons as inadequate legal counsel, error in the ruling by the trial judge, or the discovery of new evidence; however, the courts are not required to grant a new trial based on new evidence. If the reviewing court finds an error occurred that requires reversal, a new full trial or sentencing hearing is set. In many cases, with competent representation at the new trial, the defendant receives a sentence other than death.[4] Law professor James Liebman and his colleagues found that the number of death penalty cases with mistakes was so high that the upper courts found reversible error in 68% of all cases. When new trials were granted, nearly half the defendants ultimately received a sentence other than death.[5] But reversal of sentence is a slow process, and it takes an average of 7.6 years to find and rectify a problem.[6] The mistake is most disturbing in cases where the error is not recognized before the execution or the defendant is found not guilty. Although there are no proven cases that an innocent defendant was executed, there is speculation that some cases exist, including from chapter 4 that of Robert Coe.[7]

Life without the Possibility of Parole

Because restorative justice is a holistic approach, the determination of just outcomes includes consideration of harm caused by the criminal justice system. When handing out punishment and deciding the best way to deal with crime, society should consider the consequences of different forms of punishment. For family members of the offender, the death penalty seems to produce more negative consequences, such as trauma, depression, and health issues than consequences associated with a sentence of life without parole.

Next to the death penalty, life without parole is the most severe sentence handed down in the United States. Although life without parole means that their loved one will die in prison, for the family members interviewed here, this alternative is unanimously preferred to the death penalty. Consider the change in the tenor of life for three generations of Nathaniel's family when, 6 years into his death sentence, he accepted a plea bargain that resulted in a sentence of life without parole. Nathaniel has a large extended family, of which we interviewed his father, his brother, his sister-in-law, and their two children.

Nathaniel's mother died when he was an infant, and his father, Karl, assumed the dual roles of dutiful and loving mother and father. The family was always close; Nathaniel's sisters and father doted on him, and his older brothers considered him their friend. When Nathaniel was in high school, he began to worry his family by running around with an older crowd, but he heeded none of their warnings. On a spring day, he and his friends had a run-in with a police officer that ended in the officer's heartbreaking murder. Nathaniel was not apprehended right away, but when he was, he confessed to the murder. He and his family maintain that he was not the shooter, although he admits to being an accomplice. After the crime, he and his friends agreed that if they got caught, Nathaniel would take responsibility, believing his juvenile status would result in leniency from the courts. His trust in his friends and his willingness to please them was a lapse of judgment that ultimately led to his death sentence.

From the beginning, Nathaniel's family stood by him, and although the family agreed that he needed to be punished for his crime and poor judgment, they saw his death sentence as profoundly unjust. Despite his imprisonment, Nathaniel's family did not relinquish their role of raising and caring for him. Karl organized his life around his son. Nathaniel's siblings also devoted time to visiting and maintaining their relationship with him. Even though the drive to prison was several hours each way, Karl visited Nathaniel on almost every visiting day. A friend of Karl's once half-jokingly suggested that Karl would move into the prison if he could.

Nathaniel's siblings often brought their young children when they visited. Christopher, his 15-year-old nephew, described Nathaniel as like a brother who gave him advice about being an adolescent. Christopher likes knowing that Nathaniel will be there for him if he ever has a problem, and he views Nathaniel as visible evidence that "it is important to listen to your parents because look at what can happen if you do not." In contrast, Nathaniel's 10-year-old niece, Lindsey, suggested that "he is like an imaginary friend." Lindsey looks forward to the weekly exchange of letters that she initiated and the prison visits, yet it seems that her interactions with Nathaniel are so unique in their circumscribed context that he has never felt entirely real to her.

The family remembered visitation as a time when they "piled into the car and spent the time listening to music and cutting up" with each other, but as they neared the prison the reality of death row quickly checked their exuberance. Christopher explained the logistics of the visit as "the worst. We all had to cram into a phone booth-size place to be able to talk through a hole in the wall. We had to bend down, and it was hot and sweaty. People would be interrupting each other, and someone would be left out. Then you might get your feelings hurt." Christopher's father, Daniel, who is Nathaniel's brother, recalled the routine surrounding the vending machine as the most painful part of the visit. The family all agreed that the food in the vending machine was "horrible," but they always got what they could for Nathaniel because to him it was a "massive improvement" over prison fare. After they bought food, Karl would beg the guard, to no avail, to let him pass the food to Nathaniel so that he could touch Nathaniel's hand. Daniel recounted, "It tears you up seeing your father do that," and Christopher agreed that watching his grandfather beg made him very sad.

When asked about their understanding of death row, the children appeared nervous. Christopher made the point that although he grew up knowing about death row and was aware that Nathaniel might be killed, it was not until a few years ago when he was sitting in a parking lot by himself that "it came to me what that really meant." At that time he "just broke down." When you have a family member on death row, "there are a lot of things that you have to worry about, and then you think that this [death] might happen to Nathaniel, it is stressful . . . every day is stressful. You are always a phone call away from it." Ten-year-old Lindsey defined death row as "when you are in prison and they want to kill you." She started to say that meant she would never see Nathaniel again, but her tears halted her sentence. She later added that his presence on death row was scary and confusing.

Each member of the family vividly remembered the day that Nathaniel was granted a new trial (a process that led to a plea agreement). Christopher came home from school, and everyone was jumping up and down crying with joy. His father and mother said that the whole family was ecstatic, and this elation continued when Nathaniel's sentence was converted to life without parole. The entire family agrees that things have "been a lot better since

Nathaniel has been off death row." Christopher explained that every time he hears his mom or someone else in the family say that Nathaniel is no longer on death row, it is a "great feeling; you don't have to worry about him eventually coming to that day." Visits to the prison have improved as well. Daniel said he was filled with joy and relief at seeing his father touch his brother for the first time in 8 years. Now the family touches and plays games together, and the vending machine rituals are much better.

No one was made more ecstatic by the commutation than Karl, who described the following Christmas as the best ever. It was the first time since Nathaniel's arrest that they were able to eat together and share the day without a piece of glass separating them. Karl is proud of Nathaniel's efforts to further himself in prison, where he is working on completing high school and has a job at the library. The prison staff often sings Nathaniel's praises to Karl.

Karl's joy has also buoyed the family. Daniel revealed that his father "was in a constant state of stress and anxiety" when Nathaniel was on death row. "Dad was definitely a lot more cynical and depressed and emotional when Nathaniel was on death row. Now as long as he is feeling good (physically), he is happy as a lark." Karl's prior unhappiness was hard for the family and particularly problematic for Christopher and Lindsey because Karl lived with them for a number of years while Nathaniel was on death row. Although the children's parents provided them with a loving environment, sometimes their grandfather's short temper was painful. Karl and Daniel clashed about visits; Karl felt that Daniel did not visit enough. Daniel, a student with a full-time job, wanted to spend precious weekends with his family. He wanted his children to have a well-rounded childhood so that they could enjoy other activities such as sports along with their visits to prison. After spending the majority of his youth living in the shadow of death, Christopher has developed his own arguments against the death penalty. He does not believe in it because it "does not really do any good. It doesn't bring the person back." He also has firsthand knowledge of what it means to come perilously close to losing someone that you love.

Once their loved one is removed from death row, family members learn to relax again and form and maintain healthy relationships. Their depression lifts, they are better able to cope with the trauma they endured while their relative was on death row, and they appreciate the numerous differences between life and death sentences. For example when Jane's and Pearl's sons were taken off of death row because they received new trials and commuted sentences, each described her son's change in sentence as a new beginning. For Jane the reversal brought a sense of peace that had been absent in her life for 8 years. Pearl said it was like a "big weight being lifted off me," as she placed her hands near her chest and opened them up, a smile and deep breath accompanied her actions. Like Karl, these mothers relish being able to touch their sons at the contact visits allowed for inmates in the general population. Jane recalled, "I cried when I saw him and hugged him and smelled him. It is wonderful to have a physical connection with him."

Jane is deeply moved that her son Eliot's life has become more expansive since death row. She explained that while on death row Eliot had needed to go to the dentist, and the guard took him on a shortcut across a grassy area. The reality of Eliot's confinement was brought home to her in a very powerful way when he described the shortcut as the first time that he had felt grass under his feet since his incarceration. After his first night in the general population, Eliot called home exclaiming that he now walks to breakfast on a grassy path. "I am on grass. I am on grass," he told his mother in disbelief.

For Pearl, comparing a death sentence to her son's sentence of life without parole has been like night and day. The first time we talked to Pearl in 1999, when her son Gilbert was on death row, she wore a housedress and no makeup, and her hair was not styled. Her attitude was timid and her voice quiet. She spent much of the interview in tears and described her days as spent "praying and crying and crying and praying." She faithfully took her medicine for depression, but it did not adequately address her condition. She kept her house dark, and she confided to us that her son's death sentence was more difficult than the death of her 19-year-old daughter. In 2004, a year after Gilbert's new trial and sentence of life without parole, we returned to talk with Pearl. She and her house were unrecognizable; the house was light and clean, and Pearl looked years younger.

Pearl clearly understands that she feels better and that she *is* better, saying that when Gilbert was on death row, she had little patience with her children and grandchildren. At that time she was so worried about him she could not parent her daughter. Instead of providing understanding and advice, all she would do was tell her struggling daughter that she was "messing up" and that she was doing the "wrong things." Pearl was short with her daughter and kept her at a distance. Now with the relief of Gilbert's new sentence, she reaches out to her daughter with phone calls and visits, and she talks with her about what is going on in her life. She no longer berates her poor choices but instead talks with her about consequences and other alternatives. Pearl is thrilled to report that her daughter has responded by making some necessary and difficult changes in her life and has leaned on Pearl for support.

The time Pearl spends with her grandchildren is fulfilling now. While Gilbert was on death row, her grandchildren made her nervous. Their noise and carrying on, even when they were happy, were like fingernails on a chalkboard to her. Now she takes pleasure in spending time with them, and she is delighted that she has the energy and patience to babysit for them. Pearl is particularly pleased that by providing child care she has also helped her daughter put her life in better order.

Both Pearl and Jane talked about their sons' futures with enthusiasm. Pearl's son, Gilbert, is writing a book about his life. He hopes that by sharing his experiences he will help other young African American men avoid his mistakes. Jane is proud that Eliot now participates in education in the prison and that she can bring him materials to augment his studies. Eliot sends letters to Jane's Sunday school classes telling students not to drink or take drugs and that what happened to him could happen to anyone who gets involved in drugs. The young students are shocked when she reads those letters and shows the class a picture of Eliot, who does not look very different from them. Both Gilbert and Eliot take responsibility for their actions and are pleased that without the constant threat of execution that they can try to meet some of the obligations they created when they committed a violent crime. By working to better themselves and educate others, they are helping repair their communities and prevent future crime, even while they are behind bars.

In addition to all of the benefits associated with the move from death row to the prison's general population, there are a whole new set of issues that are troubling to the family members. This is the first time they worry about their children's safety from other inmates. Eliot is in a section of the prison that is known for violence, and he has already been beaten up. These parents recognize that their sons will probably outlive them, and Pearl, Jane, and Karl worry about who will send their children money, visit, and otherwise be there for them when they are gone. They celebrate the life that has been saved, but they still struggle with the freedom that has been lost, and they all wish that society recognized that even serious criminals can sometimes reform their lives. Like many other families who face either the death penalty or life without parole, they wish that society would acknowledge that their children might not be beyond redemption.

William Neal Moore

Few individuals on death row are ever returned to society, especially those guilty of capital murder. William Moore's case was unique in that he was guilty but was released in large part because the victim's family members embraced restorative justice principles. In 1974 William had just returned to the United States after being stationed in Germany with the army and was assigned to Fort Gordon in Augusta, Georgia, where he drank and socialized on the weekends. One night, after hours of drinking and taking drugs, William and an acquaintance, Javier, came up with a plan to break into Javier's uncle's house while he was not home to steal from him. Their first attempt was unsuccessful, but later that evening William returned to the house, and a burglary attempt turned into murder when he shot Javier's uncle as the man tried to defend his property.

William was soon arrested and admitted his involvement in the crime. Not long after he was told about the possibility of receiving the death penalty. "And see, the day I got arrested, he [the sheriff] told me that he would see that I got the death sentence. Well, I really didn't know there was a death sentence because the last thing I heard when I was in Germany [serving in the military], in 1972, the Supreme Court had abolished capital punishment. That was it, and I just saw that in a headline in the paper."

He was shocked to find out that the death penalty was once again considered constitutional.

When William's family first heard about the crime, they assumed that there must be some mistake. William explained, "We were all a close-knit family, and when this happened, they didn't believe it. They didn't want to believe, and it was just hard for them to believe because I had done some crazy stuff as a kid, but this was far, far beyond what they would ever think I would do."

When William became a teenager he took on responsibilities well beyond his years, including taking care of his mother until he was 17 and his parents remarried. In fact, William had joined the service and left Ohio when his parents remarried to get away from some of the bad influences in his neighborhood. So his family was stunned when his sister got the phone call from William saying he was in trouble and in jail. The siblings went to the army base and asked the military for help in finding a lawyer, and they hired the attorney recommended by the military. Although his siblings were frustrated with William's determination to be held responsible for the crime and not place any blame on his codefendant, they stood by him the entire time and provided him with emotional support, traveling from Ohio to Georgia for his trial.

On the advice of his lawyer, William pled guilty and waived the right to a jury trial, thinking that the judge would take his honesty and sense of responsibility into account during sentencing. But in a gross violation of due process and presumption of innocence, the judge filed a guilty verdict and sentence of death with the court before the proceedings even began. There was no presentence investigation or presentation of mitigating evidence, and as a result William was sentenced to death. Though this type of treatment may sound unheard of today, in the 1970s in rural Georgia with a black defendant, this treatment passed for justice.

William's family was heartbroken. Each time an appeal was denied, they grieved for him, and each time he came close to his execution they experienced anxiety and anguish over the thought of losing him. William served the next 17 years on death row. From the day the police knocked on his door to arrest him, he has never denied that he committed the crime or ever tried to shift responsibility to the man who was with him on the night of the crime. In 1974, while awaiting his execution in a county jail, William accepted Christ, and after his conversion, he felt moved to contact the victim's family. He said, "I wrote them a letter to apologize. Told them that this letter is not going to change anything, but if you could find it in your heart to forgive me, I would truly appreciate it. But if not, I understand because if I was in your position, I wouldn't forgive me." To William's great surprise, within a week, the family of the man he killed wrote back offering forgiveness. He was amazed by the mercy and grace of the victim's family, a very religious family, who felt that not forgiving him and moving on would be contrary to their beliefs and would further harm their family. William had not realized that the victim's family members had been in court the day that he was sentenced to the death penalty. He said: "They were there in the courtroom, which I didn't know because they were behind my family and my lawyer didn't ask them anything. The prosecutor didn't put them on the stand because I'm sure he probably knew that they were going to say they didn't want me to get the death sentence—but they didn't get to talk." When the death sentence was given, not only was it tragic for himself and his family, but also it was inconsistent with the victim's family members' moral beliefs.

The family also went a step further and prayed for William, believing that he still had a purpose to his life. And so began a long-term relationship between William and his victim's family, and they finally convinced him it was time to forgive himself and focus his energy on others. But forgiveness was not easy. William recalled: "But, you know, a lot of times when you do stuff, you think now how could I have been so stupid to have done that and be real hard on yourself, and so they were telling me if you believe God has forgiven you and we have forgiven you, who are you not to forgive you? So you have to do it. Basically, it's a choice . . . you choose to forgive yourself, and you go on. You won't be able to fully go on and help other people if you're bound up."

William dedicated himself to God and helping other people, and in return he was helped by others. On death row, he formed a Bible study group, tutored other inmates, and wrote thousands of letters to the many friends he made with visitors from the church and the community. These individuals felt that he had a future and a contribution to make to society, even though some of them also believed in the death penalty.

Meanwhile, William watched as the men around him, men who he befriended and with whom he read the Bible were executed one by one. One of his friends, Jerome Bowden, had a severe mental handicap, and William taught him how to read so that they could study the Bible together. During a stay of execution to assess the degree of his mental handicap, Jerome was given an IQ test to establish his case and possibly avoid the death penalty. In a sickening twist of irony, Jerome, who had never before been able to pass tests and who had a tremendous desire to show that he was not "stupid," passed his final test. With an IQ of 65, a Georgia psychologist reported to the court that he was not mentally retarded. For years, William tried to forgive himself for enabling his friend's execution, and later, when he himself was sitting on deathwatch, the guards taunted him by reading the last statements of several other inmates who had been executed, including Jerome. William recalled, "The thing that Jerome said which made me feel so much better, even in that type of situation [awaiting execution], was that he was glad that he learned how to read and write. He was glad he was able to accept Christ, his life had changed, and he was happy that the things he learned made him a better person."

In 1984 it looked as if William's options had run out. His lawyers knew that his appeals were failing, and they asked if they could visit the victim's family members, who William had always tried to protect from publicity and intrusion, even from his own lawyers. He recalled, "My lawyers wanted to know, asked me if they could go talk to them but I said, 'Listen, one of the things I don't want ya'll to do is to harass the victim's family. Don't go ask them to do anything because I don't have the right to ask that. If they want to help in any way, they'll let you know or they will let me know and I'll tell you.'" Although his lawyers did not ask directly, they did go to the family and told them of his dire situation, and the family volunteered to help. William continued, "So the family said: 'write the letters.' So everybody in the family, cousins, counsel people, regular folks, everybody that knew the family wrote letters to the parole board on my behalf, asking them not to execute me, and then 7 hours prior to the execution, they gave me a stay."

Between 1984 and 1991, appeals in William's case were filed in both the Eleventh Circuit Court of Appeals and the U.S. Supreme Court. Although there were many delays and stays, in 1991 when it appeared that William had exhausted all legal options the Supreme Court granted him a final 30-day stay. Then in an unprecedented turn of events, the Georgia Board of Pardons and Paroles decided to review his case on August 21. Although William was not present for the review, the meeting with the parole board was packed. He said, "So what happens is everybody, including the victim's family, comes to the parole board, not only just the immediate family, but almost the whole community comes to the parole board. My father, brother, two sisters, and nephew were there." Others who had supported William's efforts, and in the process had become his friends, were also in attendance, including a bishop from Rome, Georgia, and a Jesuit priest who had made contact with Mother Teresa in Calcutta. Such extraordinary support paid off. The Georgia Board of Pardons and Paroles commuted William's sentence to life without parole for humanitarian reasons, including support from the victim's family, a phone call from Mother Teresa, testimony from the religious community, thousands of letters, and the fact that William was never granted a real trial.

When the board announced that they were commuting his sentence, his family, the victim's family, and the rest of the audience broke out in singing "Amazing Grace." In contrast to most death penalty cases that polarize the offender's and victim's family members and the community, the restorative justice principles used here helped build a stronger and larger community of individuals devoted to the concepts of mercy and forgiveness. Integral to this process had been William's willingness to be accountable for his own actions and to communicate his story to others, as well as the victim's family members' compassion and desire to move beyond the murder. This was not without a lot of suffering, however. He reflected how his time on death row was difficult for all of his family members, especially his young son, who has been in and out of trouble with the law, and for himself, especially when his brother died in 1984 and his mother in 1985, because he could not attend their funerals.

In another unique turn of events related to a law that has since been changed, William was granted parole on November 8, 1991. Since his release, he has become a minister, met with his victim's family, and continues to work tirelessly to help other people. He shared, "One of the things I try to teach everybody: look at people on death row from a different perspective. Society puts out how they are monsters and wants you to believe that. But if you can meet somebody and talk to them, your perception will change, and that's one of the things I desperately always try and get across wherever I go because people see me and they say: 'He was on death row? Are you serious?' And I say: yes."

William frequently gives talks on problems with the death penalty, the importance of the decisions we make, and the power of mercy and forgiveness. He concluded our discussion with the following recommendation:

> Family members need to understand that they should not be at odds with each other. Because the defendant's family had nothing to do with the crime, so they should not be ostracized like he [the offender] who committed the crime. Then the victim's family should not be victimized like they are, and they are definitely victimized by the district attorney because they will use them and use them and use them. When they're through with them, they throw them to the side. They don't need them no more. I think those two families can come together and probably help each other because they're both victims. They're both going through a situation where one's lost a family member, actually both have lost a family member—one to death and one to prison or execution.

Personal accountability and a willingness to face the obligations produced by individual actions are essential elements of restorative justice, and William embodied these principles. Although the crime caused immense suffering to the victim's family, William's family, and William himself, restorative justice principles helped them put their lives back together and strengthen their own communities. Even though this case is atypical, it speaks to the potential for restorative justice to help all involved parties in capital cases; the transformative power of mercy, compassion, and forgiveness; and the need to assess the damage that is caused by the present operation of the criminal justice system. The importance of personal accountability and obligation, however, take a different meaning in cases of innocence.

Exoneration: The Case of Joseph Amrine

Toward the end of the play *The Exonerated*, which is based on the oral histories of six exonerated death row inmates, Sunny Jacobs tells the audience, "So I'll just give you a moment to reflect: from 1976 to 1992, just remove that entire chunk from your life, and that's what happened."[8] Sunny is one of 133 people who have been freed from death row since 1973.

One hundred twenty-three were exonerated, and 10 additional people, of which Sunny was one, were released from death row because of possible or probable innocence.[9]

Between 1973 and 1998, there were on average 3.08 exonerations a year. Recently, with DNA testing and organized programs that fight for individuals on death row with innocence claims, such as the Innocence Project at the Benjamin N. Cardozo School of Law started by Barry Scheck and Peter Neufeld and the Center on Wrongful Convictions at Northwestern University Law School, that number has risen to an average of seven death row exonerations a year.[10]

Although most of the discussions regarding exonerations explore those that have occurred since 1973, they have a much longer history. In 1819, for example, a month prior to scheduled execution, Steven Boorn was exonerated. Some of the practices that wrongly convicted him were the same practices used to convict the 133 individuals released from death row since 1973, including jailhouse snitches and false confessions.[11]

Steven's case, which began in 1812, involved him, his brother Jesse, and his father, all of whom were implicated in the death of Russell Colvin, but Jesse was the only Boorn originally arrested for the murder. While awaiting trial, Jesse was placed in a jail cell with Silas Merrill. Merrill told the police that during a visit he overheard Jesse and his father discussing the murder and the roles that they and Steven had in it.[12] Like modern jailhouse informants, Merrill testified against the family in exchange for his immediate release. In an effort to avoid hanging, both Jesse and Steven confessed to the crime. Steven's confession was not corroborated by the facts of the case and was written in language beyond his education and skill level. At the trial, Jesse was sentenced to prison and Steven to death. However, in a bizarre and coincidental chain of events, it turned out that Russell Colvin had not been murdered at all, but was living in New York, and Steven and Jesse Boorn were released from prison.[13]

No matter when an exoneration takes place, the inmate has much to celebrate, but exonerations also create great challenges. These inmates exalt in their freedom, grieve the loss of years, address broken assumptions about their safety, learn to function in a changed society, and reintegrate with their family, friends, and community. They are sent back into society without money and few social supports and under the cloud of having been convicted of a brutal crime. They have no case manager to help them find a training program, assist them with a job search, or coach them through changing norms and technological developments. Nor are they provided access to a therapist who might help them address the psychological issues associated with a wrongful conviction and release into a society that has changed since their arrest. Although the exonerated rejoice in personal freedom, he or she is seldom offered a simple apology by anyone in a position of authority, and monetary compensation for the years lost is rarely given by the state or federal government.[14]

This was the case for Joseph Amrine, who in 1976, at the age of 23, was sent to prison to serve 9 years for writing bad checks, an action for which he has accepted responsibility. He confesses that at the time of his arrest and conviction, "I was not a nice person"; in fact, he says, "I had an ugliness inside of me." However, he was not a murderer, but while in prison he was accused and convicted of killing an inmate, which resulted in a death sentence. His original release date for the check forgery crime was 1985, but he remained in prison for an additional 18 years.[15]

The murder charge and subsequent conviction were based on the testimony of three other inmates, Randall, Terry, and Jerry, who said that they saw Joe commit the murder.[16] In the oral arguments involving the case, it was stated that prison officials knew that Randall wanted to escape the sexual abuse he was experiencing, and that he had been told that although he himself was a suspect in the prison murder, if he implicated Joe he would be moved to another, safer, prison. "At first [he] refused, but it did not take long . . . living under the constant threat of rape, to reconsider the investigator's offer." Terry, who had only 60 more days in prison, chose to testify against Amrine when he was told that he was also a suspect in the prison murder and feared that he might lose his release. Perhaps Jerry had the most to lose if he did not testify; not only was he a suspect, but also if he "did not do what they told him to, they would label him a 'snitch' and put him back in the general [prison] population, in which other inmates would likely kill him."[17]

Years later each of the witnesses recanted, and one of them testified, "I am really sorry for what I have done to Joe Amrine. I lied on this man because I was afraid, and I hope it is not too late to right a wrong." In fact, Randall felt so guilty for Joe's death sentence that he tried to kill himself several times.[18] The witnesses did not recant all at once but one by one over time. In this regard, Joe seems to have been lucky because all of the recantations were made after the 1995 court decision of *Schlup v. Delno*, which in narrow cases involving condemned prisoners allows the court to review new evidence of actual innocence when that evidence was not available at the trial.[19]

Equipped with the unanimous recantations and the *Schlup* decision, Joe Amrine and his attorney filed a motion for a new trial, but Federal District Judge Fernando Gaitan ruled that Joe's evidence was not new and denied the motion. Specifically, he wrote that the evidence could not be considered new because a posttrial hearing had been held in which two of the recantations were previously heard. At that time Joe reasoned that the sentence was upheld because the recantations were not unanimous. He needed to get Gaitan's decision reversed or he would be executed, and he knew that he would have to make his case public to get judicial attention. Locked behind bars, Joe had to rely on his siblings.

Joe has 10 siblings who describe themselves as stair steps, one born right after the other. When he was originally arrested for check forgery, their primary reaction was that he had committed a crime and needed to pay for it. Moreover, the family was no stranger to incarceration—all of Joe's brothers at one time or another served time in jail or prison. His family hoped that he would serve his 9 years, learn from his mistakes, and return to build a constructive life. But all of that changed in 1985 when he was charged with killing an inmate. His mother firmly believed that he had not committed the crime, and most of his siblings agreed, although some were more skeptical— they said that it is hard to know what anyone is capable of doing after spending so much time in prison. However, as the shaky evidence began to emerge, it became clear to the entire family that Joe was telling the truth.

Because of the prosecution's lack of evidence, Joe's siblings did not take the death charge seriously, believing that once the jury heard the evidence they would find him not guilty. But when he was found guilty and sentenced to death, his mother and siblings began to take a serious look at the case. One of his sisters said that "once we started [working for Joe], we became detectives." They examined the evidence, studied the case, and used each other to develop their thoughts. When Joe's mother died in 1997, his siblings took over her position as his drum major for justice. Once the case was upheld by the Supreme Court, they realized that he only had two slim chances for justice—a governor's pardon, which could be political suicide for the governor in a "tough-on-crime" state, or a reversal by the Missouri Supreme Court. The latter would also be difficult because the Missouri court had never before chosen to hear a case that had already been heard by the U.S. Supreme Court.

The family dedicated themselves to fighting for Joe, but they were unsure how they could develop the political capital to influence the governor or court. A series of coincidences worked in their favor. Professor Ed Bishop at Webster College in Missouri assigned his students the task of finding out the facts about an existing case. The students were to carefully examine both sides and determine if the person was guilty or innocent. A group of students selected the Joe Amrine case and became convinced that he was innocent; they further believed that they bore a responsibility to do something. The students then recruited another faculty member, John McHale, who worked with them to develop a 30-minute documentary about Joe's case.

The film provided a powerful tool to build the political influence necessary to win the hearts and minds of Missouri and thereby influence the governor and the Missouri court. Reflecting on the video, Joe's older sister Renee[20] said, "It felt like, damn—we finally can do something. We finally have something." After several planning sessions, the family developed a media strategy to keep Joe's case in the public arena. Two family members were selected as spokespersons, and the entire family became grassroots organizers. Helped by death penalty abolitionist college students, the family arranged for the film to play in churches, homes, community centers, and theaters across the state. They heavily publicized each showing by placing flyers in the neighborhood where the movie was to be shown. One of Joe's sisters, Tonya, remembered a particular (yet typical) event: "We were going to show the movie somewhere. We got flyers, and my sister and my brother and I, we went downtown at 12 at night, after the kids were in bed, to put flyers in the club. We were there until almost 2 in the morning, putting flyers on car windshields and talking to people."

Additionally, someone from the family attended each showing to say a few words about Joe's case and encourage people to follow up with Governor Mel Carnahan. For Joe's siblings, this meant a great deal of travel throughout the state; one sister recalled, "I drove my truck across the state like it was nothing. In the snow, I didn't care. We would talk for maybe 5 or 10 minutes." Before the family left, they made sure that people signed a petition which they developed and carried. Thousands of signatures were collected, brought to the state capital, and "boxes and boxes of petitions brought to the governor." One of the first indications that their efforts were working was editorial support in the *St. Louis Dispatch*.

Despite the support they were garnering, the family's sense of their own efficacy varied; some believed that Joe would win his freedom, while others worried. All of the family believed in the merits of his case and their ability to organize, but not all of them believed that the system would ever allow for the correction. Joe himself revealed, "Every time I was denied [a hearing], it took a little bit and a little bit more out of me. I thought I was going to get executed because of the procedures." Even while organizing, some family members were similarly afraid and preparing for tragedy; one sister reasoned if Joe was going to be executed she would try "to be prepared." She explained, "I used to dream about what we would do with the body." Another sister was "trying to mentally prepare for being a witness." If there was an execution, she wanted to be there with Joe.

The fear of execution was not the only burden that Joe's family shouldered; though none saw the work that they did to secure his freedom as a problem, it did affect their lives. Joe's older sister Venita quit college because she said there was no way that she could maintain her studies and work for his release. Another sister commented that it was stressful to be so prominent in the community, as the media often reported on the family's organizing efforts. Although the family sought media attention and was grateful for it, some of the siblings missed their anonymity and struggled with how public their lives had become. Another sister explained that she had previously been apolitical, but she learned that by standing on the street corner and telling people what was going on, she could bring about change.

Clearly the family knew that they were making a difference when Governor Carnahan publicly stated that he was sympathetic to Joe's case. But in a dramatic turn of events, all their progress seemed as though it might have been lost when Carnahan was killed in an airplane crash on October 16, 2000. However, the family was relieved when his appointed successor, Governor Holden, said that he would make good on Carnahan's commitment to support Joe. It is assumed that Holden asked the Missouri Supreme Court to hear the case, and in 2003 the court overturned Joe's conviction, in a four-to-three decision. Joe was released in July and is quoted as saying, "I feel good. It took 18 years to win this battle. There was a time when I had given up. It's hard being on death row. It can't be described."

Joe's life was transformed in prison. He entered with meanness inside of him, soon became addicted to heroin, and in many ways had given up. Twelve years into his death sentence, he began to take stock of his life and decided to change. Strengthened by his resolve to do right by his mother's memory, Joe quit drugs, became reflective, put his heart into studying, and found God. When he was finally released, however, he was a 20-year-old in a 50-year-old body.

For his brothers and sisters, the organizing has not stopped—today they are working to support the quality of his living. When Joe first got out of prison, he lived with Venita in a small but charming home. She was thrilled to have him, but there was work required; as Joe says, the family had to teach him everything. During his 27-year imprisonment, the world around him had changed considerably and being almost 50 and unable to operate a remote control or a computer was humiliating. Other adult activities, such as managing a budget and owning and operating a car, were beyond his scope.

Venita and her siblings managed Joe's reintegration with the same skill that they did his exoneration and release. They assessed his needs, divided the workload, and assigned everyone a role. Some worked on helping him get a job, others taught him to drive, and all supported his psychological needs. Without knowing it, this family was practicing restorative justice by focusing on Joe's needs and obligations. They supported him and made sure that he learned to take responsibility for his own life and did not revert to crime.

After several months of staying with Venita, Joe decided to move in permanently with his girlfriend. The siblings were concerned that he was rushing things, and without his knowledge they organized a family meeting. When Joe walked into Venita's house and saw his family, he knew immediately that something was up. His siblings expressed concerns that Joe did not know his girlfriend well enough to make a commitment, and that they thought he needed more time under their watchful eyes. Joe listened to what they said but nevertheless moved in with his girlfriend. They soon broke up. Without her income, Joe could only afford an apartment in an inner-city neighborhood full of negative influences and temptations. He recognized the dangers of drugs and violence and moved into another area, but as a result now struggles with the higher cost of living.

When he first moved, he remained close to his sisters and often leaned on them for psychological support, wisdom, and money. Now, although he still maintains regular interactions, things have changed. Concerned that Joe was not making wise decisions about money and afraid that he was becoming dependent on them, the siblings once again organized a meeting to let him know that they would be pulling back their financial assistance, which Joe saw as tough love. He may miss this assistance, but he respects their decision and says that he probably would have done the same if the roles were reversed. He is now working for his lawyer's firm and supporting himself and the death penalty abolition movement through a New Voices Ford Foundation grant. His work, which involves speaking and organizing for abolition, is his sole source of income, so money can be tight.

Prison robs people of much more than time and resources. Joe has traveled a very scary and intimidating path in finding his way outside of prison, and he credits prison in some ways for saving his life, but it had also taken away the safety, joys, and comforts of a free life. Joe now sees a therapist for PTSD. Sometimes he falls into depression and feels that both he and his life have no meaning, and he gets physically lost. He often finds himself in his car not knowing where he is driving. Joe is also struggling with hepatitis B and C, which he is sure he got from the dirty needles that he used while shooting heroin in prison.

Whereas Sunny Jacob asks people to think about the time between 1976 and 1992 and erase it from their personal history, Joe's story asks people to consider the 18 years from 1985 to 2003. Joe missed not only a good portion of his life but also the opportunity to hug his mother as a free man and attend her funeral. Although he and his family have suffered from the tragedy of his undeserved death sentence, each day they are grateful for how different their life is now. Venita says that she and her siblings tease Joe by reminding him that they "gotcha out of prison." They can find things to joke about because although his life is hard off of death row, "his story has a happy ending."

Summary

For the offenders and family members in this chapter, a change in sentence, whether through exoneration or commutation, established that "life is different." A sentence other than death instilled hope in their lives and awakened a capacity for productivity and compassionate contributions to the lives of others. They still bear the scars that come with the death row experience, as one mother divulged: "Once a death row family, always a death row family." But moving out from the shadow of death allowed them to experience a semblance of peace and provide their family members with the love and attention they deserve.

William Moore's story provides insight into how life may be different for victims. Following his release from prison, William met with the victim's family members, with whom he had been corresponding since 1975. They greeted him with open arms, welcomed him into their homes, and treated him as one of their own; to this day he has maintained contact with them. Forgiveness has allowed the victim's family to move beyond the crime and focus on their own healing and futures, and by averting execution, the family was spared any internal conflict or sadness that might have accompanied

William's death. In keeping with the restorative justice principle of accounta-bility, William requested that we not contact the victim's family. He felt that it was his responsibility to shield them from any type of publicity related to his case and that it would be unfair for him to share their information with us. We honored his request.

Nathaniel's family, the Amrine family, Pearl's family, and Jane's family each experienced hardship because of a death sentence. For Nathaniel's fam-ily, it was manifest as stress, and for Karl, Nathaniel's father, depression. The Amrines gave up years of their lives fighting for Joe's freedom. They lost time with their own children, and Venita dropped out of college. Pearl was unhappy about the decisions that her daughter was making but could only yell at her and shame her when she was consumed with terror for her son. All of the families in this chapter suffered as a result of a death sentence, yet none of them received support to deal with their pain and confusion. No one addressed the specificities of the family members' experiences and what it means to be a death row family. Additionally, even when Joe Amrine was exonerated, the criminal justice system did not provide him support for his readjustment into the free world or compensation for his lost years.

The stories in this chapter all demonstrate that death sentences produce detrimental consequences to offenders' family members beyond what they face with other sentences. Trauma, depression, and financial and emotional costs are much more severe with death sentences. These families also demon-strate that some offenders can make positive contributions to society, even from behind bars—but rarely while on death row. Restorative justice pro-grams working with death penalty cases need to address both the harm caused by the crime and the harm caused by different types of criminaljustice reactions to crime. The harm that the criminal justice system places on the wrongfully accused is profound, and yet there are few processes designed in which accountability is accepted and obligations are met. The next chapters explore the organic beginnings of restorative justice work with death penalty cases and the initial efforts of several groups aiming to meet the needs of family members of offenders and victims in capital crimes.

9

Organizing for Abolition

I created an organization in Arizona to end the death penalty. I became involved at the national level, serving on the board of the National Coalition to Abolish the Death Penalty, participating in the Journey of Hope alongside murder victim family members who were advocating for abolition, and speaking around the country. Saving John's life and ending the death penalty at first were obsessions, which eventually grew in to a calling. I am convinced my love for my family and activism ultimately saved my life.

—Katherine Norgard[1]

Family members of capital offenders live deeply involved with the legal system, yet their roles generally are limited to being witnesses as they help the legal team prepare their loved one's psychosocial history for mitigation. Only during their short time on the stand, which some are never granted, can they speak to the judge, jury, and victims' family members. Their lack of voice and participation often makes them feel helpless.

So perhaps it is not surprising that with no other satisfying way to help their loved ones, some family members join organizations working either to abolish the death penalty or provide assistance to families of capital offenders. For most family members, this is their first involvement in activism. Many individuals volunteer with preexisting groups, but a few, like Katherine Norgard, start their own advocacy or support groups. In working with such organizations, family members bond with a community that understands their issues and with whom they can express themselves openly. Consequently, many of them have said that their involvement allows them to know that they are doing something, and this sense of efficacy is vital to their well-being. Involved family members speak of the benefits of activism, but most family members of death row inmates remain isolated.

In this chapter we explore the death penalty abolition movement and the ways the family members of offenders interact with it. We begin with a brief history of the abolition movement and then describe some large national and international organizations with an aim to abolish the death penalty. Then we summarize theory that explains how families benefit by their interaction with organized groups. At the heart of the chapter are examples of organizations, groups, and individuals who have reached out to family members. None of the organizations that we discuss here could be accurately characterized as a restorative justice program. Despite this, each of the programs is a response to the needs that resulted from the crime and criminal justice process of offenders' family members and sometimes victims' family members. Programs based on the needs of involved stakeholders offer important building blocks for the development of more holistic restorative justice programs, and therefore it is important to look at these programs for lessons.

The Death Penalty Abolition Movement

Established in 1787, with the support of Benjamin Franklin, the Philadelphia Society for Alleviating the Miseries of Public Prisons was one of the first organizations with a mission of prison reform and death penalty abolition. The society also provided support for released offenders and organized prison visitation for inmates.[2] The society's philosophical rationale is rooted in the Quaker ideology of nonviolence, as well anti–death penalty arguments developed by eighteenth-century Italian philosopher and economist Cesare Beccaria, who Reverend Jesse Jackson credits as almost single-handedly starting the anti–death penalty movement with his writings.[3]

Beccaria found the practice of the death penalty to be flawed in major ways. He argued that long prison sentences and death were equally effective in deterring crime so that there was no reason to resort to death. Furthermore, he believed the state's role in execution made society more rather than less violent. Finally, understanding the fallibility of the court in its decisions, he worried that a mistake could not be remedied once an individual was executed.[4]

Sociologist Herbert Haines, who studied the history of the anti–death penalty movement, has identified four periods in abolition work and acknowledged that like many other social movements, the anti–death penalty movement oscillated between moving forward and setbacks.[5] The first active death penalty abolition movement in the United States was from 1780 to 1830. During this period the movement spread beyond the Quaker-influenced city of Philadelphia and the Society for Alleviating the Miseries of Public Prisons to the states of Maine, Michigan, Rhode Island, and Wisconsin, which all passed laws that essentially abolished the death penalty in their jurisdiction.[6]

During the Progressive Era, from the late 1800s to the early twentieth century, 10 additional states ended the death penalty. As the Progressive Era faded, the American League to Abolish Capital Punishment began in 1925 as the first organization to support and link statewide efforts. During this time attorney Clarence Darrow spoke about the necessity of abolition and successfully defended two men, Richard Loeb and Nathan Leopold Jr., against the death penalty. Darrow argued that crime resulted from external social forces that shaped individuals and their behaviors.[7] Hence, in his view criminals were unlikely to be deterred by fear of capital punishment and instead needed social services.

According to Haines, the third era in death penalty abolition began in the 1960s, with a boost both from Great Britain, which abolished the death penalty in 1968 after questioning its deterrent effect and the publicity surrounding two high-profile American executions.[8] The California executions of Barbara Graham and Caryl Chessman brought the abolition cause to the attention of a national audience, including such public figures as Eleanor Roosevelt and Marlon Brando. Graham and Chessman were executed in the gas chamber, in 1955 and 1960, respectively, despite claims of innocence. Chessman's case is particularly noteworthy because he filed his own appeals, and for 12 years he fought strongly against his execution, including writing two books about his case and his claim of innocence.[9] Two films made about his life further publicized his cause. The executions gained international attention, and the United States was criticized for supporting the practice; feeding growing international condemnation was the belief that innocent people were being executed.

What further distinguishes the third era is the anti–death penalty movement's extension beyond traditional grassroots organizing strategies into litigation-based attacks. Lawyers sought to show ways that the death penalty was not consistent with evolving standards of decency and raised a host of procedural issues designed to demonstrate that the death penalty was racially biased. The combined efforts culminated in 1972 with the *Furman v. Georgia* lawsuit, which sought to show the capricious and racist nature of the death penalty.[10] On hearing the evidence, the Supreme Court agreed that arbitrary decisions were made regarding who gets the death penalty and under what circumstances and found the implementation of the death penalty to be unconstitutional in 1972. However, the court also left the door open for the states to revise their statutes to revive the use of capital punishment.

In the wake of *Furman*, states and the federal government introduced the concept of aggravating and mitigating evidence presented in a bifurcated trial (a trial with a guilt and innocence phase and a separate sentencing phase). The presentation of aggravating and mitigating evidence was designed to support consistent decision making regarding who gets the death penalty and why. Subsequently, with the issue of arbitrariness seemingly addressed, the death penalty was reestablished in 1976, and the country entered what Haines describes as the fourth era in the death penalty abolition movement, the post-*Furman* era,[11] characterized by new legal and organizing strategies. In this era, lawyers and activists have made headway in restricting the use of capital punishment with recent cases banning the execution of juveniles,[12] banning the execution the mentally retarded,[13] as well as cases addressing inadequacy of counsel and due process violations.[14]

Currently, numerous groups are working to abolish the death penalty, including large organizations like the National Coalition to Abolish the Death Penalty (NCADP) and Amnesty International (AI) Program to Abolish the Death Penalty, both of which support national grassroots organizing efforts and buoy the hundreds of local and state organizations seeking death penalty abolition. The American Civil Liberties Union (ACLU) and the National Association for the Advancement of Colored People's (NAACP) Legal Defense and Educational Fund also seek to eradicate the death penalty by using the dual tactics of advocacy and litigation.[15]

Abolition Organizations: A Closer Look

In its statement of purpose, the NCADP indicates that since its inception in 1976 it "has been the only fully staffed national organization exclusively devoted to abolishing capital punishment. NCADP provides information, advocates for public policy, and mobilizes and supports individuals and institutions that share our unconditional rejection of capital punishment." The NCADP currently has 28 affiliated chapters in 24 states, but a quick review of their Internet home pages shows that fewer than half of these chapters include (either in their work or in their mission statement) support to defendants' family members. This omission may not mean that these groups do not work with families, only that such work was not easily identified in a review of their Web sites.[16]

In contrast, many affiliates have statements or links that involve support to victims' family members. Of the NCADP chapters that claim to support offenders' family members, the Floridians for Alternatives to the Death Penalty's mission is the broadest; it seeks to "support the many persons affected by capital crime and its punishment."[17] Another NCADP chapter, the Delaware Citizens Opposed to the Death Penalty, links to a subgroup called Because Love Allows Compassion (BLAC), which reaches out to death row inmates and their families. We will revisit BLAC later in this chapter.

Each year the NCADP hosts a large conference attended by members of affiliated chapters, other abolitionists, and people touched by capital punishment from all over the United States. Several of the family members we talked to have attended these conferences, and each of them said the conference can be a very moving and enriching experience. One mother, however, took a while to warm up to them, saying she got nothing out of her first two conferences. During her third, she was moved by a presentation given by an individual she respected. He spoke about his sense of powerlessness and isolation because he never seemed to fit in given that he was from an ethnic minority. With her experiences validated at last, she was able to voice her feelings and began to make significance progress addressing her nearly 10 years of depression.

The second large organization that supports death penalty abolition in the United States is Amnesty International USA; its Program to Abolish the Death Penalty supports local organizations while working to end the death penalty nationally and internationally.[18] One of its more visible projects is the National Weekend of Faith in Action on the Death Penalty.[19]

During a weekend in October, faith communities are encouraged to devote time to explore the death penalty and its implications from the perspective of their faith traditions. AI's Web site provides an organizing toolkit, including suggestions activists can use to support family members. Suggested ideas are organizing a carpool for family members to and from the prison; creating support groups for the victim's family members, the death row inmate's family and friends, and those who have been exonerated; and brainstorming within their faith communities to determine other ways to offer assistance.

In Atlanta, AI helps staff Georgians for Alternatives to the Death Penalty (GFADP), founded as part of the Southern Center for Human Rights, a nonprofit litigation- and advocacy-based organization. GFADP—does not offer a specific program for families, but it does provide services to families—members often drive them to the prison and organize their participation in the NCADP conference. Board members Ed and Mary Ruth Weir, whose work we detail later, provide a hospitality house for families visiting death row inmates. GFADP's board includes two family members of deceased capital offenders, one of whom is Pat Seaborn, whose experience with her cousin's deathwatch was found in chapter 4. She states that her work to end the death penalty and to give back to the community that provided support and care to her has been critical to her healing. Released death row inmate William Moore, who we met in the last chapter, is also on the board.

GFADP's work is concentrated in two areas. The first is a moratorium campaign, a legislative initiative that pushes for both a moratorium on capital punishment, and the creation of a statewide death penalty implementation study. The second entails execution alerts that mobilize letters to Georgia's governor and its Board of Pardons and Paroles after a death warrant is signed. Like most local death penalty abolition groups, they issue a public statement with every execution. On the day of an execution, the group holds candlelight vigils in 11 communities throughout the state, including outside the state capitol building, local courthouses, and the death house. According to organizer Laura Moye, a vigil's purpose is to make a statement that an execution is occurring and that certain people in the community oppose it. In essence, she says, the group seeks to "lift up the value of life." Like GFADP's predecessor, the Society for Alleviating the Miseries of Public Prisons, several members regularly visit death row inmates.

A number of student groups across the country also fight the death penalty, and both NCADP and AI have student-oriented programs. One such group from Missouri worked with the Amrine family on the documentary that led to Joseph's exoneration. Abolitionists and family members working together can save lives like Joseph's, but only a few organizations have specific programs to address the needs of offenders' family members and to give them a sense of community support.

Connecting with Others

At some point, everyone needs support. How many of us have friends, family members, neighbors, or colleagues that we call when we may be without our cars, need help looking after our children when an unforeseen circumstance occurs, or with whom we can talk when we are troubled? Many of us search for an understanding ear or a strong shoulder to see us through our weak moments, and we know that when we need to confide, we likely can find someone who will understand our experience. For family members living in the shadow of death, however, finding compassion and understanding can be next to impossible. As one mother said, it does no good to talk with friends: "They have no idea what to say or do. They cannot help me learn what to expect from my child's appeals and if he is safe. They cannot help."

Thus, not surprisingly, family members often reach out to the only people who understand their situation—other family members of death row inmates who they encounter through abolition networks or the prison visiting area. But even with this commonality, they cannot necessarily solve each other's complex emotional issues or lessen the depth of their pain. One mother used the metaphor of drowning to describe her relationships with other family members, saying that she and her friends were tangled up in deep water where they simultaneously held each other up and slowly pulled each other down. For example, due to circumstances ranging from a death warrant to a broken car, one of the family members would put extra emotional weight on the others, which strained the already tenuous system even further.

In addition to emotional support, a number of family members say that they need material help, particularly with regard to visitations and education. Access to reliable transportation and the costs associated with a long trip can be difficult or even impossible hurdles. Other family members indicate that their largest need is education; they want to know what to expect from the courts and the appeals system. They desperately want to learn how to interact with the prison system and advocate effectively for their loved one. All family members need to be sure that their loved one is safe and as comfortable as possible, and some relatives, like Katherine Norgard, need to help others.

The "empowerment process" championed by social workers provides promise for effective support of capital offenders' family members and fulfillment of some of their needs. Social work researchers Lorraine Gutierrez, Ruth Parsons, and Enid Opal Cox found that meeting individual needs through organizing work empowers those who are disenfranchised and isolated.[20] Through the empowerment process, the individual gains a sense of control within his or her own life and the ability to effect social change.

These researchers have identified four elements in the empowerment process, the first of which is belief. Here individuals work to believe in themselves and gain a sense of their own self-efficacy, which is then used to promote action and self-worth. The second element is validation of thoughts and feelings through interaction with others, where participants begin to understand that their experiences and reactions are normal, and there are others who share their feelings. Once they begin to see that they are not alone in their thoughts and experiences, participants can begin to shed the notion that there is something wrong with them or that they are going crazy; as a result, a connection with others can begin to develop. The third element is critical thinking and action; through group interaction and relationships, members begin to identify the system-level issues affecting them, challenge stereotypes associated with those beliefs, and place their issues in a sociopolitical context. The last element, praxis, refers to the process of bringing theory and action together, often for the purpose of developing a program, initiative, intervention, or just getting involved.[21]

A number of organizations that reach out to capital offenders' family members demonstrate characteristics that are found within the principles of the empowerment process. They provide offenders' family members with a safe place to tell their stories, explore the ways they are harmed by the crime and the criminal justice process, and begin to meet their needs and the needs of their communities and are therefore consistent with several restorative justice principles. The remainder of this chapter provides short case studies of a number of these groups. Some concentrate on political organizing and others on meeting individual needs. All of them exhibit some degree of success, as indicated by enthusiastic participation levels and participants' feelings of accomplishment, although they all also suffer from a lack of resources. Each organization offers lessons in how communities and other organizations can begin to address the needs of offenders' family members and empower them with a sense of self-efficacy.

Case Studies

Philadelphia's Family and Friends of Death Row Inmates

Political consultant and pundit James Carville once described Pennsylvania as "Philadelphia on one end, Pittsburgh on the other, and Alabama in between."[22] In the late 1980s, one of the authors (Elizabeth Beck) was working in Greene County, an impoverished rural area in southwestern Pennsylvania; part of her job was to respond to the growing Ku Klux Klan presence in the community. At that same time, the Greene County commissioners also were hoping to attract economic boons to the depressed area. The commissioners' plans included the development of a new maximum security prison, with a death row, called SCI Greene. The prison opened in 1993 and was touted as a great economic success because of the jobs it created.

Other aspects of SCI Greene's history are problematic at best. In November 1997, Pierre Sane, secretary-general of Amnesty International, visited SCI Greene's death row inmate Mumia Abu-Jamal and was "horrified" by the prison's death row. "Death row in Pennsylvania looks and feels like a morgue," he said. "From the moment that condemned prisoners arrive, the state tries to kill them slowly, mechanically, and deliberately—first spiritually and then physically."[23] In May 1998, the prison was mired in further controversy as word of brutalities leaked out. Reports told of employees taunting inmates, and guards beating prisoners and writing KKK across their bodies with the inmates' blood. A guard told a *Pittsburgh Post-Gazette* reporter that he was responsible for "adjusting the attitude of inmates," and inmates recounted having been viciously clubbed during such "adjustments."[24]

Visitation policies and practices also aroused the fears of family members. Most family members who visited death row inmates were African Americans or Latinos from Philadelphia, and they were well aware of and frightened by the area's history of Klan activity. Security measures at SCI Greene were particularly stringent; for example, any woman who has visited a prison knows not to wear an underwire bra because it can set off the metal detector. At SCI Greene, however, reports were common of female visitors and lawyers who were denied access to the prison when the metal clasps on their bras triggered the devices. Additionally, SCI Greene uses a drug detection device called an itemizer, which checks a skin sample for drugs. Although the itemizer does not detect most legal pharmaceuticals, family members were fearful that their heart or diabetes medicine would scan positive and make them unable to visit. Many family members would then forgo life-sustaining drugs to ensure they could visit their loved one.

Over the years, conditions at SCI Greene have improved significantly. Following the reports of improper activity in 1998, inmates contacted civil rights attorneys to initiate a lawsuit and investigation. As a result, the superintendent was demoted, and his replacement required the guards to temper their interactions with inmates and their family members, and a grievance policy was initiated.[25] However, prior experience had shaken family members, and they remained terrified of their trips to Greene County and the prison until Peggy Sims and Family and Friends entered their lives.

Wherever she goes in Philadelphia, people know Peggy and are happy to see her. She is always friendly and in command. Peggy is statuesque in the traditional African clothes that she often wears. In the 1990s when she retired from a large telecommunications company she started volunteering in her church's prison ministry. She attended a training program that qualified her to become an official visitor with the Pennsylvania Prison Society, formerly the historic Philadelphia Society for Alleviating the Miseries of Public Prisons. During the training, Peggy learned how to talk with inmates, including not being judgmental or discussing the inmate's case (because prison society visitors do not act on behalf of attorneys) and only work on nonlegal issues the inmates may have.

Inevitably, her discussions with inmates centered on two issues: prison conditions and family concerns. Most eastern Pennsylvania inmates were concerned with prison visitation. They hated that their families had to wake up at 3 A.M. to come to an area known for Klan activity, and all they would receive for their effort was a visit lasting two hours or less.[26] Peggy immediately began organizing support for family members and launched Family and Friends with a handful of people and a rented van.

Today Family and Friends is a strong organization with a three-pronged approach. The first prong addresses what Peggy calls barriers to visitation, the second advocates for changes within the prison, and the third works to abolish the death penalty and to keep young people out of the prison system. Peggy's official title is "organizer," and she credits the training she received in business with giving her the knowledge necessary to do the work.

To further their work, Family and Friends has forged a meaningful connection with the Quaker American Friends Service Committee, which provides the group with space for meetings and events. At their monthly meeting located at the Friends Center in the heart of Philadelphia, 30 to 50 people gather to discuss and plan. The monthly meeting prior to the bus trip is largely devoted to visitation. Family members receive a review of the rules and what to expect. The itemizer scanners are explained, and family members are encouraged to take their medicines, reminded not to wear underwire bras, and told to bring their identification.

Family and Friends has made large gains in reducing barriers to visitation, including transportation and cost. Thanks to the group's efforts, family members now ride in comfort, are well versed in prison procedures, and have an advocate in case something goes wrong. Four times a year Family and Friends charters a bus to SCI Greene. Nearly everyone who rides the bus is African American or Latino, and what Peggy loves most about the trips is the diversity of the passengers, who include children, teenagers, and older individuals. They are Muslims, Catholics, Baptists, and "everything else." Most riders are women—mothers specifically—though one faithful rider is a father confined to a wheelchair. Together they represent almost the entire socioeconomic spectrum.

Kelly, a mother of a death row inmate, acts as the transportation administrator, renting the bus and managing the money. The cost of the bus rental is $2,350, and each person donates $50 toward it, but when a family member is unable to contribute, he or she is not turned away. Several weeks before the visit, Kelly informs the prison administration when the bus will be coming and who will be on it, and this communication has proven to be very important. Sometimes a change of name or address can foil a visit, but prison officials now work with Kelly to iron out any issue before the family arrives, and so far no one has been denied their visit. The first thing Kelly does when she sees someone get on the bus is to ask them whether they remembered their identification; once when a mother forgot her infant's birth certificate, Kelly had it faxed to their fast food lunch stop so the visit could proceed. Kelly also organizes games and videos for the children, and the bus is abuzz with excitement and camaraderie.

Family and Friends also devotes a large amount of time to advocate for changes within the prison and uses thoughtful community organization strategies to address prison problems at their roots. Peggy and one or two family members meet every quarter with the superintendent of SCI Greene and the secretary for the state's prisons in Pittsburgh. The carefully scripted meetings are limited to two or three participants so as not to overwhelm the officials or create an adversarial climate. Before each meeting, the Family and Friends representatives confer to determine the agenda, which they follow carefully, staying focused and restrained. As a result, an atmosphere of respect and warmth has developed between the prison administrators and Family and Friends.

Once during a meeting Peggy offered up a "sort of friendly dare" to the secretary; "I always come here," she teased. "I bet you would never come to us." She proudly proclaimed, "Well, he took me up on it," and they held a meeting at the Philadelphia Friends Center. Peggy described the gathering as "packed, and the family members were thrilled; they felt like they mattered and that they were being heard." A truly collaborative relationship now has taken shape. The prison's official Web site even provides a link to the organization.

The official agenda of the meetings with prison officials always includes grievances from the men in prison. When an inmate believes that he has been wronged, he either writes to Peggy directly—and she sends him a standard letter indicating that she has received it—or he gets word to her through his family. She makes a note of the incident and then creates a chart that helps her look for a pattern. When a particular guard's behavior is found on the chart three times, she passes the information to the secretary and superintendent. Because she does not exaggerate the information, and because Family and Friends is known for its integrity, the officials take the grievances seriously.

In addition to individual grievances, Family and Friends rallies for institutional changes within the prison. Recently, they argued that conditions were needlessly repressive for inmates, and after a series of conversations, a number of improvements have been made. For example, the time that an inmate can be outside has doubled from one hour to two, and men are now allowed to buy long johns and typewriters from the prison commissary. Such progress has led inmates like Mumia Abu-Jamal to refer to Peggy as his "guardian angel."[27]

Perhaps most important to the inmate and his family members are the improvements in communications and visits. Specifically, the group advocated for more phone calls, and the prison changed its policy from allowing weekly phone calls to triweekly calls. The visiting hours for families riding the bus have been lengthened from two hours to at least a full morning.

The final area of Family and Friends' work is to develop crime prevention programs for children and educational programs about the death penalty. The group believes that youth need a message of hope to not become involved in violence and other destructive activities. The education committee is active, and programs are directed not only to the inmate's family and friends but also to include public events that support abolition activities, such as a day with Sister Helen Prejean. In 2004, Toni, the program chair for Family and Friends, spearheaded a conference based on the book *7 Habits of Highly Effective Teens* for 30 youths, most of whom had a loved one on death row.[28] The youths developed a play and talked about issues that were important to them, including teen violence, teen pregnancy, drugs, and the death penalty. At the end of the day, the teens received a certificate. Evaluations indicated that the event was very powerful for the participants; as one young person said, "It helped me to see how much I can do, not what I cannot."

Finally, although Family and Friends is not a formal support group, it provides an invaluable support network for its members. Often Peggy will get a call from a family member when a death warrant is signed at trial. She works to calm the family and reassure them that nothing will happen right away— each inmate is granted an automatic appeal. The most difficult warrant experience that Peggy has had to address involved the 11-year-old son of an inmate. The prison administration knew that an execution would not occur because the inmate's appeals had not been exhausted, but they phoned the family's home and asked the offender's young son what they wanted done with his father's body. Peggy said that the boy has not been the same since the call; he has begun acting out at home and school, and she has been working to connect him with mental health support. The work takes an emotional toll on Peggy, who often cries for the family, the inmates, and the future of the country, which, in her words, "recycles trash but not human beings."

In 2004, Family and Friends hosted a conference in which family members talked about their experiences and learned about the prison process. Some of the comments on the evaluation form included: "I needed to release energy; it was great," "God bless this effort, I feel empowered," and "The fellowship with other family members was the best part of the day." Peggy explains that family members do support each other, and the feeling of being surrounded by people "who understand what you are going through" is a great relief. Mostly, "Family and Friends provides a voice for the voiceless," she adds, and family members begin to regain a sense of self-efficacy in their own lives as they speak with one voice.

Peggy attributes the success of Family and Friends to a number of factors, not the least of which is the support of the incarcerated men. In this regard, she has developed relationships with about two-thirds of them and tries to check in on them at least once a year. Another critical factor is her belief in spending time building and maintaining relationships with prison officials, family members, and anyone who may help her with her work. Although Peggy has only attended one NCADP conference, she found it invaluable because it gave her ideas on how to work with groups like youth and clergy. Without knowing it, Family and Friends has incorporated the empowerment process into their work and demonstrates how important this process can be to family members.[29]

Because Love Allows Compassion

BLAC stands for Because Love Allows Compassion, as well as for Barbara Lewis and Anne Coleman, its founders. In 1985, Anne's daughter Frances was shot and killed while she was driving through south central Los Angeles. Although Anne says that at the time she would have happily killed the murderer herself, she was and remains opposed to the death penalty. Similarly, Barbara lost her niece, nephew, and uncle to violence. Then in 1992 her son was arrested for capital murder. Shortly after his arrest, she read in the local newspaper that the Delaware Citizens Opposed to the Death Penalty was holding a meeting, so Barbara went looking for help with her son's case. Although the group historically did not provide services to family members or get involved in legal advocacy, the trip was significant because she met Anne.

Although Barbara is African American and Anne is white and English, they have developed a connection so strong that they call each other "twins." Always ready to support each other, they quickly recognized that the support they offer each other was not available to most family members of victims and offenders, thus demonstrating the underlying restorative justice premise that both victims' and offenders' family members are stakeholders in the justice process. By working together they are able to help themselves and their communities.

In its first few years, BLAC helped offenders' family members through 13 executions, but Anne and Barbara found it hard to sustain the work. They began to grow weary, and with each day Barbara's son grew closer to his own death. The women needed help. Then they met Sandy Jones, a licensed clinical social worker with a doctorate in sociology and a longtime death penalty activist. She had recently moved to Delaware. For several years now, Barbara, Anne, and Sandy have joined together to reach out to the family members of the 17 men on Delaware's death row.

BLAC's outreach begins as soon as a death penalty trial is announced. They send a letter of introduction to the inmate, requesting him to provide family contact information or ask his family directly if they would like to talk with someone from BLAC. The response, according to Sandy, is almost always positive. The inmate is often relieved to find out that support exists for his family, and the family usually wants to talk with anyone who may be able to help.

BLAC tries to support the many needs of family members. As Sandy explains, family members need "to vent, they need to feel empowered. Many times they have lost their extended family and community support." They need everything from a ride to the prison to knowing that someone will be with them should the execution take place. At the moment, much of BLAC's work can be viewed as support services; specifically, family members interact with BLAC representatives on a one-to-one basis, but BLAC is beginning to pursue group activities, as well.

BLAC's major activities include rides to the prison and phone conversations to check in with family members, but that is not all the group does; sometimes the needs that members fill are not readily apparent. Consider Kofie, who we met in chapter 6—a 16-year-old African American man who, since our interview, served time in jail. His father is on death row, and his residency shifts frequently between his mother's and his aunt's homes. He feels that his mother barely wants him, and his aunt does not have the energy to devote to him. Moreover, Kofie has an anger problem; after his stint in jail, his probation officer told him that he needed to attend an anger management class. Kofie knew his life would be easier if he could get his temper under control, but no one was available to take him to the class. Sandy stepped in and provided the needed transportation. Kofie felt as though the anger management education was very valuable, but perhaps equally important was the stability and support that he received from Sandy. Her commitment gave him the knowledge that he mattered enough for someone to go out of their way for him on a consistent basis.

Sandy and BLAC cannot meet all of the needs of the families of individuals on death row, but they do provide some insight into the scope and breadth of services required. Because Sandy's interest is specifically with children, she has developed meaningful relationships with a number of them. The children we interviewed who worked with BLAC say that Sandy's support has been a huge help, and she has started an informal group where the children meet and support each other. She has provided a safe space to air their feelings, fears, and hopes. Like restorative justice models, BLAC uses a needs-based approach to work with family members of offenders. Both children and adults find a safe place to tell their stories, get assistance with transportation and education, and support through the execution process.

Journey of Hope from Violence to Healing

Like BLAC, the Journey of Hope from Violence to Healing (or simply the Journey, as it is often called) involves murder victims' family members and family members of capital offenders. It was started by Bill Pelke and others who lost a loved one to violence. The death penalty first entered Bill's consciousness when Paula Cooper, the 15-year-old girl who killed his grandmother, received a death sentence. Originally a supporter of Paula's punishment, years later, after she was taken off of death row by a legal commutation, he met with her in prison—and forgave her. Since then he has been an avid abolitionist. From his interaction with Paula, Bill began to see how the family members of capital offenders are "the forgotten victims" and to understand the cruelty and barbarism of capital punishment. He explained that if people knew that his grandmother was to be killed at a certain time and date, the community would mobilize to stop it. In Paula's case, had she remained on death row, community members would have likely cheered her death.[30]

Bill believes that the key to abolition lies with murder victims' family members, and thus he was also very active in forming Murder Victims' Families for Reconciliation and is now active with Murder Victims' Families for Human Rights, explored below. Both organizations are made up of "family members of all homicides including state killings [capital punishment] who oppose the death penalty in all cases."[31]

The Journey of Hope seeks to end the death penalty through education, provided by a variety of speaking tours, the most comprehensive of which is the annual Journey. During this time, murder victims' family members, defendants' family members, and others pile inside rented vans and personal vehicles to begin a 17-day speaking tour within an individual state. Organizations within the targeted state sponsor the tour and help coordinate events such as community forums. The first tour took place in 1993 and was hosted by Murder Victims' Families for Reconciliation; since then only a few years have been missed. Journey members talk with civic groups and church groups at schools, community centers, and large lecture halls, and although their audience varies, their abolition message does not.

The Journey also has become a support system for a number of the family members and provides a meeting place for families of both victims and offenders. Bill recalled that on one of the first Journey trips, three mothers of death row inmates from states across the country met, and a bond was formed instantly. Their meeting marked the first time they encountered someone who understood what the other knew as reality. Bill found it very powerful to see the women who had previously been isolated within their own communities start to develop a deep and long-lasting support system. In another case, he said that he was able to see the physical differences in a mother as she began to open up and share her story; the contours of her face lightened, and the effects of a previous stroke lessened.

It is remarkable to see the interactions between the victims' and offenders' families. For victims' family members to treat offenders' family members with respect and dignity touches the offenders' family deeply, and many experience enormous relief as they begin to see that they did nothing wrong and can be forgiven. Ken Robison, the father of a capital offender, expressed solace at "being with people who had been through the horror of losing a loved one and having them be understanding and compassionate" to him and his wife, Lois, and added that they "felt so accepted."

Now retired schoolteachers, Ken and Lois are considered the grandparents of the Journey's tour. In January 2000, their severely mentally ill son, Larry, was executed, and on the Journey, the couple talks about the horror of death row and their inability, despite a tireless effort, to get long-term and sustained mental health care for their son both before and after the crime. They have traveled the United States with the Journey and have gone on sponsored trips to the Philippines, Scandinavia, and Europe.

What is most important to Ken and Lois is education. They are convinced that the public needs to be made truly aware of the consequences of the death penalty, and as both teachers and parents of an offender, they offer a powerful message. They believe the public needs to understand that severely mentally ill people may be condemned to death despite their limited mental capacities, and in many cases the families pay a devastating price for an offender's execution.

In 2005 the Journey combined with Murder Victims' Families for Human Rights (MVFHR) to publicize the experiences of the Robisons and others like them. In Austin, Texas, the Journey's tour ended with the beginning of an initiative called No Silence, No Shame, which kicked off the annual meeting of the National Coalition to Abolish the Death Penalty. No Silence, No Shame, a project of MVFHR, brought family members of the executed together to share their stories and begin a political movement.

Murder Victims' Families for Human Rights

On October 27, 2005, in Austin, 18 people from across the country placed 36 roses in a vase. As they placed the roses, the family members of the executed—sons, mothers, sisters, brothers, nieces, nephews, and grandchildren—said the name of their loved one and the victim's name. As Susannah Sheffer, MVFHR staff writer and author of several books, including *In a Dark Time: A Prisoner's Struggle for Healing and Change*, noted: "Many abolition groups could have brought family members of the executed together through something like the rose ceremony, but few would have likely brought together symbolically or physically, the victims with the families of the executed." Like the Journey of Hope, MVFHR is unique and powerful because it was started by a family member of a murder victim, Renny Cushing, along with three other family members of individuals who had a loved one executed and nine family members of murder victims.

The seeds for MVFHR were planted on June 1, 1988, when Renny Cushing's father, Robert Cushing, a retired elementary schoolteacher, was murdered. Renny became a survivor of a homicide victim, an identity marked by things like "funerals and caskets; cemetery plots and headstones; empty chairs at holidays; maybe police investigations; hearings, trials, sentencing, appeals."[32] Renny, like so many other victims, was also concerned about who was going to clean the blood off the wall of his parents' home.

Following the death of his father, Renny entered what he called the dead zone, where his life felt like a haze of grief and trauma, and where thoughts about things like homicide and vengeance filled his head. Renny, a lifelong abolitionist, thought about how long and complicated the grieving process is and how murder continually retraumatizes the survivors. He thought about the death penalty and its cyclical effect for profound retraumatization and violence. As a supporter of social justice and member of the New Hampshire House of Representatives, Renny emerged as a leader in the victims' movement against the death penalty and has since devoted his life to abolition as a way to honor his father.

Most recently Renny has started MVFHR out of the recognition that the death penalty transcends national borders and that it is larger than a criminal justice issue—it is a human rights violation. In their newsletter, MVFHR explains that the death penalty is a violation of Article III of the Universal Declaration of Human Rights, the right to life, and Article V stating that no one should be subjected to "torture or to cruel, inhuman or degrading treatment or punishment."[33] In viewing the death penalty in this regard MVFHR is linking with "human rights, anti–death penalty, and victims' activists in this country and around the world."[34]

Renny also knows that the human rights of family members of the executed are violated, and he knows that there are similarities between the experiences of victims and family members of the executed. Each set of relatives experiences profound grief and trauma, and in many cases the death certificates of both victims and offenders are marked homicide. But the grieving process is different because family members of the executed are experiencing nonfinite loss and disenfranchised grief, and their experience is colored by shame, which takes away their power.

One of the first things the MVFHR chose to do was transform that shame into political capital and to "speak truth to power," with their No Silence, No Shame Initiative. The day, which concluded with the rose ceremony previously described, began with facilitated private discussion in which family members of the executed shared their personal stories, including their fears, thoughts, and experiences. Some individuals spoke words that they never thought that they would be able to say to another human being because it felt so shameful, but in this environment they were given something they never had before—safety among strangers and an opportunity for healing. In that room that day, the family members "had the opportunity to transfer their trauma memories into stories and to have someone to listen to them." As one participant said, the day was "life changing." For Renny it "was an amazing experience to be in a room of a couple of dozen people where having a family member executed was the norm" and to see the healing power of storytelling.

After the discussion there was the public rose ceremony followed by formal remarks from three family members, including Celia McWee and Robert Meeropol. Celia, after describing what it was like to witness Jerry's execution, said, "Some days I wonder about my ability to go on. . . . I know that we are stronger if we join together. I know that ending our silence and moving away from our shame will help us heal ourselves and help us bring about a better world."[35]

The event had meaning for individuals like Celia, who said it was amazing to see the roses together as Jerry's memory was flanked by others just like him and to participate in the beginning of a political movement. On October 28, the *Austin American-Statesman* carried an editorial, "Families Left Behind," which included the following excerpts. "We hardly give them a second thought . . . but the family members of people who have been executed are no longer willing to suffer in silence. Their stories of survival after their parents, children or siblings were executed should give the public yet another reason to abolish the death penalty."[36] The editorial exemplifies that when family members break their silence, they do have power.

The MFVHR organization seeks to harness that power and has developed an impressive list of next steps. These steps include continuing to reach out to families of the executed, documenting their stories for policymakers and the general public, supporting them to speak out against the death penalty, and joining with other efforts to educate child welfare workers, mental health professionals, and the general public about the negative effects of execution.

New Hope House

Ed and Mary Ruth Weir have raised children and foster children and have welcomed grandchildren into their family. Mary Ruth is soft-spoken, and although Ed may appear quiet at first, he actually has a wry sense of humor and enjoys telling a good story. Ed's beard speaks to his spirit and passivism; like the Amish who shave their mustache as a way of distinguishing themselves from the Europeans who persecuted them, Ed wears his beard without a mustache.

Years ago, Ed and Mary Ruth moved from their home in suburban Maryland to Georgia to live in an intentional Christian community devoted to social justice in which participants dedicated themselves to trying to live their lives in accordance with the gospel. In 1982 their community and two others met and decided to work on a project together. Murphy Davis from the Open Door community in Atlanta suggested that they provide hospitality for individuals visiting family members on death row. Six years later, Ed and Mary Ruth bought property on Possum Trout Road, about 10 minutes from Georgia's death row in the Georgia Diagnostic and Classification State Prison, commonly referred to as Jackson because it is near Jackson in Butts County.

Soon Ed and Mary Ruth built a guest house that they dubbed "New Hope House," which was filled with family members visiting Jackson's death row. For a number of years an informal support group developed as family members representing six men on death row met every Friday night for a potluck dinner and were joined by Randolph Loney, an ordained minister and author of *A Dream of the Tattered Man: Stories from Georgia's Death Row*.[37] These family members, explained Ed, "were devoted to each other. It meant a lot to them to have each other as most of them could not talk with people in their community, and some could not talk with family members. They celebrated together and mourned together." Eventually the group dissipated as members stopped their visits to Jackson. Of the six inmates, five had their sentences lessened and were moved to prisons across the state, and one was executed. Although people still come today, New Hope House does not have the number of overnight visitors that it once did. Ed and Mary Ruth both lament the decline of visitors, but this has not slowed their other efforts to support family members of capital offenders.

Indeed, pinning Ed and Mary Ruth down can be difficult because they travel the state constantly observing capital trials and offering support to family members. They have attended over 50 trials. According to Ed, with the exception of summer when things slow down, in the state of Georgia, there is a death penalty trial under way almost every day of the week; in fact, the week prior to our interview, three such trials were happening in the state.

Ed explained that they got the inspiration to attend trials when a mother told them of the shock she experienced hearing the execution date read at the conclusion of her son's trial. From that remark, Ed and Mary Ruth realized that the family members needed someone to guide them as well as "[accompany] them: to eat lunch with them or to cry, to do whatever is helpful." To offenders' family members, the Weirs not only offer warm faces when there are none, but also they provide a wealth of knowledge. Ed and Mary Ruth make sure that all relatives know what will happen if a death sentence is handed down, and they begin to explain the appeals process. On a first courtroom visit, one mother of a defendant let them know that it meant everything to have someone with her, and they have heard the same message over and over. Ed concludes that there is some advantage to "having someone who does not know you act as a support person."

As restorative justice advocates, the keys to the success of Ed and Mary Ruth's approach are that they let the individual family member's needs guide their work, and they learn from their mistakes. Mary Ruth explained that they introduce themselves to family members as people who are against the death penalty; once they had made the mistake of saying that they work with families who have members on death row, and of course the family was aghast because jury selection had not even begun.

Ed and Mary Ruth also have supported family members in telling their own story and working as activists. One young man, whose brother was on Georgia's death row, has become an active public speaker who believes that telling the story of his brother's mental illness and lack of treatment is important, though it can be emotionally draining. Mary Ruth also believes that acknowledging your loved one and making a contribution in his name is a common but personally significant occurrence that supports healing. To illustrate her point, she talked about individuals who do things like starting scholarship funds in their loved one's name following a tragic death in the family. Although death row families do not traditionally start scholarship funds, some immortalize their loved ones by speaking out against the death penalty.

Ed and Mary Ruth never planned on entering the funeral business, but they soon perceived a vacuum there, too, which they strove to fill. When an inmate has no other family, it sometimes falls on them to carry out his final wishes; at other times they have helped family members organize the funeral. A New Hope House volunteer has helped the couple raise money from churches for funeral expenses, and Ed has found a brother of a former death row inmate who contributes headstones at a largely discounted rate. In fact, Ed enjoys telling the story of the first donated headstone; when he went to pick it up, he explained, he expected something modest, but what was waiting for him was a huge marker that weighed down their truck and had to be hoisted off by a makeshift pulley and a group of people. Although Ed and Mary Ruth laugh at this story and other antics, the work is also wearing on them; to them it is "the hardest pain to imagine" to have someone on death row.

Summary

As has been discussed throughout the book, the needs of offenders' families can be grouped into emotional, informational, health, logistical, and empowerment needs. The achievements of the organizations highlighted in this chapter provide powerful examples of how those needs can be addressed through a variety of approaches. As these examples illustrate, emotional and logistical support, along with empowerment, are clearly critical to the coping and healing process.

A previous chapter noted that the experiences of family members of capital offenders provide insight for mental health professionals, particularly those who work in the areas of trauma. In this chapter it is shown that the experiences of death row families speak to the need for a holistic approach to healing, one that includes combining emotional support with regaining personal power. In this regard, a great deal can be learned from the empowerment perspective as it begins to redress the feelings of powerlessness and disconnection that create the foundation for trauma symptoms. The empowerment process uses both storytelling and political organizing as tools for healing.

Although none of the groups explored in this chapter was specifically designed using a restorative justice model, they all incorporate certain restorative justice elements. Most significant, all of them provide some sort of formal or informal storytelling forum where family members can share their experiences and express their needs in a safe environment. Most of them have adopted a needs-based approach to working with families, focusing on the needs of the family member and trying to develop ways to meet them. Whether the needs are emotional, informational, logistical, or empowerment based, each group has worked hard to help the families rebuild their lives and deal with the ongoing trauma of having a loved one on death row.

A few of these groups, such as the Journey of Hope and MVFHR, have brought offenders' and victims' family members together. The interactions have provided relief to offenders' family members and helped victims' family members cope with the pain of a loved one's death.

Restorative justice focuses on bringing people together to repair and rebuild communities that are badly damaged by crime. The groups chronicled in this chapter have begun to address community issues in two ways: first, the groups help individual family members connect with a new community of others who either share their experiences or are empathetic to their situation. Second, some of them are involved in prevention efforts that help reduce crime in the communities where the crime occurred. MVFHR sums up the work nicely with their aptly named initiative, No Silence, No Shame.

10

Reaching Out

Lyle defined himself as "a father, a provider, and a lover." So when his wife left him and won custody of their four children, as well as a large alimony and child support settlement (which ended up being over three-quarters of his meager pay) and thidated house that he had worked on to make livable, Lyle struggled with his new circumstances. The stress of trying to cope with the financial and emotional strains aggravated his mental frailties and triggered a series of psychotic episodeychotic s. Following the divorce, Lyle was committed to a psychiatric hospital twice as a result of his schizophrenic delusions and paranoia. Each time, despite the severity of his illness and the need for sustained treatment, the hospital released him on the 11th day of his stay. Coincidentally, Lyle's medical insurance only covered 11 days of inpatient care.

On release, Lyle could no longer hold a job and had to move into his parents' trailer. He tried to meet his commitments to his ex-wife and children with his paltry disability payments. He frequently contemplated suicide but struggled to maintain his role as a father and a provider. Lyle's sole possession at this point in his life was a beat-up old pickup truck. He valued this truck because it allowed him to get work and try to provide for his family. However, the paperwork for this truck was in his ex-wife's name, and to get insurance he had to have it in his name.

One Sunday afternoon Lyle returned to his ex-wife's (Donna) house to get the paperwork signed. In his old parking spot was a new truck, owned by his ex-wife's new boyfriend. Upset, he went to a neighbor's house to call one of his wife's family members to help with the situation. They did not want to be involved and advised him to handle it on his own. He grabbed a gun from his truck, and when he rang the doorbell it took a long time for anyone to answer, leaving him time to contemplate the thought of a new man in his wife's and children's lives.

Once inside the house he and his ex-wife argued while the new boyfriend, Brian, sat in a recliner with pictures of Lyle's four boys behind him on the wall. Matt Rubenstein, the lawyer who recounted this story to us, described what happened next, "during the course of the exchange, Lyle bent down to pick up his 18-month-old son, and their son called out the new boyfriend's name."

While still holding his son, Lyle shot Brian repeatedly and then shot Donna. Next he called his father and ex-father-in-law and asked them to call the police. When the police came, Lyle was standing in the middle of the room contemplating suicide. The police quickly disarmed and arrested him.

Although everyone knew that Lyle would be convicted of murder, his parents were still devastated by the guilty verdict. Rubenstein explained: "[They] can never really prepare for [the verdict]. This is 12 people just deciding your son is never going to walk free again. He's going to die in prison. And he's either going to die when we [the state] kill him, or he's going to die in God's time."

What makes this case so different from many other death penalty cases is what happened after the verdict and after the sentencing portion of the trial, when the jury returned from deliberations. "Lyle's family had been weeping and was just very emotional." They were terrified at the possibility of a death sentence. Rubenstein recalled what happened next:

> Lyle's family is on their side of the courtroom, and Donna's and Brian's families are on their side of the courtroom. And the verdict comes back with life. These two families, in the courtroom, [are] separated by the 8 feet between the two benches down the middle of the courtroom. They meet there. And the two families come together, and they exchange hugs and kind of multiple conversations. The victims' families were comforting Lyle's family! So they all sort of huddled together for 5 or 10 minutes. And it seemed the victims' families got what they wanted; they were sort of happy, not in a nasty way. Obviously this was a traumatic thing. They lost these family members they loved very much. But they felt like it's over. And, in fact, I think they may have been relieved to some degree that Lyle wasn't given a death sentence. If Lyle was given a death sentence, their grandkids, and their nephews, would experience having Daddy killed by the state.

Lyle's family felt tremendous shame and guilt for his behavior. So in many ways, it was the victims' family that provided Lyle's parents with comfort at the end of the trial. Rubenstein continued: "Donna's mother's hugged Lyle's mother, shaking hands and hugging each other, and I think on some level, there's an instance of forgiving . . . we forgive you. On a psychological level, I think that was very important for Lyle's family. Just human contact, whoever it was [over 30 of the victims' family members were at the trial], recognizing the pain and the hurt that Lyle's family was going through."

Although the court process involved in this case was based purely on the adversarial system of criminal justice, restorative justice found a way into the courtroom on the day of the final verdict when the families' recognized one another's pain and shared the loss of Brian's and Donna's lives and Lyle's life as it had been. Both families needed to express their sorrow and support healing for Donna and Lyle's four children. This spontaneous coming together of victims' and offender's families may not have happened if the verdict had been death. A death sentence, as so many offenders' families have shown us, forces people into self-preservation mode, and the adversarial stance continues through the protracted and bitter appeals process. The verdict of life in Lyle's case made it possible to focus on the loss of Donna and Brian and provide support to their survivors.

The verdict also ensured that Lyle and Donna's four children would not grow up in the shadow of an execution. And significantly, Donna's parents are currently raising the kids and allow frequent contact between the children and Lyle's parents.

Lyle's and Donna's families have shown that sometimes members on both sides of the aisle have the need to reach out; they do this both to support their own healing and to give comfort. Sometimes restorative justice occurs through formal systems and sometimes through informal channels. Just as Donna's family brought restorative justice into the courtroom, there are other examples where offender's or victim's family members sought to do the same. In this chapter we highlight the spontaneous restorative actions of victims' and offenders' family members; the work of victim outreach specialists, who help victims' family members communicate their judicial needs to the defendant and the defense team; and a model program in Texas, the Victim Offender Mediation program, that includes death penalty cases.[1] We discuss Azim Kamisa, the father of a murdered child, and Ples Felix, the grandfather and guardian of the boy who murdered Azim's son. We also recount the relationship between David Kaczynski, brother of Ted Kaczynski (the Unabomber), and Gary Wright, a survivor of one of the bombings. We start by addressing some of the many issues that must be grappled with for restorative justice to occur in murder cases.

Restorative Justice in Murder Cases

For restorative justice to move forward in murder cases two issues that need to be addressed are punishment and how to structure restorative justice initiatives in capital cases. Presently capital punishment in the criminal justice system is based on punishment and revenge. Although revenge is a natural reaction to crime, particularly violent crime, its repercussions can damage innocent parties. Coping with the violent loss of a loved one involves complex feelings of which revenge is only one, but in the adversarial system revenge holds a prominent position.

Restorative justice practitioner Tammy Krause explains that for victims' family members, justice tends to be defined by the prosecution, and the prosecution has equated justice with revenge. Although punishment is certainly a component of justice, according to Krause, justice is a much broader concept that includes helping families heal. Despite society's widespread acceptance of retribution, it has limitations. It does not encourage the offender to own up to the crime, apologize, and try to make amends. Retribution also ignores many of the needs of the victim that go beyond revenge. Connie Kotzbauer, whose daughter Lori was murdered, explains: "All sense of respect, fairness, and kindness has been lost in our system, and this is particularly true in a death penalty trial."[2] But figuring out how to get past society's reliance on retribution is a significant barrier for advocates of restorative justice.

Restorative justice theorists and practitioners also struggle to determine how best to take the successes and lessons from many restorative justice programs operating in the United States and across the globe that focus exclusively on minor or property crimes and work these principles and practices into processes that can support the healing of violent crime. Many of the programs for minor offenses revolve around a meeting between the offender and the victim, sometimes in the presence of community members. At a typical meeting, everyone gets to tell their story and be heard, the group reaches a resolution, and the process concludes, leaving the offender to do community service, pay reparations (actual or symbolic), and seek treatment to address the issues that led to the crime.

A restorative justice model in a murder case has a different structure, although the components are largely the same. The major difference is that the actual victim is absent, so the victim's family members become more central. Additionally, because of the severity of the crime, a meeting can be very difficult for victim's family members and even potentially create further harm. Communication in these cases instead occurs through intermediaries, who might, for example, help the victim's family members articulate and meet their needs. Another difference is that in the case of murder restorative justice will not replace the traditional system of justice, just augment it.

Howard Zehr argues that learning how to work with different systems of justice requires a change in focus so that rather than focusing purely on the questions that drive the current justice system, such as "What laws have been broken? Who did it? What do they deserve?" instead we should focus on the harms and the needs created by the crime and involve all stakeholders in a process to deal with these issues. We should ask questions such as "Who has been hurt? What do they need? Whose obligations and responsibilities are these? Who has a stake in this situation? What is the process that can involve the stakeholders in finding a solution?"[3] In death penalty cases, we and others in the field are jus starting to explore these questions. We start this process by looking at the needs of offenders' family members to reach out and how many of these needs fit into a restorative justice framework.

The Need to Reach Out

Many offenders' family members want to reach out. They want to connect with the victims' family members, the offender, other offenders' family members, and the larger community to help them cope with the horrendous nature of the crime and its consequences. This desire to reach out, a natural part of the human experience, is an intrinsic part of doing restorative justice.

Driven by their need to reach out, many of the offender's family members were trying, without knowing it, to do restorative justice, that is, transform the situation, in their own by attempting to connect with the victim's family. The lives of the offenders, victims' family members, and offenders' family members are painfully fused. One of the most difficult steps toward healing is acknowledging these new, often unwelcome relationships. The families we interviewed were all aware of the fact that their lives were connected to the lives of the victims' family members, even if they had been complete strangers before the crime. Charlene, an offender's mother, described the crime and the resulting collision of lives as surreal: "So if they [the courts] were looking for punishment, they got it from both of us—both sides [offender and victim families]. I have often looked about the lives of people and the ripple effect of how many lives it changes. I would sit there and think, 'What am I doing here? This is unreal. How did I get here? I don't know these people and they don't know me, and yet our lives collided.'"

Although family members did not use the specific terminology associated with restorative justice theory, many articulated their guilt, shame, and a desire to do something that might help the victims' family members deal with their loss. They realize, however, that their very presence can be a difficult reminder of the crime and loss to the victim's family member. Charlene confessed:

> It was horrible. I wanted to go over and say something to them and give all my condolences and tell them I understand for your son that you lost and your pain that your family went through, but at the same time you can't, because you see the anger and the hostility and the hatred, and you're like, I don't know what to do. What can I do to make you feel better? Is there anything? But they are looking at you like they want to hurt you, and you just sit there and you know you are sitting there and looking over, and my heart would go out like, God, if I could just speak to the mother. Just sit down mother to mother and talk with her. To let her know from my heart what I am feeling from my heart and pour my heart and let her pour her heart out to me.

Charlene also recognized, as did many other families with whom we spoke, that the criminal justice process itself was further distancing and impeding any possibility of humane communication between the offender's and victim's family members. She described to us what she wished she could say to the victim's family members: "We know we can't bring your son back. But, God, we want you to know that our hearts got torn up in two, and we aren't condoning any of this." She felt that she did not get the chance to do this because "the prosecutor has already made the family hate our guts because he's painted this picture of this monster and his monster family that goes along with it."

Other family members wanted to extend their personal condolences, send a card, flowers, or even send a formal letter of apology to the family directly or to the community through the local newspaper. Most relatives, though, were strongly discouraged from making contact by the defense attorney or other individuals who worked in the criminal justice system. Some were told to speak to a pastor about their feelings. Others approached the victim's family members' advocate, who is typically employed by the prosecutor's office, only to be told they should keep their feelings to themselves. Matt, whose son was later sentenced to the death penalty, explains, "The first day of trial, I tried to apologize about what had happened to the family. I went over—I crossed the aisle—that wasn't going to happen. The victim's advocate told me I belonged on the other side of the aisle." So without a restorative mechanism to reach out to victims' family members in a way that is acceptable to them, offenders' family members often risk remaining "on the other side of the aisle."

Several family members' efforts to make contact with the victims' family members were successful, although many of these occurred by chance in places like the courthouse bathroom, elevator, or hallway, or in public places such as a grocery store. These contacts were generally positively received and helped the offenders' family members deal with the events surrounding the murder. For some, it was a huge relief because it lessened their feelings of guilt.

Bernard, a grandfather of a capital offender, felt so strongly about apologizing that when he was called on to testify during the sentencing phase of his grandson's trial, he told the judge: "Before I answer any questions, I'll let you ask me anything, so I looked at the judge and he said, go ahead, so I said Mrs. [victim's mother], the first thing I would like to do is apologize, and I told her there is no way that I can express in words how I feel. . . . This did not make it [testifying] easier on my part. I just wanted to apologize."

Later on, during a break in the trial, Bernard wanted to talk with the family directly, especially the mother. He recalled, "I could see that she was really in agony, and she was mad and so on, but then the brothers came over. I just talked to them. They were nice." Then the victim's mother and sister approached Bernard. "I just talked to them. They were nice and they seemed to be understanding, and the mother came too, and I apologized to her and she was kind of mellower to me." This experience was redemptive for Bernard because he firmly believes that individuals should be held accountable for their actions, and if he had any role whatsoever in his grandson's life and deeds, then he needed to express his remorse for the pain the victim's family members were experiencing.

Another mother met the mother of her son's victim outside the court-room. "I sat with her one time. . . . She was outside crying . . . and I just told her, 'I'm sorry for what happened.' " It was important for this offender's mother to recognize the grief of the victim's family, even with everything that was going on in her son's trial. Although she could not do much, the act of sitting together in quiet empathy helped both mothers bridge the aisle.

Several family members that we interviewed told us of cases where victims' family members approached the offenders' family members to express their sympathy over the sentence or the actual execution. Their reaching out is a reminder that victims' families do not always seek only retribution—they, too, wish to transcend the unthinkable grief of losing a loved one.

Restorative justice solutions need to focus on victims' feelings and give them choices to decide if and how they wish to participate. Before encouraging offenders' family members to meet with victims' family members, it is important to consider how victims feel about these encounters. A recent study of victims by criminal justice researchers Mark Reed, Brenda Sims Blackwell, and Sarah Britto found that most victims, at least when initially asked in a research setting, did not want to meet with offenders or their family members.[4] When asked about a desire to meet with the boy who had killed his son, one father responded: "Couldn't do anything like that, because I would be in his face, I'd stab him."[5] Victims' family members' emotions, even years after the death of their loved ones, were often raw and unresolved. Any restorative justice solution must, first and foremost, offer victims a safe place to express these emotions and talk about the loss of their loved ones. Victims need to be empowered, have choices, and be given the opportunity to let their feelings evolve as they deal with their loss and continue with their lives.

A small number of victims in the Reed, Blackwell, and Britto study either desired to reach out to or already had met with the offender or their family members. The mother of a murder victim approached an offender's mother in court: "We were both leaving at the same time, and I told her I was sorry for what she was going through. Because she loved her son just like I loved mine. I said, now I'm not sorry that he is on trial, I want to be so clear. But I am sorry that you have to watch this and deal with this, knowing what he did. Because you are not responsible for your son pulling the trigger."[6] Another mother wrestled with forgiving the man who killed her daughter and what it meant for her: "This thing about forgiveness is I know it's something I have to do for me, but forgiveness is a process. Forgiveness is not forgetting what the person did, it's just somehow or another living with the choice and decision that they [the offender] made and somehow going on with your life, that's the only thing I can see. Forgiving is not letting them have power over me."[7]

One of the greatest needs of victims is for choice—including choosing the time frame and terms on which they process their loss. Reaching out for help can be difficult because the courtroom atmosphere seldom supports empathetic human interaction. It is clear that something more needs to be done. The criminal justice system needs to be refocused to begin to see the human needs associated with homicide. A combination of restorative justice and traditional modes of justice may better address harm found when a serious crime occurs.

Emerging Victim-Based Restorative Justice Programs in Felony Cases

This section offers descriptions of some formal efforts of agencies and individuals working with the criminal justice system to attempt to support restorative justice processes. Although these initial programs have only begun to scratch the surface in terms of developing adequate models for combining the adjudication and punishment goals of the traditional justice system with the needs-based approach of restorative justice, they do offer tremendous promise for all involved parties, surprisingly even the criminal justice system itself.

Victim Outreach Specialist

Victims' needs are central to any legitimate restorative justice effort. Services are often currently available to homicide victims' family members. Victim advocates, for example, provide a broad range of services, which typically include talking about what happened, navigating the legal process, coordinating with the prosecution team, support services through the court process, and referrals to support groups and mental health services. These advocates are frequently trained to think that meeting the victims' needs means winning the case and executing the offender. Many are employed through the prosecutor's office, and their affiliation with the state can cause them to be reluctant to encourage victims' family members to explore anything that can even remotely be seen as jeopardizing the prosecution, even in the name of healing. Restorative justice practitioners are now developing a complementary restorative justice-based model—defense-initiated victim outreach.[8]

Throughout the capital defense community, Dick Burr is respected as a compassionate and highly skilled attorney. He has been a lawyer since 1976. In 1979, he began representing people in capital cases, and by 1981, capital cases were the sole focus of his practice. He has worked as a public defender (in Palm Beach, Florida), for private nonprofit groups (Southern Prisoners' Defense Committee, the NAACP, and the Texas Resource Center), and in private practice in Oklahoma.

While working as part of Timothy McVeigh's defense team, Burr was struck by how profoundly traumatizing the whole experience was to victims' family members and their communities. Feeling an obligation to do something for the victims' family members, if only to improve the relations between them and defense teams, he contacted Howard Zehr, a criminal justice theorist and the current codirector of the restorative justice-based Center for Justice and Peacebuilding at Eastern Mennonite University. Zehr agreed to meet with Burr and other defense attorneys and brought along a talented graduate student, Tammy Krause, who had worked with victims and was well versed in the effects of trauma.

Zehr went through the principles of restorative justice with McVeigh's legal team, explaining how a needs-based approach is more likely to transform conflicts into healing than a purely retributive model. Much to her surprise, Krause was also called on to discuss trauma and explain the process that many victims go through when dealing with traumatic events. She recalls: "And so at the end of the weekend, Burr and the other attorneys said, 'Ok, ok, we get it. We need to reach out to the victims' families and [because of our agenda] we realize that we are not the right ones to do it.' And they said, 'so who can do it?' And all of the sudden, it was just one of those things where the room got really quiet, and everybody's head turned to me."

Krause agreed to try to work with the families of victims in the McVeigh case using a restorative justice framework, including addressing harms and needs, meeting obligations, and finding engagement.[9] From that moment, Zehr, Burr, and Krause began creating a practice called defense-initiated victim outreach and a new role in capital trials called a victim outreach specialist (VOS).

Defense-initiated victim outreach is based on the recognition of the following:

- The adversarial system does not support individuals in meeting their needs, including supporting the *three pillars of well-being*, which are often taken away from individuals following a traumatic event.[10] These pillars are autonomy, order/safety, and relatedness (the ability to again make connections with people and find meaning).
- Sometimes some of the needs of the victim can only be met by the offender and the defense team.
- The defense team must be a part of a restorative justice approach because their members are the only ones who have access to the defendant, and although the VOS is employed by the defense team, she or he is not a part of it.[11]
- The relationship between the VOS and the victims is unconditional during its duration.

The work of VOS began with the McVeigh trial and has been evolving ever since. A Soros Foundation postgraduate grant on Crime, Communities, and Culture and then a fellowship from Ashoka helped Krause develop the practice of defense-initiated victim outreach, and train others. There is now a cadre of individuals who have been trained by Krause, Zehr, and Burr to do defense-initiated victim outreach work across the country, and this group is growing. Additionally, VOS is now an official job within the federal defender's office. At the simplest level and from the perspective of victims' family members, the VOS is a safe person with whom to share their stories without feeling that everything they say is on the record. Krause explains: "People [victims] are so saturated with pain, if there's somebody there with as open hands as possible, just saying if you'd be willing to talk with me I would really like to listen and learn from you. I'm not a therapist, and I'm very clear with them in working with me I'm in no way trying to fulfill a counseling role. But that doesn't mean that just sitting with and talking with me can't feel therapeutic or can't feel healing. It's just a chance to tell somebody's story; you have an active listener."

To examine the work and its evolving nature it is helpful to start with the Oklahoma City bombing trial. Both Krause and Burr realize that they started work with the victims' family members in the McVeigh case much too late to fully reach all of the victims who may have been helped by this process—jury selection was already under way. However, they did not want to give up on reaching out to victims altogether, so they narrowed their approach. Rather than working with all family members, which is common practice for defense-initiated outreach work, Krause started by trying to identify and contact families that might be against the death penalty. The victims who agreed to talk with her shared their experiences with the bombing, life after it, and their desires within the judicial process.

They kept in touch during the trial and met several months later because Krause reflected: "When I went there, I saw these families feeling this enormous sense of responsibility—that they somehow felt like they could or should have done more on the behalf of Tim, you know, and the death sentence. And it was this horrible thing to think that people were feeling guilty about something that he [Tim McVeigh] chose to do."

After this meeting, Krause met with Zehr and phoned Burr to discuss the possibility of facilitating a meeting between the defense attorneys and the victims, one that would in no way help McVeigh's appeal but hopefully would help many of the victims deal with the dual trauma of the bombing and the criminal justice process. The attorneys immediately agreed, and the meeting happened 14 months after McVeigh's trial. Although not all families attended, all were welcome regardless of their feelings about the death penalty. Krause recalls, "It was an amazing experience because I think what we saw is that we were able to take off a lot of masks—the masks that victims assumed defense attorneys wore and vice versa."

During this meeting, family members wanted some very specific information about McVeigh and the defense team. Burr responded honestly to questions about the legal process and the change of venue from Oklahoma to Denver explaining the court was not trying to hurt them or give McVeigh special treatment, but that it was their duty to provide him with a fair trial. Furthermore, although the defense team tried to provide McVeigh with the best defense possible, they did not agree with his actions in the bombing and felt for all of the victims in the case. Many family members were angered and troubled by McVeigh's smiling ("shit-eating grin") and laughing coming into the courtroom. Burr explained that had McVeigh showed no emotion he would have been seen as a cold, inhuman monster. This conversation helped both the attorneys and victims to see that their perceptions fed into the tension in the courtroom.

The victims also wanted to know what McVeigh was like. Burr described how he was distrustful of the government and by extension his lawyers because they were part of the legal system, but that Burr had used jokes to connect with him. Burr also told the family members that Tim liked Peppermint Patties. Through this line of questions, victims' family members were trying, with obvious difficulty, to see McVeigh as human.

After spending time with Zehr and Krause, Burr understood the victim impact testimony at the McVeigh trial in a different way. He realized that many of their stories "had to do with their own journey of healing and what they needed in their lives." Whether or not they formally reached out to a VOS, their stories speak volumes to the significance of a needs-based approach and the importance of healing.

As a result of the experience, Burr, on behalf of the Federal Death Penalty Resource Council, asked Krause to continue her work on another federal death penalty case. Krause agreed on the condition that her official job would be grounded in restorative justice principles, include the needs of the victims, and specifically focus on offender responsibility. She emphasized the questions, "What obligations did the crime create, and who should be held accountable for those obligations?" Everyone—Krause, Zehr, and Burr—was committed to developing a practice based on restorative justice. As Burr explained, "I understood it some from the work we'd done in the McVeigh case, but as I became more conversive in restorative justice, I realized that it made complete sense and gave the work integrity." Perhaps most important, because restorative justice supports the pillars of well-being, and autonomy is one such pillar, as Burr explained, it is "a safeguard against trying to push victims to somewhere they didn't want to be or didn't want to go," including their own decision to seek the death penalty.

The work of the VOS and the ways in which defense-initiated victim outreach repairs harm are illustrated in *United States v. Stayner*. On July 21, 1999, Joie Armstrong, a beloved naturalist who taught children that it was bad to kill bugs and who lived and worked in Yosemite National Park, was murdered. She was beheaded, her body left in a creek. Joie left behind her mother, Leslie Armstrong, who adored her, a large group of immediate and extended family who also loved her, a fiancé, and many friends and children who had been touched by all that she had to offer.

Carey Stayner, a severely mentally ill man, confessed to killing her and three other people (Carol and Juli Sund and Silvina Pelosso) five months earlier. Because Yosemite is federal property, the case went to federal court, and Krause was asked to participate. She wrote a letter to Joie's mother in which she was very clear that she was associated with the defense team and wanted to assist her. The first letter went unanswered, but Leslie responded to Krause's follow-up. She called Krause, skeptical about how anyone from the defense team could possibly help her.

As Krause explained her role, Leslie softened and agreed to meet with her. Krause flew to Florida and found Leslie to be a lovely person in desperate need of support. She told Krause that she first needed to know Joie and sent her back to her hotel room with letters and memorials. When Krause returned, she encouraged Leslie in a critical aspect of restorative justice—storytelling. Not as a therapist or counselor but as a VOS, Krause listened to Leslie with nothing but empathy and time. She calls this process of listening and storytelling "bearing witness" to someone's pain and believes that it is critical to establish connection. Although Krause gave Leslie all the time she needed to talk about Joie, she would sometimes steer the conversation to Leslie's needs and the trial.

On the third day, Leslie began to question Krause's motives. "What gives?" she asked suspiciously. Krause explained that the defense team wanted to plead the case out, and she explained that two judicial tracks were possible—labeled as Track A and Track B. Krause said that if the case went to Track A, it would go to trial, and if that were to occur, Leslie would listen to two phases of the trial, the guilt/innocence phase and the sentencing phase. She explained what content would be covered in each phase of the trial and some of the things that the prosecution and defense might say about both Stayner and Joie. She also explained the appeals process and what would be required of Leslie if Stayner received a death sentence. Krause said that it would be many years before Stayner would be executed. Still suspicious of someone associated with the defense team, Leslie checked all of the information with the prosecutor. The prosecutor confirmed what Krause had to say, showing Leslie that the defense was more forthcoming with her than anyone else in the criminal justice system. Always working toward full disclosure, Krause explained to Leslie that she had to determine for herself what her needs were: did she need the judicial closure that could result from Track B—a plea bargain (which guaranteed that there would be no more appeals) and would limit the details of Joie's death rehashed in the court? Or did she need to hear a jury say "death?" Although employed by the defense team, Krause wanted every move, even if it was to go ahead with the trial, to support Leslie's autonomy and therefore her healing.

Leslie determined that her primary need was to try to move forward with her life, and she reasoned it would be more likely to occur with a plea agreement where there would be no appeals. Leslie and Krause made a list of things that Leslie wanted from Stayner and the defense. She wanted him to stop giving press and radio interviews from his prison cell. Given the high-profile nature of the crime, this was a common occurrence and one that would catch Leslie off guard. Leslie wanted Stayner to give up the literary rights to his story, so that any money made from it would go to the Joie Armstrong Memorial Fund. Although Leslie had no desire to meet with Stayner at the time, she wanted to reserve the right to victim-offender conferencing if she ever chose to talk to him at a later date. Leslie's needs were placed in the plea agreement that Stayner signed, and on the day that it was read in court he said: "I am so sorry. I wish there was a reason [for the murder], but there isn't. It's senseless. . . . If there is a God in heaven, I pray for his forgiveness. I cannot expect the forgiveness from Mrs. Armstrong or her family from taking Joie from them."[12]

After the proceedings, Leslie told the press: "He is devastated. I'm devastated. I ached for him. I ached for me. I ached for everything." However, within that pain, Leslie is also very grateful to Krause for her role in her life and assistance in ensuring that the plea agreement met her needs.

The effort to reach out to victim family members from within the defense team was groundbreaking in many ways, but it was not without institutional and ethical challenges. This work defied both the traditional adversarial criminal justice process where the defense and the victims' interests are pitted against each other and restorative justice models that typically occur outside of the courtroom and are based on accountability rather than retribution and punishment.

While every case is unique and victims can respond to similar situations in very different ways, some common needs were expressed to us by Burr and VOSs Tammy Krause and Pamela Blume Leonard. Victims' families need others to listen to them and acknowledge the loss that they have experienced. Burr explained: "They have an enormous need to tell their story to other people and to talk about who it is that has died. There's just a need for everybody in the process to know their loved one was a good person and to know what pain they're feeling." Family members often want information about how and why a crime happened and specifics about their loved one in the last moments of their lives. This information can often be communicated through the offender to the defense and VOS. Family members need offender accountability, including admitting guilt and acknowledging the loss of their loved one. Although this information can be conveyed in a written letter or through the VOS, Leonard says that some family members may need to have "a face to face and make sure that the person who killed their loved one is aware of how profoundly it hurt them." Some family members, like Leslie, may need to have the option to meet the offender face to face at some point if they choose.

Many family members' needs relate to the criminal justice process. Some families want judicial closure, which can often come from a plea agreement. Judicial closure is very different from the emotional closure that most victims' family members believe they will never find. Krause says:

> To actually have the case legally finished means something huge. One, it means that there's a conviction. That means they're going to feel safe, that this person's not going to be out on the streets, [that] this person has accepted guilt. The second thing that it means [is] they're not going to be harassed by the court, saying, "Oh we have an appeal coming up." They're not going to get these nagging letters that are going to drag them right back to the night their loved one was murdered. The third thing is, when a case is legally over, well, the media goes away. They're not going to open the paper on some random Tuesday morning, and, *wham*, it's not going to be in front of them all the time.

Some family members need information about the legal process and the actions of the defense team. This was apparent in the McVeigh case. For some families, the pressure of the death penalty is a huge burden to them. Krause argues, "There's almost an unspoken rule; your loved one is important enough to get the ultimate sentence. But a family typically, if they are given another option and if they see that the other option can be actively met and directly addresses them, it takes away the weight or pressure of the death penalty. Additionally, it doesn't put any moral weight on whether a person believes or doesn't believe in the death penalty."

Perhaps the most difficult need for restorative justice advocates to handle is that some family members need to see the offender receive the death penalty. Krause explains: "If we continue to maintain a relationship with the victim's family, even if they believe in the death penalty . . . you know, we're respecting them as humans and that's the deepest sense of humanity we can give. It's saying, you know, I might disagree with you . . . but I'm still . . . if you're willing to let me, I will walk with you through this journey."

Though no VOS can guarantee that all the needs of a victim's family members are met, the opportunity for a victim's family member to speak directly to someone whose work is rooted in restorative justice, who has direct access to the defense team and is not part of the adversarial process, opens up the process for many new possibilities. A defense team that knows the needs of the victims may be able to meet them and may also be able to work with the offender to meet his obligations in the process. Offenders' obligations include being held accountable for a crime in the form of admitting guilt, expressing apology, and trying to transform his own future; giving the victim information about the crime and the last moments of their loved one's life; answering other questions about the motivation for the crime; not making statements to the media about the crime; and possibly meeting with the victims' family members. This process is quite new, and empirical studies measuring its success have not yet taken place, but anecdotal evidence shows that the outcomes of cases handled in this manner are satisfactory for all involved parties (offenders, victims' family members, offenders' family members, the legal system, and the community).

Defense-initiated victim outreach only works because it is rooted in restorative justice principles. If it was not, the ethics might become very confusing. Pamela Blume Leonard, a VOS and project director of the Georgia Council for Restorative Justice and a graduate of the Conflict Transformation at Eastern Mennonite University, described the ethics of restorative justice require that the process be "completely voluntary. There are some people who will not want to do this, or they may not want to do it now or at a particular time. But the idea is to try to keep the door open."

The work of the VOS is helping more than individuals like Leslie Armstrong; in some circles, it is reorienting the nature of the adversarial process. Since Burr has been introduced to restorative justice and started using a VOS in some of his cases, he finds that he is "more mindful and sensitive to, and I hope empathetic toward, victims' family members."

He elaborated: "I'm beginning to develop a reflexive sense of wanting to make sure family members of victims know about what is going on. . . . I think, as a defense person, making a genuine and unconditional outreach to family members, it is [a] recognition that we understand what this is all about. And, I think, to begin to take some of the hostility out of the process, I can't say tangibly results in life sentences for my clients, but I think that it might contribute to that." Burr is not alone—there are a number of attorneys who seek a VOS for their cases, and many have learned from Krause, other VOSs, and victims themselves what it means to be a victim and have sought to interact with victims with compassion.

Though there are some prosecutors who are supportive of the VOS, that is not always the case; some prosecutors actively discourage it. Moreover, restorative justice theorists and practitioners have had concerns about the process from the beginning. According to Zehr, there were those who believed that the process would be too offender oriented, a reasonable concern given that the defense pays for this service.

Krause, Burr, and Leonard stress the importance of training for making sure VOS is "done right." For the process to work, the VOS should have extensive training in dealing with individuals suffering from trauma, restorative justice principles, ethics, and a working knowledge of the adversarial model. Additionally, training should include how to reach out to victims' family members in a way that does not produce further harm. Connie Kotzbauer, a victim's mother, explained: "I believe in the defense specialist coming and helping the families. I can see that as a win-win situation for both families, *if* it is done right. I can see no way that a family could be hurt. If it is victim-centered, it has to be victim-centered."[13]

Each of the three experts also mentioned that offenders' family members were occasionally called on to provide information for the defense or for victims' family members, but they lament that no one was playing the role of an outreach specialist for offenders' family members. They agreed that offenders' family members also needed help meeting their needs and responding to the crime, the criminal justice process, and the sentences received by their loved ones.

Victim-Offender Mediation

Restorative justice researchers Mark Umbreit and Betty Vos studied another effort to help bring restorative justice into capital cases by providing victim-offender mediation/dialogue sessions between a surviving family member and the death row inmate.[14] Early work in this area was done by David Doerfler, the state coordinator for the Victim-Offender Mediation/Dialogue (VOMD) Program of the Texas Department of Criminal Justice, Victim Services Unit. This program was not initially designed for capital cases, but was piloted in a small number of these cases. In each of these cases mediation occurred after the formal court process and never influenced the punishment of the offender. The mediation for these sessions was dialogue driven and designed to meet the needs of victim's family members and offenders.

The meetings described in Umbreit and Vos's article and in the book *Facing Violence: The Path of Restorative Justice and Dialogue* were initiated by the victims.[15] Doerfler met several times with the offender and victims' family members to prepare them for the meeting, making sure they knew what they wanted to express, and what emotions might overwhelm them. The authors concluded that the mediation sessions were very powerful and positive experiences for all involved, even though the process itself was very difficult. They use the family members' own words to describe how they felt about the offender after meeting with him. A granddaughter replied: "Before, he was just, you know, a murderer. . . . After, he was a human being." One victim's sister's view of the offender also changed. "I pictured him as just an animal . . . but after meeting with him it was just so hard to." Finally, the victim's mother describes the meeting: "I saw a person and not just the man who murdered my daughter. In no way did this shift toward perceiving the offender as more human make the offender any less accountable."[16] Similarly, the offenders found that the dialogue sessions were helpful. Umbreit and Vos explain, "Each felt that having participated in the mediation made it easier to face his own impending death." Furthermore, both victims' family members and offenders found the process healing.[17]

With the growth of these initial efforts and increasing numbers of violent crime victims, including death penalty crimes, requesting the opportunity for dialogue, the program was expanded to meet their needs. The Texas program, under the guidance of Doerfler and more recently Eddie Mendoza, trains volunteers to assist both victims' family members and offenders through the mediation process. For many of the participants, the preparation for the dialogue is even more important than the dialogue itself, and many individuals drop out of the program before the actual dialogue happens. The VOMD has grown, and although meetings with victims' family members and offenders on death row are still rare, Texas and other states are increasingly providing it as an option.[18]

Survivors' reasons for wanting to meet with the individual who murdered their loved one vary from a desire to meet the offender "eye to eye," to having questions answered about their relative's last moments, to express their pain over their loss, to make the offender personally accountable, and sometimes to offer forgiveness.[19] Similarly, offenders agreed to participate because they wanted to answer questions victims had, apologize and seek forgiveness, and do the right thing for themselves and their religious beliefs.[20] Umbreit and Vos and several of their colleagues sum up the outcomes of the mediation and dialogue sessions they studied as: "Both the family members and the death row offenders who participated in these three meetings were grateful they had the opportunity to do so, and none of them had any regrets. All seven participants were moved beyond their expectations, all were relieved, and all reported significant impact on their healing. And all seven pointed to the same set of components to account for their response: careful, compassionate preparation, gentle and unobtrusive guidance during the session; and above all the opportunity for [a] genuine, human face-to-face encounter which increased, rather than decreased, offender accountability and responsibility."[21]

Victim outreach specialists and the VOMD program recognize that the needs of victims in death penalty cases go beyond the services offered by the typical criminal justice process. By using a restorative justice conception of a crime as harm to individual relationships that creates obligations to help repair that harm, the programs have made great advancements in trying to meet the needs of victims' family members and offenders while at the same time centering the relationship between the two parties around responsibility and accountability.

Forging a Better World Together

Defense-initiated victim outreach and VOMD programs open the door to the potential of blending restorative justice and traditional justice, but they have not specifically targeted offenders' family members. The challenge of the next stage of restorative justice programs is to become more inclusive or to build separate programs that address the needs of offenders' family members. As mentioned at the beginning of this chapter, a restorative justice model in homicide cases does not necessarily mean that all of the groups have to come together at one place but that communication about needs and obligations between groups is necessary. Additionally, more efforts are needed to define the community that is affected by homicide and include these individuals in solutions that heal communities and prevent crime.

One example of bringing the injured parties together to improve communities was described in Rachel King's book about capital offenders' families.[22] In 1995, Tariq Khamisa was gunned down while he was delivering pizza by a young gang member named Tony Hicks. Tariq was a college student with his entire future ahead of him. "Believing that there were 'victims at both ends of the gun,' Azim Khamisa, Tariq's father, reached out in forgiveness to Tony's grandfather and guardian, Ples Felix, to begin the process of healing."[23] Azim also made an effort to meet Tony in prison and continues to exchange letters with him to this day.

Rather than limiting their healing journey to meeting and forgiveness, Azim began a nonprofit organization that reaches out to the larger community to try to curtail youth violence. Both Azim and Ples are actively involved with the Tariq Khamisa Foundation. They travel to elementary schools to offer programs such as the Violence Impact Forum, where they tell the story of Tariq and Tony, including reading a letter written by Tony in prison, discussing the consequences of violence and teaching peacemaking alternatives. In the words of Azim: "I will mourn Tariq's death for the rest of my life. Now, however, my grief has been transformed into a powerful commitment to change."[24]

Sometimes forging a better world begins with forming new relationships. In *Wounds that Do Not Bind: Victim-Based Perspectives on the Death Penalty*, an edited book, David Kaczynski and Gary Wright explore their relationship.[25] The two began their relationship because David's brother, Ted, known as the Unabomber, placed a bomb on a street. Thinking it was a traffic hazard, Gary picked it up, and it exploded. Gary survived the ordeal, although his whole body sustained injury, and he needed multiple surgeries. As a result of the bombing, Gary worried much more about his personal safety. In time, he wrestled with the idea of forgiveness, but it was not until he realized that if Christ could forgive, then he could, too.

Although the Unabomber had injured 29 people and killed 3 through package bombs over several years, it was difficult to get insight into him— that is, until he started publishing his manifestos. Only then did David Kaczynski see the connection between the man who did such horrible things and his own mentally ill, reclusive brother. David and his mother followed their own consciences and contacted the FBI with information about Ted that led to his apprehension. They negotiated with the FBI so that Ted did not face the death penalty in his trial, and Ted was convicted for his crimes and is now serving life in prison without the possibility of parole.

David and his wife, Linda, wanted to let Ted's victims and their families know how sorry they were for their pain and that David's working against the death penalty was not meant to minimize his brother's actions. David was not able to get an address for Gary, but he did have a phone number, so he asked a friend to call Gary and ask if David might give him a call on behalf of the Kaczynski family. Gary agreed. David called him, and Gary made it clear to David that he "could not bear the burden of his brother's actions." This meant everything to David and his family—to be told by this man who was so harmed by his brother that he was a good guy. The two have since developed a friendship.[26]

Gary and David now refer to their relationship as "bridge building." Gary explains this bridge "connects two families that are looking across a great abyss and feel isolated from one another and helpless or uncomfortable to offer any assistance or consolation."[27] For Gary, their relationship has meant healing as it allowed him to "humanize the event and understand things that I otherwise would not have known."[28] He is grateful for the support that he and David have provided each other and grateful to have "been blessed with the gift of friendship."[29]

Summary

In the past, especially in the United States, the application of restorative justice has been limited primarily to property offenses or violent crimes with only minor injuries. The majority of these programs have focused on juvenile offenders. What we are now witnessing is the opening up of both the theory and practices of restorative justice to explore new ground. Applying restorative justice to murder cases in general and death penalty cases in particular presents some daunting challenges, including

- keeping the needs of the victims' family members central to the entire process,
- including offenders' family members and their needs in the process,
- developing services and programs that allow restorative justice to operate in conjunction with a retributive justice system, and
- defining and including community in the process.

The programs discussed in this chapter are in their infancy, but they are beginning to meet some of these challenges. VOSs work on behalf of victims' family members to make sure that they have an open line of communication with the defense if they so desire it. Additionally, these individuals allow victims' family members to tell their stories in a safe environment and provide emotional support and needed information about the criminal justice system. In the next chapter we propose that a similar role be created for offenders' family members.

VOMD has taken promising steps toward actualizing restorative justice dialogue sessions within the traditional criminal justice system. In death penalty cases, these conferences have given victims a chance to talk with the offenders in their loved one's case before execution. This process has stimulated healing on the part of both victims' family members and offenders, although many still argue that the death penalty may overshadow some of these interactions because the execution does not allow the offender to live his accountability by becoming a better person.[30] The death penalty also creates another round of victims' family members because the offenders' family members suffer the loss of their loved ones.

Azim Khamisa, Ples Felix, and Tony Hicks have all tackled tremendously difficult emotions that come with murder by using restorative justice. Together, they honor the memory of Tariq Khamisa by serving the community and trying to prevent other young boys like Tony from getting involved with crime. When Azim graciously understood that Ples (the grandfather and guardian of Tony Hicks) was suffering from the crime, it allowed them to join forces and work for community justice—something that was missing in the criminal justice system. Similarly, David Kaczynski and Gary Wright have bonded and transformed their awkward connection based on violent crime into a healing friendship.

The many stories in this book demonstrate the need to expand the restorative justice umbrella to encompass the needs of offenders' family members, especially in death penalty cases when they, too, suffer the loss of a loved one's life. The work of VOSs, VOMD, and individual victim's and offender's family members demonstrates that the current criminal justice system underestimates the humanity of all parties involved in the death penalty process and that restorative justice may help us rectify this deficiency. The next chapter explores how restorative justice may play a role in repairing community institutions and building social capital among community members to help reduce future crime.

11

Systems Failure

Ken and Lois Robison described their home life as average. It revolved around things like Sunday school, Boy Scouts, and family time. Lois taught third grade, and Ken was a Spanish teacher. Their son, Larry, played Little League. But all that changed when Larry turned 12 and his behavior became bizarre. He disrupted class. His grades dropped. He collected strange objects—lots of pencils and staplers. Things deteriorated even further in high school when he began running away from home, suffering bouts of irrational fear, and hearing voices.[1]

After high school Larry joined the U.S. Air Force. He was discharged from the Air Force after only 1 year because of his frightening behavior. He thought people were able to read his mind and wanted to hurt him. He also said that he could read other people's minds. Lois and Ken took their son to the emergency room, where he was diagnosed as a paranoid schizophrenic and hospitalized. Lois explained that at the hospital, "They told us that he was paranoid schizophrenic, one of the worst that they had ever seen, and that he needed long-term treatment. Then they asked us who our insurance was with. When we told them that Larry had just turned 21, our insurance did not cover him, and he did not have any on his job, they discharged him. We were advised to take him to the county hospital."[2]

At a hospital in Fort Worth, Larry was admitted for inpatient care, but "after 30 days of treatment he was discharged because he was 'not violent' and they 'needed the bed.' We were told that we should not take him home under any circumstances," wrote Lois in a letter to the Texas Parole Board.[3] But Lois and Ken did take Larry home. In preparation, they asked his doctors a number of questions about his medications and how to handle his bizarre behavior, but they did not receive helpful answers. After Larry's discharge from the county hospital and his subsequent deterioration, Lois and Ken brought Larry to the VA Hospital in Waco. He was again admitted and kept for 30 days; on the 31st day he was discharged and placed on a bus headed home. For 6 weeks no treatment was available because the hospital administration had neglected to sign his release. All the while his condition worsened, and he ended up in jail, having stolen a truck from a car lot. Lois and Ken begged the district attorney to have Larry committed, but he served his time and was released. From that day on, Lois and Ken devoted their time to trying to get help for Larry. Unfortunately his illness escalated to the point where the voices in his head told him to kill to protect the ones he loved, and he brutally murdered five people. He began with his friend Ricky Bryant, who he decapitated and sexually mutilated. Then he went next door and killed neighbor Georgia Reed and her son and mother. When Bruce Gardener came to the door to pick up Georgia for a date, Larry also killed him.[4] Ken and Lois fought to save Larry's life prior to his execution and have always wondered what else they could have done to save his victims' lives and the life of their son.

"If only we were able to get him the help that he needed. If only we had the help that we needed to be better parents." Families echo this refrain as they berate the system and themselves for their inability to control or resolve the problems that escalated in their loved ones' lives. In virtually every family we interviewed, someone tried to get help for their loved one, but many were lost in a maze of systems purportedly designed to promote health, safety, mental health, education, justice, faith, economic self-sufficiency, equity, and general well-being. Once support was found, it was woefully inadequate and destructive in some cases, as we will see. Because one of its major components is accountability, restorative justice provides insights for improving inadequate social systems.

Throughout this book we stress the importance of offender accountability and the need to encourage offenders to accept responsibility. William Moore demonstrated this by clearly owning up to murder and expressing guilt and shame. He spoke of his remorse and apologized to the victims' family members, as well as to the criminal justice system and the community. Presently he lives each day trying to meet the obligations he incurred from his actions and to help other offenders and victims.

In this chapter we will look at ways to develop community accountability as suggested by restorative justice theorists Dennis Sullivan and Larry Tifft, who argue that restorative justice's belief in needs and obligations goes beyond interactions between individuals to interaction between individuals and their communities.[5] Using the 14 psychosocial histories we analyzed (see Table 3.2 for a review of these cases), we consider how systems failure can lead to violence and how restorative justice can be used to address community needs and obligations related to violent crime. The refrain *if only* is used to indicate that these failures are not destined to be repeated. We recommend specific ways that institutions can be improved. We also suggest several examples of innovative restorative justice programs that address systems failure. By starting this chapter with an overview of published studies, we link social environments and social systems to individual development, specifically involvement in violent crime. From there we highlight the numerous systems that shape the if only statements of offenders' family members and suggest ways institutions can improve past practice.

The Social Environment

Multiple community systems—such as school, child welfare, juvenile justice, and mental health—touch our lives. Each of us lives in a constantly evolving social environment comprising both affirming and threatening forces embedded in our family, social network, neighborhood, broader community, and society.[6] A social environment includes informal social forces, such as networks of people who live, work, and play near our family and with whom we socially interact, as well as formal social systems that may directly influence an individual's, child's, or family's life. The most universal formal systems are schools and health care services; others include alcohol and drug treatment services, economic assistance programs such as public assistance (e.g., Aid for Families with Dependent Children, Temporary Assistance for Needy Families [TANF], and food stamp programs) and emergency assistance (e.g., from private agencies that provide food, shelter, clothing, payment of utility bills, recreational programs, and enrichment programs, such as music, arts, or drama), and religious organizations and faith communities.

A child's development is also affected by broader social forces that are typically expressed through laws, norms, and customs in a community, which can be helpful in many instances, but there are also times when these laws, norms, and customs are expressed in hurtful ways. For example, racial and ethnic bias can be manifested as housing discrimination, unequal school funding, inequitable employment, and income and health status disparities. Federal economic policies may lead to industry closings that trigger the demise of large communities. Zero-tolerance behavioral discipline policies may lead to children being excluded from school. Generalized homophobia can cause gay, lesbian, bisexual, and transgendered youth to be marginalized. Sexism can harm a girl's self-efficacy, impair her ability to deter exploitation, induce hypermasculinity in boys, and provide tacit support of men's violence against women. The social forces of stigma and norms of self-reliance can cause parents to avoid seeking help for their own problems as well as those of their children.

Starting at an early age, people learn to relate to others through interaction with their family and their family's social environment. To the extent that social environments nurture and support a child, the child will learn self-worth, competence, and trust. If the environment is hostile or confusing, the child will learn behaviors such as withdrawal or aggression, behaviors that may be harmful to themselves or others.

All of the defendants in this book had some contact with systems that were designed to promote positive development. Though aspects of the systems did meet some needs, they were also riddled with problems—problems that let people down and may have ultimately meant the difference between life and death. Public health researchers Freedman and Hemenway found similar system failure in their review of 15 death row inmates, observing that in all cases, overwhelming evidence showed that schools, juvenile programs, medical and psychiatric services, and other systems failed to recognize and remediate the children's needs or provide equal access to services.[7]

When children come into contact with systems that fail them, they learn and remember an unfortunate lesson: that the system causes harm and should be avoided. Thus when stressors mount, they are unlikely to look for outside assistance. In every case reviewed in our research, the crime was committed while the defendant was going through a period of intense emotional distress and alienation; when a disturbed person perceives no sources of support he or she is at risk of impulsive and irrational behavior.

When family members sought assistance and received little or none, they also learned hard lessons. They felt isolated and frustrated, and they also began to distrust social service systems. Offenders' family members could not get over the irony of the government's paucity of help when it came to social services, especially for their mentally ill loved ones, and later its abundance of resources and energy to pursue an execution. They perceived the government's behavior as bizarre and inhumane.

Tommy provides a potent example of systems failure as he had contact with the local department of social services, department of juvenile justice, area mental health center, schools, family court, and local law enforcement officials. All of these entities were aware of Tommy's family difficulties, but none effectively intervened to protect him or the people he hurt.

According to Tommy's aunts, his mother, Deborah, never really wanted him; they say she beat him regularly from the time he was only a few weeks old. Family members routinely saw Tommy with bruises and welts as he grew up. Deborah's abuse also included calling him degrading names and threatening his life. On many occasions, Tommy feared that his mother would kill him. He did not know it then, but his mother had untreated borderline personality disorder and an addiction to alcohol and cocaine. Deborah had grown up in an unsafe home, and her father had also been impulsive and threatening.

Not wanting to be a full-time parent, Deborah often pawned Tommy off so that his home base floated among his mother's, father's, and maternal grandmother's homes. Between the moves, his needs were consistently overlooked by personnel from community agencies involved in his life. Once when his mother fired a gun at him, the mental health center focused on his resistant adolescent behavior instead of his mother's violence. When he was 10, a family court judge asked him which parent he wanted to live with, and Tommy chose his father. The court inexplicably placed him with his mother, and the beatings escalated. In 1983, after his mother attacked him with a baseball bat and he reciprocated with violence, law enforcement authorities and the court took action against him but not her. Naturally, Tommy was confused and enraged by what he interpreted as official support for his mother's abuse. Consequently, he never learned to develop appropriate standards of behavior.

Tommy perceived that no one was available to help him. He believed that the school officials regarded him only as a problem after some of the teachers made a point of reminding him that his parents had also been troublemakers. Both of his parents had dropped out of school and derided the value of education. Under such circumstances, it is not surprising that Tommy never thought to ask for help at school. He particularly distrusted personnel from community agencies like law enforcement because he believed that his mother had influence over them through her sexual and social relations.

Perhaps what is most tragic about Tommy's case was that there had been sporadic moments when he had some support in his life and did well, these include when his grandfather was alive, at a Department of Juvenile Justice group home, with a foster family, and during visits to his adult cousin Rose's home. During these times Tommy's behavior was positive and appropriate; he responded well to support, guidance, and structure, suggesting that if he had been given consistent care, his victims might very well be alive today.

Types of Systems Failure

Child Protective Services

If only . . . Child Protective Services really did listen to and protect children.
If only . . . abused and neglected children received mental health treatment and support.

Many of the offender's families desperately needed help from Child Protective Services (CPS). In five cases CPS was contacted by a neighbor or teacher, and they did intervene. But in each case, the intervention was completely ineffective in protecting the child from further harm. For example, in two cases, the child welfare system arranged residential care for the children because of neglect. But the children were subsequently subjected to abuse in foster care. In four cases of physical abuse, no one ever sought help from CPS or law enforcement resources. In several cases, CPS workers went to the home, but a file was never opened. This happened to Jonathan, whose father stripped him naked and beat him 50 times with a leather thong. When CPS went to Jonathan's house, his mother denied the father was abusive, and his father explained to the case worker that they were having a hard time.

In two other examples, the cases of Arnold and Garth, the CPS investigations into their lives went further, but the boys never got the help they desperately needed. Arnold's parents fought several times a week and beat the children with belts and switches. Police came when neighbors reported domestic disturbances, but they usually left after talking to the parents. A couple of times Arnold's mother took the children to a battered women's shelter. CPS once came to the home on a day when the parents were relatively sober and the house had been put in order. The investigators observed that in spite of the family's poverty, there was food in the refrigerator. Both parents denied hitting the children, and the children did not dare disagree. The family was given information about how to get emergency food and other material help, which Arnold's mother took advantage of. Because everything seemed to be normal, the CPS worker violated protocol and did not interview neighbors or talk to the children away from their parents. Ultimately CPS determined that abuse did not occur and the case was unfounded.

Garth's father also beat his children regularly, but his abuse went further—he also repeatedly raped his daughter. Garth's father still laughs sarcastically about the social worker who came to his home to see about the children. He would not let her in the front door. He quoted the Bible to her and told her that when his children gave him trouble God expected him to discipline them. In his mind, that was not abusive. He asked her to pray with him. This case was also deemed unfounded.

A lack of follow-up by CPS in Alfred and Yvette's cases ensured that they were never safe. Alfred's father beat him, neglected him, and forced him to have sex with his cousin. CPS opened a case on him four different times, finding that Alfred was neglected by his father at age 4, physically abused at age 7, neglected at age 8, and sexually abused at age 10. Each time they placed him with a family member and monitored the case for a few months. Each time they closed the case, and the family member with custody promptly returned Alfred to his father. CPS did not know that Alfred was returned to his father or about the additional abuse that continued between open cases. CPS also did not know that he was exposed to domestic violence, even though there were numerous police records based on calls from his father's partners. Furthermore, every time a CPS worker saw Alfred, it was a new individual who was not familiar with the previous referrals in his case. His family hated meddling by the government and taught him never to trust the police or CPS workers because they were the enemy.

Yvette's parents separated when she was 4 years old, and several times following the separation her father came to her house waving a gun and threatening to kill her mother and himself. Police came to calm him down and take him back to his place, but they never suggested that the mother should get help for her child who was exposed to these traumatic events repeatedly. Even after her father came to her mother's house raving mad one day and then went home and killed himself, no one encouraged the family to get help for Yvette.

However, after her mother remarried CPS came right away and took the case to family court when Yvette told her school counselor that her stepfather was sexually molesting her. Her stepfather was a local politician who had helped get the local prosecutor elected, so he met with the prosecutor and asked for time for the family to work out their problems, promising that they would get help. They did go to a counselor, who was inept at treating sexual abuse and regarded the problem as a family issue. This counselor met with the stepfather, mother, and Yvette as a group, thus violating standards of practice for sexual abuse treatment. Yvette denied having problems because her stepfather was in the room. Therefore, after only a few sessions the counselor closed the case. By then, the sexual assaults had resumed.

Before Yvette disclosed the abuse at age 13, she was struggling with depression, anxiety, solitude, and conflict with her mother, and she felt unloved. After the shame of disclosure and ineffectual treatment, she found comfort in her sexual relationship with her stepfather. She was honored to feel loved by him, and he taught her to keep that part of her life secret, a response that is not uncommon for victims of child abuse. Yvette learned that disclosure of the secret risked public humiliation and criticism from her mother. She continued to feel miserable in her private life and to lead the external life of a wholesome, obedient high school student. She never tried to get help again.

The effects of sexual abuse are not limited to the individual who has been raped. Recall Garth's father, who asked the CPS worker to pray with him. Every night for 5 years, Garth's father crept into his daughter's bedroom. He went so far as to install a door in the closet wall between the bedroom he shared with his wife and his daughter's room. The other children in the house were aware something was happening, and as they entered their teen years, they understood what it was. Meanwhile, his father often preached about the sin of sex and accused his sons of masturbating and his wife of having affairs. Thus Garth's childhood environment was atypically sexualized, characterized by premature and frequent exposure to sexual activity, pervasive communications about sexuality, and forced sexual contact between younger and older persons. He chronically witnessed his father's sexual obsession with his sister and was himself the victim of sexual abuse from his uncles, cousins, and male neighbors. He became quite promiscuous; while using both drugs and alcohol, after a fight with a male partner, he raped and killed a female custodian who was cleaning the house next door.

The children in these families needed protection. They needed help dealing with the emotional and mental impact of the abuse. Their stories tell of child protection systems that failed to thoroughly assess risk and to follow through to monitor outcomes. If the CPS workers had checked collateral contacts (such as teachers, neighbors, and extended family in the cases of Arnold, Garth, and Jonathan) and followed these cases long enough to make a more accurate determination of abuse, perhaps the children would have been protected physically and mentally. Alfred needed a single CPS worker with a systematic approach to his case. Given the chaos in his life, a consistent CPS worker may have provided some stability and a perspective that might have mitigated the harm being done by the turbulence in his home. Perhaps Yvette's mental health would not have deteriorated and she may not have committed murder if her therapist had followed professional standards for effective sexual abuse treatment.

In addition to not providing support, as was the case for Garth and Jonathan, too often child protection programs and law enforcement agencies fail to work together, as illustrated by Arnold, Yvette, and Alfred—so that the harmful effects of exposure to domestic violence are not identified and therefore not addressed. In most states, CPS workers have caseloads that are too large to provide effective services, and the training that workers are given is often inadequate.[8] States need to make effective functioning of CPS a priority. This means employing an adequate number of workers who are well-trained and compensated for a professional service.

Interpersonal Violence Services

If only . . . abusers were held accountable for their actions and victims were supported in getting help.

If only . . . adults and children found to be abused or neglected received effective treatment.

If only . . . policies and practices that supported women's equal status were fully adopted.

Only one of seven battered mothers from our sample sought help from interpersonal violence programs. Some of the defendants, however, grew up before the 1980s, when community action to address domestic violence had not yet evolved. Consequently, shelters and other domestic violence services were not widely available. Moreover, until recently, interpersonal violence was something to be ashamed of and hidden, making some women too embarrassed to admit a problem. In several cases, the mothers did call for law enforcement protection, but the police typically asked the abuser to calm down and took no assertive action.

Much has been done to address the needs of battered women and make public the issue of interpersonal violence. Today police officers are trained to address domestic abuse, and emergency rooms and other community-based services provide referrals and outreach. Programs for battered women provide for such needs as safety and job training. Additionally, offending men are often remanded to batterer intervention programs that have had varying degrees of success.[9]

Battering often occurs within a context of rigid gender roles. Each of the two female defendants developed a dependent personality disorder as a means to buffer the exploitation she was experiencing. Several of the male defendants tried to be patriarchal men as a way to reduce their feelings of powerlessness and low self-worth.

Garth's parents provide an example of a dependent mother and domineering father with rigid gender role expectations. Franklin's view toward his wife, Helen, was patriarchal: "She began to disappoint me 1 week after we were married. She cussed, smoked, and didn't keep the house clean like a woman should." Franklin married Helen when she was 16 years old and trying to escape her abusive home. Helen's mother died when she was a young girl, and she was raised by her father. She and her sister did all the housework on the farm while the men, her father and brothers, hung around. Helen said Franklin was just like her father: "It was his way or no way." She knew Franklin was hurting the children and that her brothers had sexually abused Garth, but given her history she felt helpless to stop the men in her family from doing such things. For her mistakes, she believes "I should be the one on death row."

Research shows that girls abused as children are often victims of domestic violence in their adult relationships, as several of these defendants' mothers can attest.[10] We located details about the mothers in 13 of the 14 cases we reviewed; in 8 of the 13 cases, the defendants' mothers started bearing children while they were still teenagers. Two of the women bore children by their own fathers. These babies were placed for adoption, and the mothers received no treatment for the incest that occurred and no postadoptive support. Seven of the defendants' mothers attempted to escape chaotic families by leaving school and getting married or moving in with a boyfriend before age 18. When interviewed, the mothers generally explained that they thought setting up a home of their own would give them relief from past agonies. All too soon realized they were wrong. They had replaced the misery of one home with that of another.

Just as abuse produces victims, it also produces more abusers. Boys who have been abused are more likely than those who have not to grow up to be abusive men.[11] This was the case for Jonathan's father, Daniel, who was raised in a strict home that demanded obedience at all costs. When Daniel was at home, the entire tone of the household changed; everyone stayed quiet and alert to his expectations. From an early age, Jonathan had a hard time meeting his father's expectations, and he suffered the consequences. Daniel beat him severely for minor offenses and once set the pants Jonathan was wearing on fire.

Jonathan's father needed to be placed in a batterer's intervention program, but he also needed to understand positive parenting and address the pain of his own abuse as a child. Boys should learn through educational programs at all age levels that violence in the home is not appropriate and that feelings of frustration or depression can be managed in other ways.

Society did nothing to hold Jonathan's father accountable for his actions, and this inaction may have planted the seeds of a capital murder long before the crime actually occurred. Helping batterers and their victims through programs that recognize each of their needs while working on issues of accountability is integral to preventing future generations from becoming involved in violent crime. Jonathan and other children might have prospered from a restorative justice response that would have sought accountability on the part of the abusing parent and services for the victims.

Currently many advocates and experts in interpersonal violence view it as a human rights issue. The connection between human rights and safety will never be realized as long as oppression exists and gender determines one's worth, along with other attributes such as race. The institution of sexism, however, remains and gives permission for men to belittle, berate, and batter women. To ensure women's safety, all practices that degrade and undervalue women must end, and boys should be taught how to address their feelings in productive ways.

Mental Health Treatment

If only . . . mental health treatment provided the type, length, and quality of care needed by all mentally ill individuals.

If only . . . mental health treatment were accessible, stigma free, effective, family focused, and culturally competent.

As we saw in Larry Robison's story, mental health problems are often prevalent among offenders and their families. Retrospective interviews with various family members reveal symptoms of mental disorders that went undiagnosed in many cases. In the few instances where family members or the defendant did get services for mental health conditions, the services were highly ineffectual, particularly for trauma-related problems.

Darius, who we met in chapter 3, as well as Martha and Yvette illustrate what can happen when inadequate mental health services are provided. After the accident that killed his friends, Darius's uncle took him to the mental health center. He saw the center's psychiatrist, who told him that he had the devil in him and should go to church. The psychiatrist refused to see him again, saying that Darius had a drinking problem. Darius's PTSD went undiagnosed and untreated.

Martha, who at the age of 50 killed her husband with poison, experienced ineffectual mental health services. Although she had a long history of mental health problems, she did not get help until about 6 years before the crime, and then the clinicians underestimated the intensity of her symptoms. Martha had rigid expectations for herself and others, avoided conflict and anger, worked to the point of exhaustion, and required order and control in her environment. She regarded men as powerful, mis-trusted them, anticipated their moral code violations, and expected to be disappointed by them. She also expected women to be inadequate. Martha dreaded feeling humiliated or ashamed and spent a large part of her life pretending to be happy. Her compulsion to repress her emotions had apparently contributed to numerous stress-related physical ailments, including chronic incontinence and diarrhea, sleep disturbances, headaches, asthma, and exhaustion. Research and clinical mental health studies document that all the symptoms exhibited by Martha are commonly found in adult survivors of unresolved, untreated, severe childhood trauma, yet no one ever treated her for trauma.[12] While she was in treatment for her depression, she slowly murdered her husband by serving poison to him.

Yvette's disastrous experience with unethical therapy following her father's molestation of her ensured that she would never seek help again. Help might have made a difference for Yvette. Two months before the crime, which involved killing her children, Yvette was in the process of divorce, and during this time the accumulated stressors in her life and her maladaptive compulsions increased. In the 10 days before the crime she cried continually, displayed classic trauma symptoms, could never be truly calm, and sank deeper into depression. Overwhelmed by fear and a sense of doom, her earlier encounter with therapy prohibited any consideration of help.

Only three defendants received help from providers who seemed to diagnose the problem accurately and recommended a treatment plan. Donnie's needs, however, were so severe that the treatment he required was not possible in his home. Donnie was adopted at the age of 4 months after being almost starved to death by his birth parents. By elementary school, psychiatrists at a large facility diagnosed him with organic brain damage that led to severe behavioral problems. Donnie tried in vain to control his impulsive behavioral outbursts. His teachers and mental health consultants diligently tried to affirm his positive abilities, but they were stumped by the persistence of his problems. Maintaining a consistent and positive environment was much more difficult for Donnie's parents because his mother was an alcoholic and his father worked long hours and had heart disease. Instead of working with Donnie, his parents set strict expectations for him; when he did not meet their expectations, they punished him with beatings.

The mental health experts in Donnie's life recognized the problem he faced: that his brain damage affected his emotional and behavioral control. But the adults around him in his daily life could not seem to give him the support he needed to adapt positively to the condition. Donnie's community did not have what he needed, which was a good wraparound course of treatment, one that would involve coordinated planning and case management to ensure that he had psychologically available caregiving, hour by hour, with plenty of attention and consistent behavioral reinforcements from adults with primary responsibility for his care. Instead he faced shifting environments, changing teachers, psychologically unavailable parents, solitude, and punishments.

Another prevailing issue with respect to seeking mental health help is the family's inability to recognize symptoms of major mental illness, which we consider in the following brief examples. In Jamal's case, he was hearing voices that his parents believed were spiritual messages from angels and demons, when in fact he had schizophrenia. Darius's family had never heard of PTSD. Martha's family thought she was quiet, not depressed. Graham had been dissociating, seeing things, and hearing voices since he used to hide naked in the woods after his father's beatings. His family just let him keep to himself and live a vagrant life because seeking mental health assistance did not seem to be an option in their rural community. In other cases, family members minimized distress. This was certainly the case for Yvette's family, who never addressed her father's suicide or her stepfather's molestation of her.

Intensive care is not available to many who need it, and as a result prisons and jails have become the halfway houses, psychiatric facilities, community-based care, and housing that so many people need. Communities should reassess the way they allocate resources and focus much needed attention on appropriate and supportive mental health care and away from primarily punitive responses to crime.

The U.S. Center of Mental Health Services of the Department of Health and Human Services has initiated a major antistigma campaign so that families and the general public will not feel shame or experience stigma from receiving mental health services. They also seek to educate the general public and health practitioners about signs of mental disorders, just as they have general information about early warning signs of heart disease or cancer. Had this been in effect earlier, there might have been help for Jamal. Additional initiatives are needed to create systems so that families have information and support for their children as they deal with major life transitions and losses. Moreover, therapists need to understand more fully the effects of trauma and identify its symptoms, and research needs to begin to find its antidotes.

Alcohol and Drug Treatment

If only . . . families had access to effective alcohol and drug abuse prevention and treatment resources.

If only . . . prenatal maternal health screening detected potential fetal alcohol or drug exposure and led to effective treatment.

If only . . . alcohol and drug treatment programs focused on the entire family to help children actually recover from the effects of parental alcohol and other drug abuse.

Alcohol and drug abuse appear like ripe apples all over the family trees of most capital defendants. The defendants in 12 of our 14 cases had at least one and usually several family members who were addicted to alcohol and involved in their direct care as children. Of the two who were not so directly exposed, one was raised in an institution because his mother was raped by an alcoholic foster father, and the other one was raised in a fundamentalist family with a sexually and physically abusive father who had himself been raised by an alcoholic. The defendant from the latter family became addicted. The chemical addiction had skipped his father's generation, though psychological maladaptations were manifest in other ways. Such intergenerational effects are profound among the family members; in 10 of the 14 cases, the defendant was heavily under the influence of a chemical substance at the time of the crime.

In all cases, the families seemed never to seek professional help for the substance abusers; however, some short-term interventions occurred—after trouble with the law, usually traffic violations or property crimes. In some cases, the substance use was tolerated, if not approved, and the problems in behavior were attributed to other causes, such as a temper or justified provocation. Even though research-based information exists about how substance abuse can affect family dynamics through multiple generations, none of the families received education that might have motivated them to seek help. Often someone in each family knew it was a problem but seemed at a loss about what to do.

Most families expected men to drink but were less tolerant of women's drinking. A mother's addiction during pregnancy can have both early and long-term effects, as was the case with Arnold, whose mother drank daily while pregnant with him. Though his birth seemed normal, he developed signs of fetal alcohol syndrome at an early age, including problems with behavior management and cognitive processing. Arnold's father was also an alcoholic, so he and his siblings were raised by parents who were almost constantly intoxicated or hung over. They provided little discipline or supervision. Not unexpectedly, the children developed drinking habits themselves; Arnold, one of the youngest children in his family, followed his older brothers' lead and started drinking at age 9 and stealing to help support himself.

From an early age, Arnold showed signs of problems in social functioning related to unresolved family issues and the drinking within his family, including many symptoms of fetal alcohol effects:

- learning disability, educational failure, difficulty with abstract reasoning;
- impaired ability to express himself, including stuttering;
- emotional problems, anxiety and depression, attempted suicide, insecure attachment, yearning for family, and dependency on others;
- yearning for attention manifested often as physical ailments and seeking attention from health professionals;
- behavior disorder, identification as different from others, resistance to authority;
- disrespect for personal property, chronic stealing and lying to get money or material goods;
- absence of vocational ambition, living day by day;
- social isolation and impaired ability to form intimate relationships;
- promiscuous sexual relations;
- heavy alcohol and drug abuse and addiction;
- premature autonomy and transition to adult-like roles; and
- perpetrating abuse in domestic relationships, especially when under the influence of alcohol or drugs.

Arnold's school placed him in special classes for children with emotional disorders, and teachers noticed that his parents smelled of alcohol, but no one sought sustained help for the child's exposure to alcohol abuse. CPS workers came, but they did not find severe abuse or neglect and did not insist that the parents get help for their addictions. Their letter carrier seemed genuinely concerned for the children and would sometimes come by and take them on outings. Otherwise, neighbors and formal systems employees seemed to think that the parents were drunks and disorderly but the children were managing fine. They were oblivious to the way exposure to such chronic alcohol use can damage a child.

In cases like Arnold's, CPS should have sought a court order seeking involuntary treatment of the parents for the sake of the children. In an effective system, Arnold and his siblings would receive support while their parents were in long-term treatment and recovery so that they would be less at risk of developing addictions themselves.

Schools

If only . . . schools at all levels, preschool through high school, provided quality education and support for special education needs.

If only . . . schools could effectively work with families for the sake of their children's education.

If only . . . schools paid attention to underachievers who are not overt troublemakers—the quiet ones, the loners.

All of the defendants for whom school records exist had learning, emotional, or behavioral problems recorded in their school files. In most cases, the problems emerged in the elementary years. Ten of the defendants dropped out before graduating from high school. Nine of the male defendants displayed what are clear signs of attention hyperactivity deficit disorder that affected their ability to concentrate and master school material. In two cases, the school handled the hyperactivity by sending home notes to parents or asking for parent meetings, which usually resulted in the child being severely beaten. Martha was the only defendant in this sample who performed at or above her potential at school.

Only one defendant was identified as having mental retardation, although several tested low on measures of intelligence. Most of the defendants were placed for some period of their education in special education classes for children with emotional and behavioral problems. Alfred's school found him to be compliant but a poor learner. Tommy's school records suggest the teachers just thought he was lazy. Martin was educated in an institution for people with retardation.

Several defendants changed schools often during their upbringing because their families kept relocating. Several had poor attendance records related to neglect or chaos at home, resulting in poor school performance. When interviewed, teachers and school officials often say they did what they could while the child was in the classroom, but they could do little to affect his or her life outside of school. Twelve of the defendants' had very poor school attendance. The schools did not work with the parents to determine the reason that the children were absent. Further, parents and teachers blamed the children for poor performance, and the children were left unassisted.

Research about child development has established that children's perception of their success in school significantly affects their self-confidence, emotional well-being, and behavior. Educational ideology promotes helping each child feel successful in some way. Unfortunately, the ideology often fails to get translated into concrete intervention in a child's educational settings. Even when academic instruction is tailored to a child's needs, his or her emotional problems interfere with learning. The current trend is for mental health services to be provided in school settings, but such programs were unavailable at the time these defendants were in school.

Many of the offenders might have developed differently if their parents had been encouraged to support their education and been taught specific skills about how to help them succeed in school. At the same time, schools need to ensure that all children are learning. School personnel should look out for mental health problems in students, which might have helped lonely children like Alfred, Jonathan, Yvette, Tommy, Arnold, and Garth. There should be programs in schools that support interaction with family members and school social workers to conduct home visits and assist families.

Juvenile Justice

If only . . . juvenile justice systems offered restorative assistance rather than punishment.

If only . . . early intervention by juvenile justice systems would promote the youth's acquisition of prosocial skills.

Eight of the 14 defendants were in trouble with the law before they turned 18, mostly for nonviolent offenses such as theft and truancy. These defendants did not get into legal trouble until they were suspended or expelled from school, typically for minor infractions such as shoving another student or talking back to the teacher. Given that most of them had hyperactivity attention deficit disorder, they also exhibited oppositional behavioral incidents at school, such as talking back to teachers or fighting with other students. By the time they dropped out, usually about ninth grade or age 14, they were failing and generally unhappy at school. Once out of school, their communities had no juvenile crime prevention programs so they hung out with other kids who were also suspended or expelled from school, as well as older youth. Their use of alcohol and drugs escalated, as did their involvement in petty crime, always with peers.

Six of the eight defendants adjudicated as juveniles were ordered by juvenile court to spend several months to over a year in residential treatment centers with schools, and three completed their GED this way. Each of the defendants tends to recall these periods with fondness, appreciating the predictability of the center's schedule and the sense of accomplishment he or she achieved. None of the programs adequately addressed and treated their mental health behaviors and substance abuse, and none of the programs had follow-through to help the youth adapt to the less predictable environments in their homes and communities, and none of the defendants seemed to have a consistent youth worker or counselor who tried to help guide them.

Of course, to effectively deter children and youth from delinquency, the juvenile justice, child welfare, and mental health systems need to collaborate with the child's family and schools. Often this does not occur, as we saw in Tommy's case. Too many juvenile justice programs focus on punishment at the expense of addressing underlying issues that lead to crime. If only juvenile justice authorities had handled these interventions using restorative justice, Tommy's needs and his family issues might have been revealed, and agencies could have worked together to meet them. Furthermore, a reparations plan would have helped Tommy learn that he is accountable for his own actions and to recognize the harm to others that his actions produced.

The juvenile justice system represents an opportunity for society to respond to troubled youth in a way that prevents future harm, rather than aggravates it. Focusing attention on why children are committing crimes and providing them with needed services, teaching them accountability and responsibility, self-respect, and awareness of how their actions hurt their victims and others would do much to reduce future crime.

Faith Communities

If only . . . faith communities stopped turning a blind eye to family violence and held offenders accountable.

If only . . . faith communities had more effective interventions to help family members cope with their own severe problems.

If only . . . faith communities could reach out to children who have been religiously abused.

Information is available about the faith community involvement of 12 of the 14 defendants. Each was raised in a family system that had some members who actively attended a Christian church; one was Roman Catholic, the others were various Protestant denominations. Of the 12, five can be considered to have suffered religious abuse.

Garth's father was a self-appointed preacher in a Pentecostal Holiness church, who lined up his family every night and read to them from the Bible for over an hour. If one of them grew sleepy or acted disinterested, he beat them all with a belt. Then after bedtime, he crawled into his daughter's bed and raped her. The family was in church "every time the doors opened," with bruises and welts showing. Helen, Garth's mother, once went to the deacons to seek help, so they reprimanded her husband, but the abuse continued. After his daughter could no longer tolerate the sexual abuse and called the police, the church removed him from a preaching role. Soon thereafter, Garth's father stood before the congregation and confessed his sin, saying that he loved his daughter so much he had shown it in ways that were wrong; he asked their forgiveness, and they gave it. He no longer was a preacher but remained an active church member. He resumed sexual abuse of his daughter, using enticements and coercion rather than physical force.

Yvette's stepfather was an active member of a local congregation of a mainstream protestant denomination and president of his local Christian Coalition. He sexually molested Yvette, and after she did not get support when she reported the crime, she assented to the rape and convinced herself it was okay because she thought of her stepfather as a righteous man.

Martha's father became one of her victims, and the moral inconsistencies and religious abuse in her upbringing help explain her personality disorder. She was born into a home where her mother and older siblings had long coped with her father's abuse. Martha's father frequently and unpredictably wielded knives and threatened to kill her mother and all the children. He repeatedly beat his wife and all the older children with belts, firewood, and fists. He once stabbed Martha's 11-year-old throat when she had tried to intervene in his beating her mother. He grabbed her from behind, pinned her, and jabbed the knife several times into her neck and upper chest, telling her that he was going to kill her.

His fluctuations were extreme, shifting from periods of sanctimonious behavior to monstrous abuse. Exposure to these fluctuations had powerful significance for Martha, who grew up attending a fundamentalist church with her mother. Their church had strict behavioral expectations and a theology that emphasized hell and damnation for violators. The church also advocated repentance and forgiveness. Her father "repented" several times, but inevitably the abuse resumed.[13]

Martha's mother had given up any hope of escape and became withdrawn and compliant, seeking solace through her faith and religious practice, which taught that women should be submissive and that men should be protectors and providers. Following her mother's survival pattern, Martha learned early to be compliant, nonassertive with men, and compulsive about creating order so tempers would not flair. She was known for her good cheer, attempts to make people happy, housekeeping, and her care of her younger siblings to ease her mother's strain. Martha, her mother's namesake, aligned with her mother in anticipating her father's rage and doing whatever was necessary to avert it.

Martha seems to feel that she was insignificant, expendable in her father's eyes. No matter how hard she tried, she could not please him—he always indicated only what she did was wrong. Unlike her brother Sam, who tried to forget his father ("I acted like he was dead") after he left home, Martha never stopped trying to win his affection. She always hoped he would repent and return to her mother after he left her, but his remarriage showed that he did not intend to do so. Martha could not resolve the inconsistencies in her life, and in the end she killed her father slowly, over a year with poison, as she did her husband.

Religious abuse creates significant barriers to healthy development. For example, when a parent lives a hypocritical life, calling for love and righteousness while committing physical and sexual abuse, the child identifies the powerful parent with the church from which the parent claims to gain authority. The child is thus cut off from developing a relationship with a supportive religious community, and his or her spiritual development is inhibited.

Faith communities often seem ambivalent about how to help victims of their own members. Garth and Martha and their mothers were involved in churches, but even after their fathers confessed maltreatment, no one monitored their safety or promoted their emotional recovery. Yvette's stepfather was affiliated with a religious group, but they did not step in when they became aware of his rage or sexual abuse. Jamal had the unfortunate experience of living with a separatist faith group, so his parents were not open to seeing what most people would regard as signs of psychotic illness. Some children, like Willie, were abused physically and psychologically in faith-based children's homes. Surely not all faith communities are passive in the face of family problems, but people who face the death penalty seem to have come across many that are.

Using Restorative Justice to Address Systems Failure

Systems failures must be addressed to create a restorative community. Based on restorative justice principles, we offer three ideas that could begin to address these failures. These include community review panels, offender family outreach specialists (OFOSs), and restorative work within the prisons.

Community Review Panel

We propose a restorative justice approach utilizing community review panels to explore the system failures found throughout offenders' histories. The processes in which the panels work would be reflexive and based on future crime prevention. Before we sketch the review panel, we explore some underlying assumptions.

Our notion of a community review panel is informed by Tifft and Sullivan's view that restorative justice communities should address social, economic, and political inequities by reforming agencies responsible for providing care. We also see the significance of needs-based communities, and for a picture of what that looks like, we turn to the United Nations Convention on the Rights of the Child (CRC), which calls for all nations to ensure that children are nourished, protected, educated, allowed to participate in decisions about their lives, and generally supported in ways that promote healthy and prosocial development. The CRC also advocates that every child has a right to be raised in a family environment that is supported by community and government resources. Even though the United States has not ratified the CRC, laws and policies that the federal government and states have recognized ensure children are entitled to care and protection through a vast system of schools and organizations addressing child welfare, mental health, health, and juvenile justice.[14] Presently the public system works together with resources that are available through the nonprofit, faith-based, and business sectors. But despite these efforts, children still fall through the cracks.

To meet the standards of the CRC, it is important to evaluate the services available to children under the present system, and in this effort, we go back to the notion that a key to crime prevention often lies in the psychosocial histories of individuals who have committed violent crime. Given the level of detailed information that becomes available when a death penalty trial is well conducted, mitigation evidence might be an effective starting point for supporting the goals of the CRC and implementing a community review panel.

The review panel would be informed of the psychosocial history of the defendant. The panel would first bring together representatives from each of the systems involved in the defendant's life, a representative from the defendant's family, and a representative from the victim's family, if they choose. This group would talk about the needs that the offender had in his childhood that were not met by public or private resources, and in an effort to foster accountability without blame, the panel would review policies, practices, and records to determine what changes could be made to help future children and to reduce the number of future victims. Recommendations would include ways to procure better funding, staffing, volunteers, and other missing or inadequate components.

With such a process, the community is accountable for its institutions, and the institutions are accountable to the community. Although poor practices would likely need to be addressed, it does not have to be a punitive process for agencies, as progress can be celebrated, new ideas developed, and community alliances made. In those situations where agencies' hands are tied by bureaucracies, the review panel could work with institutions to remedy a policy or a funding constraint that might affect the agencies' ability to provide services.

Offender Family Outreach Specialist

As the numerous stories in this chapter illustrate, capital crimes often reveal families that have suffered from a cycle of abuse that has spanned generations. Practices based on restorative justice principles can alter the negative focus that a capital crime places on a family and use it to help them recover, rather than relegate them to further ignominy. Offenders' family members need help to cope with their own issues of abuse, as well as the harm they face throughout their loved ones' trials and punishments.

Family members should have access to a support person throughout the trial, a position that could be modeled after the victim outreach specialist. The offender family outreach specialist (OFOS) can listen to the offenders' family members and help them discover and articulate their needs, as well as communicate with the offender, defense, prosecution, and victim's family members when appropriate. The OFOS would be trained to recognize various problems, including trauma and depression, and would offer referrals for mental health, medical care, substance abuse, and other social support services.

A number of the family members we interviewed talked about the healing effect of telling their story to us. For many of them, our interview was the first time they could share their experience and emotions with an unbiased and uninvolved individual. Several family members said that this must be what therapy felt like; others were able to confront their feelings of shame for the first time anywhere.[15]

The pain caused by a capital crime, a trial, and an execution can be compared to a layered onion. The outer and strongest layer is the family members' desire to escape the shadow of death and to participate in a criminal justice system that is fair. The next layer is the family members' need to be differentiated from the crime that their loved one committed. They do not want to be made to feel like villains or monsters. They need people to stop harassing them at work, home, and school, and they need to feel safe. The inner layers of the onion are specific to the family members themselves and the individual circumstances of their life histories and relationships.

Recall Paul from chapter 4, who never reentered college after the trauma of his brother's offense and death penalty trial. Had an OFOS been available to him, the specialist could have become an educational advocate to support him in getting the help he needed to overcome the obstacles to reentering school. This person could also have assisted him and his father as they prepared for trial by helping them confront the history of Paul's father's abuse. An OFOS could have helped Paul testify with accuracy and force without fearing the loss of his father, and perhaps some more of what Paul called "his demons" would have been laid to rest. Moreover, it is possible that some of his hesitancy to reenter school was an attempt to distance himself psychologically from the stress associated with his brother's crime, as he tends to associate his time in college with his brother's murder conviction. An OFOS could have referred Paul to get the help he needs to overcome trauma.

An OFOS could also encourage and support interactions between offenders' family members and other community organizations, such as churches and other religious groups. Examples of faith-based organizations' positive involvement with family members are found in the interviews and can provide some lessons for the specialist as he or she might seek to facilitate involvement with religious organizations. Pearl, an African American mother, explained that her church was supportive, and that within 2 hours of hearing the news of the arrest, church members and the pastor were at her house bringing food and prayer. The pastor brought a van of people to the trial to show support for her son. In another case, Matt, a father, stated that his son's preacher drove "5 hours to testify on the defendant's behalf, not even knowing whether he would be called to the stand."

Matt also credits his experience with pastoral counseling for his ability to overcome his depression and anxiety following his son's arrest. Furthermore, Patty said that at Christmas her father's church sent money to her nephew to use in the prison commissary. Finally, in the days leading up to Robert Coe's execution, Bonnie explained that the anti–death penalty community, including church members and leaders, came to the aid of her and her siblings. One community-based organization communicated regularly with the condemned man's family to offer words of support and tangible resources. Bonnie explained, "Strangers took us in and brought us food. We would not have made it through without them. . . . They were like family to us, and we would be sitting around and they would try to make it easier for us."

Family members need to be recognized within the criminal justice system not as offenders but as individuals who need to understand its workings. Although the present justice system offers some support to crime victims and their family members, it does not consider the needs of the offender's family. An OFOS could help meet the plea expressed by many family members for someone from the justice system or advocacy community to help guide them through the process and offer support.

Restorative Justice in Prison

Currently, the prison system often does further harm to offenders' family members, and many of them report being treated like offenders as they try to visit their loved ones. Communication between offenders and their family members with guards and prison administrators is often strained, with neither side fully understanding the perspective and needs of the other. Prison administrators and guards need to maintain safety and security to protect the general public and the inmates. At the same time family members and offenders wish to have meaningful interactions with their loved ones. Restorative justice practices in prisons would facilitate communication between inmates and their family members.

For the needs of all groups to be met, a process of communication, perhaps modeled after the one used by Philadelphia's Friends and Family, should be developed whereby representatives of family members and offenders can meet to discuss concerns with prison administrators. Such meetings could help family members feel less fearful about their visits, have respectful interactions with the prison authorities, interact with their loved one in a satisfactory way, and know that their relative is safe. The families should be able to express their concerns in a frank way, without fearing repercussions to their loved one.

Family members need information from the prison about visits. With simple language, a letter could walk family members through a visit, including some details about the locked doors they might encounter, screenings that occur, and how to attend to their own eating and bathroom needs. The letter might also provide tips on bringing children to visits, including how they might talk to their child about a visit, concerns that the child might have, and suggesting that parents let children know what to expect from their visits.

A prison social worker, counselor, or trained volunteer would be helpful in working with offenders to prepare for family visits and to learn how to communicate with their children. Positive parent-child interactions during visits are of vital importance and can reduce problems in children's development. There are some prisons that have implemented programs to support the development of children of incarcerated parents by strengthening parents' interactions with their children. Behind No Bars is one such program operating in Cambria County Prison, Pennsylvania.

At Cambria, grant money was raised to create a playroom in a section of the prison. The room is brightly furnished and includes toys and educational activities. With the consent of the administration and after attending a parenting course, parents visit with their children in this area. During the parenting course, the inmates learn about conflict resolution, discipline, and communication, and parents are also asked to keep a journal that explores their thoughts on parenting and provides them a place to engage in self-examination.[16]

It is true that most of the offenders mentioned in this book will never get out of prison, but they can still contribute to society. Stanley "Tookie" Williams provides a powerful example of how a person can change from behind bars. In 1971, Williams founded the notorious gang the Crips, and he was on death row from 1982 until his execution in 2005. From death row he wrote a series of books for children debunking the romance of gang life and focusing on issues like self-esteem as a way to keep out of trouble. Through an antigang organization in California, he contributed letters to Tookie's Corner, an interactive Web site for children. He also brokered gang truces and as a result saved numerous lives. To see the profound effect that Tookie made, one can visit Tookie.com to read the mailbox, which is filled with letters from youth thanking him for inspiring them to leave gang life, disengage from violence, or veer from the destructive path they were on. Others have also contributed to their communities while on death row. Recall Eliot from chapter 8, who sent letters to the children in his mother's church group advising them to listen to their parents and to stay out of trouble, and Andre, who tries his best to parent his sons from prison to keep them on a successful life course.

Restorative justice approaches begin with accountability: an individual must come to terms with his or her own actions and the harm that they have done. William Moore wrote a letter of apology to his victim's family members and took responsibility for his actions. The prison system needs to provide offenders with counselors or restorative justice coaches who can help inmates accept accountability for their actions and support reparation.

The coach would be a trained visitor through one of the many associations that brings volunteers together with prisoners (in chapter 9 we talked about the Pennsylvania Prison Society, which makes such connections). The coach could help inmates understand and explore the repercussions of their actions and work with the inmates to determine if reparation could be made. If an inmate wanted to extend an apology to the victim's family, the coach could help him fashion a letter. But because a letter from the offender might be jarring to victim's family members, the coach could act as intermediary between the offender and the family. If a victim-offender conference were to be held, the coach could work with the mediator.

Coaches could also learn from a program started by former Wisconsin Supreme Court Justice Janine Geske, who founded the Restorative Justice Initiative at the Marquette University Law School. The initiative includes a 3-day session with offenders, generally in a maximum security prison, in which they are challenged to take an in-depth look at the effects of crime, work with crime victims, and explore ways to repair harm. Geske explained, "From my own experience, when an offender really understands and hears from the victim about the harm and its ripple effect, they are much less likely to harm anyone else."[17] Similarly, the Centerforce program in California sponsors the No More Tears project, an ongoing forum made up of inmates and community members, that attempts to address issues of violence in the community.[18]

Another program, the Texas victim-offender conference program, which is run out of the victim assistance program, refers to itself as "victim-centered, offender-sensitive." Their combined goal of supporting victims and helping offenders deal with their accountability and needs provides an important model. We believe that restorative justice in the prison system could have multiple effects, including easing some of the hostility found in the prisons, supporting relationships between offenders and their family members, encouraging offender accountability, and in some cases supporting victims' healing.

Summary

From a primary prevention perspective, the offenders' family lives are very revealing about how damaging gender role expectations, abuse and exploitation, attachment disruptions, substance abuse, and unresolved trauma, loss, and grief are to an individual and a family. Every community should have family support programs that can help with these fundamental issues. The cases in this chapter suggest that parents who are very young, very old, or have their own mental health or substance abuse problems particularly need help. Keeping our children off death row begins early in life by identifying risk factors and following through with effective treatment. We saw appalling stories of abuse and neglect, and although the abuse and neglect often occurred within the offender's home environment, it was also found within the community and the social systems designed to provide support. Thereby crime, its causes, and prevention become elevated from a problem between individuals to one that in some cases has roots within a community.

When a state overlooks or directly harms a child, it is an affront to justice when the state then seeks to execute that child for a crime that might not have happened with proper intervention—the contradiction is bewildering. The restorative justice approach to crime that we advocate in this book supports the development of caring communities that are proactive in preventing crime by addressing systems failure and structural inequality in communities. These communities also incorporate the needs and obligations of its members into its social fabric.

It is important to note that the offenders in this book have been influenced by multiple factors. Yvette did not commit capital murder *only* because her father killed himself or her stepfather raped her or because of religious abuse or even her own mental illness; we will never know the exact confluence of factors that caused her to commit murder. But we do know that appropriate support and intervention are the key to preventing such crime and strengthening families and communities. The restorative justice approaches we have introduced are meant to provide blueprints for reform: strategies for keeping community members off death row and supporting recovery when it is too late.

12

Shining Light in the Shadows

Restorative justice is not a simple Band-Aid solution that we can place on capital cases and expect the pain and suffering associated with murder and its aftermath to go away. It is a philosophy that assumes that the people who comprise a society can develop a vision of how humans can live peaceably and constructively with one another and put this vision into practice. In the aftermath of a horrendous crime, restorative justice requires all involved parties—offenders, victims' family members, offenders' family members, and community members (you and me)—to wrestle with issues of accountability and repair. When a capital crime is committed, a death sentence does not always ease the survivors' pain and does not address the factors that contribute to crime in the community. Instead, further personal harm occurs, as we have seen over and over again throughout this book, and the cohesiveness of our community and trust in our neighbors often erodes. Restorative justice requires us to ask and answer tough questions about the consequences of specific crimes and how people want to live in community. Facing violent crime, exploring its roots and subsequent damage, and responding from a place of understanding and compassion rather than fear may ultimately create a safer, more just society.

Howard Zehr sets out specific questions that any restorative justice initiative should address.

1. Who has been hurt?
2. What are their needs?
3. Whose obligations are these?
4. Who has a stake in this situation?
5. What is the appropriate process to involve stakeholders in an effort to put things right?[1]

Because restorative justice is so new in capital cases, this final chapter does not provide all the answers. The ideas we offer are grounded in restorative justice theory and should further conversations about responses to violent crime and support the development of pilot initiatives. We use Zehr's questions to structure our summary of restorative justice in capital cases.

Who Has Been Hurt?

"No mother should have to go through this." The same sentiments are echoed by victims' and offenders' family members as they suffer through the aftermath of a violent murder. The first goal of restorative justice is to establish who has been hurt by a crime. The harms resulting from a murder are innumerable, and it would be impossible to explore in any depth even a portion of the damage experienced by those who have lost a loved one to murder, their communities, and those involved with the life of the offender. Instead, in the following pages we briefly summarize many of the harms incurred by victims' family and friends, offenders' family members, the offender, and criminal justice personnel.

Victims' family members and friends suffer a series of devastating losses when a loved one is murdered. Initially they must cope with the physical absence of their loved one. This loss is then multiplied as they face the future without their loved one; all the emotional, physical, spiritual, and even financial aspects of their relationship are cut short. They must live with the terrible images of their loved one's last moments, and as a result they suffer from a loss of safety, trust, and belief in human goodness. The murder creates feelings of fear, anxiety, anger, and often a desire for raw revenge, something that many family members never experienced prior to the murder. Victims' family members frequently suffer from depression, PTSD, and related health problems that may result in an inability to work and exacerbate stress over finances.[2] Their lives never return to what they were before the murder.

Offenders' family members, too, are hurt when their relative commits a murder. In this book, family members lay bare their stories of how they suffered for their loved one's wrongdoing. They told us about how dealing with the agony of murder was hard enough, but facing the specter of death by state execution was devastating. For Phillip, the father who committed suicide, and Sarah, the mother who died of a broken heart, the agony was more than they could bear.

When the crime occurred, the offender's family's world changed forever. They instantly had to face the awareness that their loved one had hurt others in the worst possible way. They grieved for the victim and their family. They were thrust into a humiliating public limelight that dehumanizes their loved one in order to sanction his death. The family faces a long march through a confusing legal process, marking dates on the calendar as they pass through hearings, prison visits, the trial and sentencing, appeals hearings, and eventually the dreaded execution date. They confessed guilt, depression, and problems with physical and mental health associated with grief and trauma. Although they did not commit the crime, they feel desperately responsible for making amends, even knowing that it is impossible to repair a murder or to protect their loved one from the consequences of his actions. Their sense of efficacy as parents, brothers, sisters, grandparents, or other loved ones suffers because they are unable to help. They live with both anger and love every day.

In answering the question, "Who has been hurt?" by a capital crime, we must also look at the harm that offenders have done to themselves. Many, like Jerry McWee and William Neal Moore, feel tremendous regret, guilt, and sorrow over their actions. Offenders must live with the fact that they have killed another human. They must live with the burden of awareness that they have brought immense pain and suffering on the victim's family members as well as their own. The offender is harmed by the adversarial court process because the defense discourages him from taking responsibility for the crime by shifting attention away from accountability toward the effort to save his life. He is also obviously harmed by the execution itself and the restrictions of death row.

Communities, too, can be torn apart by murder, especially when it is highly publicized. Individuals who live in the same geographic area where the murder occurred or near the victim or offender are often found on the nightly news expressing their feelings of anger, shock, and fear. Another community harmed is the people in the social networks of both families. These individuals include friends, church acquaintances, and classmates who interact with members of both families and share in the loss. Finally, communities of individuals who share similar characteristics such as race, or mental illness with the offender are often harmed by the crime as these marginalized communities once again are scrutinized.

The general public reacts with revulsion, fear, anger, distrust, vengeance, compassion, and many other feelings. Human brutality stimulates a protective response among members of a community and an opportunity to bond together in responding to the crime and to protect and prevent future harm to the community.

Communities often do not bond after a crime because in many cases the only information the public receives about the crime is the "good" versus "evil" characterization, which does not explore the causes of crime. As a result, the public is not only damaged by the fear and anger that they feel as a result of the crime, but also is robbed of the chance to understand the crime and be a part of solutions that may help prevent similar crimes in the future. Many community members feel that showing compassion for the offender's family members and friends somehow dishonors the victim. The notion that you are either for the victim or for the offender can divide communities when they should be uniting.

The murder causes obvious harm to many people. But under the retributive justice system, capital sentencing inflicts additional harm. In addition to the anguish of offenders' family members detailed in this book, the death penalty places emotional burdens on people who work in the corrections system to guard, care for, and execute people on death row. Wardens, guards, members of the Board of Pardons and Paroles, and governors all carry the moral weight of being responsible, at least in part, for the death of another human being. Fred Allen worked in prisons for 16 years and played a part in numerous executions. He recalled one day when he was home working in the shop in his garage: "And all of a sudden something just triggered in me and I started shaking. And then I walked back into the house and my wife asked 'What's the matter?' and I said, 'I don't feel good.' And tears—uncontrollable tears—were coming out of my eyes. And she said, 'What's the matter?' And I said, 'I just thought about that execution that I did 2 days ago and everybody else's that I was involved with.' And what it was, something triggered within, and it just—everybody—all of these executions all of a sudden all sprung forward."[3] Allen decided he could no longer participate in the executions of other humans, and he is now a full-time carpenter. Because the scope of harm is broad, identifying and talking about the ways that crime and criminal justice responses to crime affect stakeholders is an important step to making changes in the way society responds to crime.

What Are Their Needs?

Victims' and offenders' family members, offenders, community members, and the various people who participate in the act of an execution are hurt by the murder of the victim, and many are often harmed by the death of the offender. Restorative justice recognizes that the needs of each of the involved parties are unique and may be quite different from case to case. But generally there are shared concerns. We review common needs that often permeate the experiences of victims' family members, offenders' family members, offenders, and communities.

The largest organization in the United States providing support and advocacy to crime victims is the National Organization for Victim Assistance (NOVA). NOVA has come up with seven principles or rights that each crime victim should have. Although they are articulated as rights, an explanation of the rights reveals common needs of victims.

- Victims and witnesses have a right to protection from intimidation and harm.
- Victims and witnesses have a right to be informed concerning the criminal justice process.
- Victims and witnesses have a right to reparations.
- Victims and witnesses have a right to preservation of property and employment.
- Victims and witnesses have a right to due process in criminal court proceedings.
- Victims and witnesses have a right to be treated with dignity and compassion.
- Victims and witnesses have a right to counsel.[4]

The rights of victims as defined by NOVA are a starting place, but there are additional needs that crime victims have that victims, therapists, academics, and victim outreach specialists (VOSs) have identified. Some of the categories of needs they specify include telling their story and the story of their lost loved one in a safe environment; this often includes the need to retell their story many times. They need to honor the memory of their loved one, feel assured that the offender is held accountable, and feel protected from the press. Some victims' family members need to confront the offender and tell him personally about the victim and how the loss has destroyed or changed their lives. Others are more comfortable talking with a VOS who can communicate with the defense team to help answer their questions. They may need mental health assistance or spiritual guidance. They need to feel connection with their community and understanding when they express feelings of anger, sadness, and mistrust. Many individuals cannot readily articulate their own needs following a violent crime, so they will need assistance with this process.

The NOVA rights can also provide a meaningful starting place to explore the needs of offenders' family members. With the exception of reparations, these issues are applicable to offenders' family members as well, and, as one mother in a focus group said, this is "more than a reasonable request." A first step toward applying restorative justice principles in death penalty cases would be to provide trained individuals to assist family members of victims, family members of offenders, offenders, community members, and criminal justice professionals in identifying their needs. This role was described in chapter 11 with the position of the Offender Family Outreach Specialist who would listen to offenders' family members and help them negotiate the criminal justice system. Offenders' family members need assistance from mental health professionals, spiritual leaders, and support groups. They need humane prison policies that allow them to interact meaningfully with their loved one. They need to have access to their loved one, and they need to know that he is safe behind bars and not mistreated. Children and young siblings of offenders need support to help them overcome the trauma of losing regular contact with their parent or brother. They need for their loved one not to be executed, and if they are executed, they need support through the process, and they need to be empowered to speak about their political views if they so choose.

Family members need understanding from their communities and a press that presents accurate reports. They need communities to make a concerted effort to help prevent future crime by improving mental health services, addressing child abuse, and providing more equitable access to child care and work opportunities. They also wish for help for the offender.

Many offenders needed help long before the crime ever happened, and following a crime, that need escalates. In prison, they need help to address the roots of crime, including assistance with depression, trauma, anger management, physical abuse, sexual abuse, neglect, substance abuse treatment, education, medical attention, and spiritual care. Although some offenders do not immediately recognize this need, many have an underlying need to be held responsible for their actions and to receive help with the many factors that led them to a place where they chose to commit a horrendous crime.[5] Society should encourage accountability by giving offenders a safe place to tell their own stories, an opportunity to know the effect that their crime has had on the victims, competent legal aid to help them through the death penalty process, and assistance communicating with the victim's family and their own family and loved ones, particularly their children.

Following a capital crime, community members often change their patterns of daily living and interactions as a result of both fear and anger. Community members need to be able to talk about their feelings and mourn the loss of the victim; they also need a sense of efficacy that they can help prevent future crimes. Community members need to know that mental health systems, child protective systems, domestic violence and substance abuse services, as well as many others systems are available and meeting the needs of families and individuals so that systems failure is not a factor in perpetuating criminal behavior. Community members need a sense of justice, which means different things to different people. For some, justice means revenge: an eye for an eye, a life for a life. For others, justice means a sentence other than death but one that fits the profound severity of the crime. Still others have a broader conception of justice that attempts not only to deal with past crimes but also to create a more humane society by addressing inequality, racism, and other risk factors explored in this book.

Whose Obligations Are These?

Under a restorative justice model, each harm and need created by a crime is matched with an obligation to attempt to repair harm as best as possible or meet a need. Violent crime is inherently unfair. A victim is physically hurt or killed in an action that is beyond his or her control, and the obligation of repairing a violent crime can never be completely met. At first glance it may appear that the only individual with any obligation in these situations is the violent offender, but no violent crime is ever that simple. Although offenders have many obligations to meet as a result of crime, just societies should collectively contribute to meeting the needs of crime victims, offenders' family members, and community members through publicly sponsored resources, religious institutions, nonprofit organizations, and the actions of individual citizens and businesses. Agencies and individuals that have failed the offender in the past should face the obligations created by their actions and inactions, help repair harm by meeting the needs of involved parties, and developing practices that may reduce the likelihood of future violent crimes.

Under retributive justice models, communities assume obligations in response to crime by investing enormous resources into prosecuting and condemning offenders. Proponents of restorative justice should try to move away from blame toward accountability by rechanneling some of these resources into creating more adequate responses to the needs of all the people who have been hurt by crime and building a safer and more socially cohesive future for the community.

Who Has a Stake in This Situation?

Restorative justice is a collective response to crime that involves anyone who has a stake in the situation and is willing to participate. By definition, capital murder cases involve more stakeholders than most other crimes because we all suffer when our communities lose valuable members, and we all have a stake in creating a society without violence. We have already articulated the various groups that have a stake in responding to crime: victims' and offenders' family members and their social networks, the criminal justice system, human services and the educational system, businesses, and the community at large. For example, the Oklahoma City bombings and the terrorist attacks on September 11 affected the entire United States. We collectively mourned for the victims, and many Americans responded with calls for revenge, whereas others responded with calls for compassion and a greater understanding of what causes offenders to choose to commit crimes of terror.

The media play an essential role in creating a just society and informing the public of crimes and official reactions to crimes. As a result they, too, are stakeholders in this process. News editors and reporters need education concerning the causes of murder and how to incorporate context into crime reporting so they can provide more balanced perspectives that do not solely prey on the fears of readers and viewers.

Case by case, stakeholders should be identified and involved in the restorative justice process. Once identified, it is important to include and engage all stakeholders in a way that is true to their own feelings and respectful of other participants in the process. Individuals who do not wish to be involved in the process, particularly survivors of victims, should never be required to participate.

How Do We Involve Stakeholders?

For years, pioneers in the restorative justice movement have wrestled with developing appropriate processes to deal with criminality and the resulting needs, harms, and obligations. As we illustrated in chapters 2 and 10, these efforts have typically focused on bringing offenders and victims together in some format. Developing processes that honor victims without their presence and input is challenging. The nature of the extreme harm experienced by all stakeholders in murder cases makes this process more daunting and also more critical to participants if they are going to move toward recovery and healing.

Restorative justice processes are based on open and active communication, which is most often through face-to-face interaction but may also be through written, electronic, or third-party communication. Some stakeholders prefer not to meet together because it would be emotionally draining and in some cases traumatic. Understandably, many victims' family members may mistrust the process. It is important for restorative justice processes to be open enough to work with offenders, victims, and their family members who are not ready to or do not ever desire to meet other parties. Although meetings are often useful for fulfilling many of the needs of stakeholders, they should not be seen as the only way to do restorative justice.

We believe restorative justice principles and practices can be used to help stakeholders deal with homicide and capital punishment through many different possible practices. We do not propose a protocol for a particular process but advocate flexibility and empowerment of all stakeholders in developing the process. We suggest resources and programs that could provide ideas for individuals working with offenders, victims' family members, offenders' family members, and communities that are attempting to blend restorative justice with traditional justice practices in the case of serious violent crimes.

For many who are familiar with current restorative justice programs, these ideas may seem incomplete, as if they do not fully reflect a restorative justice solution. Much like Zehr, we argue that there are degrees of restorative justice practices and that traditional criminal justice and restorative justice are not mutually exclusive. The criminal justice system can meet the safety, due process, and legal needs that are critical to cases that involve the loss of life and the possible execution of an offender, whereas restorative justice practice may help meet other needs, including information, communication, understanding, mental health, reflection, personal accountability, crime prevention, and building stronger communities. We now turn our attention to a more specific conversation about what these processes might look like for each of the stakeholders.

Victims

To support crime victims, the victim advocacy movement has pushed hard for policies and programs that provide services for victims and their survivors. Although victim advocates and the victims' rights movement have made impressive improvements in services, many needs still remain unmet, and victims continue to be harmed by the criminal justice system. Additionally, the adversarial position that many victim advocates are trained to take and the fact that a number of them are located in the prosecutor's office can inhibit their ability to assist family members with needs that do not relate to the prosecution of the offender, such as mental health treatment or communication with the offender or his family members. There is a belief among many community members and criminal justice practitioners that murder victims deserve the death penalty and that anything less devalues the victim. Yet there are victims' family members who oppose the death penalty and who are marginalized both in the criminal justice process and in their own communities because of this belief.

When working with the victims advocate, the victim outreach specialists (VOSs), as we discussed earlier, represent a more comprehensive approach. VOSs work as liaisons with the defense team when the victims desire to communicate with the offender or his legal team. Whether it is a victim advocate, VOS, friend, religious leader, mental health professional, or a combination of supports needed to put things in order, the principles found in victim outreach that allow the victim to define his or her needs and address them are critical to healing.

Some victims want to face the offender who killed their loved one. In these cases, victims should have a trained facilitator who will help them prepare for the meeting. Preparations include making sure that the survivor is emotionally prepared for the interaction; helping the survivors focus on what they want to get out of the meeting, including what types of questions they want to ask and what information they want to share; and communicating with a facilitator who is working with the offender to ensure that he, too, is prepared for the meeting.[6]

The way the criminal justice system or other sources revictimize or harm victim's families should be explored, identified, and corrected. It is important that a victim's healing not be impeded by the lack of understanding from individuals involved in the criminal justice system. Police departments and prosecutors' offices should implement a communication protocol between victims' family members and someone in their offices to help avoid revictimization and repair the damage caused when it does happen. Jeremy's father went to court one day thinking he was attending his son's trial when in fact the constitutionality of the electric chair was being debated that day. The images he was left with haunted him throughout his son's case. Information from the prosecutor informing him not only of trial dates but also of the content of the arguments would have spared him this trauma.

Offenders

Dick Burr, the attorney we met in chapter 10 who helped develop the VOS position, now purports that there are five stages of a death penalty mitigation investigation. The defense team must determine

- What went wrong in the offender's life?
- What is the kaleidoscope of his life—including all of the good and bad factors that influence who he is today?

- What is possible in the present based on his mental capacity after the crime? This includes exploring such issues as what he has learned, what kind of inmate he can be, or what kind of father he can be.
- What are the possibilities for the offender's future? This includes his own sense of redemption and determining if he can take responsibility for his actions.
- How has he responded to the crime, and what capacity does he have to make symbolic reparations to the victims' family members?

Jerry McWee, as well as others, would have given anything to offer some type of reparation and would have actively participated in an opportunity to meet with the victim's family members and answer their questions, apologize, and provide other information they desired.

Correctional institutions should foster restorative justice processes that include the offender taking responsibility for the crime and for other decisions in his past, present, and future. Offenders must also learn how to parent from jail. Like Andre, the father we met in chapter 6 who is facing execution, they need to learn ways to describe their role in the crime to deter their children from following a similar path. An expert could help them learn the difficult process of parenting without touch. A coach such as a prison social worker, chaplain, or specialist working in the area can help the death row fathers learn how to have meaningful relationships with and support positive outcomes for their children. At the same time, basic information about children's developmental issues and appropriate parenting tasks should be provided to the offender. Misty might be healthier today if Jerry could have helped her open up about her issues and fears.

Meeting or corresponding with the victims' family members or providing them with information through a liaison can help offenders meet some of the obligations they created by committing a crime. These interactions, if properly facilitated, can also help the offenders meet many of their own needs. Offenders should take responsibility for their actions and be willing to be held accountable before communication between an offender and a victim should occur. Without this recognition and sense of moral responsibility for their actions, a meeting can do further damage to the victim's family members.

For this reason, restorative justice solutions should recognize that the factors that contributed to the offender's behavior need to be addressed before any steps are taken toward meeting with the victims' family members. The offender should have assistance in the form of a coach or other trained support person who can listen to the offender's story and help identify some of the problems that led to the crime. Chapter 11 explored the many ways that institutional failure often plays a large part in the histories of men and women on death row. Dealing with issues such as child abuse and neglect, PTSD, depression, substance abuse, fetal alcohol syndrome, and anger management problems will help the offender heal and more fully understand how his actions hurt the victim, the victim's family members, and the offender's family. Adequate medical and mental health treatment in prisons will help prepare offenders to own their responsibility in the crime and to meet their obligations to victims' family members, as well as members of their own family.

Empathy for the offender is a central element of reconciliation.[7] Public confessions and sincere apologies seem to be critical for instigating an empathetic response from survivors of deceased victims.[8] After the offender's apology and disclosure of truth, some victims feel moved to forgive, but that is entirely an individual choice. Forgiveness essentially is a conscious decision to let go of bitterness and vengeance.[9] Forgiving does not mean the victim forgets, condones, or excuses the crime; releases the offender from accountability; or is ready for reconciliation or trust.[10] Victims who forgive typically still wish the offender to be punished, but forgiveness is more likely to precede mercy and acceptance of a less harsh consequence than when vengeance is sought.

Through meeting and dialogue, offenders have an opportunity to better understand the harm they caused, the victims' needs, and how they can live in a way that prevents such damage from happening again. Victims have an opportunity to release some of the anger, overcome confusion about the crime, and accept the humanity of the offender if they choose. They may be able to move forward in daily life with a diminished burden and more hope for the future.

Researchers who have studied victim-offender mediation/dialogue have reported that many offenders wish to meet their victim's family members because they feel it is the least they can do, given their actions. They often want to apologize. Some also would like to explain the process that led up to the crime and how they have changed while in prison. Even offenders who are scheduled for an execution express a desire to participate in these meetings.[11]

Some offenders, because of mental illness, mental retardation, or other reasons, may never get to a point where they are able to understand and accept responsibility for their crimes. In these cases, the offenders' family members may be a vital source of information for victims' family members. The offenders' relatives can often provide background information about the offenders' illness or pattern of behavior that can help victims' family members answer questions about the crime and why it happened.

Restorative justice processes may be stalled when condemned offenders feel that their need to avoid execution outweighs the needs of their victim's family. Whether restorative justice principles and practices can help involved parties in death penalty cases deserves more exploration. It is also possible, as happened in the case of William Moore described in chapter 8, that when survivors, offenders, family members, and communities come together in a restorative justice process, the belief that the death penalty and in some cases even life without parole meet the needs of the survivors and community members will be discarded.

Offenders' Family Members

Bud Welch immediately recognized the pain on Bill McVeigh's face when he saw a picture of him on television. He empathized with him as a father who has lost a child, and later he made arrangements to meet him to let him know that he cared. Too many offenders' family members suffer in silence and are racked with guilt, shame, and embarrassment over the crime of their family member. Finding a way to include offenders' family members in the restorative justice process is essential.

Offenders' family members are devastated by the murder committed by their loved ones and the capital trial, but perhaps even more damaging, they become family members of a murder victim when their loved one is executed by the state. In the course of these three events (the murder, trial, and execution), they frequently find themselves without supports and ostracized by the press, their community, and sometimes even their religious organization.

For offenders' family members, the first step toward meeting their needs should be providing them with a safe space where they can talk about their experiences and have their pain and loss recognized rather than demonized. This could be done through an OFOS employed by an advocacy organization or the defense or through a support group facilitator who works with offenders' family members in serious cases. Service providers should have training and experience in dealing with capital cases so they can provide the family members with information about death penalty trials and appeals. Additionally, this service provider should be able to recognize and provide referrals for depression, trauma, domestic violence, and other related issues so that the family members can get the services they need to cope with the case, provide their loved one with the support he needs as he goes through the criminal justice process, and be available to other family members who also rely on them for care and support.

A similar support system should be in place to help children, siblings, nieces, and nephews of offenders in capital murder cases. Children of incarcerated parents are a concern for society. Their trajectory toward adulthood is fraught with obstacles and pitfalls. They must be able to explore their feelings in a constructive way so that they do not harm themselves or harm others as Jerry's daughter Misty did following his execution. As chapter 6 demonstrated, the resiliency of children in these situations is tied to the support they receive at home, their understanding of their loved one's situation, interactions with their relative while in prison, and safety at school and play.

Adult and child family members of prison inmates need meaningful prison visits with the offender. The obligation for these visits is shared among the offender, the offenders' family members, and the correctional system. In chapter 9, Peggy Sims of Philadelphia's Family and Friends of Death Row Inmates demonstrated the success of working with these groups to improve prison visits while still maintaining the security of the institution. All prisons should have a representative who is willing and able to listen to family members' concerns about visitation, including their need to have contact visits with the inmate, access to food and water during the visit, and respectful treatment by the prison staff. This person should possess the communication skills to interact with both the families and the prison system to make changes in visitation that reflect safety and security needs as well as interpersonal familial needs.

Developing programs to assist offenders' family members in the area of personal efficacy—to feel that they can help their loved one, the victim's family members, and other members of society—is critical to their self-worth. Social service interventions should include empowerment processes whenever possible. Examples included talking with us in the hope that their stories would help other family members; others become involved in the abolitionist movement or crime prevention and education programs that may prevent future crime; still others worked to raise children in this environment who are strong enough to survive these experiences and avoid their own criminal involvement.

Each family member of an offender on death row in the United States carries with him or her a tragic story, which could be used to help heal themselves and their communities. For these stories to be transformed from tragedy into hope, the world must listen to them, care about them, and learn from them. For some family members, talking with a researcher in the privacy of their own homes is currently the only way that they can communicate with community members about the experiences of their families that led to a tragic crime and what they have faced interacting with the criminal justice system. With the help of restorative justice principles, it may be possible for other family members to one day share their experiences in meetings with community members and social service agencies. These meetings would have to be held in a safe environment, and family members would need support in the process, but these conversations, if handled constructively, could help communities develop crime prevention strategies.

Communities

Depending on the circumstances of the crime, the affected community may be as small as a neighborhood or as large as the whole world in cases that receive international news attention. Restorative justice models that focus on meetings between the victim or survivor and offender have struggled with how to include community members in meaningful ways and decide which individuals can best represent community members in the process.[12] When community members are included in such mediated sessions, issues of confidentiality arise because some stakeholders are reluctant for the public to know their private concerns.[13] From a different perspective, some stakeholders have sought full truth and transparency to counter the tendency for offenders to minimize or deny their actions, as the South African

Truth and Reconciliation process demonstrated.[14] When deciding how best to use restorative justice, victims' family members' right to privacy and need for truth should be balanced and respected as decisions are made about how to include the community in restorative processes.

In reviewing the stories of offenders' family members and the criminal court cases of their loved ones, we noticed tremendous institutional failure. Many of the stories told in chapter 11 would not have ended in a violent murder if the communities where the offender resided had adequate social services to assist individuals when issues such as child abuse, mental health problems, poverty, juvenile delinquency, and learning disabilities threaten to disrupt the life of a child. For many of the offenders on death row, it was not just one problem that led to their involvement in crime but a history of cumulative disadvantage where multiple problems were heaped on them without the necessary skills and resources to cope. Restorative justice requires a focus on accountability. Although this has traditionally been presented as the offender's accountability, we support a wider view of accountability that includes public systems.

The kindly shop owner killed by Marcus might still be alive today if Marcus received the mental health care that he needed. The individuals that Bobby killed, including his father, might be alive today had Bobby's mother, Lesa, had a place to seek refuge and rebuild her life after the abuse that her husband inflicted. Fred Gilreath may not have killed his wife if his childhood issues with drugs and alcohol had been caught and addressed.

It is easy to play the blame game and point fingers at all of the individuals and agencies who could possibly have prevented the crime, but for restorative justice solutions to work, it is critical to move beyond blame and fear of punishment. Community review panels, such as those proposed in chapter 11 with representatives from local institutions and social service agencies, could meet with victims' and offenders' family members—separately if that is more comfortable for either party—to talk about the crime, its causes, and ways to offer assistance as well as to develop better practices and programs so that future crimes could be prevented.

Envisioning a Better Future

We have repeatedly demonstrated the harm and devastation caused by a murder to victims and their family members, offenders and their family members, and the communities where they reside. Too often politicians and the general public hide behind "tough-on-crime" rhetoric, rather than attacking the root causes of crime and providing assistance to individuals whose lives are harmed by crime. Restorative justice solutions are not soft on crime—they are premised on personal accountability for the offender and others whose behavior contributed to the conditions that lead to crime. To fight the crime problem in the United States, we cannot hide behind the death penalty and long prison sentences without facing the personal harm caused by violent crime.

Restorative justice, combined with traditional justice, may help all those harmed by violent crimes cope, heal, and gain hope for the future. Years of experience have shown us that the criminal justice system does not do this on its own and that simply matching harm with a punishment may provide a superficial sense of justice, while the obligations created by the crime still go largely unmet. A future built on principles of restorative justice may include many of the suggestions mentioned, as well as numerous practices and programs that are yet to be developed by victims' family members, offenders, offenders' family members, community members, and service providers working together.

By sharing their stories, offenders' family members have shed light on how communities can prevent future victimization. They have clearly demonstrated the horrendous consequences of not addressing issues of abuse, neglect, mental illness, and alcohol and drug addiction. Community members who many have overlooked, forsaken, or condemned offenders' family members can gain valuable insight by carefully listening to them. By engaging in the lives of victims and their family members and offenders and their family members, we can work together as communities to heal from crime and develop ways to prevent it.

Afterword

All of us who have worked on death penalty cases, whether for the defense or the prosecution, have witnessed the ongoing misery of the families of victims and defendants. We have seen their faces and heard their voices of woe. Sometimes, even most of the time, I (as a member of the defense team) have failed to comprehend the depth of their suffering.

A mother taught me about the bottomless shame and sorrow experienced by family members of capital defendants. Ruby, whose son was accused of fatally shooting a man during a robbery, did not understand why the defense team sought so much information about her, her past, and her son's upbringing. On the other hand, the defense had little understanding of the pain she felt every time one of us arrived at her door. Throughout trial preparation, we agreed that Ruby, like her son, was suspicious, difficult, and uncooperative. We predicted that she was unlikely to provide helpful testimony during the sentencing phase of the trial. We were wrong. She gave eloquent testimony about her sorrow for the victim's family and her struggle to get mental health treatment for her son, and she pleaded for mercy for him. Ruby was able to hold herself together and walk out of the courtroom with composure. However, after she passed through the doors to the hall, she surrendered to a wail of deepest sorrow that echoed through the courtroom. I never will forget her cry, and I never want to forget the terrible cost she paid when she faced the magnitude of her son's crime and the punishment that she would endure along with him. Still, I had no idea what to do to help her and the many others like her.

In this book, Elizabeth Beck, Arlene Andrews, and Sarah Britto ventured into the shadows of the death penalty to bring us stories of the people who suffer there. Sitting in the fire with these family members is often too much for their friends, neighbors, pastors, and even their own family members. The authors' willingness to listen deeply to the pain of capital defendants' families has shown us that Ruby's anguish was not unique. They have also shown us that in the wake of the most serious violent crimes, restorative justice can reduce the suffering encompassed by our adversarial criminal justice system—even in death penalty cases, should victims' families voluntarily decide to interact with the defense.

A young girl whose father was murdered when she was still a toddler taught me that it is possible for dialogue to occur between victims' families and a capital defense team. She and I met when one of the several defendants convicted of killing her father was in the midst of a retrial. Barely a teenager, this girl read the testimony her terminally ill mother had given at the first trial to the jury. During a break in the proceedings, the daughter, more confused than angry, confronted me and asked how I could help defend a man who killed her father. She listened intently to my belief that killing in response to killing helps no one and hurts many. We had a brief but profound interchange. In this girl, who would soon be an orphan, I saw dignity and courage, but I did not have adequate skills to respond to her concerns and needs.

Years later, when Dick Burr, Howard Zehr, and Tammy Krause invented defense-initiated victim outreach, that young girl's voice helped me recognize the integrity of their victim-centered approach. Today, a growing group of victim-centered professionals offers survivors a bridge to the defense team in death penalty cases and potentially some relief from the trauma implicit in death penalty proceedings. Some of the questions about the effectiveness of this approach were answered in the trial of Zacarias Moussaoui, the only person charged in regard to the terrorist attacks of September 11, 2001. Approximately 40 bereft victim-survivors testified as government witnesses, with the implication that they favored a death sentence for Mr. Moussaoui. Subsequently, more than a dozen victim-survivors testified as victim impact witnesses for the defense, including family members of two "heroes of Flight 93." The attorneys for Moussaoui believe that their courageous testimony helped jurors envision and implement a punishment other than death. A news correspondent put it well when he declared their testimony made it clear that neither side "owns the victims."

From the many voices in this book we have learned that the harm flowing from a capital crime is a tsunami that engulfs victims, defendants, their families, and communities for the duration of the case and beyond. Often it feels that there is no way out. However, the authors lead us out of the shadow of the death penalty toward a more humane approach: restorative justice. No effort can undo murder, but offenders need the opportunity to take responsibility for their crimes without facing death as a result; their families need to make personally significant meaning out of the tragedy caused by their loved one and do so without fear of reprisal from their community. Likewise, victims must be given the opportunity to envision rebuilding their lives and the resources to do so.

In the three decades of the modern death penalty, social science has revealed numerous flaws—legal, social, and moral—in the application of this punishment. I urge the authors to continue their exploration of the human costs and effects that occur when the state seeks the death penalty. We need rigorous investigation of the effects of capital trials on families. Our society needs to take into account the long-term effects of executions on victims and on the children and grandchildren of the executed. Thus, there is a need for evaluation of defense-based victim outreach initiatives and victim advocacy functions in capital cases. There are additional questions that need to be addressed. What are the effects of the specter of the death penalty on the individuals who defend and prosecute these cases? Do these participants in the criminal justice system experience trauma? How can communities, including educational and religious institutions, more effectively support victims, offenders, and their families?

I believe that data from such studies will provide additional evidence to support the argument that restorative justice is a compassionate, effective, and cost-efficient framework for responding to aggravated murder.

—Pamela Blume Leonard
former Deputy Director of Georgia Capital Defender and
currently Project Director of Georgia Council for Restorative Justice

Appendix A: Methods for Gathering Information about Offenders' Families

The stories and supporting information in this book are the stories of offenders' family members as told to us by the family members themselves, their lawyers, activists, and victim outreach specialists or revealed through our own experiences with them in a research or job-related capacity.

We worked to capture the lived experiences of family members, but we also wanted an objective understanding as well. We realized that when talking about the court system, the crime, and other facts that family members' views are shaped by their specific experiences, perspectives, and their own memories. Therefore these subjectivities may not give a complete or even accurate picture of the workings of the criminal justice system or the perceptions of other involved parties. Whenever possible and appropriate, these stories were supplemented and confirmed (triangulated) by data from public records including court documents, newspaper articles, and published books and papers. In most cases where a story is described in detail, we have fact-checked the story with newspaper articles, and the attorney on record has reviewed the segment for accuracy.

Questions regarding subjectivities are not necessarily restricted to the participants, as we had previous interactions with members of the population that helped shape our data collection and theoretical orientation. Although we tried to guard against these particular subjectivities influencing the data collection efforts, these perceptions cannot help but affect the types of questions that were included in our instruments.

We examine the specific methods that we used to collect and analyze data. Our techniques include focus groups, in-depth individual interviews, case studies from court records, and ethnography. Before we describe the methods, however, we explore some of the ethical issues and obstacles related to interviewing individuals on such sensitive topics as the death sentence and the execution of a loved one.

Interview Protocol: Ethics and Obstacles

We had two issues that we needed to address in the development of the interview protocol. First we were asking vulnerable people about sensitive topics, as we asked participants (the family members) to discuss such things as their experience with child abuse and neglect, trauma, depression, suicide, and health issues, which brings up a host of ethical issues. Although we thought that the data collection was important, we did not want to retraumatize our respondents by talking about these sensitive subjects in ways that opened psychological wounds.[1]

Our second concern was related to recruiting participants directly, and we identified several reasons why many would not want to interact with us, including:

- distrust of the criminal justice system;
- fear that their words or actions would adversely influence a family member's court case;
- fear that the media would get the information obtained during an interview and use it to hurt them or their loved ones;
- guilt that their own actions or inactions may have contributed to the crime;
- shame and embarrassment about the crime and their own family; and
- emotional reactions to their loved one's arrest that could be triggered and lead to retraumatization.[2]

To address these issues, we developed a protocol for interviewing respondents and conducting focus groups about sensitive issues. Our work was guided by the dual goals of minimizing harm to participants and collecting reliable and valid data. We developed this protocol by turning to ideas found in feminist methods and restorative justice.[3]

Alison Jaggar, a feminist scholar, argues that feminist methods require praxis or a coming together of both research and practice.[4] Carol Gilligan, an internationally known psychologist, views women's essentialist nature as based on an ethic of care.[5] This ethic includes responsibility within particular human relationships, the placement of self-in-relationship, and avoidance of hurt. Both theorists maintain that ethical research should keep the humanity of the subject central to all parts of a study, and this includes recognition that research involves a relationship based on trust and a commitment to using the information obtained from the research for the larger good of society.

In addition to exploring restorative justice as a possible response to criminal wrongdoing, we also used it to inform our research methodology. Specifically, restorative justice emphasizes the value of storytelling to all participants. Part of the healing process after a crime includes telling the story of the crime from one's own perspective without being judged.

Additionally, restorative justice emphasizes the need for creating a safe space where participants can talk freely, cry openly, and express other emotions without restraint.[6] In each of our interactions with family members, we tried to create an environment where they felt heard and not judged.

General guidelines for the interview and specific strategies to support constructive storytelling focused on protecting respondents from harm and ensuring that the research would be used in the interests of the participants. All of us read books and journal articles about the death penalty so that we would have an understanding of the unique culture surrounding these cases, as well as an appreciation of race, class, and religious issues in the participants' lives. Beck, a social worker, conducted all of the interviews with family members and also participated in all of the focus groups so that if necessary she was available to assist people with personal issues, identify trauma symptoms, and refer people for treatment. Interviews and focus groups were conducted in a comfortable and safe place (usually in the respondent's home). Before conducting the interviews and focus groups, we reviewed available data from newspapers and lawyers to gain an understanding of the crime and the court processes, so that family members did not have to focus on the details of the crime when they spoke with us.[7]

All participants in this study signed informed consent forms explaining the benefits and the possible harms that would result from their participation in the study. These consent forms guaranteed the respondents that their identities would be kept confidential. Because of this, in most cases, we use pseudonyms to refer to offenders and their family members. We chose to use pseudonyms for two reasons. First, we wanted to grant anonymity to individuals who have to contend with public scrutiny and judgment. Our second reason was out of concern for the death penalty process. Given that most of the cases found in this book are under appeals, we wanted family members to speak with assurance that nothing that they said might impact their loved ones' cases. In a limited number of cases, the respondents chose to have their identity revealed. When a full name is used, the person signed an additional consent form. Each of these informed consent forms and the research protocols were reviewed by the Institutional Review Board at Georgia State University, Central Washington University, or the University of South Carolina. The specific protocols for each different methodology will be reviewed in more detail next.

Methodological Considerations

In addition to using methodology that supported storytelling and tried to minimize exploitation, we also were concerned with issues of objectivity, reliability, validity, and representativeness of the sample. Sandra Harding described "objectivism" as the research subject becoming the sole object of scrutiny and the researcher shielding his or her "own subjectivities, beliefs, and practices" from the research participant to support "value neutral or interest-free" research.[8] Whether any researcher can be value-neutral has long been the subject of philosophy of science debates.[9] Researcher Leslie Roman rejects the efficacy of objectivism, believing instead that researchers bring their own experiences and biases, and these experiences contribute to their ability to do research well.[10]

In the case of capital offenders' family members, we determined that support and empathy are appropriate and in fact critical to ensuring that respondents feel safe enough to reveal information. However, we guarded against extensive discussion of the researchers' perspectives to avoid bias. Because the ethics of care required the inclusion of self, we gave the interviewer permission to move away from objectivism in specific areas by showing signs of empathy, providing encouragement, and expressing her wish for the loved one facing execution to live.

Additionally, we wanted to ensure that our questions and the way they were asked would yield reliable and valid information. For each transcript that was reviewed, interrater reliability tests were conducted and revealed over 90% consistency in the coding of themes and subthemes. Because we used mixed methodology, we were able to compare the results from each of these sources, and we found a high level of consistency in our findings. This is particularly significant because some of the interviews were conducted by different members of the research team, demonstrating that the same protocol yielded similar results regardless of who conducted the interviews.

To obtain validity, we implemented the five standards of validity in qualitative research as described by Margaret Eisenhart and Kenneth Howe, which include (1) that there is a fit between the research question and methods; (2) that there is a comprehensive understanding of the issues; (3) that there is an awareness of prior knowledge, that the study is useful; (4) that bias is addressed and removed; and (5) that data collection and analysis are systematic.[11] First, we sought research methods that supported the research question, which is "how are offenders' family members affected by their loved one's crime, the death penalty trial, incarceration, and execution?" Due to the sensitive and exploratory nature of this topic, the depth of the issues, as well as the emotional content of the topics, we chose qualitative methods. Second, the study question was built on our multidisciplinary backgrounds of social work and criminal justice. Third, the research question was based on prior knowledge of all authors, one who worked as an expert witness in death penalty cases, one who has worked with mitigation on death penalty cases, and one whose experience was with research in the area of criminal justice and restorative justice. Fourth, we sought to provide context in the text to each of the cases so that readers may reach their own conclusions, and we have explicated our personal biases and subjectivities. Fifth, our data collection included use of trauma and depression scales in some cases, newspaper articles, court records, and discussions with lawyers to triangulate the qualitative results. Finally, some study participants have read aspects of the findings, and each agreed that we captured their experiences.

In addition to the challenges of developing an ethical research protocol that collects meaningful, reliable, and valid data, we faced the challenge of contacting subjects in the population of interest and gaining their consent. Offenders' family members in death penalty cases are a relatively small group compared to many other study populations. As of January 1, 2005, there were 113 inmates on death row in Georgia and 74 in South Carolina, where most of the stories in this book take place.[12] Family members are often difficult to identify and locate. Some possibilities for locating them include researchers going through court transcripts to find any indication of a family member mentioned during court proceedings and then trying to find contact information using phonebooks or the Internet, gaining access to capital offenders themselves and then requesting referrals, identifying names through advocacy groups (which are limited), or getting referrals from defense attorneys working on capital cases.

Unfortunately, none of these methods ensures a representative sample of the population, and no matter which strategy is used, those most likely to be included are also likely to be different in marked ways from those not included. For example, if a researcher chose to go through court transcripts, the data would be skewed toward competent attorneys because less detail-oriented attorneys may not include family members as witnesses. Gaining access to the offenders in the prison system also involves getting prior permission from both the correctional system and the inmate. Additionally, by going through the offenders directly, it is likely that severely mentally ill offenders would self-select out or be unable to provide information. By going through lawyers, it is likely that individuals who have closer relationships with the offender are most likely to be included because these are the family members the lawyers will know about, and individuals who are estranged or do not maintain close contact are least likely to be included in a study. This reality may have the unintended consequence of biasing any study of this population in favor of restorative justice because individuals with strong ties to offenders are more likely to be supportive of programs designed to assist offenders, victims, and community members in healing.

To try to minimize the possibility of bias, in addition to using lawyer referrals, advocacy group contact information, and meetings with several of these individuals at death penalty conferences, we also included the case studies of 14 death penalty cases in which author Arlene Andrews had been an expert witness. These case files, which are all a matter of public record, included interviews with numerous family members (some of whom were not supportive of their loved one's case).

Data Collection

To gather robust data from this population, we used multiple methods, including

1. Three groups of semistructured qualitative interviews between 2002 and 2005
   - general interviews that began the study
   - interviews with children
   - specific interviews that focus on individuals who were chosen because of their particular experiences
2. Focus groups that centered on the particular needs of offenders' family members between 2003 and 2004
3. Case studies of psychosocial histories conducted in the course of one of the research team member's work as expert witness

Each of the methods used in this book is outlined next.

Semi-Structured Interviews: General Interviews

The largest source of data came from interviews with 24 family members of capital offenders who represented 24 different offenders and the unique factors in their cases. We used a purposive sampling technique in which individuals were selected because of their participation in the life of a family member in a capital case. The names for the majority of these family members came from contacts with 17 defense attorneys who represented capital offenders in four southeastern states. Additional family members were recruited through advocacy organizations and one of the authors during a death penalty conference.

The main criterion for participation was that the family member maintained a relationship with the offender during the trial and its aftermath. Notably, the respondents of this study may be different from a general sample of capital offenders for the following reasons: (1) some capital offenders go through the process alone due to disrupted family bonds or other barriers to family participation, (2) using lawyer referrals may have led to particularly cooperative family members, and (3) the only families reached were those who had phones and traceable addresses. A total of 27 people were targeted for participation. Twenty-five of them were contacted for interviews, two were unreachable, and one declined. The response rate for this portion of the study was an impressive 88%.

Most of the interviews took place one-on-one between the participant and the interviewer, but in four cases, participants asked that another family member join them. In two of these four cases, the family members asked that others join them to provide emotional support, and in the other two cases, the family members asked a relative with whom they intimately shared the experience to join the interview. The interviews lasted between 90 minutes and 4 hours. A semistructured interview protocol was used. All participants received $50 for their time. At the time of the interview, the family members were involved in various stages of capital proceedings.

These interviews were conducted solely for the purpose of data collection. Participants were queried on their interactions with the criminal justice system and their attorneys; their relationships with family, loved ones, and their community; and changes within their lives during the capital proceedings. The interviews were taped and transcribed. The transcriptions were coded and categorized using a variant of qualitative researchers Strauss and Corbin's grounded theory.[13] This coding scheme uses inductive reasoning to build on and expand on current restorative justice theory. The interviews were analyzed and coded using a qualitative coding scheme that emphasized themes related to restorative justice. We systematically indexed the interviews.[14] Interrater reliability yielded a 94% agreement on major themes. Responses were annotated and then reanalyzed to sort the responses based on subthemes within each thematic area identified during the initial coding process.

Semistructured Interviews with Children

A separate protocol was developed to interview the minor siblings of defendants and the children of defendants. The children for the interview were identified based on information given to us from the general semistructured interviews and the psychosocial case study records.

Eight children of offenders were interviewed, as well as two siblings who had been minors at the time of the arrest of their respective brothers. The interview protocol asked children to talk about their visits to the prison, their interaction with their loved one, and what it meant to them to have a family member imprisoned. For children to be included in the sample, they had to be actively engaged with their father or brother. Before conducting the interviews with minors, Beck asked all of the caregivers what the child knew about the imprisonment so that she would not inadvertently provide any new information to the child.

Semistructured Topic-Based Interviews

A third set of semistructured interviews focused on individuals whose experiences represented a particular issue that we wanted to focus on in more depth. A purposive sample was used to identify subjects for this part of the study, so any generalizations made about the larger population should be viewed with caution. These individual case studies were chosen for inclusion not because they are representative but because they provide insight into specific experiences and alternative options. These included face-to-face interviews with the family members of offenders who had their cases commuted or were exonerated, an offender whose victims' family members helped get his death sentence commuted and whose case exemplified restorative justice, lawyers who had knowledge of specific cases, organizers involved in efforts to either abolish the death penalty or provide services to offenders' family members, and victim-offender specialists who work within a restorative justice framework as liaisons between victims' family members and the defense team. Three individuals spoke to us about commutations, five sisters and a brother from one family spoke with us about exoneration, and one offender spoke to us about his own commutation. Three lawyers, six organizers, and three victim offender specialists were interviewed for this book.

All of the interviews were conducted face to face with the exception of some lawyer interviews and the victim outreach specialist interviews, which occurred over the phone because they did not pose the same emotional risks to the respondents that the other interviews did. Family members were each paid $50 for their time. Because the interview focused on their profession and remuneration could present a conflict of interest, lawyers and victim outreach specialists were not paid for their interviews.

Focus Groups

In addition to interviews, we held two focus groups to understand the issues more holistically from the participants' point of view and because we were interested in the interactions among people from various offenders' families. In particular, we wanted to mirror a natural setting and explore the perceptions and opinions of family members interacting with other family members and assess whether anyone was helping them meet these needs.

Participants were recruited using a list of inmates' family members that an advocacy group held for their state. To maximize the participation rate, we held focus groups on different sides of the state, and individuals were selected for participation in a specific focus group based on their proximity to the site. Fifteen family members were contacted, and 12 participated, for a participation rate of 80%. Focus group participants received $50 for their time.

Focus group meetings consisted of a meet-and-greet with refreshments and then 2 hours of directed questions and probes. These groups met after we had a chance to analyze the exploratory data from the semistructured interviews, and the content of the questions was shaped by many of the issues brought up in the interviews. This group is also not fully representative of death row family members because the individuals on the contact list chose to give their name and contact information to an advocacy organization and thus again represented family members who are intimately involved with an offender.

Questions included feelings toward the criminal justice system and its particular members, the prison system, the media, their communities, and what was lacking in their lives in terms of services and support. Respondents were also asked about their feelings toward the victim and the victim's family. Probes asked family members to discuss physical and mental health issues that arose as a result of their family member's case, people who have supported them and how, and things they wished that could have been done differently. The moderator tried to encourage a natural interaction between the respondents while at the same time keeping them focused on their responses to their loved ones' cases.

The overwhelming majority of the participants were forthcoming, and most of them openly expressed their feelings verbally and through tears and other body language. Other focus group members were very supportive of these expressions. The moderators of the focus group stayed with the participants for some time after the meeting to debrief and ensure that everyone left the meeting feeling comfortable about their participation. The focus group proceedings were taped and transcribed, and the results were analyzed similarly to the methods used in the semistructured interviews described in the previous section.

Psychosocial History Case Studies

Another data source included public records of psychosocial histories developed by one of the authors who has served as an expert witness in the sentencing phase of capital trials. Over a period of 15 years, Arlene Andrews conducted extensive social histories for 14 defendants referred to her by defense attorneys in 5 states. Each case required interviews with 5 to 100 family members, friends, and associates. Additionally, she conducted extensive reviews of records about family members and social networks from such sources as physical and mental health care providers, schools, social service agencies, and courts. The information in each case became a matter of public record through court testimony. Her discussion in this book is based on a meta-analysis of themes that emerged in these independent cases. This particular methodology is more representative of the entire population of offenders' family members than the semistructured interviews and focus groups because family members estranged from or who have poor relationships with offenders were also included.

Each of these cases is a matter of public record, but the names and other identifying information have been changed to protect the privacy of family members. The cases include 2 African American male, 11 white male, and 2 white female defendants. All families of origin live in the Deep South of the United States. Four received life sentences at the capital trial. Ten received death; three of these received life at retrials, one is on death row but cannot be executed because he is so mentally ill he cannot comprehend death, one was executed, one is awaiting execution, and four are still in appeals.

Conclusion

Our methods aim to create an accurate, reliable, and valid illustration of the types of families who face the death penalty with their loved ones and the issues that are important to them. They also seek to explore the specific needs of offenders' family members and how they are being met with an eye toward exploring the potential for restorative justice processes. We have used their voices whenever possible to honor their expressions. Several family members reviewed our drafts and affirmed that the information presented here captures the essence of their experience.

Appendix B: Process of a Death Penalty Trial

Many family members of defendants interviewed for this book found the criminal justice process intimidating, confusing, and unfair. The system in practice was different from anything they read about in civics class or saw on television dramas. Much of the depression and trauma suffered by family members was linked to the system itself. Family members often felt misled by the police before the arrest of their loved ones, confused by the number of court appearances and the roles of the many different actors in the court, responsible for the sentence that their loved one faced because of their behavior or testimony in the process, and finally betrayed by a system that they often saw as discriminating by race and class. What follows is a brief description of the typical (if any capital case can be considered typical) process involved in capital cases.

All capital cases begin with a crime, and in most jurisdictions this crime must include murder and usually requires murder accompanied by one or more aggravating factors (such as being committed during the process of another felony, multiple deaths, or occurring in a particularly heinous manner). A couple of notable exceptions are Georgia capital crimes, including aircraft hijacking and treason; Florida's capital drug trafficking laws; and New Jersey's narcotics conspiracy law. Similarly the federal government also has the death penalty for a few nonhomicide crimes, such as espionage, treason, trafficking in large quantities of drugs, and hiring someone to kill a juror or witness. Since the 1970s, however, no one in the United States has actually been sentenced to death for a nonhomicide offense.[1]

Following the commission of a crime, there is an investigation. Investigations of capital crimes differ from other crimes in several ways. Many murders garner media attention, but this is especially the case in capital cases. Some argue that it is the uniqueness of a particular crime that fascinates the media, but frequently it is the prosecutor's announcement that the death penalty is being sought that baits the media into extensive coverage. A study of prosecutorial discretion found that it is less often characteristics of a crime than racial characteristics of the offender and victim and political factors that influence the decision to seek the death penalty.[2] Furthermore, a prosecutor's decision to seek the death penalty is rarely part of the judicial review of the case at the state or federal level.[3] Media coverage of the crime is frequently fear-producing and serves to agitate the community into calling for the immediate capture of the guilty party. This creates intense pressure on both the police and prosecutors to make an arrest and calm community fears. Additionally, the victim's family members face constant reminders of their loved one's death in the media. Unfortunately, this can also lead to shortcuts in the investigation process.

The investigation can be terrifying for family members whose loved one is identified as a suspect, especially when a prosecutor announces the intention to seek the death penalty. Families are torn in two by their fear and sometimes anger for their family member and the grief they feel over the victim's family's loss. If their loved one is on the run, they fear for his safety, and they sometimes join forces with the police to help in his capture. When a death sentence is given these family members feel extreme guilt for providing assistance to the police. In their minds, they are responsible for the execution of their loved ones and constantly ask themselves, "What if?"

A criminal investigation often leads to the arrest and the initial appearance of a suspect before a judge. An arrest involves taking an individual into legal custody (probable cause or a reasonable belief that a suspect committed a particular crime is the minimum requirement for an arrest) and informing him of his Miranda rights, which include the right "to remain silent" and to "have an attorney present during questioning."[4] Following an arrest, the defendant is typically "booked." During booking, an official record is made of the suspect, including a photograph and fingerprints. The suspect can also be questioned by the police and placed in a police line-up for witness identification. Booking ends with filing specific charges against a defendant.[5]

The courts have a responsibility to see the defendant "without unnecessary delay" at the initial appearance.[6] During this appearance, the defendant is informed of his or her rights, and the court proceedings are explained. The judge determines whether the case is strong enough to pass on to the grand jury. If the judge decides to continue the case, which he or she usually does in felony cases, the flight risk of a defendant and dangerousness to the community are also determined, and based on this risk, bail is either set or denied. Most individuals facing capital crimes are denied bail. When an individual is denied bail or cannot post a bond, he or she remains in custody of the state, usually at the local jail, until trial.

At the grand jury, it is the prosecutor's responsibility to convince the majority of the grand jury members that there is probable cause to believe that the defendant committed a felony.[7] If the majority of jurors feel there is enough evidence, the grand jury returns a true bill, and the prosecutor files an indictment charging the defendant with a capital crime. This bill of information (or indictment) is formally presented to the defendant at an arraignment. At this point, the defendant can enter a plea of guilty or not guilty. Capital cases are much more likely to go to trial than noncapital crimes, and most capital defendants plead not guilty at this stage.

In capital cases, there are a number of pretrial activities, including both sides continuing to gather information and build cases, pretrial motions, and plea bargaining. During this time, the prosecutor must also formally announce his or her intention to seek the death penalty.[8] The pretrial time period can be very confusing to family members. Some relatives interviewed actually thought they were going to the trial when they were really attending hearings on pretrial motions. Some family members must assist their loved one with a Faustian choice: plead guilty, give up the right to appeals, and accept life without parole or go to trial and face the death penalty. Another aspect of this process that devastates many families is the negotiation of lesser sentences with codefendants in exchange for turning state's evidence. Too often, the defendant who agrees to talk with the prosecutors first, regardless of the validity of his statements, receives a reduced sentence, and the remaining defendant faces more serious punishment, including the death penalty.

During pretrial motion hearings, a judge hears issues of law filed by the defense such as motions to change the venue, suppress evidence, suppress a confession, or "discover" evidence held by the prosecutor. Judges also hear motions filed by the prosecutors to produce documents, blood samples, and so on.[9] The defense may also request a competency hearing to argue that their client is unable to comprehend the charges against him or her or assist the lawyers in his or her defense. Pretrial activities can proceed for many months and even years. Family members describe intense anxiety during this period. This perpetual state of not knowing and worrying about the fate of their loved one often causes both emotional and physical problems. Trials in capital cases are separated into two stages: (1) the guilt/innocence phase of the trial when the prosecutor attempts to establish the guilt of the defendant and (2) the penalty or sentencing phase of the trial when the judge or jury decide the punishment of an offender who is found guilty.

The first part of the guilt/innocence stage of a trial is to select a jury. Some states also allow a defendant to choose a bench trial where only a judge hears and decides on the case, but this option is rarely used in death penalty cases because it places the fate of the defendant in the hands of 1 person, rather than in the hands of each of the 12 members of a jury among which a unanimous decision is required to convict. During voir dire (the process of questioning jurors by the prosecution and defense to determine their selection to the jury),[10] potential jurors are questioned about their beliefs and attitudes related to crime, punishment, race, gender, and so on to establish their potential fit for the current trial.[11] One thing that makes capital cases unique in terms of jury selection is that each potential juror must be death qualified to be eligible to serve.[12] A death-qualified juror is one who is not morally opposed to the death penalty and one who is able to weigh both mitigating and aggravating circumstances in the determination of the appropriate punishment for the defendant. Potential jurors can also be eliminated from serving on the jury by both the prosecution and defense. There are two different means by which this may be accomplished. The first mechanism is to challenge the juror for cause, asserting that the juror, because of prejudice, bias, exposure to pretrial publicity, or assorted other reasons, is not fit to serve on the jury. The attorney seeking to remove the juror must convince the court that the presence of that potential juror on the final jury would deny the state or defendant a fair trial. The second manner to eliminate a juror is through the exercise of the peremptory challenge. As long as the exercise of the peremptory challenge is not based on constitutionally impermissible grounds, that is, race or gender, the party exercising the strike need not offer any explanation for removing the potential juror. There is no constitutional right to be permitted to exercise peremptory challenges, and their existence is usually derived by state statute, common law, or local practice. The number of peremptory challenges is limited; the number varies from state to state.[13]

Several parts of jury selection troubled family members, most notably the requirement of a death-qualified jury. They reported feelings that death-qualified jurors were less compassionate and more supportive of punishment in general than people opposed to the death penalty. This may make it more likely that their loved one is convicted. And because more minorities oppose the death penalty, as a result of this process the number of minorities on capital trials is reduced.

Once a jury and alternate jurors have been selected the actual trial begins. This process starts with opening statements made by the prosecution and the defense. These statements are just outlines of the evidence that each side intends to present. Following opening statements, the prosecution and defense teams both present their cases, including evidence, witnesses, and expert testimony. The burden of proof is on the prosecutor, while the defense tries to establish reasonable doubt. Both sides can call rebuttal witnesses to discredit information presented during the case. Closing arguments summarize the cases presented. Many family members feel disadvantaged by this process because of the quality of the defense team they could afford or the fact that they had to rely on the indigent defense system (the quality of which varies dramatically among jurisdictions), while it appeared that the prosecution had unlimited resources, including police investigators, investigators with the prosecutor's office, and a large legal team. They are also often perplexed or disagree with the direction the defense's legal argument takes and by the information that is not presented to the judge.

This stage of the trial closes with the judge providing the jury with instructions, jury deliberations, and a verdict. Jury instructions include a description of the particular laws involved in the case and an explanation of the meaning of reasonable doubt. The jury must be unanimous in their decisions in capital cases, and a failure to reach consensus results in a hung jury and a retrial.[14] If a guilty verdict is reached, the judge announces plans for the penalty phase of the trial.

The transition between the guilt phase and the sentencing phase is often difficult for defense teams and family members because they must shift from maintaining the defendant's innocence and trying to avoid responsibility for the crime to a position of contrition where taking responsibility and signs of remorse are often viewed positively by the jury or judge. Some family members expressed distress with an adversarial system that actually discourages admission and accountability in the first stage. One grandfather regretted telling his son to tell the police the truth and cooperate because this information was later used to seek a death sentence for his grandson. Another confusing aspect of the process is the fact that most defense teams begin gathering information and preparing to present mitigating evidence which will be used in the sentencing phase before guilt or innocence has been determined. So while family members are providing information to the trial lawyers about their loved one's possible innocence, alibis, evidence, and codefendants, they are also providing information to the mitigation team about reasons why their loved one may have committed the crime, including early childhood abuse and neglect, drug and alcohol use, psychiatric problems, marital problems, community issues, and the negative influence of other offenders.

In the penalty phase of a capital trial, the defense tries to convince the jury that the defendant deserves to live, whereas the prosecution is typically advocating the death penalty. Two types of evidence are admissible during this phase of the trial. The first is evidence of mitigating circumstances or reasons why the defendant may be less morally culpable for the crime, including life histories that show physical, emotional, or sexual abuse; drug or alcohol abuse or use at the time of the crime; dysfunctional family systems; dysfunctional community institutions; mental illness, such as schizophrenia, PTSD, fetal alcohol syndrome, attention deficit disorder, and educational disorders; age of the defendant at the time of the crime; the presence of an authoritarian codefendant; and other pertinent family information. Preparing a thorough mitigation report is quite time consuming and expensive and requires the offender, his family members, and friends to air their dirty laundry. Family members were often afraid to reveal this information because of guilt, shame, and embarrassment.

Additionally, information demonstrating an offender's contrition and past good deeds are also presented. Family members who testified in court felt a tremendous burden—the burden of saving their loved one's life. The thought of saying the wrong thing or missing something plagued relatives before they testified. If their loved one received the death penalty, they frequently blamed themselves.

The jury hears aggravating circumstances from the prosecution. Aggravating circumstances include past criminal history (especially violent criminal history), committing a crime for financial gain, committing the crime during the commission of another felony, committing a particularly "heinous, atrocious, or cruel" crime,[15] premeditation, murdering a police officer, multiple victims and/or the crime placed many individuals in harm's way.[16] After hearing evidence of both mitigating and aggravating circumstances, the victim's family members may also choose to make statements concerning the impact of the crime on their lives. Following what are called victim impact statements, the jury deliberates and decides the sentence. In a bench trial, the judge would make the decision. In most states the jury decision must be unanimous for a death sentence. The final sentence is then read to the defendant by the judge, and if it is a sentence of death, the defendant is issued an initial death warrant. The day specified on this warrant is usually within a month or two.

One mother could not believe it when the judge read that her son was sentenced to death by lethal injection, but even more shocking was when the judge read the date of the execution, which was a month away. Not knowing that the automatic appeal always changes this date can be disturbing to family members and to offenders. William Moore, a man convicted of murder in Georgia whose story is told elsewhere in this book, was never told that his death warrant date was changed after his trial. On the day listed on the warrant, he waited all day long for officers to come and take him to his execution. He did not ask any of the guards about it because he did not want to remind them or bring it up in case by some miracle they had forgotten. All day he prepared himself to die, only to find out later that the original date on the death warrant is always delayed because of an automatic direct appeal.

All defendants get an automatic direct appeal to the state appellate court. After the direct appeal, defendants have a "dual system of collateral review: that is, they may challenge their convictions and/or sentences through both state post-conviction proceedings and federal habeas corpus petitions."[17] These processes are extremely confusing even for lawyers, and for family members, the myriad different petitions, forms, hearings, interviews, and other legal proceedings may be more than they can keep track of. Many are stuck in a perpetual state of anxiety as the family member's case is reviewed in different courts. On the other hand, some family members draw on the process for hope; they believe that as long as there is another chance for review, their loved one still has a chance. Families in Georgia face another challenge: the state does not provide counsel in state postconviction proceedings,[18] and they must either pay for the legal defense themselves or find a lawyer who is willing to work pro bono.

Once a state appeals court affirms the conviction and the sentence during a direct appeal, a defendant can than file for a writ of certiorari that asks the U.S. Supreme Court to review the case. The Supreme Court usually denies cert petitions.[19] He can also file a postconviction appeal with the state court. Most states have a very short time period during which the postconviction appeal must be filed and limit the types of issues that may be reviewed. Following this review, another request may be made to the U.S. Supreme Court for a writ of certiorari to review the postconviction appeal.

Three layers of federal review are left: federal habeas corpus appeals in the U.S. District Court, the Circuit Court, and finally another writ of certiorari in the Supreme Court. Habeas corpus appeals focus only on federal constitutional issues, such as violations of due process, the cruel and unusual nature of a punishment, and factors that may have made the trial unfair; ordinarily the federal court will only hear issues that have already been raised in state court. Innocence claims are not allowed, and there are strict time guidelines for filing for each appeal.[20]

When a death row inmate's appeals are exhausted, the state attorney general, the trial court, or another body such as the governor (depending on who has the authority in that particular state) issues a death warrant to the inmate notifying him of the execution date. An inmate must be sane to be executed, meaning he must recognize that he or she is being executed and why. If this is in doubt, a sanity hearing may be requested to determine the sanity of a defendant. One last possibility for avoiding execution is a clemency hearing with the parole board. If a parole board recommends clemency, the case then goes to the governor, who makes a final decision. Some state governors are legally bound to follow the recommendation of the state parole board.[21] The president of the United States may pardon a federal inmate on the U.S. death row. Barring the success of any of these avenues of review, the defendant is executed.

Notes

Note to Readers

1. The 14 cases that Arlene has worked on are part of the data for this book and are identified as the 14 psychosocial histories. One family member from Arlene's work was also included as an individual interview for this book.
2. Mitigation evidence is evidence that describes the defendant's life history. Specifically explored are issues of mental health, childhood abuse and neglect, age, and a host of other factors that the jury may take into consideration to mitigate against a death sentence. The social history is the document that describes the defendant's life, including frailties and achievement.
3. As of October 1, 2005, there were 52 women on death row (1.5% of the death row population). In the past 100 years, over 40 women have been executed, 11 of these executions having occurred since 1976 when the death penalty was reinstated. Death Penalty Information Center, "Women and the Death Penalty: Facts and Figures," available online at http://www. deathpenaltyinfo.org (accessed February 26, 2006).
4. *Furman v. Georgia,* 408 U.S. 238 (1972); *Gregg v. Georgia,* 428 U.S. 153 (1976).
5. *Woodson v. North Carolina,* 428 U.S. 280 (1976).
6. *Coker v. Georgia,* 433 U.S. 584 (1977).
7. *Atkins v. Virginia,* 536 U.S. 304 (2002).
8. *Roper v. Simmons,* 543 U.S. 551 (2005).
9. Howard Zehr, *Transcending: Reflections of Crime Victims* (Intercourse, Pa.: Good Books, 2001); *Howard Zehr, Changing Lenses: A New Focus for Crime and Justice* (Scottsdale, Penn.: Herald Press, 1990).

Chapter 1

1. In keeping with the restorative justice literature, we generally use the term *offender.* However, when the offender is discussed in a particular context, we use words that describe the context, such as defendant or condemned.
2. Katherine Gabel and Denise Johnston, eds., *Children of Incarcerated Parents* (New York: Lexington Books, 1995).
3. The use of first and last names here indicates that this is the actual name of the victim, not a pseudonym.

4. Jason DeParle, conversation with Elizabeth Beck, February 2005.

5. Robert M. Bohm, *DeathQuest II* (Cincinnati: Anderson, 2003).

6. M. Watt Espy and Martin O. Smykl, comp., *Executions in the United States, 1608–1987: The Espy File* (Ann Arbor, Mich.: Inter-University Consortium for Political and Social Research, 1987), available online at http://www.icpsr. umich.edu/cgi-bin/bob/newark?study=8451&path=NACJD (accessed February 26, 2006).

7. Death Penalty Information Center, "Executions by Year," available online at http://www.deathpenaltyinfo.org (accessed February 26, 2006).

8. Death Penalty Information Center, "Size of Death Row by Year," available online at http://www.deathpenaltyinfo.org (accessed February 26, 2006).

9. Death Penalty Information Center, "Defendants Sentenced to Death 1977–2004," available online at http://www.deathpenaltyinfo.org (accessed February 26, 2006).

10. Death Penalty Information Center, "Innocence: List of Those Freed from Death Row," available online at http://www.deathpenaltyinfo.org (accessed February 26, 2006).

11. For a more complete discussion of Linda White's story, see Rachel King, *Don't Kill in Our Name: Families of Murder Victims Speak Out against the Death Penalty* (New Brunswick, N.J.: Rutgers University Press, 2003).

12. "Fedor Mikhailovich Dostoyevesky (1821–1881)," in *Respectfully Quoted: A Dictionary of Quotations Requested from the Congressional Research Service*, ed. Suzy Platt, available online at http://www.bartleby.com/73/1527.html (accessed August 24, 2006).

Chapter 2

1. CNN Interactive, "Oklahoma City Tragedy: The Bombing," CNN Interactive, 1996, available online at http://www.cnn.com/US/OKC/bombing. html (accessed June 14, 2005).

2. Bud Welch, "Revenge and Hate Is what Resulted in the Death of 167 People," Peacework (presentation to the Human Rights Commission, Kennedy School of Government, Harvard University, Cambridge, Mass., March 16, 1999), available online at http://www.peaceworkmagazine.org/ pwork/0499/049918.htm (accessed September 19, 2006).

3. Ibid.

4. Ibid.

5. Bud Welch, "The Forgiveness Project Stories: Bud Welch," *Forgiveness Project: Stories: Bud Welch*, available online at http://www.theforgivenessproject.com/ stories/bud-welch (accessed February 20, 2006).

6. Ibid.

7. Renny Cushing and Bud Welch, "Transcript of an Address by Renny Cushing, Executive Director, and Bud Welch, Board President at Harvard Univ. in 1999," Murder Victims' Families for Human Rights: Reports and Articles (presentation to the Human Rights Commission, Kennedy School of Government, Harvard University, Cambridge, Mass., March 16, 1999), available online at http://www.murdervictimsfamilies.org (accessed February 28, 2006).

8. Ibid.

9. Howard Zehr, *The Little Book of Restorative Justice* (Intercourse, Pa.: Good Books, 2002).

10. Mark Umbreit et al., *Facing Violence: The Path of Restorative Justice and Dialogue* (Monsey, N.Y.: Criminal Justice Press, 2003).

11. Michael L. Radelet and Marian J. Borg, "Comment on Umbreit and Vos," *Homicide Studies* 4, no. 1 (2000): 88–92; Howard Zehr, *Changing Lenses* (Scottsdale, Pa.: Herald Press, 1990).

12. Umbreit et al., *Facing Violence*; Zehr, *Little Book*.

13. Immanuel Kant, *Critique of Practical Reason*, trans. Lewis White Beck (Chicago: University of Chicago Press, 1949).

14. James O. Fickenauer, "Public Support for the Death Penalty: Retribution as Just Desserts or Retribution as Revenge?" *Justice Quarterly* 5 (1988): 81–100.

15. Kai T. Erikson, *Wayward Puritans* (New York: Macmillan, 1966).

16. Leon Pearl, "A Case against the Kantian Retributivist Theory of Punishment: A Response to Professor Pugsley," *Hofstra Law Review* 273 (Fall 1982): 273–306.

17. Paul Boudreaux, "*Booth v. Maryland* and the Individual Vengeance Rationale for Criminal Punishment," *Journal of Criminal Law and Criminology* 80, no. 1 (1989): 177–196.

18. Jeffery Reiman, "Against the Death Penalty," in *Criminal Justice Ethics*, ed. Paul Leighton and Jeffrey Reiman (Upper Saddle River, N.J.: Prentice Hall, 2001).

19. Jeremy Bentham, *Introduction to the Principles of Morals and Legislation* (London: Payne, 1789); Cesare Beccaria, *An Essay on Crimes and Punishment* (Philadelphia: P. H. Nicklin, 1819).

20. Robert Blecker, *The Worst of the Worst: Who Deserves to Die?* (New York: Basic Books, 2005).

21. Hugo Adam Bedau, *The Death Penalty in America* (New York: Oxford University Press, 1997); Robert Bohm, *Deathquest: An Introduction to the Theory and Practice of Capital Punishment in the United States*, 2nd ed. (Cincinnati: Anderson, 2003).

22. Daniel W. Van Ness and Karen H. Strong, *Restoring Justice* (Cincinnati: Anderson, 2002); Michael L. Hadley, *The Spiritual Roots of Restorative Justice* (New York: State University of New York Press, 2001).

23. Zehr, *Changing Lenses*.

24. Zehr, *Little Book*.

25. Dennis Sullivan and Larry Tifft, *Restorative Justice: Healing the Foundations of Our Everyday Lives* (Monsey, N.Y.: Willow Tree Press, 2001); Zehr, *Changing Lenses*.

26. Zehr, *Little Book*.

27. Gordon Bazemore and Kay Pranis, "Hazards along the Way: Practitioners Should Stay True to the Principles behind Restorative Justice," *Corrections Today* 59, no. 7 (1997): 84–86; Gordon Bazemore and Mark Umbreit, "Rethinking the Sanctioning Function in Juvenile Court: Retributive or Restorative Responses to Youth Crime," *Crime and Delinquency* 41, no. 3 (1995): 296–316; Leena Kurki, "Incorporating Restorative and Community Justice into American Sentencing and Corrections," in *Sentencing and Corrections 3* (Washington, D.C.: U.S. Department of Justice Papers from the Executive Sessions on Sentencing and Corrections, 1999); Wayne Northey,

"Restorative Justice: Rebirth of an Ancient Practice," *New Perspectives on Crime and Justice*, Occasional Paper No. 14 (Akron, Pa.: Mennonite Central Committee Canada Victim Offender Ministries Program and the MCC U.S. Office of Criminal Justice, 1994); Mara F. Schiff, "Restorative Justice Interventions for Juvenile Offenders: A Research Agenda for the Next Decade" *Western Criminology Review* 1, no. 1 (1998): 1–16; Howard Zehr, "Retributive Justice, Restorative Justice," *New Perspectives on Crime and Justice*, Occasional Paper No. 4 (Akron, Pa.: Mennonite Central Committee Canada Victim Offender Ministries Program and the MCC U.S. Office of Criminal Justice, 1985).

28. Zehr, *Little Book*.

29. Pope John Paul II, *Memory and Identity: Conversations at the Dawn of the Millennium* (New York: Rizzoli, 2005).

30. Gerry Johnstone, *Restorative Justice: Ideas, Values, Debates* (Portland, Ore.: Willan, 2002); Sullivan and Tifft, *Restorative Justice*.

31. Todd Clear and Dina Rose, "Incarceration, Social Capital, and Crime: Implications for Social Disorganization Theory," *Criminology* 36, no. 3 (1998): 441–479.

32. Mark Umbreit, "Restorative Justice through Victim-Offender Mediation: A Multi-Site Assessment," *Western Criminology Review* 1, no. 1 (1998): 1–27.

33. John Braithwaite, *Restorative Justice and Responsive Regulation* (Oxford: Oxford University Press, 2002); Mark Umbreit and Betty Vos, "Homicide Survivors Meet the Offender Prior to Execution," *Homicide Studies* 4, no. 1 (2000): 63–87.

34. Zehr, *Little Book*.

35. Gilles Launay and Peter Murray, "Victim/Offender Groups," in *Meditation and Criminal Justice*, ed. Martin Wright and Burt Galaway (Newbury Park, Calif.: Sage, 1989); Van Ness and Strong, *Restoring Justice*.

36. Nils Christie, "Conflicts as Property," *British Journal of Criminology* 17, no. 1 (1977): 1–15.

37. Desmond Tutu, *No Future without Forgiveness* (New York: Image Doubleday, 1999).

38. Martin Meredith and Tina Rosenberg, *Coming to Terms: South Africa's Search for Truth* (New York: Public Affairs, 1999).

39. Ibid.

40. Ibid.

41. Ibid. The truth and reconciliation process was criticized by many victims who felt that they had to relive their painful experiences and that their storytelling did not ensure that offenders would come forward to tell their stories. Many were frustrated with the fact that amnesty did not include punishment other than public shame and humiliation. The National Party criticized the process because of its public nature and because it revealed so much information about the inhumanity and racism in South Africa's past. Even the African National Congress (ANC) was upset about many of the findings of the TRC, which included criticism of the violent tactics used by ANC to try to liberate the South African people.

42. Mark Umbreit and Jean Greenwood, *National Survey of Victim-Offender Mediation Programs in the United States* (Washington, D.C.: U.S. Department of Justice, Office of Justice Programs, Office for Victims of Crime, 2000),

NCJ 176350, available online at http://www.ovc.gov/ publications/infores/ restorative_justice/96520-national_survey/welcome.html (accessed February 28, 2006).

43. Mark Umbreit, *Family Group Conferencing: Implications for Crime Victims* (Washington, D.C.: U.S. Department of Justice, Office of Justice Programs, Office for Victims of Crime, 2000), NCJ 176347, available online at http:// www.ovc.gov/infores/restorative_justice/96523-family_group/welcome.html (accessed February 28, 2006).

44. Gordon Bazemore and Mark Umbreit, *A Comparison of Four Restorative Conferencing Models* (Washington, D.C.: U.S. Department of Justice, Office of Juvenile Justice and Delinquency Programs, 1997); Braithwaite, *Restorative Justice and Responsive Regulation*; Umbreit, "Restorative Justice"; Van Ness and Strong, *Restoring Justice*.

45. Caren L. Flaten, "Victim-Offender Mediation: Application with Serious Offenses Committed by Juveniles," in *Restorative Justice: An International Perspective*, ed. Burt Galaway and Joe Hudson (Monsey, N.Y.: Criminal Justice Press, 1996), 387–402; Braithwaite, *Restorative Justice and Responsive Regulation*; Umbreit and Vos, "Homicide Survivors."

46. William Bradshaw and Mark S. Umbreit, "Crime Victims Meet Juvenile Offenders: Contributing Factors to Victim Satisfaction with Mediated Dialogue in Minneapolis," *Juvenile and Family Court Journal* 49 (1998): 17–25; Burt Galaway, "Restitution as Innovation or Unfilled Promise?" *Federal Probation* 52, no. 3 (1988): 3–14; Mark Umbreit and Ann W. Roberts, *Mediation of Criminal Conflict in England: An Assessment of Services in Coventry and Leeds* (St. Paul: University of Minnesota, Center for Restorative Justice and Mediation, 1996); Umbreit et al., *Facing Violence*.

47. William Nugent et al., "Participation in Victim-Offender Mediation and Reoffense: Successful Replications?" *Research on Social Work Practice* 11, no. 1 (2001): 5–23.

48. Umbreit et al., *Facing Violence*

49. Umbreit and Vos, "Homicide Survivors"; Van Ness and Strong, *Restoring Justice*.

50. Marty Price, "The Mediation of a Drunk-Driving Death: A Case Development Study," paper presented at the International Conference of the Victim-Offender Mediation Association, Winnipeg, Manitoba, Canada, June 4, 1994, available online at http://www.vorp.com/articles/ddcasest.html (accessed February 28, 2006); Tim Roberts, *Evaluation of the Victim Offender Mediation Program in Langley, B.C.* (Victoria, Canada: Focus Consultants, 1995); Mark Umbreit, "Violent Offenders and Their Victims," in *Mediation and Criminal Justice*, ed. Martin Wright and Burt Galaway (London: Sage, 1989), 337–352; Flaten, "Victim-Offender Mediation"; Umbreit et al., *Facing Violence*; Zehr, *Little Book*.

51. Umbreit et al., *Facing Violence*; Zehr, *Little Book*.

52. Tutu, *No Future without Forgiveness*.

53. Flaten, "Victim-Offender Mediation"; Umbreit, "Violent Offenders"; Umbreit, "Restorative Justice"; Umbreit and Vos, "Homicide Survivors."

54. Umbreit, "Violent Offenders."

55. Flaten, "Victim-Offender Mediation."

56. Roberts, *Evaluation of the Victim Offender Mediation.*

57. Radelet and Borg, "Comment on Umbreit and Vos."
58. Umbreit and Vos, "Homicide Survivors."
59. Ibid.
60. Ibid.
61. Umbreit et al., *Facing Violence*.
62. Ibid.
63. Elizabeth Beck et al., "Seeking Sanctuary: Interviews with Family Members of Capital Defendants," *Cornell Law Review* 88, no. 2 (2003): 382–418; Elizabeth Beck and Sarah Britto, "Using Feminist Methods and Restorative Justice to Interview Capital Offenders' Family Members," *Affilia: Journal of Women and Social Work* 21, no. 1 (2006): 59–70; Sarah Eschholz et al., "Offenders' Family Members' Responses to Capital Crimes," *Homicide Studies* 7, no. 2 (2003): 154–181.
64. Umbreit and Vos, "Homicide Survivors."

Chapter 3

1. Social histories are collected and used by effective defense teams to develop mitigating evidence for the sentencing phase of a death penalty trial. A complete and accurate psychosocial history requires three generations of data, as individuals often show traits that reflect patterns passed on through their ancestors.
2. It is not uncommon for schizophrenia to "sneak up" on family members. Generally the associated behaviors become pronounced following adolescence and are often visible when the affected person is in his or her 20s. Therefore it is not uncommon for family members to be bewildered because the change can be startling and confusing.
3. See, for example, Mark D. Cunningham and Mark P. Vigen, "Death Row Inmate Characteristics, Adjustment, and Confinement: A Critical Review of the Literature," *Behavioral Sciences and the Law* 20 (2002): 191–210; James Garbarino, *Lost Boys: Why Our Sons Turn Violent and How We Can Save Them* (New York: Free Press, 1999); Kathleen M. Heide, "Youth Homicide: A Review of the Literature and Blueprint for Action," *International Journal of Offender Therapy and Comparative Criminology* 47 (1999): 6–36.
4. Cunningham and Vigen, "Death Row Inmate Characteristics."
5. Dorothy Van Soest, "Different Paths to Death Row: A Comparison of Men Who Committed Heinous and Less Heinous Crimes," *Violence and Victims* 18 (2003): 15–33.
6. David Freedman and David Hemenway, "Precursors of Lethal Violence: A Death Row Sample," *Social Science and Medicine* 50 (2000): 1757–1770.
7. Kristin D. Schaefer and James J. Hennessy, "Intrinsic and Environmental Vulnerabilities among Executed Capital Offenders: Revisiting the Bio-Psycho-Social Model of Criminal Aggression," *Journal of Offender Rehabilitation* 34, no. 2 (2001): 1–19.
8. It is important to note that our sample may be a bit biased and therefore atypical, as some of the cases were referred to Arlene Andrews because of her expertise in interpersonal violence.

9. This story was told to us anecdotally by a defense lawyer who asked not to be named.

10. U.S. Census Bureau, "United States Census 2000," U.S. Census, n.d., available online at http://www.census.gov (accessed March 7, 2006).

11. Carel Bailey Germain, *Human Behavior in the Social Environment: An Ecological View* (New York: Columbia University Press, 1991).

12. Mary D. Salter Ainsworth, "Attachments beyond Infancy," *American Psychologist* 44, no. 4 (1989): 709–716; John Bowlby, *Attachment and Loss Vol. 1: Attachment* (New York: Basic Books, 1969); John Bowlby, *Attachment and Loss Vol. 2: Separation Anxiety and Anger* (New York: Basic Books, 1973); John Bowlby, *Attachment and Loss Vol. 3: Sadness and Depression* (New York: Basic Books, 1980).

13. Ross A. Thompson, "Empathy and Its Origins in Early Development," in *Intersubjective Communication and Emotion in Early Ontology*, ed. S. Braten (Cambridge: Cambridge University Press, 1998), 144–157.

14. Jack P. Shonkoff and Deborah A. Phillips, eds., *From Neurons to Neighborhoods: The Science of Early Childhood Development* (Washington, D.C.: National Academy Press, 2000).

15. John B. Reid, Gerald R. Patterson, and James Snyder, *Antisocial Behavior in Children and Adolescents: A Developmental Analysis and Model for Intervention* (Washington, D.C.: American Psychological Association, 2002).

16. E. Mavis Hetherington and W. Glenn Clingempeel, "Coping with Marital Transitions," *Monographs of the Society for Research in Child Development* 57 (1992): serial nos. 2–3; Theodore D. Wachs, "Proximal Experience and Early Cognitive-Intellectual Development: The Social Environment," in *Home Environment and Cognitive Development*, ed. A. W. Gottfried (London: Academic Press, 1984), 273–328.

17. Gary W. Evans, "The Environment of Childhood Poverty," *American Psychologist* 59, no. 2 (2004): 77–92.

18. G. Roger Jarjoura, Ruth A. Triplett, and Gregory P. Brinker, "Growing Up Poor: Examining the Link between Persistent Childhood Poverty and Delinquency," *Journal of Quantitative Criminology* 18, no. 2 (2002): 159–187.

19. Froma Walsh, *Strengthening Family Resilience* (New York: Guilford, 1998).

20. Timothy Dugan and Robert Coles, eds., *The Child in Our Times: Studies in the Development of Resiliency* (New York: Brunner/Mazel, 1989); James Garbarino, *Raising Children in a Socially Toxic Environment* (San Francisco: Jossey-Bass, 1997); Norman Garmezy, "Resiliency and Vulnerability to Adverse Developmental Outcomes Associated with Poverty," *American Behavioral Scientist* 34 (1991): 416–430; Rune J. Simeonsson, *Risk, Resilience, and Prevention: Promoting the Well-Being of All Children* (Baltimore: Paul H. Brookes, 1995).

21. Hamilton I. McCubbin et al., eds., *Stress, Coping and Health in Families: Sense of Coherence and Resiliency* (Thousand Oaks, Calif.: Sage, 1998).

Chapter 4

1. The judicial process associated with a typical death penalty case is found in Appendix B.

2. David Krajicek, *Scooped! Media Miss Real Story on Crime While Chasing Sex, Sleaze and Celebrities* (New York: Columbia University Press, 1998); Ray Surrette, *Media, Crime and Criminal Justice: Images and Realities*, 2nd ed. (Pacific Grove, Calif.: Wadsworth, 1998).

3. Barry Glassner, *The Culture of Fear: Why Americans Are Afraid of the Wrong Things* (New York: Basic Books, 2000).

4. David Croteau and William Hoynes, *The Business of Media: Corporate Media and Public Interest* (Thousand Oaks, Calif.: Pine Forge Press, 2001).

5. We were able to access newspaper coverage for 13 of the 24 cases that involved a general interview. The access came from the Internet, attorneys' records, and family members themselves.

6. Chapter 7 discusses PTSD in more detail, including the inherent difficulties in treatment.

7. Although it is difficult to know how many murders are committed as a result of an individual wanting to receive the death penalty, there are definitely some inmates who have committed heinous murders with that precise hope. Once these inmates give up their appeals, they are considered volunteers. At times, David was a volunteer; however, when his medicine was properly adjusted, he would state that he wanted to go through with the appeals process.

8. David's schizophrenia had what could be considered a normal onset. Often full-blown delusions occur when an individual is in his or her early twenties, which follows several years of what can be considered abnormal or strange behaviors. Edwin Fuller Torrey, *Surviving Schizophrenia: A Manual for Families, Consumers, and Providers* (New York: Harper Perennial, 1995).

9. See Rachel King, "A Mother's Love," in *Don't Kill in Our Names: Families of Murder Victims Speak Out against the Death Penalty* (New Brunswick, N.J.: Rutgers University Press, 2003).

10. Augusta Chronicle Editorial Staff, "Opinion: Stick It to Him," *Augusta Chronicle*, March 12, 2001, available online at http://www.augustachronicle. com/stories/031201/opi_240-5391.shtml (accessed March 10, 2006). Ron Spivey's execution and the debate surrounding lethal injection, both subjects of this editorial, are explored in chapter 5.

11. James S. Liebman, Jeffrey Fagan, and Valerie West, "A Broken System: Error Rates in Capital Cases, 1973–1995," The Justice Project—Campaign for Criminal Justice Reform, 2000, available online at http://www.thejustice project.org/press/reports/liebman-part-1.html (accessed March 10, 2006).

12. The researchers indicated that the reversal rate could be construed as evidence that the system works, because it is able to address mistakes. Their final interpretation was not so optimistic—they believe that the error rate is higher than their actual findings. Not all errors can be caught by the system because not all wrongly convicted offenders are granted a new trial (which is where the reversal occurs), and not all inmates on death row have an appellate lawyer who brings the errors to light. Second, the researchers found that many of the errors have been caught through extralegal efforts, including those of first-year journalism students and volunteer attorneys.

13. Studies have been commissioned by Maryland and Indiana governors, the New Jersey Supreme Court, the University of North Carolina, the Virginia American Civil Liberties Union, and the U.S. Justice Department. See Death Penalty Information Center, "Race and the Death Penalty," *Death*

Penalty Information Center: Issues: Race, available online at http://www. deathpenaltyinfo.org (accessed February 26, 2006); David C. Baldus, George G. Woodworth, and Charles A. Pulaski, eds., *Equal Justice and the Death Penalty: A Legal and Empirical Analysis* (Boston: Northeastern University Press, 1990).

14. Steven Bright, "Counsel for the Poor: The Death Penalty Not for the Worst Crime but for the Worst Lawyer," *Yale Law Journal* 103 (1994): 1835–1844; Steven Bright, "Neither Equal nor Just: The Rationing and Denial of Legal Services to the Poor When Life and Liberty Are at Stake," *Annual Survey of American Law* (1997): 783–838.

15. Given the layers of appeals in capital cases, it is not uncommon for a defendant to have a different legal team for various levels of the case and appeals. For example, there are defense teams who specialize in trials and those who specialize in appellate work. Often pro bono lawyers or nonprofit legal centers that specialize in capital appeals will take a case during its last stage. These appellate lawyers can be among the best capital defenders in the country, but they often begin their work with numerous structural obstacles. See *Gregg v. Georgia,* 428 U.S. 153 (1976). Moreover, representation at this stage is extremely grueling, and in many examples where the case has not been picked up by a resource center or nonprofit group, the case can be severely compromised by the limited funding made available for counsel. Additionally, some offenders languish on death row with no legal support whatsoever.

16. Dissociation is a hallmark of PTSD. This disorder is discussed in detail in chapter 7 and involves psychological distress and dysfunction based on surviving a traumatic event. *Diagnostic and Statistical Manual of Mental Disorders (DSM-IV-TR),* 4th ed., revised (Washington, D.C.: American Psychiatric Association, 2000), 463–468.

17. Ibid.

18. *Coe v. Tennessee,* 1998 Tenn. Crim. App. LEXIS 96 (Tenn. Ct. App. 1998).

19. Charles Doyle, "Antiterrorism and Effective Death Penalty Act of 1996: A Summary," Federation of American Scientists, available online at http:// www.fas.org/irp/crs/96-499.htm (accessed March 10, 2006).

20. To get the evidence heard, Troy and his lawyers must show two things: (1) that there is good reason to not have presented the evidence earlier in the process, and (2) that no reasonable juror would convict Troy following the presentation of new evidence. Bill Rankin and Alan Judd, "Witnesses Recant; Law Stymies Death Row Appeal," *Atlanta Journal-Constitution,* September 21, 2003, A1.

21. Ibid.; Martina Correia, "Request for Help: Troy Davis Innocent on Death Row in Georgia," Coalition for Truth and Justice, available online at http:// membres.lycos.fr/cftj2/html/modules.php?name=News&file-article&sid= 277 (accessed March 10, 2006).

22. Ibid.

23. Troy Anthony Davis, "Troy Anthony Davis: An Innocent Man on Georgia's Death Row," available online at http://www.troyanthonydavis.org (accessed March 10, 2006); Rankin and Judd, "Witnesses Recant," A1.

24. Troy Anthony Davis, "Letter to Members of the Media," Troy Anthony Davis: Legal Process, available online at http://www.troyanthonydavis.org/ legal-process.html (accessed March 10, 2006).

25. Maurice Possley and Steven Mills, "Clemency for All: Ryan Commutes 164 Death Sentences to Life in Prison without Parole; 'There Is No Honorable Way to Kill,' He Says," *Chicago Tribune,* January 12, 2001, 1.

26. Stuart P. Green, "Uncovering the Cover-Up Crimes," *American Criminal Law Review* 42, no. 9 (2005): 9–43.

27. Possley and Mills, "Clemency for All," 1.

28. George Ryan, "An Address on the Death Penalty," speech given at the University of Chicago Divinity School, Chicago, June 3, 2002, available online at http://pewforum.org/events/index/php?EventID=28 (accessed March 10, 2006).

29. Jeffrey Collins, "McWee Put to Death for Killing Aiken County Store Clerk," April 16, 2004, Clark County (Indiana) Prosecuting Attorney: Death Penalty: U.S. Executions since 1976: Jerry Bridwell McWee, available online at http://www.clarkprosecutor.org/html/death/US/mcwee908.htm (accessed March 10, 2006); Rick Halperin, "South Carolina—Impending Execution: A Case Where Clemency is Appropriate," *News— USA, Ind., Calif., S.C., LA* (e-mail list), available online at http://venus.soci.niu.edu/~archives/ABOLISH/oct04/0601.html (accessed March 10, 2006).

30. Jeffrey M. Shaman, "The Impartial Judge: Detachment or Passion?" *DePaul Law Review* (1996): 605–631.

31. Ted Chiricos and Charles Crawford, "Race and Imprisonment: A Contextual Assessment of the Evidence," in *Ethnicity, Race and Crime,* ed. Darnell Hawkins (Albany: State University of New York Press, 1995), 281–308.

32. Ronald S. Everett and Roger A. Wojkiewicz, "Difference, Disparity, and Race/Ethnic Bias in Federal Sentencing," *Journal of Quantitative Criminology* 18, no. 2 (2002): 189–211.

33. David C. Baldus, George Woodworth, David Zuckerman, and Neil Alan Weiner, "Racial Discrimination and the Death Penalty in the Post-Furman Era: An Empirical and Legal Overview, with Recent Findings from Philadelphia," *Cornell Law Review* 83 (1998): 1638–1756; *McClesky v. Kemp,* 481 U.S. 279, 309, 333 (1987); Baldus et al., eds., *Equal Justice.*

34. U.S. Government Accountability Office, *Death Penalty Sentencing: Research Indicates Pattern of Racial Disparities* (Washington, D.C.: Government Printing Office, February 1990), available online at http://archive.gao.gov/t2pbat11/140845.pdf (accessed March 10, 2006).

35. American Bar Association, "Georgia Death Penalty Assessment Report," American Bar Association Death Penalty Implementation Project, 2006, available online at http://www.abanet.org/moratorium/assessmentproject/georgia.html (accessed March 10, 2006); Death Penalty Information Center, "Race and the Death Penalty."

36. Death Penalty Information Center, "The Death Penalty in Black and White: Who Lives, Who Dies, Who Decides," available online at http://www.deathpenaltyinfo.org (accessed February 26, 2006).

37. Death Penalty Information Center, "Race of Death Row Inmates Executed since 1976," available online at http://www.deathpenaltyinfo.org (accessed February 26, 2006).

Chapter 5

1. See *South Carolina v. Shafer,* 531 S.E.2d 524 (South Carolina 2000), *rev'd and remand.,* 532 U.S. 36 (2001). In *Shafer,* the U.S. Supreme Court, in overturning the South Carolina Supreme Court's decision, ruled that due process is violated when the court fails to correct a jury's "speculative misunderstanding" about a death penalty case. In addition to the jury issue, Jerry's case was further complicated by his codefendant, George Scott, who testified that Jerry was completely at fault for the shooting. Jerry had never been in trouble with the law, whereas Scott had an extensive criminal record. However, Scott received a lighter sentence in exchange for cooperating with the authorities as they built a case against Jerry. Associated Press journalist Jeffrey Collins, in examining Jerry's case, noted the "gross disparity in sentencing." Jeffrey Collins, "U.S. Supreme Court Refuses to Stop Execution," April 14, 2004, Clark County (Indiana) Prosecuting Attorney: Death Penalty: U.S. Executions since 1976: Jerry Bridwell McWee, available online at http://www.clarkprosecutor.org/html/death/US/mcwee908.htm (accessed March 10, 2006).
2. Jeffrey Collins, "McWee Put to Death for Killing Aiken County Store Clerk," April 16, 2004, Clark County (Indiana) Prosecuting Attorney: Death Penalty: U.S. Executions since 1976: Jerry Bridwell McWee, available online at http://www.clarkprosecutor.org/html/death/US/mcwee908.htm (accessed March 10, 2006).
3. Collins, "McWee Put to Death."
4. Leonidas Koniaris et al., "Inadequate Anesthesia in Lethal Injection for Execution," *Lancet* 365 (2005): 1412–1414. This article describes a study in which researchers examined postmortem toxicology reports and discovered that 43 of the 49 men who were given lethal injection had anesthesia substance levels below that which was required for surgery, and 21 had levels that were consistent with being aware of what was happening. The researchers concluded, "Our data suggest that anesthesia methods in lethal injections in the USA are flawed. Failures in protocol design, implementation, monitoring, and review might have led to the unnecessary suffering of at least some of those executed." Koniaris et al., "Inadequate Anesthesia," 1413.
5. Stuart Banner, *The Death Penalty: An American History* (Cambridge, Mass.: Harvard University Press, 2002); Norval Morris and David J. Rothman, eds., *The Oxford History of the Prison: The Practice of Punishment in Western Society* (New York: Oxford University Press, 1995).
6. Michel Foucault, *Discipline and Punish: The Birth of the Prison* (New York: Pantheon Books, 1977).
7. Morris and Rothman, *The Oxford History of the Prison.*
8. Ibid.
9. Ibid.
10. Perry T. Ryan, *The Last Public Execution in America* (Kentucky: Perry T. Ryan, 1992).
11. Ibid.
12. Robert J. Lifton and Greg Mitchell, *Who Owns Death? Capital Punishment, the American Conscience, and the End of Executions* (New York: Morrow, 2002), 144.

13. Ibid.

14. Margaret Vandiver, "The Impact of the Death Penalty on Family Members of the Homicide Victims and of Condemned Prisoners," in *America's Experiment with Capital Punishment: Reflections on the Past, Present, and Future of the Ultimate Penal Sanction*, ed. James Acker et al., 2nd ed. (Durham, N.C.: Carolina Academic Press, 2003), 477–505.

15. Rhonda Cook, "Pardons and Paroles Board Rejects Clemency; Gilreath Can Now Turn Only to Courts," *Atlanta Journal-Constitution*, November 15, 2001, E1.

16. Bill Rankin, "Son Hopes Execution Halted Mother Slain, Now His Father Set to Pay Price," *Atlanta Journal-Constitution*, November 8, 2001, F3.

17. Amnesty International, "Further Information on Death Penalty, Ronald Keith Spivey," Amnesty International, available online at http://web.amnesty.org/library/Index/ENGAMR510122002?open&of=ENG-2AM (accessed March 29, 2006).

18. CNNfyi.com, "Death Penalty by Electrocution on Trial: Georgia Seeks to Resolve Constitutionality of Electric Chair," CNNfyi.com, March 7, 2001, available online at http://cnnstudentnews.cnn.com/2001/fyi/news/03/07/electric.chair (accessed March 17, 2006).

19. Ibid.

20. Augusta Chronicle Editorial Staff, "Stick It to Him," *Augusta Chronicle*, March 12, 2001, available online at http://chronicle.augusta.com/stories/031201/opi_240-5391.shtml (accessed March 17, 2006).

21. Rhonda Cook, "State Executes Columbus Cop Killer; Spivey Apologizes, Blasts Punishment," *Atlanta Journal-Constitution*, January 25, 2005, p. C3.

22. American Medical Association, "E-2.06: Capital Punishment," *American Medical Association: AMA Agenda: Be Informed: PolicyFinder*, available online at http://www.ama-assn.org (accessed March 17, 2006).

23. When an execution is botched, physicians are asked to play a more active role with such tasks as finding a vein or adjusting the amount of a needed drug. For a discussion on doctors' roles, see Sherri Edwards and Suzanne McBride, "Doctor's Aid in Injection Violated Ethics Rule: Physician Helped Insert the Lethal Tube in a Breach of AMA's Policy Forbidding Active Role in Execution," *Indianapolis Star*, July 19, 1996, A1. Jose High's execution provides one example of a physician having to insert a needle.

24. Several weeks before Felicia's father's execution, Jose High was pronounced dead 69 minutes after the execution started. After 39 minutes of searching for a vein, the emergency medical technicians called for support from a physician, who then inserted the needle between High's shoulder and neck. Rhonda Cook, "Gang Leader Executed by Injection: Death Comes 25 Years after Boy, 11, Slain," *Atlanta Journal-Constitution*, November 7, 2001, B1.

Chapter 6

1. Jeremy Travis, Elizabeth Cincotta, and Amy Solomon, *Families Left Behind: The Hidden Costs of Incarceration and Re-Entry* (Washington, D.C.: Urban Institute Justice Policy Center, 2003).

2. U.S. Department of Justice, *Report on Minor Children Who Have a Mother or Father in Prison* (Washington D.C.: U.S. Department of Justice, Bureau of Justice Statistics, 2002). The literature review in this section does not touch on the research involving children of incarcerated mothers because the vast majority of death row inmates are male.

3. Denise Johnston, "Effects of Parental Incarceration," in *Children of Incarcerated Parents,* ed. Katherine Gabel and Denise Johnston (New York: Lexington Books, 1995), 59–88; Travis A. Fritsch and John D. Burkhead, "Behavioral Reactions of Children to Parental Absence Due to Imprisonment," *Family Relations* 30 (1982): 83–88; William Sack, "Children of Imprisoned Fathers," *Psychiatry* 40 (1977): 163–174; William Sack, Jack Seidler, and Susan Thomas, "The Children of Imprisoned Parents: A Psychosocial Exploration," *American Journal of Orthopsychiatry* 46 (1976): 618–628; Stewart Gabel and Richard Shindledecker, "Aggressive Behavior in Youth: Characteristics, Outcome and Psychiatric Diagnosis," *Journal of American Academy of Child and Adolescent Psychiatry* 30 (1991): 982–988; Denise Johnston, *Children of Offenders* (Pasadena, Calif.: Pacific Oaks Center for Children of Incarcerated Parents); Katherine Gabel and Denise Johnston, *Children of Incarcerated Parents* (New York: Lexington Books, 1995).

4. See Fox Butterfield, "Parents in Prison: A Special Report; As Inmate Population Grows, So Does a Focus on Children," *New York Times,* April 7, 1999, A1.

5. Susan Phillips et al., "Parental Incarceration among Adolescents Receiving Mental Health Services," *Journal of Child and Family Studies* 11 (2002): 385–399; Fritsch and Burkhead, "Behavioral Reactions of Children."

6. Stewart Gable, "Behavioral Problems in Sons of Incarcerated or Otherwise Absent Fathers: The Issue of Separation," *Family Process* 31 (1992): 303–313.

7. Ibid.

8. Johnston, "Effects of Parental Incarceration," 68.

9. Creasy Hairston, "Men in Prison: Family Characteristics and Family Views," *Journal of Offender Counseling, Services and Rehabilitation* 14 (1989): 123–130.

10. Robert Meeropol and Michael Meeropol, *We Are Your Sons* (Boston: Houghton Mifflin, 1975); see also Michael Meeropol, comp., *The Rosenberg Letters: A Complete Edition of the Prison Correspondence of Ethel and Julius Rosenberg* (New York: Garland, 1994).

11. Meeropol, *The Rosenberg Letters,* 137; see also Meeropol and Meeropol, *We Are Your Sons.*

12. Meeropol, *The Rosenberg Letters,* 141; *see also* Meeropol and Meeropol, *We Are Your Sons.*

13. Meeropol, *The Rosenberg Letters,* 235; see also Meeropol and Meeropol, *We Are Your Sons.*

14. Robert Meeropol, *An Execution in the Family: One Son's Journey* (New York: St. Martin's Griffin, 2003), 32.

15. Rachel King, *Don't Kill in Our Names: Families of Murder Victims Speak Out against the Death Penalty* (New Brunswick, N.J.: Rutgers University Press, 2003).

16. Ibid., 138.

17. Ibid.

18. Meeropol, *An Execution in the Family*, 273.

19. Ibid., 118.

20. Ibid.

21. Robert believes that his parents did not commit the crime for which they were executed, and he believes that his mother was not involved in any interactions with the Soviets. Presently, Robert will not emphatically say that his father did not interact with the Soviet Union. It is possible that Julius may have given industrial (but not atomic) information to the Soviet Union with the idea that the information could help the Soviets defeat the Nazis. However, because so many of the documents have either been tampered with or remain sealed, Robert is aware that his father may have never had any dealings with the Soviet Union. The documents that point to Julius as providing industrial secrets also exonerate Ethel.

22. Meeropol, *An Execution in the Family*, 121.

23. Rosenberg Fund for Children, "Mission Statement and Background," available online at http://www.rfc.org (accessed March 20, 2006).

24. Meeropol, *An Execution in the Family*, 201, 193.

25. United Nations Office of the High Commissioner of Human Rights, "Universal Declaration of Human Rights," available online at http://www.unhchr.ch/udhr/lang/eng.htm (accessed April 7, 2006).

Chapter 7

1. John O. Smykla, "The Human Impact of Capital Punishment: Interviews with Families of Persons on Death Row," *Journal of Criminal Justice* 15 (1987): 331–347.

2. There are no typical grief reactions, but the following resources describe adaptive experiences: Thomas Attig, *How We Grieve: Relearning the World* (New York: Oxford University Press, 1996); Charles A. Corr and Kenneth J. Doka, "Master Concepts in the Field of Death, Dying, and Bereavement: Coping versus Adaptive Strategies," *Omega* 43 (2001): 183–199; and Elisabeth Kübler-Ross, *On Death and Dying* (New York: Macmillan, 1969).

3. Eric Linemann, "Symptoms and Management of Acute Grief," *American Journal of Psychiatry* 101 (1944): 141–148.

4. Katharine Norgard, "Beyond Grief," in *Capital Consequences: Families of the Condemned Tell Their Stories*, ed. Rachel King (New Brunswick, N.J.: Rutgers University Press, 2005).

5. For the Norgard family, the years of appeals ultimately led to joy as their son was given a new trial and a subsequent sentence of life without parole.

6. Elizabeth J. Bruce and Cynthia L. Schultz, *Nonfinite Loss and Grief: A Psychoeducational Approach* (Baltimore: Paul H. Brooks, 2001).

7. Ibid.

8. This support group is for family members who have a loved one in the general prison population. At the time of this writing, a support group specifically for death row inmate family members did not exist.

9. Margaret Vandiver, "The Impact of the Death Penalty on Family Members of the Homicide Victims and of Condemned Prisoners," in *America's Experiment with Capital Punishment: Reflections on the Past, Present, and Future of the Ultimate Penal Sanction*, 2nd ed., ed. James Acker et al. (Durham, N.C.: Carolina Academic Press, 2003), 477–505.

10. Kenneth J. Doka, ed., *Disenfranchised Grief: Recognizing Hidden Sorrows* (Lexington, Mass.: Lexington Books, 1989), 4.

11. Bronna D. Romanoff and Marion Terenzio, "Rituals and the Grieving Process," *Death Studies* 22, no. 8 (1998): 697–712.

12. Smykla, "The Human Impact"; Vandiver, "The Impact of the Death Penalty."

13. American Psychiatric Association, *Diagnostic and Statistical Manual of Mental Disorders (DSM-IV-TR)*, 4th ed., revised (Washington, D.C.: American Psychiatric Association, 2000), 209–220.

14. Anne Sheffield, *Depression Fallout: The Impact of Depression on Couples and What You Can Do to Preserve the Bond* (New York: Quill, 2003).

15. Aaron T. Beck, Robert A. Steer, and Gregory K. Brown, *BDI-II, Beck Depression Inventory: Manual*, 2nd ed. (Boston: Harcourt Brace, 1996).

16. "Women and Depression," *Harvard Mental Health Letter* 20, no. 11 (2002): 1–4.

17. It is possible that some of the family members' pain is a result of accumulated loss, that is, the death of two children, though each did talk about the different nature of the loss with execution being harder.

18. "Women and Depression"; Jonathan R. Davidson, "Recognition and Treatment of Posttraumatic Stress Disorder," *Journal of the American Medical Association* 286, no. 5 (2001): 584–589.

19. Nicoletta Brunello et al., "Posttraumatic Stress Disorder: Diagnosis and Epidemiology, Comorbidity and Social Consequences, Biology and Treatment," *Neuropsychobiology* 43, no. 3 (2001): 150–163; Rosario B. Hidalgo and Johnathan R. Davidson, "Selective Serotonin Reuptake Inhibitors in Post-Traumatic Stress Disorder," *Journal of Psychopharmacology* 14, no. 1 (2000): 70–77.

20. Judith Herman, *Trauma and Recovery* (New York: Basic Books, 1997), 33.

21. Ibid., 4.

22. Davidson, "Recognition and Treatment."

23. Viktor E. Frankl, "The Unheard Cry for Meaning: Psychotherapy and Humanism," in *Traumatic Stress: The Effects of Overwhelming Experience on Mind, Body, and Society*, ed. Bessel A. van der Kolk et al. (New York: Guilford Press, 1996).

24. *DSM-IV-TR*; Davidson, "Recognition and Treatment."

25. *DSM-IV-TR*.

26. Article reprinted from the (St. Paul/Minesota) *PioneerPlanet*, Abolitionist Action Committee, n.d., available online at http://www.abolition.org/earle_interview.html (accessed March 23, 2006).

27. Jonathan Davidson, "Davidson Trauma Scale," *Multi-Health Systems* (1996).

28. *DSM-IV-TR*.

29. Ibid.; Davidson, "Recognition and Treatment."

30. Ralph J. DiClemente et al., "Adverse Health Consequences That Co-occur with Depression: A Longitudinal Study of Black Adolescent Females," *Pediatrics* 116, no. 1 (2005): 78.

31. John Briere and Joseph Spinazzola, "Phenomenology and Psychological Assessment of Complex Post-traumatic States," *Journal of Traumatic Stress* 18, no. 5 (2005): 401–412.

32. James Gilligan, *Preventing Violence* (New York: Thames and Hudson, 2001).

33. We also reviewed the public records found in Mike's story. Not all family members were able to discuss the feelings of other members, and his and the following story were told to us by members of their defense team and are a part of public record.

34. Sandra Bloom, *Creating Sanctuary: Toward an Evolution of Sane Societies* (New York: Routledge, 1997).

35. Ibid.; Janine Karen Beck, Kathryn Gow, and Poppy Liossis, "Holocaust Survivors' Delay in Child Rearing and the Psychological Health of Their Children," *Journal of Loss and Trauma* 10, no. 2 (2005): 205–220; Natan Kellerman, "Transmission of Holocaust Trauma—An Integrative View," *Psychiatry: Interpersonal and Biological Processes* 64, no. 3 (2001): 256–268.

36. Howard Zehr, *Restorative Justice: A Short Introduction for Defense-Based Victim Outreach Training based on the Little Book of Restorative Justice* (Intercourse, Pa.: Good Books, 2002); training seminar for "Just Bridges," Eastern Mennonites University, June 2005.

Chapter 8

1. Jeff Flock, "'Blanket Commutation' Empties Illinois Death Row: Incoming Governor Criticizes Decision," CNN.com, January 13 2003, available online at http://www.cnn.com/2003/LAW/01/11/illinois.death.row/ (accessed December 7, 2005).

2. Northwestern University School of Law Center on Wrongful Convictions, "Illinois Death Penalty Exonerations," Northwestern University School of Law: Faculty and Research: Programs and Centers: Center on Wrongful Convictions, available online at http://www.law.northwestern.edu/depts/clinic/wrongful/exonerations/Illinois.htm (accessed April 22, 2006).

3. *Roper v. Simmons*, 543 U.S. 551 (2005); *Atkins v. Virginia*, 536 U.S. 304 (2002).

4. James S. Liebman, Jeffrey Fagan, and Valerie West, "A Broken System: Error Rates in Capital Cases, 1973–1995," The Justice Project Campaign for Criminal Justice Reform, 2000, available online at http://www.thejusticeproject.org/press/reports/liebman-part-1.html (accessed March 10, 2006).

5. Ibid

6. Ibid.

7. Helen Prejean, *The Death of Innocents: An Eyewitness Account of Wrongful Executions* (New York: Random House, 2004); Michael L. Radelet, Hugo Adam Bedau, and Constance E. Putnam, *In Spite of Innocence: Erroneous Convictions in Capital Cases* (Boston: Northeastern University Press, 1992).

8. Jessica Blank and Erick Johnson, "The Exonerated," *The Exonerated*, available online at http://theexonerated.com (accessed April 22, 2006).

9. Death Penalty Information Center, "Innocence: List of Those Freed from Death Row," available online at http://www.deathpenaltyinfo.org (accessed February 26, 2006).

10. Ibid.

11. Ibid.

12. Max Hirshberg, "Wrongful Convictions," *Rocky Mountain Law Review* 13 (1940): 20–46.

13. Ibid.

14. Illinois Criminal Justice Authority's Research and Analysis Unit, *The Needs of the Wrongfully Convicted: A Report on a Panel Discussion*, report to the Governor's Commission on Capital Punishment, March 15, 2002, Center for Wrongful Convictions, available online at http://www.law.northwestern. edu/depts/clinic/wrongful/documents/ILLPanelRPt.htm (accessed April 30, 2006).

15. National Coalition to Abolish the Death Penalty Conference, Nashville, Tenn., October 19, 2003.

16. University of Missouri–Columbia School of Law American Civil Liberties Union Chapter and Christian Legal Society, "Petition Submitted to Governor Holden for Joseph Amrine," University of Missouri–Columbia School of Law: ACLU: View MU Law School ACLU Clemency Petition, available online at http://mail.law.missouri.edu/aclu/amrinepetition.html (accessed April 30, 2006).

17. Application for pardon to Governor Bob Holden by Sean D. O'Brien and Kent E. Gipson, in the matter of Joseph Amrine, CP48, available online at http://www.umsl.edu/divisions/artscience/forlanglit/mbp/amrinej.html (accessed April 30, 2006).

18. University of Missouri–Columbia School of Law American Civil Liberties Union Chapter and Christian Legal Society, "Petition submitted."

19. *Schlup v. Delno*, 513 U.S. 298 (1995).

20. Joe's sisters asked that only their first names be used.

Chapter 9

1. Quoted in Rachel King, *Capital Consequences: Families of the Condemned Tell Their Stories* (Piscataway, N.J.: Rutgers University Press, 2005), 4.

2. Herbert H. Haines, *Against Capital Punishment: The Anti–Death Penalty Movement in America, 1972–1994* (New York: Oxford University Press, 1996); Norman Johnston, "Prison Reform in Pennsylvania," Pennsylvania Prison Society, available online at http://www.prisonsociety.org/about/ history.shtml (accessed April 5, 2006).

3. Cesare Beccaria, *An Essay on Crimes and Punishment* (Philadelphia: Prentice Hall, 1819); Jesse Jackson, *Legal Lynching: Racism, Injustice and the Death Penalty* (New York: Marlowe, 1996).

4. Beccaria, *An Essay on Crimes*.

5. Haines, *Against Capital Punishment*.

6. Ibid.

7. Ibid.

8. Ibid.
9. See, for example, Theodore Hamm, *Rebel and a Cause: Caryl Chessman and the Politics of the Death Penalty in Postwar California, 1948–1974* (Berkeley: University of California Press, 2001); William M. Kunstler, *Beyond a Reasonable Doubt? The Original Trial of Caryl Chessman* (Westport, Conn.: Greenwood Press, 1973).
10. Haines, *Against Capital Punishment.*
11. Ibid.
12. *Roper v. Simmons,* 543 U.S. 551 (2005).
13. *Atkins v. Virginia,* 536 U.S. 304 (2002).
14. *Ring v. Arizona,* 536 U.S. 584 (2002); *Wiggins v. Smith,* 539 U.S. 510 (2003).
15. Haines, *Against Capital Punishment.*
16. National Coalition to Abolish the Death Penalty, "About Us," available online at http://www.ncadp.org/about_us.html (accessed April 5, 2006).
17. Floridians for Alternatives to the Death Penalty, "Floridians for Alternatives to the Death Penalty," available online at http://www.fadp.org (accessed April 5, 2006).
18. Amnesty International USA, available online at http://web.amnest.org/pages/deathpenalty-index-eng (accessed January 12, 2005).
19. Amnesty International USA, "National Weekend of Faith in Action on the Death Penalty," available online at http://www.amnestyusa.org/faithinaction (accessed April 5, 2006).
20. Lorraine Gutierrez, Ruth Parsons, and Enid Opal Cox, *Empowerment in Social Work Practice* (Pacific Grove, Calif.: Brooks Cole, 1997).
21. Ibid.
22. James Carville, "James Carville on Bob Casey," interviewed by Kathryn Jean Lopez, *National Review,* June 1, 2000, available online at http://www.nationalreview.com/interrogatory/interrogatoryprint060100.html (accessed April 12, 2006).
23. Pierre Sane, "News Release Issued by the International Secretariat of Amnesty International," AI Index: AMR 51/76/97 25 November 1997, Action Alert, available online at http://home4.inet.tele.dk/lepan/lene/pennsy.htm (accessed April 12, 2006).
24. Mike Bucsko and Robert Dvorchak, "Firings, Charges Shake up SCI Greene," *Pittsburgh Post-Gazette,* August 9, 1998; Robert Dvorchak, "State-of-Art SCI Greene Criticized as Repressive," *Pittsburgh Post-Gazette,* August 10, 1998; Gwen Schaffer, "Dead Serious: Anti–Death Penalty Activists Are Traveling Across the State to Spread Their Message," Philadephia Citypaper. net, May 18–June 4, 1998, available online at http://www.citypaper.net/articles/052898/cb.caravan.shtml (accessed April 12, 2006).
25. Robert Dvorchak and Mike Bucsko, "Guards Applaud Prison Official's Swift Demotion," *Pittsburgh Post-Gazette,* April 21, 1998.
26. Pennsylvania Department of Corrections, "Visiting Information," available online at http://www.cor.state.pa.us/greene/cwp/view.asp?a=428&q=129545&greeneNav=| (accessed April 12, 2006).
27. Mumia Abu-Jamal has been on death row for over 23 years. His case has received a great deal of media attention because he has always proclaimed his innocence, and he is the author of several books, including *Live from Death Row* (Reading, Mass.: Addison Wesley, 1995).

28. Sean Covey, *The 7 Habits of Highly Effective Teens* (New York: Fireside, 1998).

29. Since the time of our interview, Peggy has started Reunification Transportation Services, which provides transportation to family members of general population inmates.

30. Bill Pelke, *Journey of Hope . . . From Violence to Healing* (Philadelphia: Xlibris, 2003).

31. Murder Victims' Families for Human Rights, "Murder Victims' Families for Human Rights: Home," available online at http://www.mvfhr.org (accessed April 12, 2006).

32. Renny Cushing and Bud Welch, "Transcript of an Address by Renny Cushing, Executive Director, and Bud Welch, Board President at Harvard Univ. in 1999," Murder Victims' Families for Human Rights: Reports and Articles (presentation to the Human Rights Commission, Kennedy School of Government, Harvard University, Cambridge, Mass., March 16, 1999), available online at http://www.murdervictimsfamilies.org (accessed February 28, 2006).

33. Murder Victims' Families for Human Rights, "Home"; United Nations Office of the High Commissioner of Human Rights, "Universal Declaration of Human Rights," available online at http://www.unhchr.ch/udhr/lang/eng.htm (accessed April 7, 2006).

34. Murder Victims' Families for Human Rights, "Home."

35. Celia McWee, "Celia McWee," *WBJ Press & Will's World* (presentation at the No Silence, No Shame Inaugural Event, Austin, Texas, October 27, 2005), available online at http://www.willsworld.com/~mvfhr/nsstatements.htm (accessed April 22, 2006).

36. *Austin American-Statesman*, "The Families Left Behind," *Austin American-Statesman,* October 28, 2005, available online at http://www.willsworld.com/~mvfhr/nsns2.htm (accessed April 22, 2006).

37. Randolph Loney, *A Dream of the Tattered Man: Stories from Georgia's Death Row* (Grand Rapids, Mich.: William B. Eerdmans, 2001).

Chapter 10

1. Mark Umbreit et al., *Facing Violence: The Path of Restorative Justice and Dialogue* (Monsey, N.Y.: Criminal Justice Press, 2003).

2. Just Bridges, *Video Interview with the Kotzbauer Family*, Summer Peace Building Institute: Defense Based Victim Outreach Training, Harrisonburg, Va., June 2005.

3. Howard Zehr, *The Little Book of Restorative Justice* (Intercourse, Pa.: Good Books, 2002), 62–63.

4. Mark Reed, Sarah Britto, and Brenda Blackwell, "The Source and Nature of Secondary Victimization Among Homicide Co-Victims," paper presented at the annual meeting for the American Society of Criminology, Nashville, Tenn., November 17, 2002. For a further discussion of victims' thoughts about the death penalty, see James Acker and David Karp, *Wounds That Do Not Bind: Victim-Based Perspectives on the Death Penalty* (Durham, N.C.: Carolina Academic Press, 2006).

5. Ibid.

6. Ibid.

7. Ibid.

8. For a further discussion on defense-based victim outreach, see Tammy Krause, "Reaching out to the Other Side: Defense Based Victim Outreach in Capital Cases," in *Wounds That Do Not Bind: Victim Based Perspectives on the Death Penalty*, ed. James Acker and David Karp (Durham, N.C.: Carolina Academic Press, 2006), 379–396.

9. Zehr, *Little Book*.

10. Ibid.

11. Burr further explained that although the VOS is connected to the defense team, he or she is more like an expert witness than a team member. "The victim outreach specialist needs to have a little distance and needs not to have all the information that's inside the defense team. Because many questions arise in talking with family members that if the person knew everything, they could immediately be conflicted because they wouldn't know whether to disclose it or not. So it's better for them to say, 'I don't know but I can go talk to the defense team and see what they say.' This also allows the victim outreach specialist to become centered with the victim's family and then reach back to the defense team."

12. Christine Hanley, "At His Sentencing, Yosemite Killer Apologizes to Family," *Los Angeles Times*, October 4, 2000, A3.

13. Connie Kotzbauer speaks of this in a training video for VOSs. Just Bridges, *Video Interview with the Kotzbauer Family*.

14. Mark Umbreit and Betty Vos, "Homicide Survivors Meet the Offender Prior to Execution," *Homicide Studies* 4, no. 1 (2000): 63–87.

15. Umbreit et al., *Facing Violence*.

16. Umbreit and Vos, "Homicide Survivors."

17. Ibid.

18. Ibid.; Umbreit et al., *Facing Violence*.

19. Umbreit et al., *Facing Violence*, 353.

20. Ibid., 355.

21. Ibid., 369.

22. Rachel King, *Don't Kill in Our Names: Families of Murder Victims Speak Out against the Death Penalty* (New Brunswick, N.J.: Rutgers University Press, 2003).

23. Tariq Khamisa Foundation, "Planting Seeds of Hope: TKF," available online at http://www.tkf.org (accessed March 22, 2006).

24. Ibid.

25. David Kaczynski and Gary Wright, "Building a Bridge," in *Wounds That Do Not Bind: Victim Based Perspectives on the Death Penalty*, ed. James Acker and David Karp (Durham, N.C.: Carolina Academic Press, 2006), 85–101.

26. Ibid., 96.

27. Ibid., 99.

28. Ibid.

29. Ibid.

30. Michael L. Radelet and Marian J. Borg, "Comment on Umbreit and Vos," *Homicide Studies* 4, no. 1 (2000): 88–92.

Chapter 11

1. Lois Robison to Texas Board of Pardons and Paroles and Governor George W. Bush, July 22, 1999, Letters of Support for Larry Robison, Letters

of Support: Lois Robison Letter to Governor, available online at http://www.larryrobison.org/pages/momgov.htm (accessed April 27, 2006); Rachel King, *Capital Consequences: Families of the Condemned Tell Their Stories* (New Brunswick, NJ: Rutgers University Press, 2005).

2. Robison to Texas Board of Pardons.

3. Ibid.

4. Ibid.; Clark County (Indiana) Prosecuting Attorney, "Larry Keith Robison," Clark County Prosecuting Attorney: Death Penalty: U.S. Executions since 1976: Larry Keith Robison, available online at http://www.clarkprosecutor.org/html/death/US/robison607.htm(accessed April 28, 2006); King, *Capital Consequences.*

5. Dennis Sullivan and Larry Tifft, *Restorative Justice: Healing the Foundations of Our Everyday Lives* (Monsey, N.Y.: Willow Tree Press, 2001).

6. Urie Bronfenbrenner, *The Ecology of Human Development* (Cambridge, Mass.: Harvard University Press, 1979); Urie Bronfenbrenner, "Environments in Developmental Perspective: Theoretical and Operational Models," in *Measuring Environment across the Life Span: Emerging Methods and Concepts,* ed. Sarah L. Friedman and Theodore D. Wachs (Washington, D.C.: American Psychological Association Press, 1999), 3–28; Carel B. Germain, *Human Behavior in the Social Environment: An Ecological View* (New York: Columbia University Press, 1991).

7. David Freedman and David Hemenway, "Precursors of Lethal Violence: A Death Row Sample," *Social Science and Medicine* 50 (2000): 1757–1770.

8. Mary Bissell and Jess McDonald, "Dedicated, Overworked, Underfunded; Child Welfare Workers," *Miami Herald,* September 5, 2005, available online at http://www.newamerica.net/index.cfm?pg=article&DocID=2535 (accessed April 28, 2006).

9. Edward Gondolf, "Treating the Batterer," in *Battering and Family Therapy: A Feminist Perspective,* ed. Marsali Hanse and Michele Harway (Newbury Park, Calif.: Sage Publications, 1993).

10. Jennie G. Noll, "Does Childhood Sexual Abuse Set in Motion a Cycle of Violence against Women?" *Journal of Interpersonal Violence* 20, no. 4 (2005): 455–463.

11. Edward Gondolf, "Anger and Oppression in Men Who Batter: Empiricist and Feminist Perspectives and Their Implication for Research," *Victimology* 10 (1985): 311–324; Edward Gondolf "Who Are the Guys? Toward a Typology of Men Who Batter," *Violence and Victims* 3 (1988): 187–203.

12. Sandra L. Bloom and Michael Reichert, *Bearing Witness: Violence and Collective Responsibility* (Binghamton, N.Y.: Hawthorne Press, 1998).

13. The intermittent nature of negative behavior induces anticipatory anxiety and learned helplessness. If Martha's father had been "all bad," the family could have coped by accepting the worst and learning to live with it. Instead, he had good periods, when the family would forgive him and focus instead on his stature in the church and the relative peace in the household. Chronic victims of intermittent family violence often feel worse during these good periods than the bad periods because the bad is unpredictable, and they are constantly anxious about the next bad period. The victim becomes vigilant, anticipating the worst, and often mistrusts good intentions. Drew Westen, *Psychology: Mind, Brain, and Culture* (New York: Wiley, 1999).

14. The United States has a history of being hesitant about signing international treaties, including those related to human rights.

15. The positive effects of these interviews are described in Elizabeth Beck and Sarah Britto, "Using Feminist Methods and Restorative Justice to Interview Capital Offenders' Family Members," *Affilia: Journal of Women and Social Work* 21, no. 1 (2006): 59–70.

16. Charlotte H. Rudel and Margaret L. Hayes, "Behind No Bars—Cambria County Prison's Innovative Family Visiting Program," *Children Today,* May–June 1990, available online at http://www.findarticles.com/p/artiesl/mi_m1053/is_n3_v19/ai_8944320 (accessed April 28, 2006).

17. Tony Anderson, "Restorative Justice Places Power in Victims' Hands," *Wisconsin Law Journal,* November 24, 2004, available online at http://www.wislawjournal.com/archive/2004/1142/justice-1124.html (accessed April 28, 2006).

18. This is one of many programs described on the Centerforce Web site. Centerforce, "Centerforce: Our Programs," available online at http://www.centerforce.org/programs (accessed April 28, 2006).

Chapter 12

1. Howard Zehr, *The Little Book of Restorative Justice* (Intercourse, Pa.: Good Books, 2002), 62–63.

2. Camille B. Wortman, Esther S. Battle, and Jeanne Parr Lemkau, "Coming to Terms with the Sudden, Traumatic Death of a Spouse or Child," in *Victims of Crime,* ed. Arthur J. Lurigio, Wesley G. Skogan, and Robert C. Davis (Thousand Oaks, Calif.: Sage Publications, 1997), 108–133; Angelynne Amick-McMullen, D. Kilpatrick, L. J. Veronen, and S. Smith, "Family Survivors of Homicide Victims: A Behavioral Analysis," *Behavioral Therapist* 77 (1989); Ronnie Janoff-Bulman and Irene Frieze, "Theoretical Perspective for Understanding Reactions to Victimization," *Journal of Social Issues* 39 (1983).

3. "Witness to an Execution," All Things Considered, NPR, October 20, 2000, available online at http://www.mindfully.org/Reform/Texas-Executioner-Huntsville2.htm (accessed May 3, 2006).

4. NOVA, *Crime Victim and Witness Rights,* available online at http://www.trynova.org/victimrights.

5. Mark Umbreit, Betty Vos, Robert Coates, and Katherine Brown, *Facing Violence: The Path of Restorative Justice Dialogue* (Monsey, N.Y.: Criminal Justice Press, 2003); Zehr, *Little Book,* 62–63; Caren L. Flaten, "Victim-Offender Mediation: Application with Serious Offenses Committed by Juveniles," in *Restorative Justice: An International Perspective,* ed. Burt Galaway and Joe Hudson (Monsey, N.Y.: Criminal Justice Press, 1996), 387–402; Mark Umbreit and Betty Vos, "Homicide Survivors Meet the Offender Prior to Execution," *Homicide Studies* 4, no. 1 (2000): 63–87; Tim Roberts, *Evaluation of the Victim Offender Mediation Program in Langley, B.C.* (Victoria, Canada: Focus Consultants, 1995); Marty Price, "The Mediation of a Drunk Driving Death: A Case Development Study,"

paper presented at the International Conference of the Victim-Offender Mediation Association, Winnipeg, Manitoba, Canada, June 4, 1994, available online at http://www.vorp.com/articles/ddcasest.html (accessed February 28, 2006).

6. Umbreit et al., *Facing Violence*; Zehr, *Little Book,* 62–63.

7. Michael E. McCullough, Everett L. Worthington, and K. C. Rachel, "Interpersonal Forgiving in Close Relationships," *Journal of Personality and Social Psychology* 73 (1997): 321–336.

8. B. Weiner, S. Graham, O. Peter, and M. Zmuidinas, "Public Confessions and Forgiveness," *Journal of Personality* 59 (1991): 218–312.

9. Robert D. Enright and Joanna North, eds., *Exploring Forgiveness* (Madison: University of Wisconsin Press, 1998).

10. Julie J. Exline, Everett L. Worthington, Peter Hill, and Michael E. McCullough, "Forgiveness and Justice: A Research Agenda for Social and Personality Psychology," *Personality and Social Psychology Review* 7, no. 4 (2003): 337–348.

11. Umbreit et al., *Facing Violence*; Zehr, *Little Book,* 62–63.

12. Gerry Johnstone, *Restorative Justice: Ideas, Values, Debates* (Portland, Ore.: Willan , 2002).

13. Mary Ellen Reimund, "Confidentiality in Victim Offender Mediation: A False Promise?" *Journal of Dispute Resolution* 2 (2004): 401–427.

14. See, for example, International Reconciliation Coalition, online at http://www.reconcile.org.

Appendix A

1. For an expanded discussion, see Elizabeth Beck and Sarah Britto, "Using Feminist Methods and Restorative Justice to Interview Capital Offenders' Family Members," *Affilia: Journal of Women and Social Work* 21, no. 1 (2006): 59–70.

2. Ibid.

3. Ibid.

4. Alison Jaggar, *Feminist Politics and Human Nature* (Totowa, N.J.: Rowman and Allenheld, 1983).

5. Carol Gilligan, *In a Different Voice: Psychological Theory and Women's Development* (Cambridge, Mass.: Harvard University Press, 1982).

6. Daniel W. Van Ness and Karen Heetderks Strong, *Restoring Justice* (Cincinnati: Anderson, 2002); Howard Zehr, *The Little Book of Restorative Justice* (Intercourse, Pa.: Good Books, 2002); Mark S. Umbreit, Robert B. Coates, and Betty Vos, *The Impact of Restorative Justice Conferencing: A Review of 63 Empirical Studies in 5 Countries* (St. Paul: Center for Restorative Justice and Peacemaking, University of Minnesota, 2002); Gerry Johnstone, *Restorative Justice: Ideas, Values, Debates* (Portland, Ore.: Willan, 2002).

7. Beck and Britto, "Using Feminist Methods."

8. Sanda Harding, *The Research Question in Feminism* (Ithaca, N.Y.: Cornell University Press, 1986).

9. Max Weber, "Science as Vocation," in *From Max Weber: Essays in Sociology,*
ed. Hans Gerth and C. Wright Mills (New York: Oxford University Press,
1946); Karl Marx, *Revue Socialist,* 5 July, reprinted in *Karl Marx: Selected
Writings in Sociology and Social Philosophy,* ed. Tom B. Bottomore and
Maximilien Rubel (New York: McGraw-Hill, 1956); Earl Babbie, *The
Practice of Social Research,* 7th ed. (Belmont, Calif.: Wadsworth, 1995).

10. Leslie G. Roman, "A Feminist Material Approach," in *The Handbook of
Qualitative Research in Education,* ed. Margaret D. Le Compte, Wendy L.
Millroy, and Judith Preissle (New York: Academic Press, 1992), 555–594.

11. Margaret Eisenhart and Kenneth Howe, "Validity in Educational Research,"
in *The Handbook of Qualitative Research in Education,* ed. Margaret D.
LeCompte, Wendy L. Millroy, and Judith Preissle (New York: Academic Press,
1992), 643–680.

12. NAACP Legal Defense Fund, *Death Row U.S.A.* (Winter 2005), available
online at http://www.naacpldf.org/content/pdf/pubs/drusa/DRUSA_Winter_
2005.pdf (accessed June 29, 2005).

13. Anselm Strauss and Juliet Corbin, *Basics of Qualitative Theory Procedures
and Techniques* (Newbury Park, Calif.: Sage, 1990).

14. Bruce Berg, *Qualitative Research Methods for the Social Sciences* (Needham
Heights, Mass.: Allyn and Bacon, 1989).

Appendix B

1. Death Penalty Information Center. Last updated July 15, 2004, available
online at http://www.deathpenaltyinfo.org/article.php?scid=8&did=480
(accessed September 21, 2004).

2. Jon Sorenson, and Donald H. Wallace, "Prosecutorial Discretion in Seeking
Death: An Analysis of Racial Disparity in the Pretrial Stages of Case Processing
in a Midwestern County." *Justice Quarterly* 16, no. 3 (1999): 559–576.

3. Jessie Larson, "Unequal Justice: The Supreme Court's Failure to Curtail
Selective Prosecution for the Death Penalty." *Journal of Criminal Law and
Criminology* 93, no. 4 (2003): 1009–1031.

4. *Miranda v. Arizona,* 384 U.S. 436 (1966).

5. Matthew Robinson, *Justice Blind? Ideals and Realities of American Criminal
Justice* (Upper Saddle River, N.J.: Prentice Hall, 2002).

6. David Neubauer, *America's Courts and the Criminal Justice System* (Pacific
Grove, Calif.: Brooks/Cole Publishing Company, 1988).

7. Ibid.

8. Georgia Death Penalty Process, available online at http://www.geocities.
com/gfadp/ga_process.htm (accessed July 23, 2005).

9. Ibid.

10. John Gandy and Burt Galaway, "Restitution as a Sanction for Offenders:
A Public's View," in *Victims, Offenders and Alternative Sanctions,* ed. Joe
Hudson and Burt Galaway (Lexington, Mass.: D.C. Heath/Lexington
Books, 1980), 89–100.

11. Robinson, *Justice Blind?*

12. Georgia Death Penalty Process.

13. Robinson, *Justice Blind?*

14. Ibid.
15. Florida Death Penalty Statute, available online at http://home.c2i.net/sissel.norway/flori.html (accessed July 23, 2005).
16. Ibid.
17. Robert Bohm, *Deathquest: An Introduction to the Theory and Practice of Capital Punishment in the United States* (Cincinnati: Anderson, 2003, 1999).
18. Probono.net, available online at http://www.probono.net/.
19. Oklahoma Coalition to Abolish the Death Penalty (OCADP). Available online at http://www.ocadp.org/.
20. Ibid.
21. Texas Department of Criminal Justice: Death Row Information, available online at http://www.tdcj.state.tx.us/stat/deathrow.htm.

Bibliography

Augusta Chronicle Editorial Staff. "Opinion: Stick It to Him." *Augusta Chronicle,* March 12, 2001. Available online at http://www.augustachronicle.com/stories/031201/opi_240–5391.shtml (accessed March 10, 2006).

Austin American-Statesman Editorial Board. "The Families Left Behind." *Austin American-Statesman,* October 28, 2005. Available online at http://www.willsworld.com/~mvfhr/nsns2.htm (accessed April 22, 2006).

Baldus, David C., George G. Woodworth, and Charles A. Pulaski, eds. *Equal Justice and the Death Penalty: A Legal and Empirical Analysis.* Boston: Northeastern University Press, 1990.

Baldus, David C., George Woodworth, David Zuckerman, and Neil Alan Weiner. "Racial Discrimination and the Death Penalty in the Post-Furman Era: An Empirical and Legal Overview, with Recent Findings from Philadelphia." *Cornell Law Review* 83 (1998): 1638–1756.

Banner, Stuart. *The Death Penalty: An American History.* Cambridge, Mass.: Harvard University Press, 2002.

Bazemore, Gordon and Kay Pranis. "Hazards along the Way: Practitioners Should Stay True to the Principles behind Restorative Justice?" *Corrections Today* 59, no. 7 (1997): 84–86.

Bazemore, Gordon and Mark Umbreit. *A Comparison of Four Restorative Conferencing Models.* Washington, D.C.: U.S. Department of Justice, Office of Juvenile Justice and Delinquency Programs, 1997.

Bazemore, Gordon and Mark Umbreit. "Rethinking the Sanctioning Function in Juvenile Court: Retributive or Restorative Responses to Youth Crime." *Crime and Delinquency* 41, no. 3 (1995): 296–316.

Beccaria, Cesare. *An Essay on Crimes and Punishment.* Philadelphia: P. H. Nicklin, 1819.

Beck, Aaron T., Robert A. Steer, and Gregory K. Brown. *BDI–II, Beck Depression Inventory: Manual,* 2nd ed. Boston: Harcourt Brace, 1996.

Beck, Elizabeth, Brenda Sims Blackwell, Pamela Blume Leonard, and Michael Mears. "Seeking Sanctuary: Interviews with Family Members of Capital Defendants." *Cornell Law Review* 88, no. 2 (2003): 382–418.

Beck, Elizabeth and Sarah Britto. "Using Feminist Methods and Restorative Justice to Interview Capital Offenders' Family Members." *Affilia: Journal of Women and Social Work* 21, no. 1 (2006): 59–70.

Beck, Janine Karen, Kathryn Gow, and Poppy Liossis. "Holocaust Survivors' Delay in Child Rearing and the Psychological Health of Their Children." *Journal of Loss and Trauma* 10, no. 2 (2005): 205–220.

Bedau, Hugo Adam. *The Death Penalty in America.* New York: Oxford University Press, 1997.

Bentham, Jeremy. *Introduction to the Principles of Morals and Legislation.* London: Payne, 1789.

Berg, Bruce. *Qualitative Research Methods for the Social Sciences.* Boston: Allyn and Bacon, 1989.

Bissell, Mary and Jess McDonald. "Dedicated, Overworked, Underfunded; Child-Welfare Workers." *Miami Herald,* September 5, 2005. Available online at http://www.newamerica.net/index.cfm?pg=article&DocID=2535 (accessed April 28, 2006).

Blank, Jessica and Erick Johnson. "The Exonerated." Available online at http://theexonerated.com (accessed April 22, 2006).

Blecker, Robert. *The Worst of the Worst: Who Deserves to Die?* New York: Basic Books, 2005.

Bloom, Sandra L. *Creating Sanctuary: Toward the Evolution of Sane Societies.* New York: Routledge, 1997.

Bloom, Sandra L. and Michael Reichert. *Bearing Witness: Violence and Collective Responsibility.* Binghamton, N.Y.: Hawthorne Press, 1998.

Bohm, Robert. *Deathquest: An Introduction to the Theory and Practice of Capital Punishment in the United States,* 2nd ed. Cincinnati: Anderson, 2003.

Bohm, Robert M. *DeathQuest II.* Cincinnati: Anderson, 2003.

Bosco, Antoinette. *Choosing Mercy: A Mother of Murder Victims Pleads to End the Death Penalty.* Maryknoll, N.Y.: Orbis Books, 2001.

Boudreaux, Paul. "*Booth v. Maryland* and the Individual Vengeance Rationale for Criminal Punishment." *Journal of Criminal Law and Criminology* 80, no. 1 (1989): 177–196.

Bowlby, John. *Attachment and Loss—Vol. 1: Attachment.* New York: Basic Books, 1969.

Bowlby, John. *Attachment and Loss—Vol. 2: Separation Anxiety and Anger.* New York: Basic Books, 1973.

Bowlby, John. *Attachment and Loss—Vol. 3: Sadness and Depression.* New York: Basic Books, 1980.

Bradshaw, William and Mark S. Umbreit. "Crime Victims Meet Juvenile Offenders: Contributing Factors to Victim Satisfaction with Mediated Dialogue in Minneapolis." *Juvenile and Family Court Journal* 49 (1998): 17–25.

Braithwaite, John. *Restorative Justice and Responsive Regulation.* Oxford: Oxford University Press, 2002.

Bright, Steven. "Counsel for the Poor: The Death Penalty Not for the Worst Crime but for the Worst Lawyer." *Yale Law Journal* 103 (1994): 1835–1844.

Bronfenbrenner, Urie. *The Ecology of Human Development.* Cambridge, Mass.: Harvard University Press, 1979.

Bruce, Elizabeth J. and Cynthia L. Schultz. *Nonfinite Loss and Grief: A Psychoeducational Approach.* Baltimore: Paul H. Brooks, 2001.

Brunello, Nicoletta, Jonathan R. Davidson, Martin Deahl, Ronald C. Kessler, Julien Mendlwicz, Giorgio Racagni, Arieh Y. Shalev, and Joseph Zohar. "Posttraumatic Stress Disorder: Diagnosis and Epidemiology, Comorbidity and Social Consequences, Biology and Treatment." *Neuropsychobiology* 43, no. 3 (2001): 150–163.

Carville, James. "James Carville on Bob Casey." Interviewed by Kathryn Jean Lopez. *National Review,* June 1, 2000. Available online at http://www.nationalreview.com/interrogatory/interrogatoryprint060100.html (accessed April 12, 2006).

Centerforce. "Centerforce: Our Programs." Available online at http://www.centerforce.org/
    programs (accessed April 28, 2006).

Chiricos, Ted and Charles Crawford. "Race and Imprisonment: A Contextual
    Assessment of the Evidence." In *Ethnicity, Race, and Crime,* ed. Darnell Hawkins.
    Albany: State University of New York Press, 1995, 281–309.

Christie, Nils. "Conflicts as Property." *British Journal of Criminology* 17, no. 1 (1977):
    1–15.

Clark County (Indiana) Prosecuting Attorney. "Larry Keith Robison." Clark County
    Prosecuting Attorney: Death Penalty: U.S. Executions since 1976: Larry Keith
    Robison. Available online at http://www.clarkprosecutor.org/html/death/
    US/robison607.htm (accessed April 28, 2006).

Clear, Todd and Dina Rose. "Incarceration, Social Capital, and Crime: Implications for
    Social Disorganization Theory." *Criminology* 36, no. 3 (1998): 441–479.

CNN Interactive. "Oklahoma City Tragedy: The Bombing." CNN Interactive, 1996.
    Available online at http://www.cnn.com/US/OKC/bombing.html (accessed
    February 28, 2006).

CNNfyi.com. "Death Penalty by Electrocution on Trial: Georgia Seeks to Resolve
    Constitutionality of Electric Chair." CNNfyi.com, March 7, 2001. Available
    online at http://www.cnnstudentnews.cnn.com/2001/fyi/news/03/07/
    electric.chair (accessed March 17, 2006).

Coe v. Tennessee, 1998 Tenn. Crim. App. LEXIS 96 (Tenn. Ct.App. 1998).

Collins, Jeffrey. "McWee Put to Death for Killing Aiken County Store Clerk."
    April 16, 2004. Clark County (Indiana) Prosecuting Attorney: Death Penalty:
    U.S. Executions since 1976: Jerry Bridwell McWee. Available online at
    http://www.clarkprosecutor.org/html/death/US/mcwee908.htm (accessed
    March 10, 2006).

Collins, Jeffrey. "U.S. Supreme Court Refuses to Stop Execution." April 14, 2004.
    Clark County (Indiana) Prosecuting Attorney: Death Penalty: U.S. Executions
    since 1976: Jerry Bridwell McWee. Available online at http://www.
    clarkprosecutor.org/html/death/US/mcwee908.htm (accessed March 10, 2006).

Corr, Charles A. and Kenneth J. Doka. "Master Concepts in the Field of Death, Dying,
    and Bereavement: Coping versus Adaptive Strategies." *Omega* 43 (2001):
    183–199.

Correia, Martina. "Request for Help: Troy Davis Innocent on Death Row in Georgia."
    Coalition for Truth and Justice. Available online at http://membres.lycos.fr/
    cftj2/html/modules.php?name=News&file=article&sid=277 (accessed March
    10, 2006).

Covey, Sean. *The 7 Habits of Highly Effective Teens.* New York: Fireside, 1998.

Croteau, David and William Hoynes. *The Business of Media: Corporate Media and
    Public Interest.* Thousand Oaks, Calif.: Pine Forge Press, 2001.

Cunningham, Mark D. and Mark P. Vigen. "Death Row Inmate Characteristics,
    Adjustment, and Confinement: A Critical Review of the Literature." *Behavioral
    Sciences and the Law* 20 (2002): 191–210.

Cushing, Renny. To the Murder Victims' Families for Reconciliation. "Message from the
    Executive Director." WBJ Press and Will's World, n.d. Available online at
    http://www.willsworld.com/~mvfhr/EDmessage.htm (accessed April 12, 2006).

Cushing, Renny and Bud Welch. "Transcript of an Address by Renny Cushing,
    Executive Director, and Bud Welch, Board President at Harvard Univ. in 1999."
    Murder Victims' Families for Human Rights: Reports and Articles. Presentation

to the Human Rights Commission, Kennedy School of Government, Harvard University, Cambridge, Mass., March 16, 1999. Available online at http://www.murdervictimsfamilies.org (accessed February 28, 2006).

Davidson, Jonathan R. "Recognition and Treatment of Posttraumatic Stress Disorder." *Journal of the American Medical Association* 286, no. 5 (2001): 584–589.

Davis, Troy Anthony. "Letter to Members of the Media." Troy Anthony Davis: Legal Process. Available online at http://www.troyanthonydavis.org/legal-process.html (accessed March 10, 2006).

Davis, Troy Anthony. "Troy Anthony Davis: An Innocent Man on Georgia's Death Row." Troy Anthony Davis. Available online at http://www.troyanthonydavis.org (accessed March 10, 2006).

Death Penalty Information Center. "The Death Penalty in Black and White: Who Lives, Who Dies, Who Decides." Death Penalty Information Center: Issues: Race. Available online at available online at http://www.deathpenaltyinfo.org (accessed February 26, 2006).

Death Penalty Information Center. "Defendants Sentenced to Death 1977–2004." Death Penalty Information Center: Facts: Sentencing: Death Sentences by State, 1977–Present. Available online at http://www.deathpenaltyinfo.org (accessed February 26, 2006).

Death Penalty Information Center. "Executions by Year." Death Penalty Information Center: Facts: Executions: Execution Facts—Modern Era. Available online at http://www.deathpenaltyinfo.org (accessed February 26, 2006).

Death Penalty Information Center. "Innocence: List of Those Freed from Death Row." Death Penalty Information Center: Issues: Innocence: List of Exonerees Since 1973. Available online at http://www.deathpenaltyinfo.org (accessed February 26, 2006).

Death Penalty Information Center. "Race and the Death Penalty." Death Penalty Information Center: Issues: Race. Available online at http://www.deathpenaltyinfo.org (accessed March 10, 2006).

Death Penalty Information Center. "Race of Death Row Inmates Executed since 1976." Death Penalty Information Center: Issues: Race: Executions by Race of Defendants Executed. Available online at http://www.deathpenaltyinfo.org (accessed February 26, 2006).

Death Penalty Information Center. "Women and the Death Penalty: Facts and Figures." Death Penalty Information Center: Issues: Women: Facts and Figures. Available online at http://www.deathpenaltyinfo.org (accessed February 26, 2006).

Death Penalty Information Center. "Size of Death Row by Year." Death Penalty Information Center: Facts: Death Row: Size of Death Row Population from 1968 to the Present. Available online at http://www.deathpenaltyinfo.org (accessed February 26, 2006).

Diagnostic and Statistical Manual of Mental Disorders (DSM-IV), 4th ed., revised. Washington, D.C.: American Psychiatric Association, 2000.

DiClemente, Ralph J., Gina M. Wingood, Delia L. Lang, Richard A. Crosby, Laura F. Salazar, Kathy Harrington, and Vicki Stover Hertzberg. "Adverse Health Consequences That Co-occur with Depression: A Longitudinal Study of Black Adolescent Females." *Pediatrics* 116, no. 1 (2005): 78.

Doka, Kenneth J., ed. *Disenfranchised Grief: Recognizing Hidden Sorrows.* Lexington, Mass.: Lexington Books, 1989.

Doyle, Charles. "Antiterrorism and Effective Death Penalty Act of 1996: A Summary." *Federation of American Scientists.* Available online at http://www.fas.org/irp/crs/96-499.htm (accessed March 10, 2006).

Dugan, Timothy and Robert Coles, eds. *The Child in Our Times: Studies in the Development of Resiliency.* New York: Brunner/Mazel, 1989.

Eisenhart, Margaret and Kenneth Howe. "Validity in Educational Research." In *The Handbook of Qualitative Research in Education,* ed. Margaret D. LeCompte, Wendy L. Millroy, and Judith Preissle. New York: Academic Press, 1992, 643–680.

Erikson, Kai T. *Wayward Puritans.* New York: Macmillan, 1966.

Eschholz, Sarah, Mark Reed, Elizabeth Beck, and Pamela Blume Leonard. "Offenders' Family Members' Responses to Capital Crimes." *Homicide Studies* 7, no. 2 (2003): 154–181.

Espy, M. Watt and Martin O. Smykl, comp. *Executions in the United States, 1608–1987: The Espy File.* Ann Arbor, Mich.: Inter-University Consortium for Political and Social Research, 1987.

Evans, Gary W. "The Environment of Childhood Poverty." *American Psychologist* 59, no. 2 (2004): 77–92.

Everett, Ronald S. and Roger A. Wojkiewicz. "Difference, Disparity, and Race/Ethnic Bias in Federal Sentencing." *Journal of Quantitative Criminology* 18, no. 2 (2002): 189–211.

Fickenauer, James O. "Public Support for the Death Penalty: Retribution as Just Desserts or Retribution as Revenge?" *Justice Quarterly* 5 (1988): 81–100.

Flaten, Caren L. "Victim-Offender Mediation: Application with Serious Offenses Committed by Juveniles." In *Restorative Justice: An International Perspective.* ed. Burt Galaway and Joe Hudson. Monsey, N.Y.: Criminal Justice Press, 1996, 387–402.

Flock, Jeff. "'Blanket Commutation' Empties Illinois Death Row: Incoming Governor Criticizes Decision." CNN.com, January 13, 2003. Available online at http:// www.cnn.com/2003/law/01/11/illinois.death.row/ (accessed December 7, 2005).

Floridians for Alternatives to the Death Penalty. "Floridians for Alternatives to the Death Penalty." Available online at http://www.fadp.org (accessed April 5, 2006).

Foucault, Michel. *Discipline and Punish: The Birth of the Prison.* New York: Pantheon Books, 1977.

Frankl, Viktor E. *The Unheard Cry for Meaning: Psychotherapy and Humanism.* New York: Washington Square Press, 1997.

Freedman, David and David Hemenway. "Precursors of Lethal Violence: A Death Row Sample." *Social Science and Medicine* 50 (2000): 1757–1770.

Fritsch, Travis A. and John D. Burkhead. "Behavioral Reactions of Children to Parental Absence Due to Imprisonment." *Family Relations* 30 (1982): 83–88.

Gable, Stewart. "Behavioral Problems in Sons of Incarcerated or Otherwise Absent Fathers: The Issue of Separation." *Family Process* 31 (1992): 303–313.

Gable, Stewart and R. Shindledecker. "Aggressive Behavior in Youth: Characteristics, Outcome and Psychiatric Diagnosis." *Journal of American Academy of Child and Adolescent Psychiatry* 30 (1991): 982–989.

Galaway, Burt. "Restitution as Innovation or Unfilled Promise?" *Federal Probation* 52, no. 3 (1988): 3–14.

Garbarino, James. *Lost Boys: Why Our Sons Turn Violent and How We Can Save Them.* New York: Free Press, 1999.

Garbarino, James. *Raising Children in a Socially Toxic Environment.* San Francisco: Jossey-Bass, 1997.

Garmezy, Norman. "Resiliency and Vulnerability to Adverse Developmental Outcomes Associated with Poverty." *American Behavioral Scientist* 34 (1991): 416–430.

Germain, Carel Bailey. *Human Behavior in the Social Environment: An Ecological View.* New York: Columbia University Press, 1991.

Gilligan, Carol. *In a Different Voice: Psychological Theory and Women's Development.* Cambridge, Mass.: Harvard University Press, 1982.

Gilligan, James. *Preventing Violence.* New York: Thames and Hudson, 2001.

Glassner, Barry. *The Culture of Fear: Why Americans Are Afraid of the Wrong Things.* New York: Basic Books, 2000.

Gondolf, Edward. "Anger and Oppression in Men Who Batter: Empiricist and Feminist Perspectives and Their Implication for Research." *Victimology* 10 (1985): 311–324.

Gondolf, Edward. "Treating the Batterer." In *Battering and Family Therapy: A Feminist Perspective,* ed. Marsali Hanse and Michele Harway. Newbury Park, Calif.: Sage, 1993.

Greenberg, Paul E., Laura E. Stiglin, Stan N. Finkelstein, and Ernst R. Berndt. "The Economic Burden of Depression in 1990." *Journal of Clinical Psychiatry* 54, no. 11 (1993): 405–418.

Gregg v. Georgia, 428 U.S. 153 (1976).

Gutierrez, Lorraine, Ruth Parsons, and Enid Opal Cox. *Empowerment in Social Work Practice.* Pacific Grove, Calif.: Brooks Cole, 1997.

Hadley, Michael L. *The Spiritual Roots of Restorative Justice.* New York: State University of New York Press, 2001.

Haines, Herbert H. *Against Capital Punishment: The Anti–Death Penalty Movement in America, 1972–1994.* New York: Oxford University Press, 1996.

Hairston, Creasy. "Men in Prison: Family Characteristics and Family Views." *Journal of Offender Counseling, Services and Rehabilitation* 14 (1989): 123–130.

Halperin, Rick. "South Carolina—Impending Execution: A Case Where Clemency Is Appropriate." News—USA, Ind., Calif., S.C., LA [email list]. Available online at http://venus.soci.niu.edu/~archives/ABOLISH/oct04/0601.html (accessed March 10, 2006).

Hamm, Theodore. *Rebel and a Cause: Caryl Chessman and the Politics of the Death Penalty in Postwar California, 1948–1974.* Berkeley: University of California Press, 2001.

Harding, Sandra. *The Research Question in Feminism.* Ithaca, N.Y.: Cornell University Press, 1986.

Harrison, Dwight and Susannah Sheffer. *In a Dark Time: A Prisoner's Struggle for Healing and Change.* Amherst, Mass.: Stone Lion Press, 2005.

Heide, Kathleen M. "Youth Homicide: A Review of the Literature and Blueprint for Action." *International Journal of Offender Therapy and Comparative Criminology* 47 (1999): 6–36.

Herman, Judith. *Trauma and Recovery.* New York: Basic Books, 1997.

Hetherington, E. Mavis and W. Glenn Clingempeel. "Coping with Marital Transitions." *Monographs of the Society for Research in Child Development* 57 (1992): serial nos. 2–3.

Hidalgo, Rosario B. and Jonathan R. Davidson. "Selective Serotonin Reuptake Inhibitors in Post-Traumatic Stress Disorder." *Journal of Psychopharmacology* 14, no. 1 (2000): 70–77.

Hirshberg, Max. "Wrongful Convictions." *Rocky Mountain Law Review 13* (1940): 20–46.

Illinois Criminal Justice Authority's Research and Analysis Unit. *The Needs of the Wrongfully Convicted: A Report on a Panel Discussion.* Report to the Governor's Commission on Capital Punishment. March 15, 2002. Center for Wrongful Convictions. Available online at http://www.law.northwestern.edu/depts/clinic/wrongful/documents/ILLPanelRPt.htm (accessed April 30, 2006).

Jackson, Jesse. *Legal Lynching Racism, Injustice and the Death Penalty.* New York: Marlowe, 1996.

Jaggar, Alison. *Feminist Politics and Human Nature.* Totowa, N.J.: Rowman and Allenheld, 1983.

Jarjoura, G. Roger, Ruth A. Triplett, and Gregory P. Brinker. "Growing up Poor: Examining the Link between Persistent Childhood Poverty and Delinquency." *Journal of Quantitative Criminology* 18, no. 2 (2002): 159–187.

Johnston, Denise. *Children of Offenders.* Pasadena, Calif.: Pacific Oaks Center for Children of Incarcerated Parents, 1992.

Johnston, Denise. "Effects of Parental Incarceration." In *Children of Incarcerated Parents,* ed. Katherine Gable and Denise Johnston. New York: Lexington Books, 1995.

Johnston, Norman. "Prison Reform in Pennsylvania." Pennsylvania Prison Society: About: History. Available online at http://www.prisonsociety.org/about/history.sthml (accessed April 5, 2006).

Johnstone, Gerry. *Restorative Justice: Ideas, Values, Debates.* Portland, Ore.: Willan, 2002.

Just Bridges. *Video Interview with the Kotzbauer Family.* Summer Peace Building Institute, Defense Based Victim Outreach Training. Harrisonburg, Va. June 2005.

Kant, Immannel. *Critique of Practical Reason.* Trans. Lewis White Beck. Chicago: University of Chicago Press, 1949.

Kellerman, Natan. "Transmission of Holocaust Trauma—An Integrative View." *Psychiatry: Interpersonal and Biological Processes* 64, no. 3 (2001): 256–268.

King, Rachel. *Capital Consequences: Families of the Condemned Tell Their Stories.* New Brunswick, N.J.: Rutgers University Press, 2005.

King, Rachel. *Don't Kill in Our Names: Families of Murder Victims Speak Out against the Death Penalty.* Piscataway, N.J.: Rutgers University Press, 2003.

King, Rachel. "A Mother's Love." In *Don't Kill in Our Names.* New Brunswick, N.J.: Rutgers University Press, 2003.

Koniaris, Leonidas, Teresa Zimmers, David Lubarsky, and Jonathan P. Sheldon. "Inadequate Anesthesia in Lethal Injection for Execution." *Lancet* 365 (2005): 1412–1414.

Krajicek, David. *Scooped! Media Miss Real Story on Crime While Chasing Sex, Sleaze and Celebrities.* New York: Columbia University Press, 1998.

Kübler-Ross, Elisabeth. *On Death and Dying.* New York: Macmillan, 1969.

Kuntsler, William M. *Beyond a Reasonable Doubt? The Original Trial of Caryl Chessman.* Westport, CT: Greenwood Press, 1973.

Kurki, Leena. "Incorporating Restorative and Community Justice into American Sentencing and Corrections." In *Sentencing and Corrections 3.* Washington, D.C.: U.S. Department of Justice Papers from the Executive Sessions on Sentencing and Corrections, 1999.

Launay, Gilles and Peter Murray. "Victim/Offender Groups." In *Meditation and Criminal Justice*, ed. Martin Wright and Burt Galaway. Newbury Park, Calif.: Sage, 1989.

Liebman, James S., Jeffrey Fagan, and Valerie West. "A Broken System: Error Rates in Capital Cases, 1973–1995." Justice Project—Campaign for Criminal Justice Reform, 2000. Available online at http://www.thejusticeproject.org/press/reports/liebman-part-1.html (accessed March 10, 2006).

Lifton, Robert J. and Greg Mitchell. *Who Owns Death? Capital Punishment, the American Conscience, and the End of Executions.* New York: Morrow, 2002.

Linemann, Eric. "Symptoms and Management of Acute Grief." *American Journal of Psychiatry* 101 (1944): 141–148.

Loney, Randolph. *A Dream of the Tattered Man: Stories from Georgia's Death Row.* Grand Rapids, Mich.: William B. Eerdmans, 2001.

Marx, Karl. *Revue Socialist*, 5 July. Reprinted in *Karl Marx: Selected Writings in Sociology and Social Philosophy*, ed. Tom B. Bottomore and Maximilien Rubel. New York: McGraw-Hill, 1956.

McClesky v. Kemp, 481 U.S. 279 (1987).

McCubbin, Hamilton I., Elizabeth A. Thompson, Anne I. Thompson, and Julie E. Fromer, eds. *Stress, Coping and Health in Families: Sense of Coherence and Resiliency.* Thousand Oaks, Calif.: Sage, 1998.

McWee, Celia. "Celia McWee." WBJ Press and Will's World. Presentation at the No Silence, No Shame Inaugural Event, Austin, Texas, October 27, 2005. Available online at http://www.willsworld.com/~mvfhr/nsstatements.htm (accessed April 22, 2006).

Meeropol, Michael, comp. *The Rosenberg Letters: A Complete Edition of the Prison Correspondence of Ethel and Julius Rosenberg.* New York: Garland, 1994.

Meeropol, Robert. *An Execution in the Family: One Son's Journey.* New York: St. Martin's Griffin, 2003.

Meeropol, Robert and Michael Meeropol. *We Are Your Sons.* Boston: Houghton Mifflin, 1975.

Meredith, Martin and Tina Rosenberg. *Coming to Terms: South Africa's Search for Truth.* New York: Public Affairs, 1999.

Morris, Norval and David J. Rothman, eds. *The Oxford History of the Prison: The Practice of Punishment in Western Society.* New York: Oxford University Press, 1995.

Murder Victims' Families for Reconciliation. "Murder Victims' Families for Reconciliation: Home." Available online at http://www.mvfr.org (accessed April 12, 2006).

NAACP Legal Defense Fund. Death Row USA. Winter 2005. Available online at http://www.naacpldf.org/content.pdf/pubs/drusa/DRUSA/_Winter_2005 (accessed June 25, 2005).

National Coalition to Abolish the Death Penalty. "About Us." Available online at http://www.ncadp.org./about_us.html (accessed April 5, 2006).

Noll, Jennie G. "Does Childhood Sexual Abuse Set in Motion a Cycle of Violence against Women?" *Journal of Interpersonal Violence* 20, no. 4 (2005): 455–463.

Norgard, Katharine. "Beyond Grief." In *Capital Consequences: Families of the Condemned Tell Their Stories*, ed. Rachel King. New Brunswick, N.J.: Rutgers University Press, 2005.

Northey, Wayne. "Restorative Justice: Rebirth of an Ancient Practice. New Perspectives on Crime and Justice." Occasional Paper No. 14. Akron, Pa.: Mennonite Central

Committee, Canada Victim Offender Ministries Program, and the MCC U.S. Office of Criminal Justice, 1994.

Northwestern University School of Law Center on Wrongful Convictions. "Illinois Death Penalty Exonerations." Northwestern University School of Law: Faculty and Research: Programs and Centers: Center on Wrongful Convictions. Available online at http://www.law.northwestern.edu/depts/clinic/wrongful/exonerations/Illinois.htm (accessed April 22, 2006).

Nugent, William, Mark Umbreit, Lizabeth Wiinamaki, and Jeff Paddock. "Participation in Victim-Offender Mediation and Reoffense: Successful Replications?" *Research on Social Work Practice* 11, no. 1 (2001): 5–23.

Pearl, Leon. "A Case against the Kantian Retributivist Theory of Punishment: A Response to Professor Pugsley." *Hofstra Law Review* 273 (1982): 273–306.

Pelke, Bill. *Journey of Hope . . . From Violence to Healing.* Philadelphia: Xlibris, 2003.

Pennsylvania Department of Corrections. "Visiting Information." Available online at http://www.cor.state.pa.us/greene/cwp/view.asp?a=428&q=129545&greeneNav =| (accessed April 12, 2006).

Phillips, Susan, Barbara Burns, Ryan Wagner, Theresa Kramer, and James Robbins. "Parental Incarceration among Adolescents Receiving Mental Health Services." *Journal of Child and Family Studies* 11 (2002): 385–399.

Pope John Paul II. *Memory and Identity: Conversations at the Dawn of the Millennium.* New York: Rizzoli, 2005.

Possley, Maurice and Steven Mills. "Clemency for All: Ryan Commutes 164 Death Sentences to Life in Prison without Parole; 'There Is No Honorable Way to Kill,' He Says." *Chicago Tribune,* JaBradshaw, William and Mark S. Umbreit. *"Crime Victims Meet Juvenile Offenders: Contributing Factors to Vic*tim Satisfaction with Mediated Dialogue in Minneapolis." Juvenile and Family Court Journal 49 (1998): 17–25.

Braithwaite, John. Restorre, John. Restor/nference of the Victim-Offender Mediation Association, Winnipeg, Manitoba, Canada, June 4, 1994. Available online at http://www.vorp.com/articles/ddcasest.html (accessed February 28, 2006).

Radelet, Michael L., Hugo Adam Bedau, and Constance E. Putnam. *In Spite of Innocence: Erroneous Convictions in Capital Cases.* Boston: Northeastern University Press, 1992.

Radelet, Michael L. and Marian J. Borg. "Comment on Umbreit and Vos." *Homicide Studies* 4, no. 1 (2000): 88–92.

Reed, Mark, Sarah Britto, and Brenda Blackwell. "The Source and Nature of Secondary Victimization Among Homicide Co-victims." Paper presented at the annual meeting for the American Society of Criminology, Nashville, Tennessee, November 17, 2002.

Reid, John B., Gerald R. Patterson, and James Snyder. *Antisocial Behavior in Children and Adolescents: A Developmental Analysis and Model for Intervention.* Washington, D.C.: American Psychological Association, 2002.

Reiman, Jeffery. "Against the Death Penalty." In *Criminal Justice Ethics*, ed. Paul Leighton and Jeffrey Reiman. Upper Saddle River, N.J.: Prentice Hall, 2001.

Ring v. Arizona, 536 U.S. 584 (2002).

Roberts, Tim. *Evaluation of the Victim Offender Mediation Program in Langley, B.C.* Victoria, Canada: Focus Consultants, 1995.

Robison, Lois to Texas Board of Pardons and Paroles and Governor George W. Bush. July 22, 1999. Letters of Support for Larry Robison. Welcome to the Larry Robison Website: Letters of Support: Lois Robison Letter to Governor. Available online at http://www.larryrobison.org/pages/momgov.htm (accessed April 27, 2006).

Rock, Paul. *After Homicide: Practical and Political Responses to Bereavement.* Oxford: Clarendon Press, 1998.

Roman, Leslie G. "A Feminist Material Approach." In *The Handbook of Qualitative Research in Education*, ed. Margaret D. Le Compte, Wendy L. Millroy, and Judith Preissle. New York: Academic Press, 1992, 555–594.

Romanoff, Bronna D. and Marion Terenzio. "Rituals and the Grieving Process." *Death Studies* 22, no. 8 (1998): 697–712.

Roper v. Simmons, 543 U.S. 551 (2005).

Rosenberg Fund for Children. "Mission Statement and Background." Available online at http://www.rfc.org (accessed March 20, 2006).

Rudel, Charlotte H. and Margaret L. Hayes. "Behind No Bars—Cambria County Prison's Innovative Family Visiting Program." *Children Today* (May–June 1990). Available online at http://www.findarticles.com/p/articles/mi_m1053/is_n3_v19/ai_8944320 (accessed April 28, 2006).

Ryan, George. "An Address on the Death Penalty." Speech given at the University of Chicago Divinity School, Chicago, June 3, 2002. Available online at http://pewforum.org/events/index.php?EventID=28 (accessed March 10, 2006).

Ryan, Perry T. *The Last Public Execution in America.* Kentucky: Perry T. Ryan, 1992.

Sack, William. "Children of Imprisoned Fathers." *Psychiatry* 40 (1977): 163–174.

Sack, William, Jack Seidler, and Susan Thomas. "The Children of Imprisoned Parents: A Psychosocial Exploration." *American Journal of Orthopsychiatry* 46 (1976): 618–628.

Sane, Pierre. "News Release Issued by the International Secretariat of Amnesty International, AI Index: AMR 51/76/97 25 November 1997." *Action Alert.* Available online at http://home4.inet.tele.dk/lepan/lene/pennsy.htm (accessed April 12, 2006).

Schaefer, Kristin D. and James J. Hennessy. "Intrinsic and Environmental Vulnerabilities Among Executed Capital Offenders: Revisiting the Bio-Psycho-Social Model of Criminal Aggression." *Journal of Offender Rehabilitation* 34, no. 2 (2001): 1–19.

Schaffer, Gwen. "Dead Serious: Anti–Death Penalty Activists Are Traveling across the State to Spread Their Message." *Philadephia Citypaper.net.* May 18–June 4, 1998. Available online at http://www.citypaper.net/articles/052898/cb.caravan.shtml (accessed April 12, 2006).

Schiff, Mara F. "Restorative Justice Interventions for Juvenile Offenders: A Research Agenda for the Next Decade." *Western Criminology Review* 1, no 1. (1998): 1–16.

Schlup v. Delno, 513 U.S. 298 (1995).

Shaman, Jeffrey M. "The Impartial Judge: Detachment or Passion?" *DePaul Law Review* (1996): 605–631.

Sharp, Susan F. *Hidden Victims: The Effects of the Death Penalty on Families of the Accused.* New Brunswick, N.J.: Rutgers University Press, 2005.

Sheffield, Anne. *Depression Fallout: The Impact of Depression on Couples and What You Can Do to Preserve the Bond.* New York: Quill, 2003.

Shonkoff, Jack P. and Deborah A. Phillips, eds. *From Neurons to Neighborhoods: The Science of Early Childhood Development.* Washington, D.C.: National Academy Press, 2000.

Simeonsson, Rune J. *Risk, Resilience, and Prevention: Promoting the Well-Being of All Children.* Baltimore: Paul H. Brookes, 1995.

Smykla, John O. "The Human Impact of Capital Punishment: Interviews with Families of Persons on Death Row." *Journal of Criminal Justice* 15 (1987): 331–347.

South Carolina v. Shafer, 531 S.E.2d 524 (South Carolina 2000), *rev'd and remand.,* 532 U.S. 36 (2001).

Spungen, Deborah. *Homicide: The Hidden Victims: A Resource for Professionals.* Thousand Oaks, Calif.: Sage, 1998.

Strauss, Anselm and Juliet Corbin. *Basics of Qualitative Research: Grounded Theory Procedures and Techniques.* Thousand Oaks, Calif.: Sage, 1990.

Sullivan, Dennis and Larry Tifft. *Restorative Justice: Healing the Foundations of Our Everyday Lives.* Monsey, N.Y.: Willow Tree Press, 2001.

Surrette, Ray. *Media, Crime and Criminal Justice: Images and Realities,* 2nd ed. Pacific Grove, Calif.: Wadsworth, 1998.

Tariq Khamisa Foundation. "Planting Seeds of Hope: TKF." Available online at http://www.tkf.org (accessed March 22, 2006).

"This Article is from the (St. Paul/Minesota) PioneerPlanet." Abolitionist Action Committee, n.d. Available online at http://www.abolition.org/earle_interview.html (accessed March 23, 2006).

Thompson, Ross A. "Empathy and Its Origins in Early Development." In *Intersubjective Communication and Emotion in Early Ontology,* ed. S. Braten. Cambridge: Cambridge University Press, 1998, 144–157.

Torrey, Edwin Fuller. *Surviving Schizophrenia: A Manual for Families, Consumers, and Providers.* New York: Harper Perennial, 1995.

Travis, Jeremy, Elizabeth Cincotta, and Amy Solomon. *Families Left Behind: The Hidden Costs of Incarceration and Re-Entry.* Washington, D.C.: Urban Institute Justice Policy Center, 2003.

Tutu, Desmond. *No Future without Forgiveness.* New York: Image Doubleday, 1999.

Twist, Steven J. "The Crime Victims' Rights Amendment and Two Good and Perfect Things." *Utah Law Review* 14 (1999): 369–382.

Umbreit, Mark. *Family Group Conferencing: Implications for Crime Victims.* Washington, D.C.: U.S. Department of Justice, Office of Justice Programs, Office for Victims of Crime, 2000. NCJ 176347. Also available online at http://www.ovc.gov/publications/infores/restorative_justice/96523-family_group/welcome.html (accessed February 28, 2006).

Umbreit, Mark. "Restorative Justice through Victim-Offender Mediation: A Multi-Site Assessment." *Western Criminology Review* 1, no. 1 (1998): 1–27.

Umbreit, Mark. "Violent Offenders and Their Victims." In *Mediation and Criminal Justice,* ed. Martin Wright and Burt Galaway. London: Sage, 1989, 337–352.

Umbreit, Mark and Jean Greenwood. *National Survey of Victim-Offender Mediation Programs in the United States.* Washington, D.C.: U.S. Department of Justice, Office of Justice Programs, Office for Victims of Crime, 2000. NCJ 176350. Also available online at http://www.ovc.gov/publications/infores/restorative_justice/96520-national_survey/welcome.html (accessed February 28, 2006).

Umbreit, Mark and Ann W. Roberts. *Mediation of Criminal Conflict in England: An Assessment of Services in Coventry and Leeds.* St. Paul: University of Minnesota, Center for Restorative Justice and Mediation, 1996.

Umbreit, Mark and Betty Vos. "Homicide Survivors Meet the Offender Prior to Execution." *Homicide Studies* 4, no. 1 (2000): 63–87.

Umbreit, Mark, Betty Vos, Robert Coates, and Katherine Brown. *Facing Violence: The Path of Restorative Justice and Dialogue.* Monsey, N.Y.: Criminal Justice Press, 2003.

University of Missouri–Columbia School of Law American Civil Liberties Union Chapter and Christian Legal Society. "Petition Submitted to Governor Holden for Joseph Amrine." University of Missouri–Columbia School of Law: ACLU: View MU Law School ACLU Clemency Petition. Available online at http://mail.law.missouri.edu/aclu/amrinepetition.html (accessed April 30, 2006).

U.S. Census Bureau. "United States Census 2000." U.S. Census, n.d. Available online at http://www.census.gov (accessed March 7, 2006).

U.S. Department of Justice. *Report on Minor Children Who Have a Mother or Father in Prison.* Washington D.C.: U.S. Department of Justice, Bureau of Justice Statistics, 2002.

U.S. Government Accountability Office. *Death Penalty Sentencing: Research Indicates Pattern of Racial Disparities.* Washington, D.C.: Government Printing Office, February 1990. Also available online at http://archive.gao.gov/t2pbat11/140845.pdf (accessed March 10, 2006).

Vandiver, Margaret. "The Impact of the Death Penalty on Family Members of the Homicide Victims and of Condemned Prisoners." In *America's Experiment with Capital Punishment: Reflections on the Past, Present, and Future of the Ultimate Penal Sanction*, 2nd ed., ed. James Acker, Robert Bohm, and Charles Lanier. Durham, N.C.: Carolina Academic Press, 2003.

Van Ness, Daniel W. and Karen H. Strong. *Restoring Justice.* Cincinnati: Anderson, 2002.

Van Soest, Dorothy. "Different Paths to Death Row: A Comparison of Men Who Committed Heinous and Less Heinous Crimes." *Violence and Victims* 18 (2003): 15–33.

Wachs, Theodore D. "Proximal Experience and Early Cognitive-Intellectual Development: The Social Environment." In *Home Environment and Cognitive Development*, ed. A. W. Gottfried. London: Academic Press, 1984, 273–328.

Walsh, Froma. *Strengthening Family Resilience.* New York: Guilford, 1998.

Welch, Bud. "The Forgiveness Project Stories: Bud Welch." *The Forgiveness Project: Stories: Bud Welch.* Available online at http://www.theforgivenessprohect.com/stories/bud-welch (accessed February 20, 2006).

Welch, Bud. "Revenge and Hate Is what Resulted in the Death of 167 People," *Peacework.* Presentation to the Human Rights Commission, Kennedy School of Government, Harvard University, Cambridge, Mass., March 16, 1999. Available online at http://www.peaceworkmagazine.org/pwork/0499/049918.htm (accessed September 19, 2006).

Westen, Drew. *Psychology: Mind, Brain, and Culture.* New York: Wiley, 1999.

Wiggins v. Smith, 539 U.S. 510 (2003).

"Women and Depression." *Harvard Mental Health Letter* 20, no. 11 (2002): 1–4.

Zehr, Howard. *The Little Book of Restorative Justice.* Intercourse, Pa.: Good Books, 2002.

Zehr, Howard. "Retributive Justice, Restorative Justice." New Perspectives on Crime and Justice—Occasional Paper No. 4. Akron, Pa.: Mennonite Central Committee, Canada Victim Offender Ministries Program, and the MCC U.S. Office of Criminal Justice, 1985.

Zehr, Howard. *Transcending: Reflections of Crime Victims.* Intercourse, Pa.: Good Books, 2001.

Index

Notes are indicated by n and the note number following the page number